Lord of Misrule

My family Coat of Arms

Lord of Misrule

THE AUTOBIOGRAPHY OF
CHRISTOPHER LEE

ORION

First published in Great Britain in hardback as
Tall, Dark and Gruesome in 1977 by W.H. Allen
New hardback edition published in 1997 by Victor Gollancz

This new hardback edition published in 2003 by Orion
An imprint of Orion Books Ltd
Orion House, 5 Upper St Martin's Lane, London WC2H 9EA

Second impression 2003

A CIP catalogue record for this book is
available from the British Library.

ISBN 0 75285 770 3

Typeset by Deltatype Ltd Birkenhead, Merseyside

Printed and bound in Great Britain by
Clays Ltd, St Ives plc

PICTURE CREDITS

Every effort has been made to trace every copyright holder of the photographs
but, if any have been inadvertently overlooked, the author and publishers will be
pleased to make the necessary changes at the first opportunity. Unless otherwise
indicated, photographs are from the author's collection.

1 – Royal Collection © HM Queen Elizabeth II, 2003; 9 – Aquarius Library; 26
– *The Man with the Golden Gun* © 1974 Danjaq Inc and United Artists
Corporation. All rights reserved; 27 – 1974, Danjaq LLC and United Artists
Corporation; 30 – Canal+ Image UK; 43 – Ronald Grant Archives/Warner
Brothers; 46 – Ronald Grant Archives; 47 & 49 – © MMII, NLP Inc™ Tolkien
Ent. Licensed to NLP Inc. All rights reserved; 50 – © 2002 Lucasfilm™. All
rights reserved. Used under authorisation. Unauthorised duplication is a violation
of applicable law; 51 & 52 World Connection; 53 – Camera Press

To Gitte and Christina
with all my love
and to Alex,
without whom . . .

'You're writing an autobiography? Who's it about?'

PR girl for United Artists, during tour
of USA for *The Man with the Golden Gun*

Contents

Illustrations

With Gitte and Christina
With Gitte
Peter and I – the happiest of screen enemies
As Scaramanga in *The Man With The Golden Gun*
Discussing the next shot with Roger Moore and Cubby Broccoli
About to assault the 'absolutely fabulous' Joanna Lumley
'Chris, you are the best in the biz, John Belushi – second best.'

Plate section 3

As the pagan Lord Summerisle in front of the Wicker Man
As the Comte de Rochefort
As a gay biker in *Serial*
as Rasputin
With Rasputin's real-life daughter
At a party with Shirley MacLaine
With Peter Cushing, Vincent Price and John Carradine
Birthday celebrations with Joe Dante . . .
And 'the Champion'
With Gitte
Christina's wedding day
Playing golf with Greg Norman and Seve Ballesteros
With Arnold Palmer at Bay Hill, Orlando in 1975

Plate section 4

In Gremlins 2, 1990
My last meeting with Peter, May 1994
Peter's drawing of our working life
As Jinnah
As Saruman in *The Lord of the Rings*
In *Sleepy Hollow*
As Count Dooku in *Star Wars Episode II: Attack of the Clones*
At the World Awards in 2002
With Mikhail Gorbachev
My investiture at Buckingham Palace

Introduction

Monday the 7th of July 2003 was Christopher Lee's last day as Saruman the White. It was a cold day in Wellington, New Zealand and by evening it had turned freezing. Despite the chill, despite having to gather in a huge draughty studio, the crew stayed on set to honour this wonderful actor. After changing out of Saruman's heavy, white robes, Christopher re-entered the studio, smoking a large cigar. The entire film crew burst into spontaneous and sustained applause, saluting this fine actor, who, at the age of eighty-one had just added another movie to his incredible résumé.

Looking around the room that night, I realised that we weren't just Christopher Lee fans – for my generation, he is an icon; somebody we have grown up with. I look back on the last thirty-five years, and I can connect many moments of my life with Christopher's screen appearances.

As a six year old, I was allowed to stay up on Saturday nights to watch *The Avengers*, when I was eleven, I taught myself sculpting and plaster moulding by making a replica of Christopher's *Curse of Frankenstein* make-up; *The Man with the Golden Gun* was the first movie I saw four times in a row; our school film club screened *The Three Musketeers*; I built a tiny cinema under my parents' house when I was seventeen and a terribly scratched 16mm print of *Dracula, Prince of Darkness* became my opening-night movie.

Had anyone told me back in those summery days of childhood that I would not only fulfil my dream of directing movies, but would find myself directing Christopher Lee in *The Lord of the Rings* it would have simply been too much for my teenage mind to handle.

However, some dreams come true and in 1999 we cast Christopher as Tolkien's wizard Saruman. He was perfect for the role – in fact he is perfect for every role he plays. He always seems so *right* – impossible to miscast. So for many weeks I found myself on set with Christopher Lee, calling on all my reserves of self control to behave like a professional film director instead of a fan. He turned out to be a wonderful gentleman, with a delightfully playful sense of humour. He celebrated his eightieth birthday while I was forty – 'Now it's official', he announced, 'You're only half the man I am!'

Throughout filming *The Lord of the Rings* trilogy I was lucky enough to hear him retell parts of his extraordinary life. I would happily sit with Christopher whilst waiting for the camera and lights to be set up and listen to another of his fascinating stories – true experiences spanning the last eighty years.

When he holds up his right hand, displaying a permanently crooked little finger, and says 'Errol Flynn did this to me', you realise Christopher is himself a legend. Whilst his memories and experiences are entertaining, they are also valuable, because they offer a direct connection to a world of history, personalities and cinema that seems quite unreal to most of us.

I'm so pleased that Christopher has found time to commit his memories to paper, to record the story of a life that has more surprises, laughter and human drama than could be found in any motion picture film.

Peter Jackson
Wellington, August 2003

'It's Theer Noo!'

When a film is made, the first take is usually the best. I hope this applies to books too, because after discarding seventeen bright descriptions of the way I made my very first entrance, on Saturday 27 May 1922, I've decided to print the one I first thought of. I wish I could use the marvellous booming phrase that I heard from Orson Welles on the only occasion he ever directed me in a film, and 'print – with enthusiasm!' But the truth is that neither I nor this book would ever have come about if nature had paid any heed to the convenience of my parents. I was 'a mistake'. My mother often told me so.

In her late eighties she was still firm in her original opinion. Whereas I am not altogether sorry and even dare think that the perpetrators of many terrible scripts are not sorry!

At about the time I took shape as one more Lee, embryonic wonders of all shapes and sizes were teasing the public imagination. In the actual week of my birth, not only my mother but the whole world seemed pregnant with possibilities.

Poor mother! It was phenomenally hot. The temperatures had climbed into the eighties and stuck there. All Europe was like a sun-trap. People said it was August masquerading as May, and the drought was getting serious. At the end of the week a thunderstorm, which may or may not have triggered me into action, was welcomed as a brief respite. At Epsom, with the Derby imminent, at Ranelagh where the brilliant Argentine polo team was due, and at Wimbledon which was in the midst of declaring its confidence in the future with a mass of new courts and a splendid stand, groundsmen shook their heads over the parched turf and rushed out to greet the storm with cries of 'Send it down, St Peter!'

St Peter did not oblige for long. There was a universal outcry against the difficulties of obtaining small chips of ice. The Belgravia hostesses

1

who were my mother's chums were in dire peril of having to make love to their butchers and fishmongers to get the ice they needed to chill the Niagara of white wine from Chablis and Barsac which was coursing down the throats of their menfolk.

Another grave threat to the peace of mind of Belgravia was the vast number of wasps which took part in every open-air festivity. To answer the emergency a machine was announced which would wipe out wasps altogether. It was meant to replace the standard method used by picnickers and gardeners of swiping at them piecemeal with a tennis racket. Sadly there must have been a fault in the invention, because the *modus operandi* of this weapon has remained secret to this day, and wasps along with many other killjoys swarm about us still.

For the inhabitants of my home patch the big news that week was that the King and Queen had pronounced for a brilliant Season. Now they *were* all right! For the first time since 1914, when that squalid business with Germany had put a damper on social fireworks, the girls could put their best foot forward and turn out in full fig. Not merely evening courts but full state dress courts were coming back. It was being said that trains would be shorter than in Edwardian days – eighteen inches on the ground would be just about the strength of it – and plumes would be worn lower. Naturally nobody was dissatisfied with *that*, except the girls and their mothers who'd bobbed their hair. Bouquets would be optional and despite the rumour that the Queen was made sick by the smell, put about by some silly goose who'd got her mixed up with Victoria, it was all right to carry one.

In Ireland the bitterness worsened, and the news came through of an outbreak of fire-raising and murder by terrorists in Belfast. With their aplomb undented, London fashion writers were thrilled to report many bargains in Irish linen a stone's throw from the scene of the outrage.

Unemployment was very high, and nowhere higher than in the theatre, where the heat had made a bad situation more acute by closing many shows. An actors' co-operative was mooted, which put on *East Lynne* at Battersea, Stratford and Wallasey, lost money at all three and was wound up owing £312.

The Times on the day I was born carried a lengthy feature advising its readers of the amazing phenomenon of the sudden huge expansion of radio in America, where in six months the number of receivers in private households had leaped from two to seven million. The paper's special correspondent wondered if he was present at the birth of a force for good or evil, but either way a power that must alter society. If the programmes were good, he hoped, people might be kept away from drinking dens, and to ensure this, drinking dens ought not to be allowed a wireless licence.

Country Life, The Field and *Illustrated London News* were my father's staple reading. *Country Life* was more concerned with the gathering popularity of the cinema. It was deeply disturbed by the zest with which rustic communities were greeting American films. To offset the impact of so many bedroom scenes on the developing mind, it put forward in all seriousness the delicious idea of schools banding together to form production companies. These would make wholesome movies with material lifted from the English literary canon.

Some people may feel, as the British picture industry subsequently matured, that such companies managed by high-minded babes and sucklings would hardly have done any worse. But I'm only a poor bloody actor, so it's not for me to speculate on the possible outcome of such missed opportunities.

It gives me a curious feeling to reflect that on that Saturday, the list of attractions offered by London's picture palaces was headed by *The Adventures of Sherlock Holmes*. Had my mother known that one day I would myself be playing Sherlock – and that in Germany – she would certainly have felt that she had wasted her weekend! What is more, I went on to support my dear friend Peter Cushing, when *he* played Sherlock and rescued me on Dartmoor from the terrible Hound of the Baskervilles. And I've played Sherlock's brother Mycroft as well. I have to admit that owing to the genius of Billy Wilder my Mycroft was greatly superior to my Sherlock.

One more odd little coincidence strikes me which, albeit not a superstitious man, I feel I ought to set down. Had my parents at the time perceived the connection they would have been truly appalled and astonished, and wished even more fervently that they had restricted themselves in the way of progeny to their one child, my sister Xandra, then aged five. At the same time that I was being made, so was *Nosferatu*, otherwise *Dracula*, in the great silent version by the German F. W. Murnau.

It seems to me that by comparison with today the picturegoer that Saturday in London was spoilt for choice. Cecil B. De Mille offered *Forbidden Fruit* at the Palaseum and Mary Pickford did her best to snatch it away in *The Love Light*. Pearl White scraped through with her life, or lives, in *The Thief* and Tom Mix blazed away in *Prairie Trails*. Not only was Betty Blythe packing them in at the Kensal Rise Pavilion with *The Queen of Sheba*, but Theda Bara was giving the editors of *Country Life* the jitters with *Salome* at the Empire Kinema. If mere talent and entertainment weren't enough, there were two great artists on in town: Charlie Chaplin in *The Kid* and Buster Keaton in *High Sign*.

If I hadn't been otherwise engaged, I should have been strongly tempted to spend all that gorgeous weekend gnawing at a pig's trotter in the dark and glutting myself with the sheer style of these highline entertainers.

As it was, I stayed home and got born at 51 Lower Belgrave Street. My mother was attended by an old Scots doctor who'd given her no sympathy at all when she'd gone to him and complained of the great nuisance of being pregnant. He'd simply retorted, 'It's theer noo, ye maun pu' up wi' it. When it's theer, it's theer.' He was able to go downstairs and repeat the phrase to my father at about the same time in the afternoon that the news of the winner of the 2.45 at Lingfield came through.

A succinct statement of the event did percolate through to *The Times*. But not until the following Tuesday, when a paid announcement baldly observed that a son had been born to the wife of Lieutenant Colonel Geoffrey Lee, late of the King's Royal Rifle Corps. Otherwise, not a ripple. With their usual poor sense of priorities, the papers had fixed on another birth to splash, which had taken place at exactly the same time as my own. This was a baby sea lion, born at the London Zoo. He was given a great deal of attention, with photographs. On the grounds, I suppose, that he was likely to prove a great money-spinner, and keep the turnstiles clicking.

A Wind on the Heath

It's obvious that nature was half-inclined to make a matinée idol of me. This is not quite the conceit that it may sound to all but cinema buffs. These will know that if you coldly scrutinize a range of your average idols, you will get some fairly cold stares back. You will notice somewhat inflexible features, set above chins like breakwaters. You will see heads made for helmets, not hats. People conceivably love such creatures; it's hard to imagine how they could *like* them.

Anyway, I suspect that the engineers of my genetic blueprint tinkered with the notion. Either they failed to concentrate, or I failed to follow the scheme through, but they must have been very tempted. After all, my mother was a society beauty and my father a fine athlete and a gallant officer.

At the last moment, however, when the mould was all but ready to have 'Seven Year Contract' stamped on its behind, some exuberant imp couched among the stars tossed in that little bit extra. As a result I rose on the legs of a heron and by the time I was seventeen years old I was six foot four inches tall. Whatever fortune tellers and people who give instruction in waltzing may say, there are quite a number of disadvantages to being tall, especially in Britain.

The average height of the British Army during the war against the Axis was, I read somewhere, five foot four inches. Even allowing for the fact that a gross proportion of the poor bloody infantry had bandy legs owing to malnutrition and rickets, there's a general presumption among British designers of all kinds that I'm something like a foot taller than I have any right to be. Cars are made to be steered by pygmies. The only buildings with doorways of sufficient clearance for men of my stature are cathedrals. The normal sizes of cricket bats and golf clubs look like conductors' wands in my hands.

Trousers and shirts for the tall man have to be made privately. He is obliged to sit in the back row of the cinema or theatre if he is not to incur the loathing of all those behind him. Long before he has done anything to justify his being the cynosure of all eyes, he is conspicuous in any gathering as soon as he enters the room. In most strange beds he will find himself obliged to sleep diagonally. Nothing off the peg or made to a standard measure is ever right for him. Waggish strangers feel free to address him as 'Lofty' or 'Tiny' before ever they learn his real name. I went through my school days in a constant state of embarrassment that I could never be overlooked.

In due course I found myself to be too tall for playing the romantic lead in the cinema. I had almost written that I was too tall to play anything whatsoever in the cinema – the accident of my landing some hundred and seventy-five roles on the big screen and sixty-odd more on the small one shouldn't mislead anybody into thinking the industry ever got used to the sheer length of me – but essentially the problem lay in convincing the backers that any 100 per cent nice guy could be such a long streak. Of course a leading lady doesn't like to speak her lines to her lover as if she had a hinge at the back of her neck, nor play to a man's belt buckle, but I did feel sometimes that the industry went too far in its preference for midgets. To me anybody under six foot is a midget. The reader is more than likely a midget. I am surrounded by midgets. Their midgetry is enviable.

My father was not a midget; nor was he specially tall. He was a shade over six foot and broad, as they say, in proportion. He would have regarded without enthusiasm any suggestion that it was his function in life to sire actors for the cinema, however well paid or skilful. Since in 1915 he had trained a contingent of Australian troops in Egypt and commanded them the next year in the shambles of the Somme, I believe that in his professional life as a regular soldier he must have had a backbone of steel. In his personal life he was easy-going, good-natured and gentle.

He was a tremendous natural athlete. At Radley Public School, at the Royal Military Academy of Sandhurst, in the Army and around and about he garnered a massive pile of cups and trophies. He was a champion at squash, fives, rackets, court tennis, épée, foil, sabre – and bayonet! I wouldn't have believed that one could win kudos as a sportsman through proficiency with the bayonet, and certainly the Olympic movement remains reluctant to embrace bayonetry as a sport likely to foment goodwill among nations. But my father had no such hesitations. It says something perhaps about the attitudes to war of that time: in some ways, my father's medals, won in the Transvaal during the

Boer War and in France during the Great War, belong with all the rest of his trophies.

Nevertheless the Great War brought an end to this notion of war as a branch of sporting life, for everybody, not excepting my father. He was not quite forty when he retired, in 1919. From then on he confined himself to cricket and golf, and blazing away at wildlife. As a young man about to receive his first commission he had, almost inevitably, come top of the musketry tests, and the game books of the great country houses of the days of Edward VII and George V show him as one of the best half-dozen shots in the land. This in itself, even without my mother's dark Italianate beauty, would have been sufficient to get them invited to some agreeable spread every weekend of the season.

Even being a guest, at a certain level of society, becomes quite expensive. They couldn't have gone the pace merely on an officer's pay. They both had some private income of their own, from their parents. I never knew my paternal grandparents, they had died before I was born, but I did know my grandmother had been a Trollope; no ties with the Victorian novelist, alas, but the majority view in my family was that there was ample compensation in her connection with a growing firm of builders. My grandfather was . . . another colonel.

On my mama's side I had a whole crescent of senior relatives alive and present with their music, so that must partly explain why as a boy I heard so little about the people who filled my father's half of the church when, with a guard of honour made up of colour sergeants from his regiment, the 60th Rifles, he married the Contessa Estelle Marie Carandini.

There was another reason why I always heard more about the Carandinis than the Lees. When I was not long past my fourth birthday, and after sixteen years of marriage, my father suddenly and, as it seemed to me, inexplicably left my mother.

Two years later they were divorced. I was left with the idea of a father like the hero of a tale from *Boy's Own Paper*. There also survived the actual physical memory of a tall burly man cheerfully and busily sawing logs on a wintry day of woodsmoke in a country garden. And with that went the sensation of him holding me upside down by the ankles and shaking me to dislodge a lollipop stick which had caught in my throat. I can still see the waiting plate on the brown carpet below me, coming close and receding again.

Many years later in a Dublin pub I was given a peculiar flash on the wanderings of the Lees in the byways of the past. I'd gone into the pub to refuel and relax during a break in the shooting of the German version of a Sherlock Holmes story and I was wearing the great detective's deerstalker and cloak. Most of the pub's patrons knocking it back in there were, like me, in their working clothes and I soon became restive under the appraising stare of a group of men sitting at one wall. It struck me that their appearance was scarcely less quaint than mine, since with blue-black ringlets and very dark skins, ear-rings and Romany rig they were patently made up as gypsies.

Then, as the oldest-looking of the bunch rose and made towards me, I realized that it is seldom outside the friezes of the Pyramids that you see such a profile, and scanning his companions who also had the kind of face you see at Karnak and Abu Simbel I saw that they presented a degree of gypsyness not to be expected from the make-up of a low-budget production. The spokesman stopped before me, peering slightly under my deerstalker. Then he said, in slow and formal style:

'Sir. Might one enquire your name?'

It was on the tip of my tongue to reply, 'Sherlock Holmes', but he didn't look as if he would take kindly to Irish banter, so I awkwardly told him the truth.

He said his name was Lavelle. He paused and in an unhurried way resumed his study of me under the deerstalker. I took it off. He turned about to his colleagues and raised his chin enquiringly. They all nodded.

'Might one enquire,' suggested Lavelle, 'the origins of your family?'

I immediately thought of my father. 'He was a big, dark man, not quite as tall as me, who came from Hampshire.'

This brought on another nodding manifestation. I remembered the old story of the New Forest being the rightful kingdom of the gypsies.

'You have confirmed our conclusions,' pronounced Lavelle. 'You are *chal.*' He stood aside, for all the world like a satisfied immigration officer, and let me pass to drink with my compatriots.

They gave me a Romany poem which, so they said, they'd only otherwise bestowed upon the painter Augustus John, who lived some time among gypsies. And in return I recited:

> *There's likewise a wind on the heath, brother,*
> *Life is very sweet, brother*
> *Who would wish to die?*

and went back to another kind of make-believe in front of the cameras. The odd incident had put me in a good mood, since it chimed with an old fantasy. I believe it's common enough for people who are not entirely content with the disposition of their parents to dream that they were themselves changelings.

My father of gypsy stock? I wonder what his batman would have said about that!

Mars and Venus

The batman was called Smith. As if this were not anonymous enough, he was never granted any other name when the family spoke of him. Yet he and my father were deeply attached to one another through the deepest mire of the stalemate in France. He was a lean, wiry individual with a high polish on his complexion from constant exposure to sun and sand. As an Australian he was naturally no respecter of persons.

It happened that Smith was delegated by fate to be minding his own business where my father was bound to trip over him when he strode into the Australian camp near Mina, in Egypt, to take up his new command. My father's majority was newly gazetted and he was the first British officer to be given the somewhat volatile assignment of readying for battle a batch of Australian soldiers regarded as a rabble by the War Office but whom any prudent person would recognize as an assembly of extremely rough, tough private citizens in uniform.

He arrived to find nothing but a lot of tents in a sea of sand, with the Pyramids propping up the canopy of heaven and no humans visible anywhere. He identified a large tent as the Orderly Room, but there was nobody in that either to welcome or challenge him. He moved on to the next tent, which was making a half-hearted attempt to be an office. The effect of chairs and tables and in-trays and out-trays was spoilt, however, by the office's sole occupant, a man squatting on his hunkers wearing only socks and shorts while languidly caressing a pair of boots with a strip of wadding. He did not look up. 'Where's the Orderly Room NCO?' asked my father.

No answer.

'Is there a duty officer about?'

The trooper turned the boot around on his hand, and proceeded on his slow way with the cloth.

'I'm the new commanding officer,' my father remarked.

The Australian did look up for a moment, but only to return with greater concentration to his previous interest.

My father made one of those swift transitions from civility and amiability to explosive rage which seem to be characteristic of all members of my family.

'I don't know,' he barked, 'who you are or what you think you're doing here but if you aren't on your feet in something under five seconds *you're for it*!'

'Hot, ain't it?' said Smith compassionately.

Luckily this appealed to my father and it was the beginning of a durable association. Maybe it was lucky too for Smith that he had this confrontation and was elected to the vacant position of personal slave because the confrontation with the unit as a whole was a fearsome grind. The new commander had been schooled all his life to believe that discipline and unquestioning obedience were the keys to victory. He meant to have it from this hybrid 'imperial' force. To get it he often pegged men out on the sand during the heat of the day.

One trooper who objected to this treatment assaulted him with a bayonet. My father knocked him out and put him on a charge. It's not easy to imagine oneself back into the skins of warriors of another age, but perhaps it's not sentimental to think that this fellow would also have been ready to fill the position of batman, if it had not already been taken.

At all events the 46th battalion of the 12th Brigade of the 4th Australian Division did not let their foster colonel (as I think of him) down when it came to action in the trenches. On 30 June 1916, they invested the village of Pozières on the Somme, which the Allies had coveted for months and failed to take at a great cost in men. This time they got through and forty or so men lived to share in the jubilation. The regiment picked up a DSO, and Marshal Foch himself drove on to the field to present my father with the Croix de Guerre.

He was going through a phase of exotic gongs. He had only just collected the Order of the Nile from King Fuad of Egypt. My mother used to claim a slice of this decoration for herself, because according to her he became a Chevalier of the Order through skilful action on her part. She'd gone to Egypt too, for general consort duties and to operate against the bedouin (heaven knows why) in armoured cars driven by her friends the Duke of Westminster and Prince 'Drino' Battenberg. There was also the promise of singing to the troops, which she fulfilled with passionate grace not only on the banks of the Nile but later at musters behind the lines at the Somme, reducing the men to tears. The women

11

of my mother's family knew a lot of Australian airs from first-hand experience.

She sang the sad airs, knowing by instinct that they're the best therapy for men at the front and a long way from home. In Egypt she could be, and was, more sprightly. King Fuad offered to load her armoured car with jewels if she would be sprightly for him alone, but she found him stout and ungainly, with red hair and moustaches that went up like buffalo horns, and spurned him with what dignity could be saved in these skirmishes. The King took to inviting my father instead, to play chess while he mulled over his unsuccessful siege of his guest's wife. When my father was asked how he won his order, he'd reply enigmatically, 'Playing chess with the King.' The game was not my father's forte, and the King was distracted, so the standard of play scarcely rose above the level of a good brisk contest at draughts.

Taking his career all round at forty, when he gave up the Army, my father must have had a plump time of it. Tokens of courage spread across his chest like mile-a-minute creeper. In the golden twilight of the Pax Britannica, he made the most of the Edwardian round, was merciless to salmon and grouse, and 'never spared himself in pursuit of doing the golf ball a terrible injury'. He changed his horse and his girlfriend at the end of every season, and was rewarded with a captaincy shortly before meeting my mother.

Estelle Marie Carandini had herself newly been granted permission to take a step up in rank. After a great deal of correspondence with the people who kept the archives of Modena, the custodians of the Golden Book of the Italian Nobility, the Pope, the Home Secretary and sundry cousins and friends, my maternal grandfather (previously a major of Hussars and now secretary of the Travellers' Club in London) had proved his title to the Marquisate of Sarzano. This incidentally authenticated him also as Count Carandini, Patrician of Modena and Parma and Noble of Bologna. As a *bonne-bouche* his only child Estelle became Contessa Carandini, which she'd always reckoned herself to be anyway. As practically the last act of his reign, and more or less coincidental with their engagement in 1910, Edward VII granted them the right to sport these resounding titles in Britain too. It was a perfectly useless gesture from my point of view, as it turned out, though kindly meant, because to the boys I knew at school they sounded just as foreign as ever. They only called me 'wop' and 'dago' with extra gusto, and jeered at my pedantic comment that I couldn't possibly be both. I learned early that the one truly international quality among people of all races is xenophobia.

When my parents married in 1910, however, there was no fear that they were joined in a yoke of inauspicious stars. They looked a handsome couple with a great future. To press photographers they were welcome as the union of Venus and Mars. For years they remained favourites of journals like the *Tatler* and *Bystander*.

My mother enjoyed being painted, which happened often. Oswald Birley, who was wont to charge thousands, painted her for love and gave her the portrait when it was finished. Lavery sketched her in a garden with Lady Churchill and the painter's wife. Clare Sheridan made a bust which was bought by friends in the Russian émigré colony, which we seemed to know *en bloc*. This ended up with Kerensky, in the Kremlin. This led to her being painted by the Baroness Orloff-Davidoff, which was also done for love but without talent, and the result had to be got rid of by stealth and by night.

As a sitter she was a trial: there was never a time in her life when she sat still very long. She had no sense of temperance in her judgements of people, places or art. Everything was always in the last degree miraculous or calamitous. She burned with a very short fuse and in response as a boy I trimmed mine till it was practically instantaneous.

She was a fizz. Her first expectation of life, which she brought up my sister Xandra to share, was an endless supply of new people to meet. Her great dance was the tango, and if she could have danced it with Nijinsky whom she admired above every other artist, her cup would have been full. She played trifles on the piano and whipped up a gale when she sang. She played Lady Blakeney at the Slades' house in front of Fred Terry who created the part of the Pimpernel. She was just as happy at Knowle or Castle Howard, lending an ear while being promenaded by a politician. She knew Chaliapin, and had her bottom pinched by Caruso while selling programmes at a charity gala. At Knowle the Earl of Birkenhead, otherwise F. E. Smith the great advocate, burst into her room at two in the morning to advocate his own case, and for once had the verdict go against him.

She was a classic beauty. She looked like a coin, so it was only natural for her to circulate. At the same time, she knew what it was to be an Army wife, and how the lines were drawn. Her father was a soldier; she was born in the Indian Army station of Muzaffapur; her mother had been a general's daughter born in the year of the Mutiny. My parents seemed in every way complementary. At the time my sister was born in 1917 the hopes of fulfilment on either side appeared to be realized. What went wrong? Why did they break up?

The question can only be put rhetorically. I've let the matter rest for too many years to start stirring it up now. To pertinent questions in the nursery I was told by my nannies, 'Don't ask impertinent questions' and 'Little pitchers have big ears' and 'Don't speak with your mouth full.' When I was a little older and 'knew the value of money', I was given to understand that my father had gambled himself into perdition, and that this had something to do with it. He had always been known to his brother officers as 'Betcha' Lee, and would put his money down to cover any stake whatever the hazard, from the winner of the Derby to the sex of the next person to come round the corner. After the war he became more than ever addicted to games of chance and at some time in my infancy he crossed the frontiers of tolerance and began to lose money from the Carandini crock. This is not nearly complex enough to be a fair account, but it was the one I had to be satisfied with until I was a man.

His departure from the foreground gave me an uninterrupted view of the pageantry of the chronicle of the Carandinis. Carandini is my middle name – I was often made to feel it was the only one that mattered.

Two Grains of Rice

The Carandinis, one of the six 'black' families of papal nobility in Italy, trace their origins back to imperial Rome. The dynasty seemingly was founded by a *Carandus*, or maker of carts. Little glamour attaches to this occupation, but there's no doubt of its importance to a military nation. When the victor rode in his triumph into Rome, with a man at his elbow whispering 'Remember thou art mortal', there was always a man called Carandus in the crowd reflecting on the publicity he was getting for his chariot. When the charioteers rode for death or glory round the Circus, there was always a Carandus who stayed behind after the spills and thrills to pick up the bits and put them together again for second-hand. And above all there was a Carandus Carandinus in the role of quartermaster, a figure who in any army is only less vital to conquest than the general. When the family not only made carts but filled them with provender for the legions, its influence steadily waxed, and this is symbolized by two golden grains of rice in the heraldic salad.

Not wishing to tease out every skein in the history of Italy, I'll hedgehop over the centuries and pull out a few random threads on the way.

The first is the Emperor Charlemagne, who's said to have contributed a few genes. Whether he did this legit, or in the course of hoky-poky behind the arras, isn't known. Next comes the Emperor Barbarossa, and the signs are that the family shrewdly sided with him and established themselves with the help of his heavies in the district of Emilia.

The strict record, making Paolo Antonio Risi the first Count Carandini, begins in 1184. It goes in line of descent through the male heirs to my grandfather Carandini, who was Francesco Giacomo to his parents, and Frank James to us.

Along the way they collected the double-headed eagle of the Holy

Roman Empire on their arms for services to the Emperor Rudolph. As a byblow Paolo was made a Count Palatine and authorized to legitimize bastards. In the *cinquecento* the family spread out of its northern strongholds around Modena in all directions and picked up power and privileges wholesale.

They were soldiers and bishops and administrators. Elia was governor of Cento and the Frignano. His son was governor of Castro and Rinciglione. Lodovico built the castle at Marzaglia. Francesco was appointed senator in Rome. Andrea commanded a galley against the Turks and died at the battle of Lepanto. Fabrizio, a pet of Duke Alexander Farnese, with whom he served in Flanders, was chosen by Prince Ranuzzo Farnese to be his second in a duel and was made governor of Piacenza. Muzio was Vicar of Padua. Furio was a counsellor of the Princess Giulia D'Este. Fabio was secretary of S. Carlo Borromeo and might have done better yet, but he died of the plague.

And so on. For a small boy they carried a lot more muscle than the ringmasters and clowns on his bedroom curtains.

Eventually they became governors of Lazio, the province of which Rome is the principal city. Their tombs can still be seen on the Campidoglio in the Church of SS Cosima e Damiano, and there are plaques in the Vatican and the Palazzo dei Conservatori. But their own *palazzo* on the Via di Testa Spacata, near the Forum, was destroyed to make way for the colossal white marble Altare della Patria, where the eternal flame burns above the tomb of the unknown soldier, known more familiarly to Romans as 'the Wedding Cake'.

One of the more lurid tales concerned an eighteenth-century cardinal whom my grandmother always referred to as *'un mauvais sujet'*. His wickedness was to have been in love with the Princess Chigi (member of another great family), though in extenuation it must be said that it was then possible to be a Prince of the Church without carrying out sacerdotal duties. In the midst of his amorous intrigue he was snuffed out by poison.

A generation later came Cardinal Consalvi, a great figure who generated a whole new rash of political appointments for the Carandinis. He was very much Napoleon's opponent, from the time Bonaparte imprisoned Pius VII. His tomb is next to the painter Raphael's, in the Pantheon. Italy was undergoing convulsions in the first half of the nineteenth century, and the restless Carandinis were like so many Jacobins nailed to the Tree of Liberty on their estates.

My feeling of a shaping influence becomes strong with the escapades and difficulties of the 10th Marquis, Girolamo, and his brother Federico.

They became involved in the struggles of the Risorgimento against the Austrians. On this occasion the Carandinis came off second best and in 1842 Girolamo and Federico were obliged to flee the country. They chose Australia.

The reason for this was that Girolamo had already begun a career as a singer at the Opera House in Modena and he got himself hired by the high-spirited Mrs Clarke who was taking a troupe of all-round theatrical adventurers to sing, dance and act in Tasmania. In Hobart Girolamo became Jerome. He met and married another itinerant singer from Europe, Marietta Birgison, who to suit the Australians had become Marie Burgess, known as the Tasmanian Nightingale.

The company put on just about everything to keep the interest of the tiny community they served. They offered grand opera, comic opera, straight plays, farces, ballet and hornpipes, concerts and music-hall. They painted the scenery, took the money, stitched their own costumes, held talent contests and gave lessons. It was the basis of the tours they gave with their own company when they moved to the mainland. They had a very long run in Hobart for those days – four years.

They set up a dancing school in Sydney, and Marie took lessons from another émigré, Isaac Nathan, Australia's first composer. The results were splendid: she developed into a huge draw as a contralto. Her teacher looking for a Romantic subject had set Byron's *Hebrew Melodies* to music – a fairly natural choice for a Nathan, I suppose – and it's pleasant to think of her belting out 'She walks in beauty like the night' against a background of fisticuffs and breaking glass on the Bendigo diggings during the gold rush. She was enormously popular.

But before setting up her own company in the 1860s she gave the singing Marquis seven children, two boys and five girls, some of whom I knew in their old age. The first was my grandfather, born in Sydney in 1847 and christened Francesco Giacomo. The girls all became fine musicians, trekked across rough country to the unlikeliest places with their parents and gave of their best up creeks and swamps and in camps where the only juicy note normally heard came from the kookaburra. They even penetrated Queensland, the *terra incognita* for entertainers where the normal use for a stage was a hanging. Cooktown, the port for the Palmer River goldfields, gave them a great welcome.

Away from the theatre (where it probably looked good on a handbill) there wasn't much percentage, as Damon Runyon would say, in a title like Marquis or Count. Unlike his sisters, my grandfather did not go into the theatre. No doubt in his native city of Sydney he'd seen clearly enough why the gathering place of theatrical folk, where future engagements were canvassed, was called 'Poverty Point'. He opted instead for the life of a cavalry officer – which as it proved offered plenty of scope for theatrical swagger – and joined the 8th Hussars.

In 1870 the political climate of Italy had become more friendly and Jerome made a journey to Modena to become Girolamo again, and to claim his title. But he died before he could establish his right to it. Frank James soldiered on, or rather captained on, as plain Mister. In a regiment famous for its smart turn-out, he stood out as the most dapper dandy of them all. Jokes were made in the mess and the bulletins about the shine of his leathers and the glitter of his brass. He lived only to be a successful Gentleman Rider and a Preux Chevalier. When the Eighth went to India he was really given the chance to shine.

The Raj might have been designed for the express purpose of letting Captain Carandini show off. Wherever there were races to be run, pigs to be stuck, horseflesh to be handicapped, gymkhanas to be khana'ed and meetings to be met, the dashing and popular and elegant 'attaché', as they nicknamed him, was always in demand to organize, cock a seat and ride like the wind.

At Muzaffapur, forty-three years old, he showed them what he was made of. In three days' racing on fourteen mounts he ran in eleven winners, running through the card on the second day and pipping several favourites with professionals up. It was an Indian record . . .

Perhaps he did it for his bride. He'd only just married the general's daughter, Florence Clementson. It explains why he gave his consent so easily to a mere Captain Geoffrey Lee asking to marry his daughter the Contessa. Mama was born in 1889 and in no time was turning the heads of reporters by looking fetching as the star of juvenile parties, knocking them out as a Turkish Sultana in a sweet little scarlet fez, or as the White Duchess with her beautiful little face with big dark eyes and beauty patches under a white silk wig.

My grandparents I think had a true marriage. Some of this family tale may have an element of the fabulous. But here I'm on firm ground. Grandfather died in 1921 and Grandmother lived on another twenty-five years only waiting patiently to join him. At the end she very lovingly made a special effort to delay her going just long enough to welcome me home from the war against the Axis. She died in my arms with Frank's name on her lips. I'm convinced that at that moment she saw him. He was faultlessly mounted and attired, I'm sure, as for any grand occasion, with something around thirteen hands from his Elysian stable for her on a leading rein, as tractable as hands could make him.

These were only some of the ghosts on my hearth as a child. All together they made a very considerable army. I was somewhat given to introspection and to wondering if I had quite the stuff in me which leads to a marble urn.

Two mighty drawbacks marred my proprietorial interest. Firstly, they were *not English*. My youthful comrades dubbed them alien, and me with them. In retaliation I took to exalting alien things. It compounded the villainy. I shut myself away from the withering sarcasms of boys who wanted to diminish everything foreign to a Lilliputian scale.

The other complication was the sense of being excluded by the dynasty. The line of succession ran right through to my mother, and there it stopped. The law of primogeniture was restricted to the first-born male heirs. The others all got to be counts, but even this consolation was denied me. I secretly felt it was not quite fair. Now if only my mother had been a man . . . It was very confusing.

Time brings in its revenges. Many years later the cinema, always ready to make good deprivations, would bestow on me a fictional title based on a real chief terrible in history. I speak of Count Dracula.

Ingle

The family had built and bought a number of houses in Sunningdale, dotted about the golf course, of which my father was a founder member. One of my five musical great-aunts, Emma Carandini Stokes – known as Aunt Tem – had a massive pile called Middleton by the seventeenth green of the New Course. My grandparents had put up North Lodge, then South Lodge, this latter being very tiny and to a casual glance placed right in the centre of the road, causing a nasty fright to any motorist who'd spent too long at the nineteenth hole.

My parents lived for years in the White Cottage, right in the way of a sliced shot off the second tee of the Old Course. But before they parted Mama withdrew to Crowood, a sturdy brick effort with a pleasant surround of firs on the Ladies' Course. There for the first few years after Father had vanished, she lived with Xandra and me and Grandma Sarzano – who called Xandra 'my heart' and made me furiously jealous until she noticed and placated me by calling me 'my *little* heart'. She was a wonderfully peaceful old lady, in an extremely excitable household, who never used any term of disparagement stronger than 'I don't care tremendously for him'.

It may have been the nearness of the fairways and some idea that I might spot my father playing a round that caused me to wander away for hours on the course, uncaring of the commotion that my absence created. Xandra was always swanking about the occasion she'd met the Duke of York when he was playing with Papa, though I must have erased from my mind the fact that she was a tot in her bath when this happened, a very long wood shot from any fairway.

Anyway, there'd be panic and despondency and the police would be called out, and yet another nanny would give notice, and I'd be found at last pottering about in the rough, or taking a biscuit and tea in a strange house, or hanging around for the infrequent trains at the level crossing.

Most often, I was in the Greenkeepers' Shed, talking to the men who made the grass grow or raking out the bunkers with them. Xandra was five years my senior; I didn't care much for nannies; I liked to go off on my own.

It would be too gallant to call the nannies presentable – they were downright plain. I may have voiced this opinion to one of them in the outspoken way of extreme youth because to get her own back she sprang on me in the middle of the night wearing a hideous African mask. I was paralysed with fear and stricken with a lasting phobia against masks. If they were brought out at any celebration, I had to be hurried from the room uttering piercing shrieks.

They were a hard lot, these nannies. They called me conceited, opinionated and much too anxious to be the centre of attention – qualities which in adults are much prized by the media. I don't know what I called them in return – unprintable things, for sure. And I acquired a habit of throwing things. So the nannies didn't last long and as my mother always thought she knew better than the servants we became very much like a tourist attraction for domestic staff.

Only one nanny gritted her teeth and refused to be budged. Photographs of us at the time, shrimping with Nanny Winfield among rocky seaside pools, or buttoned up for a hike, show a strong facial resemblance between Nanny and Bertrand Russell. Though the parallel mustn't be bullied too far – she was no enthusiast of radical causes, for instance – she was similarly iron-willed on the domestic plane. She accepted the need mothers felt to get away from their children and have a life of their own, especially mothers like mine with a wide circle of acquaintance. In exchange for letting them have a share in What Was Going On, she demanded total control of the nursery. Mother couldn't get within a mile of it without an appointment.

Then the whole feminine caravan bore me off to Wengen in Switzerland. Mama and Xandra skied, but with the perversity that everybody now monotonously told me was the keynote of my character, I elected for the toboggan instead. I nearly paid for my independence with my life. At my very first attempt down a steep gradient, a fence reared up out of the snow to spoil my sport. At top speed the toboggan passed under it and continued on its way, while a horizontal board caught me on the forehead and stretched me out unconscious in the snow.

I was patched up only to face new hazards. A school called Miss Fisher's Academy was found for us near the village of Territet. We were there six months, during which time Mama's divorce came through, and as soon as it was spring enough for a fellow to walk a hundred yards without having a drift close above his head, I expressed my opinion of the place by running away, once a week. I was always tracked down among the vineyards and severely punished. This had no effect whatever and I repeated the performance with great regularity.

I no longer bear any animus towards Miss Fisher's Academy. And actually I owe to it my introduction to acting. I can't say if I was typecast on account of my general malice, but I was given the title role in Miss F's production of that ferocious folk tale, *Rumpelstiltskin*.

It was a good part, and I claim to have done it justice. I learned at the outset that the best lines are given to the baddies and that these make the most impact on the audience – especially if there is some pathos in their situation. Jokey parents told me I'd scared them more than if I'd been a gnome of Zurich. But I got my comeuppance at the concert party, where the joke was on me. I did a number with Xandra and the success was all hers. She was already giving signs of 'growing up into a handsome gel' and made a smashing Columbine. But as Harlequin I was caught short by stage fright and relieved myself in my costume. It was extraordinary how, on a suit that was already patchwork, the extra patch stood out.

As arbitrarily as we had gone to Switzerland, we now returned to London. I was enrolled at Wagner's, a private school in Queen's Gate. We trailed up and down the streets of London in crocodiles wearing little light-blue and black-striped caps. I was by this time used to being ticked off for villainy, and I felt I had only to breathe nervously to be beaten. With his large upbrushed moustache like the Kaiser's, Mr Wagner was very intimidating. He beat me as often as he needed exercise with a bamboo that had a hard vulcanized bottle top at the end.

'How could you do it?' my mother wailed, on hearing of this, that or the other misdemeanour, for which I'd been flogged as if it were a capital offence. How, for instance, could I have hidden Campbell's boots in the coal-bin? I was not only thrashed for hiding them, but thrashed again for lying about it. 'Everybody lies,' I pointed out with some truth. This nearly won me a third going over. Campbell, incidentally, became a distinguished member of Popski's Private Army. He reminded me of this incident quite recently.

Then straight out of the pages of Frederick Lonsdale, in a chauffeur-driven Buick and a Chrysler for weekends, Ingle swept into our lives. It was announced he would marry Mama. It began to rain silver-fox furs and diamond pendants. He was a banker. He was very short and energetic and prodigiously strong. He bent a poker round his neck for my entertainment. He began to organize us in all directions. If life did not exactly take a turn for the better, it began to revolve with great speed.

His given name was Harcourt George St-Croix Rose. The nickname Ingle must have dated back to a drollery of his time at Oxford University, because there was nothing of the catamite about him. Another peculiarity of his Oxford days was the record of having coxed the Magdalen College VIII one year, and stroked it the next. For such a relatively small man he was exceptionally powerful. He revelled in feats of strength and did odd little things to display his prowess, such as picking up a cricket bag loaded with gear in one hand and lofting it above his head. I was fascinated, but Xandra couldn't see the point. Nor indeed was there any, except sheer animal verve.

The river was very important to him, and since he was always restlessly trying out new houses, borrowed, rented or bought, we soon came to know several strips of the Thames. But first, as soon as the knot was tied with Mama, he bustled us all into a new town house, with a glaring orange door, at Elm Park Gardens in Fulham. My first impressions of the place were alarming, chiefly because our neighbour was the actor Eric Maturin, starring in a play called *Who Killed the Count?*

Maturin had an enormous dog as fierce-looking as himself. We had a large mastiff too, called Czar, and it was plain that, if ever they were allowed to meet, the Gardens would be drenched in the dogs' gore. So unbelievable efforts were made to keep them apart, and a very neurotic atmosphere resulted, until one day Czar slipped out unnoticed, charged at the hound next door and, while everybody put their heads in their hands, they slurped joyously all over one another and lay down side by side on the lawn as if they'd sprung from the same litter.

We were now fully in the business of meeting people again, with a five-storey house and garden, and a cook and a butler and a housemaid and a scullery-maid lodged under the eaves to help us meet them, not forgetting Nanny, though she was practically family, and a governess with a French accent who wheeled me round saying 'Hello' and threatened me with the guillotine if I said anything more.

We met everybody we had known before, plus all of Ingle's friends. As Ingle travelled a great deal for his bank, Speyers', was a fine linguist, and had helped blockade Sweden during the war as well as being a very free spender, this meant we were meeting a very large number of people indeed and it was white tie practically every night. Sometimes it was not till the following day that I realized how important the people were that I'd met the night before.

I was once actually hauled out of bed to meet two men, and shooed downstairs in my dressing-gown, admonished to rub the sleep out of my eyes because I would want to remember I'd met them. Well, I do remember them now – Prince Yusupoff and the Grand Duke Dmitri Pavlovich – though I was trundled back to bed without being told that they were two of the assassins of Rasputin.

I liked the Hungarians best. They were good-humoured and zesty and wore ridiculous, extravagant uniforms with dolmans. We went to Budapest, and stayed in the Hotel Duna Palota in the Pest part. Naturally the leader of the Tzigane band homed in on me, scenting my gypsy connections no doubt, and gave me a piece of music of his own composition with my name on it. Then one day in London a Hungarian arrived saying he had forty bottles of Tokay from the cellars of Franz Josef in Vienna. We took ten of them, and I was given a swig and asked if I could hear the clash of cymbals. Ingle knew a lot about drink. It was the era of the cocktail and the punch, of slings and shrubs and fixes, and Ingle could fix a daisy or a cooler as well as anybody.

Ingle's sister Evelyn was the mother of Peter and Ian Fleming, but we didn't meet them till later. Ingle and his brother Ivor were known as 'the Wild Roses', but we never met Ivor, seemingly because he'd married an Eskimo. Ingle had been married twice before and I wondered if we would meet his son Anthony or his daughter Camilla, who was said to be very beautiful. I don't think we ever did, or if we did they forgot to tell me why they were important, and why I was being introduced.

It was an extremely noisy marriage. Ingle was a jealous, passionate husband and if any man looked at Mama, he was reaching for his twelve-bore. But he did even trivial things at the top of his voice. I found it necessary to maintain a sustained barrage of eloquence if I were to be heard at all. And when we played word games, at which Ingle excelled because of his tremendous appetite for facts, they always finished with Mama and Ingle slamming out of opposite doors, Xandra weeping, myself walking to and fro yelling that I'd won and Czar barking.

There must have been discussions I didn't hear, though. It was decided that if I was to go to Eton, I had better first go to a prep school for Eton, and if I was to get into a prep school for Eton, I had better have a crammer. Or, better still, two crammers. Ingle bought me a tuckbox, which looked promising, then stuffed it with encyclopaedias. In due course I imbibed facts the way he did and acquired the besetting sin of every person with an appetite for facts, the burning wish to pass the information on to other people, whether or not they're anxious to hear it. Sundry wretches came to give my French some shape and my maths a despondent nudge. Having been in Switzerland, I was sure I had nothing more to learn about French and paid no attention to my unfortunate teacher. As to maths, I so hated it that the mere sight of the hieroglyphs on the page produced a strange tremble in my vision akin to camera wobble. I couldn't focus at all. And when it turned out that my coach had an affliction of the bladder, which required him to break off in the middle of every explanation and dash from the room, it was hard for us to get the correct answer to anything.

In the event, all the alarums and bad language were futile. Summer Fields prep school in Oxford was very magnanimous about my deficiencies. The school was confident in its own methods of whipping dunces into shape for Eton. Besides that, there was a fall-off in their numbers occasioned by victims of the Depression not being able to pay the somewhat expensive fees. So the place was possibly a bit less particular than usual about some of the young toads creeping in under the fence. And there I was sent to board, in the summer of 1931, in my tenth year.

Often I went to have lunch and spend the day with Aunt Tem out at Sunningdale. Though I looked like a piece of string I ate like a barracks, and she had the fixed idea that I wasn't being given enough to eat. 'You won't make many runs on Imperial Tokay,' she said, when I told her about Summer Fields, and instructed 'Porchie' to cook up something that would stick to my ribs. Miss Porchman, a countrywoman of awesome beam who acted as her companion, was nothing loath and trotted off to the kitchen with the air of a cook who likes to suck her own fingers.

'I'll just play something to whet our appetites,' Aunt Tem called after her.

I would much rather have heard stories of her adventures in the Australian outback, and how she'd sung from a covered wagon. But the notion was growing on her that not only my stomach but my musical wants were being neglected, so she murmured something about them 'being too rude for young ears' and settled in to play pieces by Liszt and Chopin. It was said her calibre wasn't up to Great-Aunt Rosina's but none the less she was pretty good. She'd coached the opera star John Brownlee, among others.

With her bravura performance that morning, I think she was trying to convey that music ought to fit somewhere into my scheme of things for the future. Her false teeth clicked like castanets, but I liked Aunt Tem a great deal, and tried to exclude the rattle in favour of the notes scored by

Liszt and Chopin. I stuck it out till Porchie floated back and said lunch was ready.

'Porchman,' said Aunt Tem, 'I do hope there'll be enough for the boy?'

'Enough and to spare for the angels, m'lady.' She always called her 'm'lady' though she was actually Mrs Stokes. It must have been an automatic response to the Carandini blood.

Aunt Tem took the carver. 'Porchman, this knife looks exceedingly sharp and dangerous. I do hope there's no likelihood of my cutting myself on it.'

'Bless you, m'lady, there's no danger in that edge. You could ride on your arse to London on it.'

Aunt Tem dropped the carver. The salty speech of the Australian bush was a long way in her past. She clutched her ample bosom and flew back to the piano. She thundered into a mazurka, while the lunch grew cold.

Having composed herself in this way, but still pale, she fixed me with a keen look and said she hoped that I might remember as I grew up that music was one of the higher forms of human endeavour. No doubt she was remembering the threats of encroachment from the coarser elements in her earlier life. I said I would.

We had a piano. Mama mentioned the possibility of lessons for me to Ingle. He wouldn't hear of it. 'We don't want him growing up a pansy,' said Ingle with finality. Ingle showed me many kindnesses as well as discharging the duties of a father.

He was a clever and capable man, but in some respects his understanding was limited.

Muscles of the Mind

In those days the summers were back to back. Winter hardly got a look in. It was as if my interests were handled by some divine agent who dealt only in upbeat productions. For five years I had a small part in a long-running show called Summer Fields, which had opened in 1864. Some of its rituals were quite theatrical. There was 'the Squish' when the whole school travelled from London to Oxford on the same train at the start of each term. There was 'the Black Book' where misdeeds were recorded and cancelled out with the cane at the end of the week. There were 'Borva Notes', recondite exercises in pedantry. Even the plays were moderately theatrical. Twice I appeared in works of the Bard, which were produced without a line cut from the original texts.

It was a forcing-house of scholarship. The writer John Lehmann has said that he went for his Eton scholarship stuffed like a Strasburg goose. At the same time it was, like many successful English prep schools, essentially a family affair. The mood swung from Homer to Jeffrey Farnol. One might feel raw from the sterner disciplines, but then one was larded through with fussing over minor ailments, so one emerged like a steak Diane. The place is still there, putting on dog over its famous names in politics and academe, but I can see it only as a landscape of the past. It's dotted with small, excited figures who hardly ever look much further ahead than the next carnival of sensations. Looming over them are giants called GB and JFE and AFA and CAEW, all mightier than any PM at Number 10 could be. Harold Macmillan was at Summer Fields – he would recognize the truth of that.

But also there were the gentle Misses Hill, who coaxed the new bugs out of their Stygian ignorance. The Head's daughters were Ferelith and Perdita. Perdita married a master who played golf. There was a nine-hole course at the school and one day he invited the golfing writer Bernard Darwin (an Old Boy of course) for a game, and I carried his clubs to make an impression. Bernard remained my friend for the rest of his life, though I was nearly thirty when I took to the game.

It was a higgledy-piggledy place, with a central complex of chapel and gym and classrooms and dining-room all somehow fudged together with a long connecting corridor covered with glass. There were outlying buildings in which we slept, first in dormitories and later in cubicles. There was Old Lodge and New Lodge, and Old Borva and New Borva, and Mayfield and Newton. The Head lived in Cottage. The whole little empire looked out towards Oxfordshire countryside, over a ha-ha (meant to keep cattle out of the classrooms). Immediately adjacent was a farm. Every day an old chap carried the fresh milk to the school on a yoke across his shoulders, varying his route so as not to make tracks on the field. Every year we had a hay feast in the fields.

The Cherwell meandered round the school, making one of its boundaries. We made expeditions in punts to discover its source. First we had to pass a swimming test in water shallow enough to walk, under the gaze of a short-sighted master. I'd always been scared of the Thames, lower down, but this little tributary straight away appealed to me.

Hermione Eccles Williams, the Head's wife, wrote the letters home correcting whatever false perspectives mothers were bound to have. I was both terrified and cocky, and as it proved impossible to beat either of these qualities out of me she quite often wrote to Mama. Then Mama would come down on the school like a typhoon and the wise old clergymen who ran the place would flirt with her and tease her and she'd depart all smiles. Her behaviour must have detracted from the credibility of her prime recommendation that I be protected from any strong sensation whatsoever.

I was said to be highly strung. I so longed to please and I was at the same time so suspicious that I must have appeared ultra-touchy. Mama required that when the fireworks display came round on Guy Fawkes Day I should be detached from my peers and hold the hand of Hermione Eccles Williams and watch from the safety of her drawing-room window. I was mocked for this. I was also mocked for my insistence on my foreign background. The fact that the Italians had been on our side in the war did not palliate the offence of my family connection.

We were fewer than a hundred pupils and we had about a score of masters to teach us. Private-school boys are tremendously advantaged in having very small classes. The individual attention often felt like persecution, but there's no doubt of the ultimate value. Masters like

'Liz' can fulfil themselves by teaching in their own way. Liz was the Reverend Lysaght, who wore his collar backwards only on Sundays, and taught history with the help of cartoons. He drew everything, and chipped in puzzles and diagrams. His *coup de théâtre* was to unfurl an enormous sheet and reveal Edward Longshanks (applause!).

Alas, as it seemed to me, history had taught him to regard all foreigners as potential invaders. The necessity of having allies was the curse of politics. This attitude produced a nasty moment for me. I had adopted the accent of my mother to pronounce the name of the Empress Maria Teresa. The class was convulsed with laughter. I was about to utter an indignant protest when the teacher's ruler came down on my head. 'Marya Tereezer!' he sharply corrected me, and added, 'You're English, boy, and don't you forget it!'

I did not forget it. I strove valiantly with English things, and acquitted myself quite well with some of them, especially those very English things, Latin and Greek. Which brings me to GB who took the scholarship form and, on the way to it, many other things besides. What we knew of the Classics was riveted home by the force of his personality. He loved them, and love to him meant an all-round muscular effort of the brain. He had no patience with slackers and he believed God had averted his face from those who saw no purpose in the Classics.

He was tall and thin and slightly beaky. His hair had turned totally white when he was young – it was said, as a result of shell-shock in the Great War. For the same reason, he had a volatile temper. He boiled over very easily. He was absurdly easy to provoke and since he had a passionate dislike of Lloyd George and all he stood for, a boy had only to ask him a mild question about the little Welsh wizard to see him work himself up into a rage. There's nothing small boys enjoy more than goading highly articulate men into a rage.

In the long run his was the triumph. He counted every Eton scholarship as a special victory and even, in desperation, pushed one sick candidate all around Eton in a wheelchair rather than see the lad miss his chance. All honour to his memory. I write this despite my special dislike of one of his classroom ploys, which was neither bad-tempered nor witty but simply schoolmaster's beastly. For a minor solecism in a Latin construe he would cry 'Tweaks!' and the boys on either side of the offender would fall upon him pinching him. For a significant lapse in taste or grammatical understanding he would shout 'Roots!' and everybody near enough would pull the malefactor's hair. I thanked my stars that he did not teach maths, where I continued to plough a dismal furrow.

The desire to please overwhelmed me. The only way I could think of doing so was to excel at everything. I wanted to please GB in particular. I thought I must be a run machine at cricket. I thought I should be a charging centre forward on the football field. I thought I should bowl very fast. But my strength did not match my height, so I tried to please the school secretary instead, by imitating his action. Mr Bowtell's action is not often seen on cricket grounds but Mike Procter for Gloucester and Max Walker for Australia have done well enough with it.

One rotates one's arm not once, but twice, before releasing the ball, lending a windmill appearance to the movement which certainly surprises and may well mesmerize the batsman. So that one delivers the ball off the wrong foot. This is also a valuable piece of deception. On the other hand one hasn't quite the control a normal action gives. One may very well deceive one's own side. I found it hard to release the ball at the right moment. I built up terrifically and unwound at the crease with panache: the fielders and batsmen would all stare intently at the spot they supposed the ball should land. Then nothing would materialize. A shout of derisive applause from the spectators fifty yards behind me would be the first thing to signify the ball had gone backwards at speed to the boundary. Hanging on to the ball a fraction of a second too long had turned my stylish delivery into a subject for satire.

I persevered, though. In the constellation of my character defects, obstinacy shoved its ugly muzzle forward very early. I became with the passage of the seasons a bowling replica of Mr Bowtell. It occurs to me now that it may have been out of courtesy to Mr Bowtell that I was allowed to open the bowling for the school. As a batsman I made most of my runs in the nets. I was too flash for a long innings. I was always promising something amazing but out in the middle I let it go to hell. 'Keep your eye on the ball and not on the spectators,' said GB, going to the heart of the matter. I got the comeuppance that waits for the dressing-room comic when he tries to make a paying audience laugh. I would rather be out playing a stylish stroke than stay in with a bad one. It's an attitude that makes neither runs nor friends.

But GB indulged me. My father's exploits cast a long shadow. He had kept wicket for the Gentlemen and the even more gentlemanly I. Zingari club. He had once caught the legendary W. G. Grace, though naturally the great Doctor had declined to walk, on his usual grounds that people had come to see him bat and not to lose his wicket. My father had also played football for the Corinthians, but when it came to football GB seemed to run out of patience, and dug his heels in.

In my imagination I was a thrusting centre forward, a born striker. In

GB's book I was a natural goalkeeper, on account of my height and reach, and perhaps on account also of the fact that it was the only position in which I could be obliged to pass the ball to my team-mates. But I hated goal. And I was already weary of growing like a streak, and of the facetious remarks about my overnight increase in inches (at night dreams came to me in which I was stretched on the rack). I sulked in goal. There was a lot of friction. When I thought I could get away with it without being beaten, I would dive for the ball and then let it slip through my fingers into the back of the net.

GB actually took the question up with my mother. He was always willing to oblige, he said – considering his sulphurous temper this was a slight exaggeration – and he'd taken me out of goal, but the results had justified his original opinion. What happened was one of those little catastrophes that haunt you when earthquakes are forgotten. True to my dream I broke through the opposition, and had nobody to beat but the goalkeeper. He was the stripling heir to Lord Chandos and since he was nearly blind without his thick glasses he should have been no problem. I lashed out – and missed the ball altogether. I landed on my back in the mud. The ball came to rest three yards from the Chandos lad. He stared about vaguely, wondering what had become of it and of me. GB was upset. Scenes like that detracted from the dignity of sport. I was arrested and put back in goal, while the young Chandos was liberated to trot peacefully and aimlessly up and down the wing and sometimes off the field altogether.

Amphibian

I ought now to be able to report that my display tactics brought me success as an actor at school. But the laurels deservedly went to Patrick Macnee, whose talents were somehow kept in pickle over the years until they came out sharp and sound when he made his name as John Steed in the best of all television series, *The Avengers*. Mother and Ingle and Xandra, who drove down to Oxford to see me and celebrate my first night in puff pastry and fizz at the Mitre, were all knocked out by Patrick's style.

As King he was the star of *Henry V*, in which I played the Dauphin, who has quite a lot to say for himself in two languages, notably

> *Self-love, my liege, is not so vile a sin*
> *As self-neglecting*

and

> *I will trot tomorrow a mile, and my way shall*
> *Be paved with English faces.*

The part might have been written for me. I was also Mowbray to Patrick's Bolingbroke in *Richard II*. There I was a character doomed to exile early in the proceedings. Some people thought this was very fortunate. But I had enjoyed the magnificent surcoat and chainmail, the dashing moustache and imperial beard and the splendid shield. The chain mail was made out of string heavily coated with silver paint. This left gratifying traces on the skin and as we had only cold baths they lingered on into the holidays.

I had friends, but none close enough to take home. As it happened, home was a movable feast. Ingle as the European representative of an

American bank was a great traveller. The thought brings back the smell of hot croissants mixed with steam, hastily eaten while hurrying to climb on the Blue Train in the Paris Gare de Lyon. And then in summer his restless disposition led him to rent one house after another, always in sight of waterfowl.

In later life I've had my fortune told by exponents of all the disciplines of futurology and the occult. The Tarot pack has been spread; my palm has been tendered; predictions been made with the help of tea-leaves and tea-bags and the bumps on my cranium; Margaret Ronan has written a thirty-page interpretation of my stars. The seers are agreed on one point: that water is not my element. Ingle was a great wet-bob. To me, water has spelled misadventures. If the readings had been made at the outset, I might have been spared some difficult moments.

In an incident at Shiplake, on the Thames, I used up my first life. Our house had a lawn built up on piles overlooking the river. I didn't like the look of the water. It was dark and weedy, in my eyes a straight model of the Styx. I declined to dive.

'Don't be such a coward!' jeered Mother in a picture hat. Ingle sculled about below, looking scornful. I toppled in. I did not come up. My mother began frantically signalling. Ingle rowed intrepidly round in small circles. It was a lot deeper than anybody thought and I found it horribly lacking in illumination. When at last I broke surface and was hauled ashore, Mother was convinced I had cracked my skull.

'Don't be silly, Mother,' I said.

'Lie down and don't speak,' she replied.

'I don't want to lie down,' I said crossly, 'I'm only a bit out of breath.'

She looked at me sorrowfully. 'You've banged your head,' she said.

'I can't have done, I didn't even touch bottom. Perhaps there isn't a bottom,' I said, trying to break away.

'Poor Kiffie, he banged his head so he doesn't know what he's saying.'

I shouted back that I was all right, except that I hated diving in the bloody Thames. But it was no use. I was taken into the house and treated for a fractured skull. And later beaten for swearing.

Not that narrow squeaks affected Ingle. In due course he hired a house called Sagamore from the man who invented a cleansing powder for lavatory bowls. It was a gorgeous thing of Tudor timbers perfectly proving the saying that where there's muck there's brass, and had a drawing-room which jutted out over the boathouse. When Ingle said 'Race you to the boats,' he expected me to dive out of the window. Because I wanted to please him, I did. It was always a close thing, whether I reached dry land again.

Another life went at Whitchurch lock near Pangbourne, also on the Thames. Ingle owned a mill with a rose garden on a backwater there, plus the weir and lock. I often helped the lock-keeper let the water in and out to pass the steamers through that plied the river – boats named after local villages, Goring, Streatley, Wargrave and so forth. One day, for a dare I had proposed myself and to impress people, I rode a bicycle at great speed with no hands and vanished into the lock. Mother again thought I was done for, and I don't know why I wasn't. The bicycle certainly was.

On the third occasion, it wasn't my life that went but a stag's, and there was no bringing that one back. In the West Country we rode a lot. Xandra, with the natural affinity of young women for horses, rode very well, and I thumped along behind, sometimes breaking a collarbone or getting concussion and sometimes hanging on to the mane long enough to get home in the saddle. We went out with the Devon and Somerset staghounds, and one day came down a steep gradient at Porlock to see the stag heading out to sea with the huntsmen after it in a boat. There on the crest of a wave they cut the creature's throat and towed it ashore for the *gralloch*, when the body is cut in pieces and the entrails distributed to the hounds. It put me off bloodsports for life and made me associate water with darkness and death.

Of all our summer perches the house in the Quantock Hills in Somerset, Chargot Lodge, was the most all-round certainty for an idyllic life. There were lakes and a rough shoot with pheasant and pigeon and rabbit. Ingle bought me a small .410 shotgun and taught me to use it, and how to go fly-fishing. Chargot was set in a huge estate and a great bell swung in the wind outside my bedroom window, which gave the house the reputation in the countryside for being haunted, but was actually there to summon workers from the fields at a distance for their dinner.

I found the crash of my shotgun alarming, which made Ingle somewhat impatient. He himself had a beautifully matched pair with Damascus barrels in chased brown silver. His guns were a lot smarter than his appearance when stalking. He had a green hat turned down in pork-pie style and he'd crouch for hours behind cover, though he could be smelt downwind for miles because of an evil mixture of creosote and vinegar of his own invention to keep insects off his pale skin. He'd wave irritatedly at me to keep my face down so it wouldn't give our position away. When at last something came within range, I'd fire with the safety catch on, and the only report was the bellow of rage from Ingle. My first pigeon came when I was lying behind a log with the sun in my eyes and I blazed away at the flutter of wings without ever having seen the bird. Ingle was so thrilled that I'd hit it that he came galloping over to shake my hand, oblivious of the fact that in my excitement I was still shooting in his direction.

My next bird got me into hot water. We were after pheasants at Cuckfield Place. I loosed off out of turn. It was this that was the sin, plus the fact that with it I shot Philip Magor's bird, rather than the incidental happening of my almost ending the life of that renowned polo player. After being suitably chastised I was forgiven and went to watch the polo, played by two teams of nine- and ten-goal men at Dunster Castle, headed by the Maharajah of Jaipur and Philip Magor. Then I took part in a game of bicycle polo against them and found that was no advantage to me, for they were just as good as if they'd been on horses. I kept the stick and treasured it.

I was a solitary by nature and spent much of my time reading books in trees. From Xandra's point of view I was a gadfly who spoilt her picnics by oafishly leaping out of a tree to startle her friends, screaming and knocking over tea things. I was beaten a lot for peccadilloes I no longer remember, and even my saintly grandmother said I was 'a tiresome boy' when an arrow of mine crashed through the glass of the conservatory she was napping in, and that was the roundest condemnation anybody had ever heard her utter.

My habit of throwing things had condensed into a passion for accurate knife-throwing. I threw knives as other people throw darts. I carried targets and sheath-knives about with me everywhere. I could even throw scissors with tolerable accuracy. Most of our friends had souvenirs of bloody encounters in some part of the Empire so there was never a shortage of weaponry from the walls. Though I never in all my youth matched the sporting feats of my father, nor of Ingle, neither of them ever killed a rabbit on the run, as I did, with an assegai. Some people took exception to my knife-throwing, which they said was too indiscriminate. The most angry of these was our friend Mr Steele, who forbade me entry to the house after I had forced his beautiful daughter Penelope (Xandra's close friend) to stand against a door while I threw knives all round her. I said that I was very accurate, and that the point of it was to *miss* her, and that it was ridiculous to be angry about that. Nobody cared for my logic. But when they spoke of gallantry and chivalry I did not tell them that I despised the young Lochinvar, and that in my heart I was the *grimlie knight*.

It was perfect and timeless. I was about to go up to Eton and take my scholarship, where, by insensible gradations, I achieved the eminence of

Ingle himself, who'd worn the flowered weskit and assumed the style of the most privileged society imaginable – 'Pop'. It was England at its zenith, hampers and engrossing textbooks compounded with the delicious smells of linseed oil and athletes' hair cream. And if any of the adults knew that there was a crack opening in the path before me which would shortly widen into a fissure, they never let on. Why should they? My future was no concern of mine.

Hot Pot

ngle said he was sure the Eton test would go *swimmingly*. I'd have liked a less aquatic note, but I was glad of his support. Even Mother, who monotonously told me that I was no good at anything, and therefore had nothing to be conceited about, hoped I would *sail* through.

When the hour struck I bussed along with the rest of GB's hopefuls to put up at the White Hart in Windsor, as prescribed by tradition. From there we'd launch ourselves on the Memorial Hall in College to sail, swim or *sink*. We were part of an armada of fifth forms from all over, with an identical prospect. We were glazed with the knowledge of being in the same boat. These were good years for Summer Fields; we were usually head of the scholastic river. GB was at the tiller, keeping us chipper, though he was inwardly fearful that the plague would wipe us out before we could set pen to paper.

In the event, it wasn't too bad. Our minds unwound like so many reels of film. Having briefly exposed their cargo, they rolled up again on another spool for discard. As it was wholly instinctive I felt able to look about and appraise the place and note the boys in their bumfreezers and the economic use of one top hat between two, one youth wearing the crown and the other the brim. By the time the viva voce came round I felt quite proprietorial about Eton.

The viva was held in the Museum. Among the antiquities sat the Head, the Provost, the Senior Classics beak, a historian and Bloody Bill Marsden whose intellectual speciality was obscured by the rumour current in prep schools that he was the reincarnation of Keate who had birched every boy at Eton. I was well used to beatings and couldn't imagine anybody laying it on harder than compact little Ingle, so I wasn't fussed by Bloody Bill's presence. I was, however, keeping a wary eye out for a mathematician. I'd scored alphas in Classics and French, but a double zero in maths. My papers were too bad even to be granted an omega.

The first thing I saw was a mummy in a glass case. The second was a little old man in glasses with a skin like parchment. This was the Provost, M. R. James. I knew that he was a master of the macabre, and I knew *The Ghost Stories of an Antiquary* very well. And so did all my form mates. In cubicles at school in winter, with the fire behind him, GB read the stories of P. G. Wodehouse to us as his personal favourite, but when the sun was over the yard-arm he read us the weird inventions of the pussyfooting old scholar who would interview us. Our deference was bound to be sincere. And I rather liked the look of him. I hoped to hear him read the stories to us himself.

He asked me the routine questions, to which I made the routine replies, though the answer about my reason for wanting to go should have been that I didn't particularly, but that everybody else wanted me to, and that it was practically the only school I'd ever heard of. And he wondered if I had Old Etonians in the family, and there were nods at the name Rose, though the word Ingle would have sent a ripple round the gowned figures at table.

It was all very amiable and polite. And when the results were posted on the Summer Fields board it was clear that the master plan had worked again. Six of us were in. I was placed eleventh on the overall roll of King's Scholars and I presumed that was more or less what was wanted. It then turned out that I had been living under an illusion.

To my very great surprise masters began to throw out hints in my direction about the merits of schools other than Eton. Nobody could actually bring himself to disparage Eton, that would have been as unthinkable as matricide, but they did manage to convey the idea that an interesting alternative existence was led by schoolboys elsewhere.

I couldn't see the relevance of this good news to my own situation. Had somebody been tampering with the tablets where it was written that I should go to Eton? To some extent there had been a change of plan, yes. It was a great pity that I had not exerted myself a bit more in my maths, sufficiently to be placed tenth in the order of King's Scholars.

The first ten were taken into College, called Tug. The others were not, and were called Oppidans. Oppidan life was more expensive than Tug life. Ingle had been prepared to underwrite Tug life, but Oppidan was beyond his purse. For the first time in our association something highly desirable was ruled out as too costly. It was true that we'd once failed to travel first class on the Blue Train, but that must have been a booking error.

Mother said, 'Oh dear, it's very sad, darling, but I'm afraid they can't take you at Eton for another year. So the best is to get on and find another place where you'd be just as happy. And in fact we've found another place where you'll just *sail* through the scholarship.'

The place was Wellington College. I was again greatly surprised by the answers to my enquiries on the grapevine about the new place. It was said to be a very military establishment. It was for 'heroes, and the sons of heroes'. But Mother had been specifically outspoken against my turning out like my father, so this was a great change of tack. She was herself the daughter of a cavalry officer and the granddaughter of a general officer, but we had not been soldierly at home for some years. And then Wellington had been founded by Prince Albert to make soldiers out of the sons of the fallen and I couldn't help thinking that if an entire body of young men was brought together whose fathers had been carved up in battle, they would put two and two together and see the fundamental weakness of soldiering as a career.

However, I was assured that though there was a strong military side to Wellington, there were many other sides too, including a Classics side. I had only to bone up on my maths and devote a term to polishing up my squash and it would all go *swimmingly*. And of course if I landed the scholarship, Summer Fields would have two credits for the price of one, and everybody could approach the repetition of my test in a light-hearted spirit.

So it fell out. My tally at the scholarship examination was a replica of my first score, even to the double zero in maths. I was in bed with flu at Elm Park Gardens when the news came through that I'd clicked again. Ingle and Mother came into my bedroom and flung their arms around me and carried on with an exuberance sadly missing the first time round. I found it odd, seeing that I was supposed to be a copper-keeled certainty to *sail* through. Really it was natural enough. The mixture of guilt and anxiety they felt, plus the beginnings of a slide in Ingle's banking success, were placing them both under a heavy strain. Keeping all knowledge of it from me added to Mother's burden.

Outwardly, apart from a slight switch in lines, there had been no interference in the direction of my life. I went through very similar motions. The final ritual at Summer Fields was the Leaving Talk. This was given in his study by the Head, the Rev Cyril Williams, and was the first public acknowledgement we'd had of the existence of the sex act. On the whole his information squared with ours, as bandied about in the forum called the Vinery, otherwise the lavatories. Neither did it extend our knowledge much. We remained as unclear about the way women were put together as before, and generally felt that the need to carry on the race was inadequate excuse for that degree of intimacy with girls. The more fastidious were glad that the obligation could be indefinitely shelved.

My mentors warned me that Wellington would be less solicitous about my comfort. They were right. It was in many ways an extension of the education that had gone before, but it was altogether harder, bleaker and acrid. There were many old servants of the College who felt their job was to make men of us, or kill us in the attempt. I went there when I was fourteen and early on had an encounter with a typical example.

Every house and every dormitory was named after one of Wellington's generals or a benefactor. They radiated like spokes off a central hub and through the windows at the far end you could see the statue of your eponymous hero. Mine was Combermere. The dorm had an annexe, with a corridor giving off on the bathroom, and a further annexe with a few cubicles to which you graduated with seniority.

Each dorm had a servant called a Jallyho, in our case a very bandy-legged person whose Army life had patently been spent with horses. His incoherence reinforced the impression given by his legs. When the bell for Reveille went his first task was to thump on the doors, shout at the top of his voice and hold the bathroom door wide while one shivering creature after another darted naked past him to plunge into the icy water he'd drawn. He then emptied the chamberpots, whose issue he obviously regarded as a soft, retrograde step on the part of HQ. Authority graciously allowed them, to prevent a constant traffic down to the Vinery all night. Their use after the bell was forbidden.

One day I was late in dressing. I looked for the Jally in his uniform of blue-and-white striped jacket and black trousers. Not seeing him, I used the jerry. Coming to make the beds, he discovered the crime shortly afterwards. I turned round from the mirror startled by the roar and the crash of his boots as he thundered down to me.

He shoved the pot under my nose, babbling, 'See this? See this? Oi'm takin' you orf to see Weldon!' Weldon was the head of the dorm, an eighteen-year-old with private quarters. The Jally banged hysterically on Weldon's door until that very grand being came out.

'Look at this 'ere, Mr Weldon, what this dirty young beast, this devil Lee, 'as done. In the daytoime too, Mr Weldon.'

I hotly denied it. I said it was conceivably a midnight happening. Conceivably the Jally had failed in his duty of clearing it up from the previous day. Conceivably some other villain had left his visiting card.

The Jally cut straight into my protests. 'Wotcha mean, yer did it last night? Yer done it just *now*—' He suddenly whipped his free hand over and stuck it straight in, shouting triumphantly, '*It's still waarrrm!*'

I was immediately summoned and thrashed. As I straightened up, I said to myself, 'Floreat Etona!' It seemed I had fallen among barbarians, with nothing to be done about that but grit it out for the next four years.

Stiffeners

'There are more statues to soldiers than to civilians,' remarked the young Custer entering West Point as a cadet. At least, Errol Flynn as Custer remarked it, in *They Died with Their Boots On*. I had ample scope at Wellington in the late thirties for making the same observation, without any corresponding increase in the urge to wind up either as a soldier or a statue. Yet I came to feel some loyalty towards Wellington. And this is hard to explain, since in almost every particular that I can recall, it was coarse, grotesque or harsh. Boys in their teens are generous with their loyalties; that may sum it up. To me, and I guess to many others from that belt of English public schools in the thirties, Lindsay Anderson's brilliant *If* . . . came across not so much as an essay in fantasy as virtually *ciné-vérité*.

Prince Albert in 1857 had been emphatic about the importance of a private life to a growing boy. There must be a place for him to retreat from the minatory stone faces of Wellesley, Talbot, Upton and Picton (the one who wore his top hat in battle), from Orange, Murray, Anglesey and Blücher (his fellow Hun). So we had cubicles in the dorms, wooden partitions where we could set up the furnishings of our inner being. Some set them up ascetic and bare, and others, sensuous, barring pin-ups. I fixed mine colourful and simple.

A bright orange coverlet draped the bed, which had a brass headrail and above it a hanging bookcase. Ingle bought me a small desk and a chest. I had a makeshift safe to guard intact the store of marshmallows which were my passion. A favoured guest would be offered a terrible wicker armchair. There was no place to cook, but under the window seat at the end of the dorm a very small radiator providing a brief *interregnum* of warmth between cold baths. And on it, every year between October and May, I fostered a prize crop of chilblains.

The privacy of the cubicles stopped some way short of the ceiling. If a prefect suspected you were up to no good, making yourself blind or driving yourself mad through sexual fantasy, he would jump up the far side of the wooden partition and stare down. Frequently when quietly immersed in *The Georgics* or gloating over an illustrated encyclopaedia, I was alarmed by the abrupt appearance of a disembodied head peering over the side.

Privacy was also eroded by the habit prefects had of springing about from one cubicle to another yelling 'Boy!' and lying doggo to fool the wretched slaves who were obliged to respond to this summons. Those who located the source last collected whatever unpleasant job was going, a kind of perverse Dutch auction in which the last bidder gets the prize. And those who showed slackness in locating the source were beaten. That goes almost without saying. Being already a long-time habitué of flogging chairs, I was not surprised by the Wellington system, except that the minimum ration was six, and the addition of beatings by boys was a disagreeable novelty.

We were freed from the bondage of fagging when we passed a stiff examination in knowledge of every detail in the chronicle and customs of the College. This did not strike me at the time as having any value beyond the immediate reward of ceasing to fag and of wearing the house colours, which blissfully allowed one to blend into the pack. But I can see now that it was also a way of ensuring that otherwise forgettable trivia would be recorded accurately when the sons of heroes came to write their memoirs.

Every Vinery had its own name – like 'the Pumps' – that we had to know. Every Vinery was what W. C. Fields called 'A wall of human flesh'. We waited in lines to take our turn in cold showers, baths and doorless lavatories.

Every master had his nickname. I should say, every *usher*. The ushers who were in charge of houses (which in practical terms were *dormitories*) were called tutors. Combermere's tutor, and therefore mine, was Herbert H. Wright, known as Lofty. He stood six four. It was a nickname I was growing into myself. I envied him for having stopped growing. His clothes fitted; mine never did.

As the masters were all called ushers, the way was open for the Head to be called the Master. He was called Freddie Malim, though never to his face. I believed he could not read a Christmas story without making his audience tremble, but I may have been wrong. Bobby Longden, who had succeeded him by the time I reached the Classical Sixth, was charming and I was personally saddened when in 1940 a German bomb fell on Wellington and killed him. He was the only casualty.

There were tutors called the Drain and the Egg and the Hun and the Monk. Some nicknames seemed to derive from the language of Biggles. There was Hoppy, and Mac, and Huz Guz (for Hughes Games) and Taggers (for Eustace). If I enrolled again today I'd pass the test with flying colours. I don't suppose, though, that they'd be any more willing than last time to trust me as a prefect.

The porters and coaches were not ignored. There was Mole and Gowie and Price, who had an artificial leg and there was a running controversy as to whether it was the real or the artificial leg that squeaked. A. E. Relph, however, makes an exception to my total recall. He was an England bowler who'd played against Trumper and Armstrong and Spofforth and Soforth, and a lovely bamboozling player. He would have had a nickname but if I ever knew it it was knocked out of my head by his appalling end. I think it was on the Good Friday of the year in which I was sixteen that he placed a shotgun on a chair in the Pavilion with the barrels facing towards him, knelt down in front of it, and pulled the trigger.

The fields were called Turf, Derby and Big Side. We knew all these things and the scores that had been made on them back into the mists of antiquity. And the names of the governors from the King down, through Victoria's grandson the Duke of Connaught who presented me with a Prize for Progress (meaning perhaps half a dozen beatings fewer than the previous year) all the way to the Bishop of Norwich who confirmed me and spoke at greater length than any prelate before or since.

We wore caps so constructed that the peak could not shield the eyes, nor the back guard the neck. In summer we sported boaters with ribbons. We did not doff them. Instead we saluted with one finger when passing an usher, a dwindled version of touching the forelock. They acknowledged the salute. There were many more of us than there were of them, and some of them kept their hands up permanently.

Under orders I spoke at great length myself. I delivered the whole of Cicero's *In Catilinam* speech. Likewise the whole of Demosthenes' Philippic against the tyrant of Macedon. I was by no means surprised to hear an usher called Dortsch recite the whole of *Beowulf* in the original Anglo-Saxon, a language he spoke fluently on the rare occasions that he could find anybody to understand him. I attended the Debating Society but I never once had the courage to say anything of my own.

The only time I acted in any show I had a tiny part as a raffish pirate in a production devised, written and produced by an American boy. He had a total enthusiasm for England and the play was a mixture of *The Pirates of Penzance*, Peter Pan and *Young England*. Somehow he squeezed the character of Popeye into this, which was sung by a lad called John Addison, who was already a fine pianist and went on to be a prolific and clever composer of film music, such as the Steamboat material in *Maggie*.

I sang in a raucous baritone and enjoyed being in the choir. We went to Bagshot Hall, where there was a great big room with an organ in it, and let the Duke of Connaught have the Hallelujah Chorus right between the eyes. The old chap took it well, but soon afterwards when my friend Sapper (the author of *Bulldog Drummond*) died, and I went to a service at Canterbury with his widow, I was shushed for singing too vehemently. Generally the English do not think it polite to speak to God in a voice much above a whisper.

The business of my being a semi-dago, coupled with the conflict of my desperate wish to please, continued in an accentuated form. I had an idyllic Derby day when I made 149 not out in a cricket house match, often scooping the ball on to the railway to the annoyance of the umpiring usher, then ran out of partners, flung my bat down in the pavilion and wept tears of vexation that I had not been able to get 150.

Less and less were team games my style. I achieved glory by scoring a goal with my left ear in a hockey match, with a quick flick of the head, but I was not so useful when handling a stick in the conventional way. My years of martyrdom as a goalie in soccer came to naught, because Wellington played football only with the oval ball. The brown and orange rugger shirt worn by the College XV, making them look like a swarm of angry wasps, seemed just right for this game in which, as a full-back, I was always being mauled to fragments. Again, my reach should have made me a contender as a boxer, but my strength-to-height ratio was still all wrong. I was put in the ring with dense little Rocky Marciano types who gave me a terrible going over. One broke my nose.

The rackets courts were a haven. They proved my solution to the need I had for privacy, where I could pull myself together. Rackets and fencing had no team atmosphere and I became a passable performer at both. They demanded eye and wrist more than courage and muscle. I hoped I might become quite good, though the ageing pro who taught me, Walter Hawes, always said, 'Ah, you'll never be the player your father was.'

Sometimes, very infrequently, Xandra and I now saw Father in the holidays. She had always written to him. He wasn't, himself, the player he had been. He was no great age, but he had injured himself badly running for a bus, and walked always now with a stick.

Offal on the Square

Sparta will always conquer Athens. We didn't expect to be cosseted at a military school, even if it did have a Classical side. We played on pitches frozen like lakes, and if we fell we bled, and were left to get on with it. The vivid smell of mud and blood together occur as a reprise through those years.

Of the many acrid smells of Wellington, of sweat and old games clothes and old grammars and inkwells stuffed with chalk and blotting paper, and metal polish and floor wax and brickwork, the most pervasive and detestable were those of Brasso and Blanco. The horrible green stuff that one put on one's webbing came off over everything. The Blanco came off on the brass, and the Brasso came off as a white smudge on the webbing, and couldn't be got off without scrubbing. Then you'd be faced with a light patch and the Blanco had to be put on again, and the whole rigmarole restarted from scratch. We'd sit up into the night getting it right.

Late at night, the polishing, polishing, polishing of boots, buttons, buckles, webbing, plus pressing one's trousers, ate into one's sleep, which seemed to be wiped out altogether when we got up at an ungodly hour to continue with the heartbreaking process of getting the exact amount of space between each layer of puttee. The distance was invariably wrong and they often came undone. Then, taking the stupefying smell along with us, we'd draw rifles from the armoury. Every time I thought what a terrible misuse it was of the beautiful grounds set among silver beeches to hold parades and weapon training among them.

Inevitably my uniform looked as if it had been made for someone else. Inevitably I was the automatic choice on account of my height as the Right Marker, conspicuous by definition. And I loathed that. When the order 'Markers!' came, I'd have to rocket forward into the open spaces of the square with my rifle by my side, wait for it till 'Fix!' was shouted, which jerked the rifle between my knees and the bayonet upheld, till finally 'Bayonets!' obliged me to make an exhibition of slamming that tricky bit of steel into its clasp. And as I stood there, swaying like a bare flagstaff in the wind, my puttees would slowly and shamefully unwind from my thin legs.

This phenomenon was on one occasion observed in all its detail by the OTC commander, Major Mackenzie, who glittered and gleamed through night ops and the pouring rain on field days, Sam Browne, buttons, ginger moustache and all. He hove to before me and barked the single word, 'Offal!' And at the far extreme of the rank, he said to the most diminutive khaki soul who brought up the rear, 'Ullage!'

Germany as a possible opponent wasn't mentioned, while we drilled with the Lee-Enfield .303 and the Bren. Our enemy was Eton. We marched against them across huge expanses of land between Bagshot and Crowthorne to Caesar's Camp. We looked down our noses at them in their plum-coloured uniforms with light-blue chevrons all over the place. I understood that we always won. I didn't care. One entrance to College was called the Path of Duty, the first half of a Tennyson line that ends 'is the way to glory'. That path actually led from the tuck shop, where we gorged ourselves on bananas and cream and wonderful chocolate marshmallows. To me that was the right end of the path. On field days I became 'Dead' as quickly as opportunity offered.

It was the kind of weakness Ewan Charteris felt in honour bound to bring to public notice. Charteris was a boy who appointed himself my conscience. He was the personification of bounce and virility and endeavour and I ran round corners when I saw or scented him coming. He invariably pointed a finger at me and out would come his latest accusation, 'You're yellow, Lee, I saw you funk that tackle,' or whatever it might be, and someone eminent would hear him and I'd be beaten.

Often enough, I found ways of being beaten without his intercession. My remarkable crime sheet included throwing a light bulb at an usher, forgery and being beaten too often. The forgery of signatures was a talent I discovered in myself early on, and once in the holidays I forged cheques for millions of pounds in a book of one of Ingle's friends called Guy Tylden-Wright. At Wellington I was blackmailed by a kangaroo court into forging an usher's signature to a notice cancelling a cross-country run. Then one day an usher asked me to forge the signatures of all his colleagues on one sheet, which I did, and it was hung in their common room.

The beatings were logical and therefore acceptable. You knew the rules, you broke them, you paid for it. This was brought home to me with great force once on Ascension Day, a suitable date for contrition. We'd been given the whole day off, to go where we pleased, and our tutor had stipulated only that we be back before six for evening chapel or there would be trouble, by which, he said, when making the announcement during prayers the night before, he meant trouble.

I suggested to my friend Carrington-Smith that some rich friends of my mother called Argles near Twyford would be overjoyed at the chance of giving us lunch. If he liked we could borrow some bikes and cycle over to the Argles' lovely place. Carrington-Smith was a well-behaved lad so I forbore to mention that I had not consulted our prospective hosts. He blushed and said he would like it enormously.

All went well. Though stunned by our unexpected visit they duly laid out a magnificent lunch. It was no sense of being unwelcome that made Carrington-Smith say that we should start home in good time. It was simply that he made it a rule never to be beaten. I acceded to his request. Crossing a big stretch of open common, some five miles from Crowthorne, my bicycle chain broke. It was unmendable. I had to walk. Carrington-Smith, noble friend, got off his bike and walked with me.

We were late. We missed chapel, we missed prep. We denied nothing. We told the truth. We apologized. 'Here,' we said, 'is the broken chain.' And this kind man our tutor took us in turn to his study, spreadeagled us on the sofa and gave us six with the bamboo. Poor old Carrington-Smith! He found it hard to forgive me.

After he'd beaten me, Lofty came to me with a smile where I was fighting back the tears and put his arms round my shoulder, saying, 'I'm sorry, Christopher, I had to do it. I did tell everybody six o'clock.' I replied plaintively, 'But it wasn't my fault.' He said, 'I don't suppose it was, but rules are rules.'

None the less he bore me no malice, and I bore him none for this injustice. I knew well enough where I was with him. And piecemeal I had learned where I was with each of the parts in the Wellington structure. In the Classical Sixth I was even enjoying myself with the fresh teaching of the new Master.

Then when I was seventeen, with one more year to go at Wellington, the year in which ancient civilizations really begin to make sense, a direction for the future emerges and the harvest of privileges and bounties is poured on the senior collegian, the almighty crash came.

I heard from Mother that this summer term of 1939 must be my last. The money had run out. Ingle had gone bust. He was bankrupt for twenty-five thousand pounds. Everything must be sold up. I must bend my mind to getting a job. Xandra was already working as a secretary for a charity.

Nunc animis opus, Aenea, nunc pectore firmo. Now indeed was the time for the dauntless spirit and the stout heart. My first thought was horror and the conviction that we should all starve. Then the pendulum swung and I felt a certain exhilaration at the notion that it was up to me to pull the womenfolk out of the mire. There was nothing I could immediately do about it, though, until the end of the term. But I felt driven to do *something*.

What I did was to steal a ten-shilling postal order from a locker in the changing room. It was soon detected, I was punished, felt foolish and crestfallen and was quickly allowed to forget it. It was my last and only truly indictable offence at Wellington. I worked better for Bobby Longden than at any other time of my College life. I left with his kind farewell and no idea whatever as to what I should do next.

Short Sharp Shock

There was only one wheel left on the family financial vehicle. The houses had all been sold up, the flawns and the custards had all disappeared. Mother was down to the income provided by the interest from her Burma Rail shares. Xandra was pulling in three pounds a week as a typist in a drab office of the Church of England Pensions Board in Smith Street behind Westminster Abbey. Ingle was nowhere to be seen. It gradually dawned on me that he and mother had split up. Superficially the situation was highly charged with disaster.

Nobody was unduly demoralized. Grandmother had been born in the year of the Indian Mutiny and regarded herself as a natural survivor from the beginning of her days. Mother was delighted with a minuscule house called Ramblers Cottage, oddly shaped – like half a building – which overlooked a remote part of Wentworth golf course. The garden was the size of a sheet and in place of a mastiff she now had a dachshund.

As a working girl Xandra found herself the object of curiosity among her friends. Far from being shunned by them on account of it, she was even then making up a party with Mary Woewodski and Cynthia Monteith to visit Menton on the French Riviera as per usual. It was obvious that if there was a problem, I was it. The only two futures that had been seriously canvassed for me were ruled out. The possibility of a private income of a thousand a year, which Ingle had said was essential to anybody contemplating 'the Diplomatic', had gone up in smoke. The chances of my becoming an England cricketer and MCC tourist, based on a double century in a house match when I was thirteen, had finally evaporated with the discovery that my father had forgotten to put me down for the MCC when I was born. He'd forgotten! I was horrified.

Since most employers had taken off for their summer holidays and all the people we knew who had not already departed were preparing to do so, it was decided that the best way for me to confront the crisis was to go on holiday to Menton too. It would no longer be L'Hôtel d'Angleterre, but the Russian Pension Mazirov. There would be vodka and the balalaika, and tears and laughter. It would be a chance for me to polish up the extracurricular Russian I'd been learning with a group from Wellington that visited the great expert on czarist and Soviet matters, Sir Bernard Pares.

Off I went without delay, as if discharged from a ballista, landing first in Paris. I thought on the way of Ingle and how in the past few years his rows with Mother had become rather less amusing than they had been in the early days. As his money worries deepened, he had taken to drinking more heavily. He was always intolerant; the drinking made him only more irritable. I had an image of him early on sitting with a friend in the twilight by the Thames, slightly tipsy, popping off with guns at bottles in the river. It seemed quite funny at the time. Now it was superimposed with other pictures, of him being carried home from his club, White's, and another of him brandishing a gun and yelling at Mother. I couldn't imagine what I was supposed to feel on Mother's behalf; I only knew that he'd always treated me well. I'd not seen so very much of him in my teens. He was always said to be up to his eyes in deals which took him on lengthy journeys. He never came to Wellington. He was an Etonian, I hadn't expected him to.

During my short stay in Paris, I was taken under the wing of one of Ingle's friends, Webb Miller. He was an American war correspondent and the author of *I Found No Peace*. I had just had my seventeenth birthday, and it amused him to find that in June 1939 I could have emerged from a military place of learning like Wellington with so little intimation of the build-up of hostilities in Europe.

Every aspect of my naïveté intrigued him. He soon perceived that *La Vie Parisienne* had never been my regular reading and, furthermore, that I would have been no more enthusiastic about the feminine half of Paris if it had been. He listened to my stories of College discipline and we talked quite a lot about crime and punishment. He drank a lot of wine and told me it was time I grew up and learned about life and death. He launched into graphic descriptions of executions in the electric chair, several of which he'd apparently witnessed. I was fascinated but I said it sounded ugly and a rotten way to die. He replied drily that he'd heard that Mme la Guillotine was uglier.

He spoke about various parts of the underworld he'd traversed as a journalist and of the behaviour of the Mafia, and I wished that I might have had his experience. He said that the chance might come for him to give me a glimpse in the next few days, but that I wasn't to let on to anybody because there were always killjoys about. I promised, and looked forward eagerly to the exposure of a nest of political agitators, and to contributing a few observations to Webb Miller's front-page report.

When he actually came for me, I was taken aback. It was still dark when he routed me out of bed a couple of mornings later. My watch said it was not yet four o'clock and I could not believe this was happening to me. Dry-mouthed with excitement and fear I followed him out into the street, seeing anarchists behind every tree and *pissoir*.

We took a tram with the early workmen through the empty streets, destination Versailles. Naturally I did not expect him to break the secret of our final venue by telling me with all these people about, even if they did look as if their English would be shaky. He said little until we had alighted, and with the dawn coming up, we came into an open place where there was quite a crowd and all around in the windows clusters of people were looking down.

Webb Miller said that the rooms were rented out by the tenants to spectators for quite substantial sums. The spectacle we had come to share with them was a man being guillotined. The prison lay dour and dark before us, and immediately before it, near the gate, the contraption with the knife. It was a ghastly shock. 'Oh, I don't want to see *that*!' I exclaimed, ready to burst into tears.

'I'm not trying to frighten you,' he said in avuncular tones. 'But I advise you to stick with it. You'll never forget how people behave. How people like to see blood. How cruel they can be!'

The gates opened eventually, after a long delay. The noise of trams and cars stopped, and every other sort of noise began. A great wave of howling and screams engulfed the square. Two middle-aged men came rapidly out of the prison bearing a man in white shirt and dark trousers. 'Eugen Weidmann,' said Webb Miller tersely. 'Night-club killer. Murdered a lot of women.'

They rushed Weidmann to that extraordinary structure, so that his bound feet came off the ground. His hands were tied behind him and his head was held back. They set him down by the plank and punched him in the stomach so that he fell forwards on to it, a strap went over his back, the plank tilted forward and the man they called the Photographer adjusted his head. In that instant the knife fell, and I thought I would die myself.

Webb Miller and I walked back without saying much, having stopped at the first bistro we found, for a *café cognac*. He had been right about the way the crowds behaved. I read that some had dipped their handkerchiefs and scarves in the blood on the pavement, as souvenirs.

But my friend was a bit shaken and hadn't much to add to underline the comments he'd made during the discussion when, presumably, the idea of helping me grow up had first come to him.

We were not the only people to have taken away a poor impression of this scene. It was the last public execution in France.

Webb Miller tried to divert my attention to the other attractions of Paris. But I had no interest in further sightseeing. I only wanted to get out of the place.

Wagons Lee

None the worse for having travelled third class, but afflicted (as I would be ever more) by nightmares of the guillotine, I arrived *chez* Mazirov in Menton with some curiosity as to how the other half lived. As it happened, in this old quarter of Menton, called Garavan, the other half was living quite cosily, and certainly very cheerfully. Every other guest was an exiled Russian prince, entirely at home with paintings and portraits of noble relatives looking down from the walls, and the Czar himself peering out of every corner in his anxious-looking way.

Xandra came down with her chums and her savings and correctly forecast that twenty-five pounds would see anybody of rational appetites through the summer. As well as the families – such as the Galitzins, the Zinovievs and the Mazirov octopus – the place was naturally flooded with personable young Russians seeking cultural exchange with Xandra, Mary Woewodski and Cynthia Monteith. One or two of them made themselves pleasant to me in the hope that I would put in a good word for them with my sister. When they saw that I had no influence in that quarter they desisted. I was satisfied to be left to my own devices and virtually banished from the *pension* between *le petit déjeuner* and *le dîner*. (The meals were French – I suppose they had been in Russia too.)

The food I took with me on my daily expeditions hardly ever varied. Every morning I bought a baguette, a large bunch of grapes and some gherkins from the local market. The gherkins ensured that nobody broke into my solitude. I was totally happy. It was possible at that time to sit on the beach without being trampled on or poisoned by pollution, or to hitch up at the bar of the Hôtel de Paris in Monte Carlo without sitting in somebody else's lap.

I took buses into the hinterland, to Sospel in the Alpes Maritimes, or into Italy for my first draft of authentic Italian air. And once, walking back across the frontier I pretended to be a girl, with two enormous peaches in my shirt. It was easy for me, dark and skinny as I was, though of course I would only have tried it with Italians who are only too eager to believe anything is a girl. In those days frontier guards took such deceptions in good part, and as I went by swinging my hips one of them propositioned me. I gave him a gherkin and told him to be satisfied.

If I missed the bus home I slept in the woods. In those days there was nothing in them more dangerous than a goat. There was a wonderful smell of hot earth and pines and flowers – to offset the goat. If I did get back there was dinner round a big oval table with fruit in the middle. Then we had dancing and drinking and tears rolling down nostalgic cheeks. I was encouraged to practise my Russian, but the phrase I most often used meant 'go away, Volk' to Mme Mazirov's wolfish dog.

The glamour trips were over the Corniche to Monte. I used to like watching Douglas Fairbanks all in blue sitting by the pool with his Great Dane on a leash, both of them eating ice-creams from Sorasio's. At the Sporting Club, Alberto Rabagliati and his Lecuona Cuban Boys were introducing the rumba and the samba to an international set uniformly dressed in one-piece suits and lounging pyjamas. Unfortunately for me I could only just catch the melodies of Rabagliati and his alternate, Wal Berg, strained through the walls. It was not permitted to enter the Sporting Club in casual dress, and I had no DJ. Seeing me pressed with my nose to the windows one day a very sporting fellow lent me his white tuxedo for a quick tour of the interior. He was much broader than me and it hung off me with the sleeves jutting over my hands. But that was all right. I didn't want to dance with anybody, shake hands or hold a drink. I only wanted to *know* what the place was like inside. When I came out, I knew, and there was no cause to enter the club again.

Bobby Cunningham Reed, great pillar of the local social scene, was envied for the possession of some primitive snorkelling equipment. My wish to test it was in conflict with my proven bad luck in the water, but when he invited me to come out in a boat with him and his son and a sailor, I succumbed to my wish to know. I discovered it was a kind of cement diving helmet, which enabled you to walk along the bottom, ten or fifteen feet deep, in the middle of Menton harbour. The sailor was there to pump air in. He smiled at me a lot and I said to Bobby that he seemed very nice. Absolutely charming, Bobby agreed, and added that he was a mass murderer. Flight from a vendetta in Serbia had led him to make his domicile in Menton. I thought that such a being would have little hesitation about pinching the line and cutting off my air supply just for the practice. I wanted to abandon the dive but Bobby said that would make him nervous. So I had to descend. It seemed a very long, sticky and claustrophobic experience. I had to hold my breath while the air was pumped in hot and hissing, and release it, gravely doubting the wisdom of doing so, when the sailor stopped pumping. I saw no future in snorkelling.

Had I been sentenced to remain in France for ever, I'd have been perfectly content, so long as the supply of baguettes, grapes and gherkins held up. Seeing this, Xandra arranged that I should stay on with the Mazirovs after she and her companions had returned to London. But quite suddenly, a tidal wave of panic and hysteria hit the country. The Germans were coming! The Germans were coming!

I was ordered to get on the first train I could, with my passport and a bag just big enough to accommodate a baguette, a bunch of grapes and some gherkins. I didn't like the idea of going on any old train. I preferred to wait for the Blue Train, even if I did have to go third. But I was told that tickets were absolutely meaningless. To get on was the great thing. In the *pension* grand old gentlemen were shrieking that they would don the uniform again and restore the czar.

The Mazirovs took me to the station, priming me to jump the train coming through from Rome. Mme Mazirov folded me to her ample bosom while Monsieur stood by like Ambassador Maisky, declaiming, 'You are going to fight for your king!' I didn't care for this sentiment, but I did appreciate their kindness. I was launched from Madame's bosom, when the train showed up, like a weeping greyhound from an upholstered trap, and cantered through the pandemonium on the platform just ahead of the mob.

I wriggled into a niche in the corridor, amidst cosmopolitan exhalations of fear, and was desolated to find as the train pulled out that my baguette, bunch of grapes and gherkins had somehow been dislodged from my stupid little bag in the charge to get on the train.

For hour upon hour the train chuntered along covering a pitifully small mileage. Then it stopped. Everybody got off. We transferred to another train moving in the reverse direction. Then that ground to a halt. We changed again. We lost all sense of direction after this had happened several times. Each train was more congested than the last, inevitably. We reasoned that we were moving, on the whole, north because we were being held up for more and more troop trains. Guns went by. Tanks went by. There was chaos at every station. There was nothing to eat or drink at any of them. People peed out of the windows because the effort of moving down the corridor was too great. It took a couple of days to get to Paris. There the chaos was suited to a capital city. It took most of a day just getting from one terminus to another. In the train from the Gare St Lazare I sat by a Frenchman who'd just had his hand amputated. He kept up a non-stop flow of chat, gesticulating all the time, both arms waving in my face and one of these ending in a bandage, all bloody. Wedged between us was a fat, blond German woman trying to go north to get back to *her* country before the balloon went up. All night the amputee addressed her, in a ceaseless tirade. Lord, how she wept!

We lost her at the second change on the way to Calais. The amputee had a struggle getting on the third train, which had people hanging on the sides. He declared that he was disgusted with his countrymen and that he'd rather walk. I got back to Dover on a jam-packed boat. There was a note on the mirror of Xandra's room for me, if I should turn up, saying that she was at the Odeon Cinema in Chelsea. I walked to it down the King's Road, and stumbled around the stalls till I found her. She was sitting with Micki Woewodski. I said 'Here I am' and began to tell them about the last few days. I was told not to disturb people; it could keep till the end of the film. This was *Spy in Black*, starring Conrad Veidt, the wonderful actor on whom, had I wanted to go into films, I should have most wanted to model myself.

Something in the City

Nobody we knew was much interested in the coming war. Not wanting to be known as a poltroon, nor as a young man bent on making people's flesh creep, I kept quiet about my acute sense of foreboding and my trip across France.

A couple of days after the E-flat welcome I received in the Chelsea cinema, I was sauntering across Wentworth golf course bending the ear of Dorothy Clarke, a friend of my mother's, on the subject of my great enthusiasm for Conrad Veidt, and how fantastic he had been both in silents and talkies. In common with various of Mama's cronies, she had been extolling the benefits of gainful employment and how I must do something positive to help out, but Veidt's name registered powerfully. Good heavens, she said, she had known old Connie terribly well years before. The long arm of coincidence, attached to a golf club, then chipped out of a bunker, and the ball was followed a moment later by Connie in person. We gaped at him open-mouthed as he shook us by the hand and interrupted his game for half an hour to chat.

Then we went our separate ways, he to Hollywood and a sequence of roles as Nazi officers in films that were not worthy of him, and I back to Ramblers Cottage to implement my mother's suggestion that I go to work in the City. In acknowledgement perhaps of the vast deal of custom Ingle had brought to his shipping company, the managing director of the United States Lines in Leadenhall Street interviewed me as a prospective shipping man. I wasn't at all keen on going to sea, but I was assured that it would not be necessary, a great quantity of key work remained to be done on dry land. The boss was a splendid old American called Mr Jackson, and in appearance he might have been a direct descendant of his namesake, Old Hickory. He believed I would go all the way to the top, for which the ideal point of departure was the bottom. I would accordingly start by taking care of the mail and the tea and running any errands in the City that seemed to need urgent personal attention. My pay would be one pound a week.

The assumptions behind my education were that when it was complete I would be ready to lick the world. Now that it was, it seemed I was not fit for anything but to lick stamps. A strange blank interval began in my life, rather like a dream, in which one moves to and fro perfectly aware but unable to direct one's own actions.

My only suit was a blue one, acquired from Burton's 50-Shilling Tailors, and worn with an Old Wellingtonian tie. Xandra had taken a bed-sitter in London and saw us only at weekends, so she lent me her bicycle. At a very early hour in the morning I rode out on it. First I looked out across the land that sloped away in the front of the house to woods of beech and silver birch and a small bridge that crossed the railway line, to see if I could deduce what kind of day it would be and whether my train was signalled. Then I would cycle furiously, like a clown at the circus with his knees jutting out, to catch the train at Virginia Water. From the London terminus at Waterloo I took the tube under the river called the Drain, and fetched up panting and steaming to report for duty in the office of the chief clerk at 9 a.m. It was a routine similar to that followed by a hundred thousand other office juniors and clerks and I looked in every way like them except that I wore no bowler, feeling that to add further inches would be to gild the lily.

I had hardly laid the cornerstone of my career as a shipping magnate when war broke out. Chamberlain chose to declare it on the Sabbath, which any Old Wellingtonian hearing him while looking out sombrely at a famous old golf club would recognize as par for the course. In fact he had barely started broadcasting when I made for the door. There were frowns. 'Where are you going?' I was asked. 'To telephone my aunt,' I replied. I was not referring to Aunt Tem, nor Aunt Vi, nor Aunt Liz, nor any others of the heroic Carandini mould. The phrase was a family euphemism for visiting the lavatory. It seemed the safest and best place to be, and in the lavatory I started my war, planning to feign dead and be directed back to base and the tuck shop when the first opportunity offered.

It seemed at first, however, that it was not to be nearly such an energetic war as the one we had waged against Eton at Caesar's Camp. The Army was even less bothered about enlisting my services than the City had been. Along with a few other recent schoolboys who felt neglected by the War Office, I took a journey to Finland. Our idea was that we would rescue the Finns from the Russian invaders. Our surprised hosts affected to be delighted by this callow set of volunteers, and touched that we had paid our own third-class fares. They gave us some white uniforms as camouflage in the snow, and took us up front to a perfectly safe area. We never saw any Russians, and went home after a fortnight. It was clear that the tiny Finnish army was doing rather well against the Russian colossus, without our help.

Christmas and the spring of 1940 went by and my working life was filled entirely with envelopes, papers, notes, messages, letters, stamps, tea and getting by on one pound a week. This was swiftly gone, with eight bob on fares, two bob on Woodbine's minuscule gaspers, and one shilling and sixpence a day on lunch down the steps below the concourse into Slater's in Leadenhall Market. That was made up of soup, meat and two veg, pud and coffee. I was bloated on it. I looked like an anaconda in a blue suit that had just swallowed a goat whole, until I'd spent the afternoon walking it off with urgent messages.

My evenings were blank, except for a visit to my first revue, when I was taken by Xandra's godmother Irene Carisbrooke to see *Stop Press* at the Adelphi. It was a double first – we met the star Edwin Styles backstage. He had a number based on the characters played by George Arliss – Rothschild, Disraeli and the Duke of Wellington – and every time Styles sang 'and the Duke' he winked down at me in the stalls. It was like a hand being stretched to me from a point somewhere near the horizon.

The great thrill of my week in a lifestyle which had shrunk completely was the weekend visit to the local pub at Knowle Hill called the Fox and Grapes, for bread and cheese and a pint. Even that fell short of perfection, there being no gherkins. I made do with pickled onions instead.

Nevertheless I absorbed the City and enjoyed it. I wandered with my messages down countless alleys and byways, among the sellers of jellied eels and old clothes as much as among the stockbrokers and Jews of the Exchange. Like somebody who takes the headlines of a newspaper for granted, I skirted the great institutions like St Paul's and the Tower and the Old Lady of Threadneedle Street, but the lesser institutions from the Wren churches to the Dog and Vulture all drew me in a marathon of tireless rubbernecking.

One afternoon, having wandered rather further and taken more time than the message I was on warranted, I jumped on a bus back to the office. I was standing on the top deck looking about for a seat when I recognized a familiar figure seated at the front of the bus. He was crouched forward, staring motionless out of the front window with his back to me. I would have known him anywhere, though, and had in fact spotted him in a place where I never expected to know anybody. It was Ingle. His collar was turned up, his hands were clasped before him. He looked as if he were contemplating a cast and waiting for a fish to rise.

It was the only time I had seen him since the collapse, when all his fortunes had gone out of the window. I wanted to speak to him. I wanted to say that I hadn't forgotten him. But I realized that no words would come. I was overwhelmed with sorrow and confusion. The bus drew up at a stop and passengers rose from their seats and filled the aisle, meaning to get off.

I allowed myself to be swept back by them and down the stairs. I stepped off the bus with them, and stood for some time watching the bus recede with the traffic. I never saw Ingle again.

Laocoon

Unexpectedly, a certain satisfaction with licking stamps crept into my daily round. I felt I was doing something on my own and that I was contributing. Nevertheless there were days when the position at the head of the board seemed impossibly remote and others when I felt an obscure resentment at being given a desk which was not partnered by any chair. Through contacts in the mail room I learned of a vacancy in an export corporation. There might seem to have been a poor future for export in a country beleaguered by U-boats, but my City colleagues prided themselves on taking the long-term view, so I took their advice and applied.

The chairman of my new enterprise, Mr Stanley Holmes, gave me an enthusiastic welcome on the day I took up my duties, and never spoke to me again. The firm was called Beecham's and manufactured a great range of products, all salubrious though not necessarily palatable. Commensurate with its commercial importance it had its headquarters in a large and glamorous building in Pall Mall, slap on the corner of St James's Square. Impressionable though I was, I had by now learned to take mundane practicalities into account. It was the presence of a tiny Italian sandwich place, set among the business fortresses and heavy clubs like a winkle among oysters, that clinched the matter.

The benefits of the change were largely environmental. I was still paid a pound a week, but I had a park to walk through on the way home. I still made the tea and took care of the mail, but I could also carry typewriters about and earn the smiles of the Robinson sisters and Miss Houchen and make jokes with Mr Micklem and Mr Dunbar about Olympian financiers who looked like heathen idols.

I still carried messages, but the extent of the Beecham interest in the health of the animal world was such that they provided a much more satisfactory mulch for fantasy. There was some kind of tie-up with A. F.

Shirley's veterinary interest on the Great West Road, which treated distemper and canker in dogs and possibly cats and other fauna as well. In addition to Shirley's Dog Powders the group did well with Phensic to restore ruffled nerves and Thermogen Plasters which you wore on your chest to draw the humours, and subsidiary products like Yeastvite to build you up and MacLean's toothpaste and Brylcreem to make you the sensation of the dance hall once you were built up. It gave me great pleasure to imagine a global network of communities needing these things, and to dream, for instance, of making personal delivery of twenty tons of Thermogen Plasters to Puerto Rico.

This desire to please led to my being allowed a spell as switchboard operator. I was trained in the important skill of putting plugs into sockets and pulling them out again. It was a busy nerve centre and I dare say that I looked like the statue of Laocoon wrestling with serpents, festooned in flex and hissing, as I dreamed of nosing my freighters into fantastical tropical berths, loaded up to the gunwales with Shirley's Dog Powders. But I became more competent. For once my height was on my side. I could reach the topmost sockets without leaping off the ground. I thought that in time I might evolve into an operative at the very top of the profession and manage a position on the Continental Bank of the international telephone service.

The war in 1940 became much noisier. I minded the bombs less than the sirens, which always turned my stomach over. We were warned at home that we should dig an Anderson shelter in the garden. This was reasonable because Wentworth Golf Club had been transformed into the HQ of one of the Commands, and General Ironside was in residence. But the Chief ARP Warden was thought to be officious and there was a great deal of malicious glee in the neighbourhood when the first bombs that fell around us dropped on his house. Luckily, he had believed in his own message and was in his Anderson shelter at the time.

The digging of our shelter was my responsibility. I flatly declined to do it, on the grounds that we had little enough garden as it was and that I should be bound to get into trouble with our neighbours for underground trespassing. It was in any case quite pointless, I said. Instead we slept on mattresses under the kitchen table. My sister was in the bath when the idiosyncratic vroom-vroom pulse of the German bombers first sounded unmistakably near. Mother and I were in our midget sitting-room and I grabbed her firmly by the shoulders and barked at her that everything would be all right and that they wouldn't hit us. She looked at me as if I'd gone mad, as it had not occurred to her that they would. How could any bomber aim so precisely as to hit a house that size? She writhed out of my grasp just quickly enough to see a cluster of bombs narrowly miss the railway bridge which I depended on to go to work, and score a direct hit on the greenhouses of Brigadier Critchley, whose estate filled much of the foreground. As it was then nine o'clock I persuaded her to put off inspection of the craters until the following day. She then made a tour on the Phut-Phut, a bicycle she'd bought with an auxiliary motor to help her up the hills.

As a result of it she said that our neighbours were in some jeopardy, and that we must offer to share the protection of our table with them. 'Critch', the Army's youngest and most dashing Brigadier in the First World War, courteously refused because he would not be remaining stationary for many minutes at a time during the coming months, but on the other side the offer was taken up by Valentine Smith, a distinguished scholar who was president of the society that believed that Shakespeare was a pseudonym for Bacon. I was surprised, when the raids were on, that a man with such an enormous vocabulary used a restricted language that was monotonously blue.

Then Beecham's gave up Pall Mall and moved out of London to Watford. It was too awkward for me to travel across country and I found digs with the Bowler family, made up of Ma and Pa and a nubile daughter. I was simultaneously pressed into the Home Guard, so that I was hardly ever out of my blue suit. We had neither uniforms nor guns, but my prowess at knife-throwing got me the name of being the platoon's secret weapon, and an invitation from Beecham's Mr Phypers to partner him at darts in the local league. We did very well, though many of our evenings had to be spent sitting on rooftops watching for mines to descend by parachute. None ever did.

A couple of times I escorted Miss Bowler to the cinema – no great distance as she met me outside the office when I finished for the day, and we had only to walk across the High Street to the Odeon directly opposite. Mrs Bowler was a statuesque but pleasant woman who monitored the relationship quite neutrally, her expression seeming to me to mix Keep Off with I Wonder. Rather vaguely I wondered too but I was too grossly underbriefed for any positive action.

It was fairly common in the Odeon for couples to hold hands. There were pictures when I thought Miss Bowler might have been complaisant enough to follow the fashion with me. But the idea that this licentious behaviour on my part might get back to my mother prevented me from striking any spark that might have led to an erotic conflagration. Miss Bowler never reproached me nor implied in any way that she felt slighted. In those days the cinema was a treat in itself.

During the winter, early on in 1941, my father fell ill. Though I'd been told it was serious, that he had double pneumonia, I wasn't prepared for the reality in hospital. He lay in a public ward surrounded by a wheezing apparatus feeding him oxygen. He was propped up on a heap of pillows looking straight ahead between pipes and tubes. I tried to conceal the extent to which I was upset by his appearance. It was hard keeping a brave face, but I could only think that he was himself a lion and that I must.

He could not speak nor move his head, and there was no expression at all on his features. But when I took his hand he moved it about a little in mine. I talked to him about life in Watford and at home and I said that I was thinking of joining up myself soon, while I still had some choice of service. At that point I realized that I had no inclination for the Army, and I changed the subject. He could make no reply to any of this. When the nurse drew me away, saying that he must be allowed to sleep, I left the hospital aware that he was failing.

I was manning the switchboard when my mother came through with the news of his death. She was crying and she said, 'Darling, your father is gone!' In the last fifteen years I had hardly spent as many days in his company. I really knew very little about him except that sixty-two was a nonsensically early age for a man of his vitality to go. But blood is thicker than water. I felt overwhelmed. The cords and slots of the switchboard swam together in a meaningless tangle before my eyes. I disconnected the whole works and ran into the lavatory to burst into tears.

With Xandra, our half-brother and our half-sister, I attended his funeral. Neither our mother nor theirs was present. I could remember father smiling a lot but I never ordinarily thought of him laughing. Now for some reason I could only think of a picture of him derived from something my mother had once said, describing an incident before I was born. He and my grandfather the Marquis had collected up every sort of hat from all over the house, and kept putting them on each other's heads and swapping them in endless succession, like a Laurel and Hardy routine, with the tears rolling down their faces in absolute transports of uncontrollable laughter.

And that was that. Someone of great importance to me had hovered more than a decade in the wings and then left the theatre for good without ever coming properly on stage. I returned to Watford. I bearded Mr Dunbar in his den and demanded a rise. I was granted a princely ten-bob increment. But I felt in need of a more drastic change. I went out and volunteered for the RAF. Mother wondered why I hadn't opted for my father's regiment. I said the raf was all the rage now, since they'd done so well, and I was lucky to get a ticket into the wild blue yonder, but it was only half an explanation.

Before reporting to the RAF barracks at Uxbridge I paid one last visit to the Odeon, Watford. They were screening *The Birth of a Baby*. It was the first naturalistic thing anybody had ever seen and the talk of the day. Sitting in the balcony I was very glad that I had not invited anyone else along. I thought how very embarrassing it must be for women in the audience, and how very painful it looked, and how relieved I was that it couldn't happen to me. For clarity of exposition and graphic illustration, though, I had to admit that the whole venture was a marked improvement on my previous Leaving Talks.

Lee of Babbacombe

The great thing was to get into the air. To compensate my mother for not having gone into the Army, and incidentally to please my country, I was determined to get up, stay up and drive the enemy down and out of the skies as soon as was feasible. The process was not as quick as I had thought. In the early days of the Royal Flying Corps, fifty minutes in a biplane with bicycle wheels had been enough to earn a man his wings. Twenty-five years of progress had changed all that. A long palaver had to be gone through first, plus any amount of borrowings from Army training.

The very name of the barracks at Uxbridge, 'Suvla', brought back its Crimean beginnings. Once again I was in thrall: it was a contemporary of Wellington! And the rations in the NAAFI were obviously those left on the beach when the Heights of Inkerman had been scaled. The conversation consisted mainly of commands and oaths, interspersed with a weird rococo lingo reserved to describe the group's inner life. This featured largely, if not exclusively, a tribe called F'k'nwimmin who were viewed with a mixture of fear, covetousness and derision. Sometimes the men would try to draw me into this, and I would have dearly liked to oblige but I hadn't the foggiest idea what they were talking about when they asked me if I liked muff-diving, yodelling up a canyon, or seeing to it that the old man rowed his boat.

Once again the cold and the noisome odour of Blanco. Once again I marched out on the square alone to be the fixed point on which the wavering ranks must steady themselves. But whereas before my military bearing had been the embarrassment of my platoon, by some mysterious witchcraft the situation was now turned inside out and I was remarkable only for the smartness of my turnout and the relative efficiency of my drill. I was constantly being singled out by the sergeants to demonstrate, because of my knowledge of weapons. For these things I was universally loathed. I felt it was perverse of fate to mark me out as an object of contumely among my fellows both for ignorance and excessive familiarity with the same subject.

We never saw any planes, but we had charts and diagrams and mock-ups to help us recognize them when we did see them. The silhouettes of He-IIIs and Ju-88s that we rehearsed on were shown in attacking stance, so we came away with the idea that these would be our last words as we were scythed in half by machine-gun bullets. But I found I could grasp these things quite readily. I couldn't swear, though I was willing to learn swearing as if it had been Serbo-Croat or Swahili, I didn't understand their preoccupation with the birth canal, and I was opposed to drinking much because drink tended to make people drunk. These distinguishing features, as well as my accent, which was unlike theirs, made the other fellows look at me askance.

Suvla was only marginally more unpleasant for me than for all the rest of them. Essentially we were all AC2s being given the traditional hammering. We were next moved to an Initial Training Wing by the coast. There were no more planes available at Paignton than at Uxbridge for the prospective pilots, but it was pointed out to me that there were no guns for the prospective air gunners, nor bombs for prospective bomb-aimers either, so we were all in the same f'k'n-fuselage.

A man who made a great difference to my morale was the man I bunked with at the Tenbani Hotel. This was neither as exotic nor as grand as its name suggests, but a pebble-dashed sea-front boarding house. I spent as many hours guarding it with a drawn bayonet as I did enjoying its amenities. But my companion made up for everything by his knowledge of profanity. He seemed to breathe and exhale the stuff. I was entranced. He had a gentle, monkish face from which a stream of filth poured forth in dulcet tones. It was like a sewer bursting on a bowling green. I learned certain phrases by heart and practised them on my fellows. They always knew them, but listened to me speaking them as if they'd been newly minted.

This made for greater camaraderie. I became Lofty and Tiny, Tancy to the Welsh because of a Tancy Lee who was a gypsy and their boxing champion, and also Toff and Duke. I also had to endure being called Lee of Babbacombe, which was a parallel I didn't care for. The pubs in nearby Babbacombe were popular and my companions had soon possessed themselves of all the facts in the case of a certain John Lee of Babbacombe. This Lee was sentenced to death for burning down a house and causing the death of an old woman in it. Three times at

Exeter Prison the trap at the scaffold did not open and three times the execution failed. Lee was released and later, after many years in prison, went around America billing himself as 'the man they couldn't hang'. The phrase 'third time lucky' went into the language. It became a constant joke among my mates that I wasn't to be provoked or trifled with, because I was one of the undead who cheat the gallows.

Unfortunately this sinister connection passed unnoticed by the officers. One filthy night, with the rain lashing across the road and tasting to me of salt and stale seaweed as I stood on guard outside the Tenbani, an officer came briskly up and I judged him worthy of a butt salute. This was due to all officers up to the rank of squadron leader. From there on up they could claim a 'Present'. This man ground to a halt before me and demanded of me, quivering with outrage, if I didn't know a Group Captain when I saw one? I did, but on this occasion his group captaincy was enshrouded in bad weather and a raincoat. This excuse made no impression on him nor on my CO when I was brought up on a charge and was sentenced to jankers.

I was beginning to regret that I had not after all volunteered for my father's regiment, who would have been conducting themselves in a similar style but with more panache, when the word came at last that we were to be sent to our Elementary Flying Training Schools. We were not so much told it, actually, as given evidence to infer it, when we were given jabs under each nipple at once, vaccination against all forms of tropical disorder. The immediate effect was crippling. One jab made it agony to move, the other condemned the victim to the shakes. We could only get into our wank-pits, to use the vernacular, and indulge in Egyptian PT. And we could lie there and reflect that it was in a good cause, because the flying schools were all overseas, so that the enemy could not concentrate his fire on the apprentices.

We were not in the cockpit yet, however. There was first a sojourn in Liverpool, where we took examinations in navigation and Morse, weapons and drill, and told all we knew about Hurricanes and Spitfires and Beaufighters. The hex which had been laid on my maths all my life was now temporarily lifted and my navigational guesses were allowed to pass for calculations. I trotted lightly up the gangplank of the 15,000-ton liner *Reina del Pacifico* thinking that all my troubles were over, and that I would be airborne as soon as I made landfall.

The six-week journey several thousand of us made on the *Reina del Pacifico* from West Kirby was one of the most disagreeable experiences of my life. I felt pity and horror at the life of a sailor and saw once again in a totally new way how wise I was to try to keep away from the water.

I was perhaps more sensitive to the dangers than others. Whenever anyone said there was a U-boat in the offing, all those who could find a space lined the rails and excitedly made bets as to what quarter the first torpedo would come from. Sometimes the naval escort of our convoy would change and it was always agony until the new lot had taken up station.

The food was diabolical. There was a rumour that it had been used as ballast on the Ark. Yet here I was lucky in my early training and the stomach that had survived a public school was proof against the worst the Air Force and Navy combined could do. I believe I ate horse and camel, and I most certainly ate pickled pork, and yet I was fresh and able to carry cups of tea to men in the abyss we slept in next to the engine room, where the noise and the heat and the smell of oil and the rolling made them sick enough to long for a torpedo to put them out of their misery.

The latrines were open in long lines on the deck, and here I jibbed. I sneaked quietly into the officers' quarters and risked a court martial for the sake of a bath of sea water. On one of these forays I chanced to read a menu of the officers' dinner. It was an unrivalled inventory of delicacies. I was shocked by the thoughtlessness of that particular crowd. It left an indelible impression. I had an insight, too, into the envy of the radical mind. I took the menu with me and kept it in my kit for the rest of the war.

We almost reached South America before suddenly turning sharp left, or hard aport, and setting course for Cape Town. This was the end of our journey, but through one of those mysterious illogicalities of the military mind we were forbidden to go ashore. After two years of blackout we were tantalized by the myriad lights of the South African capital. I begged and cajoled a pass on the grounds of having an important message to deliver to an export corporation which had an agency in Cape Town. The duty officer asked, 'What do they make that's so vital to the war effort?'

I replied, unthinking, 'Brylcreem.'

There was a long pause. The RAF were already being twitted as 'the Brylcreem Boys'. Then he decided to treat it as a joke. 'Be back before 23.00 hours,' he said, 'or you won't find me laughing.'

Solo at the World's End

At Hillside we had the luxury of sleeping in clean, whitewashed cattle stalls. The Hillside training field was near Bulawayo in Rhodesia, nearly a thousand miles of rail from Cape Town. We had traversed the sand and thorn of the Kalahari, learned to pick a Zulu from a Matabele and a black mamba from a spitting cobra before ever we reached the place. Some of us had abandoned all hope of ever seeing a plane that flew. But here at last was an airfield. We would emerge from the chrysalis. We would fly. It was a great thrill.

The Rhodesians of 1941 were delighted to see us; they gave us a blazing welcome. We soon saw that not only was the dispersal scheme very thorough, and that we were as far out of range of German bombers with designs on young pilots as it was possible to be, but that there were fringe benefits. There was almost a competition to take us out hunting, fishing and shooting. I was adopted by the millionaire Meikle family, who seemed virtually to own the country. I shot at wild boar from a galloping horse, I attacked huge steaks in the bright lights of Bulawayo, I floated through forty-eight-hour parties.

There is always something new out of Africa, said the old Roman encyclopaedist, perhaps with some irritation. To me everything in Africa was new. There was the pervasive fragrance of the jacaranda. Journeys into the Bundu with maize and tobacco farmers. A meeting face to face with a black mamba coiled among logs, which rose enquiringly to look me in the face and regarded me with considerable tension – and the blast of the farmer's gun that shot it from behind me. A friend with me was less lucky and had a ringhals jet venom into his eyes and was hurried off to have his eyes washed with milk. And then the first taste of mealie porridge, black and rather thin, but healthy.

Many firsts, and always with the first solo flight in anticipation to give an edge to the rest. For navigation training we were dumped unceremoniously in the jungle somewhere and told to find our way home. The animal noises at night blended us into a close-knit family. In the day we once all shinned up trees to avoid charging rhino, a short-sighted species with no sense of discrimination. Or there might be elephants, and a grand bibulous tour of the network of Rhodesian airfields, at Que Que, Gwelo, Moffat, Guinea Fowl . . . Every last one of them had a cellarful of Castle Beer.

The prospect of flying excited me intensely. In the event we used Tiger Moths with open cockpits, but I was so exhilarated that if a Heinkel had suddenly appeared I was sure I could have knocked it out of the sky, like Biggles, with a Bowie knife or the instructor's manual. I took to flying immediately. I knew I'd been right: it was my element.

Below us, during our training flights, the landscape was dominated by a dramatic landmark, Ntabaz Induna, otherwise the Chief's Rock. It was a great flat-topped rock which the chief, rather like Tiberius, had found handy when disposing of his unwanted wives by tipping them off the edge. Had my instructor told me to land on it I would have had no hesitation in doing so.

My instructor was not himself the type of man to baulk at anything dubious. He was known as Awful Alford and had the reputation of a hard man. He was a peppery little fellow who chucked the plane around the sky from the word go, and was in a hurry to introduce his pupils to the more perverse manoeuvres. He'd wait till the plane was upside down before enquiring casually of his novice if he was strapped in. Into the shimmering heat haze we took off to perform our stalls and loops and spins above a vast plain with this hypnotic rock in the middle. It was tremendous.

And then, during the last but one of the sessions that made up the eight hours' instruction before the first solo, a most peculiar thing happened. At 5,000 feet, without any preliminary warning, a grinding headache took my head as it were in a metal clasp. And simultaneously the vision in my left eye blurred over. It took me completely by surprise. I stammered out something about not being able to see and said 'You've got her, sir?' and relinquished the controls. He took over instantly. After a minute it eased slightly but only to the extent that I could hear Awful asking gently if I could see all right. I said, not terribly well. He insisted that we land straight away and that I visit the MO directly.

The medical officer was a square man with a moustache who put me through a number of tests and declared that there *was* something. He wasn't sure what, but it might be a failure of the optic nerve. He said in his kindest voice that I should rest and not put any further strain on it.

That was as far as any diagnosis ever went. I rested for a day, and I moped for several more days. I wondered what was being said, whether my trouble was being put down to a lesion, to the heat, to stress at altitude, to a psychosomatic condition, or what. The most horrible possibility that occurred to me was that 'lack of moral fibre' would be rubber-stamped across every document relating to me. After a long wait, I was summoned. I was told that I would not be allowed to fly. The optic nerve was unreliable. It was the end of my world.

I was acutely miserable in the period that followed. My sadness deepened by the freak coincidence of a boy from Summer Fields at the same flying school killing himself in a crash near the giant rock. I was inevitably left to stagnate. To my appeals for further experience a deaf ear was turned. Nobody knew what to do with me. An unreliable eye would be almost as much a handicap to an air gunner, or a bomb-aimer, as to a pilot.

With time on my hands I made an expedition to the grave of Cecil Rhodes in the Matopos Hills, where the settlers and the Matabele and the Shangan had most fiercely settled their accounts. I hopped a lift in a small open truck which rolled into the great natural mausoleum as the sun sank in flames, flashing direct in our faces, behind the range of hills at the World's End. The slab under which Rhodes lay was polished granite, flanked by mighty boulders like enormous eggs. Lower down, by the gorge called Oos, I could see the white marble memorials to the people who'd fallen in the strife over settlement. I felt subdued and reverent. At the same time my homage was divided between the historical founder of the country, and the splendid acting of Walter Huston who'd played him in *Rhodes of Africa* a couple of years before the war.

From my standpoint the place was well named. I had set off with a reasonable ambition, patently within my powers, travelled a thousand leagues to see it thwarted by the petty spite of my nervous system, and fetched up here in the middle of Africa with nothing to do, at the World's End. It occurred to me to get drunk, and make that another African first, but I was much fonder of soft drinks than alcohol.

This high tragic mood was splintered the very next morning by a scene in which I was reminded of the pleasures of mere survival. We were bowling along in our little truck with some idea of inspecting a colony of baboons which I was curious about. We found a tribe of about forty and were walking about trying to get near enough for some good pictures when it struck me, seeing some for the first time at close quarters, that their teeth were not unlike the tusks of elephants.

Furthermore I perceived that if they were to take a dislike to you in this wild, unearthly place, they would, in the words of the poet, 'unseam you from the nave unto the chaps'.

'You know,' I remarked to my friend, keeping my prey in the viewfinder but sidling backwards, 'they look *very* dangerous.' He made no comment, but replied pithily, 'Into the truck, quick!' We jumped in and drove off fast. I turned my head and saw the entire baboon nation rushing down the road in our dust. 'Faster!' I shrieked. 'They're after us!'

The road at that moment dipped through a slight depression with banks of earth on either side. As we entered it there was a crash of tearing vegetation and a thud on the hood above our heads. This was followed by clattering, scything and hissing noises and I exclaimed, 'My God, they've reached the car! We're going to be torn to pieces!' My friend replied, 'That's not baboons, it's a leopard riding with us.' That didn't seem to me to alter the case much, but he went on, 'I expect he's had some of their kids, and now they want vengeance.' However, I wasn't sure the baboons would regard us as neutral in this matter, and it was a great relief when the leopard sprang off again, and the posse of baboons veered off in pursuit of him.

Unseen arbiters then moved me about from flying station to flying station, though not to fly. Instead I picked up a comprehensive education in the miscellanea of the RAF. Coming up to Christmas 1941, I was sent to Salisbury, then a quiet country town noted for the excellence of its hospitality. On the day of the Nativity itself a group of us blue jobs attended a drinks – lunch – drinks – dinner – drinks celebration given in a private hotel. It was held to be about time I had my first cocktail, and since the cocktail in question, called granadilla, seemed no more no less than a high-octane fruit juice, I downed six or seven of the delicious things. They had no effect whatever. Inwardly I despised the cocktail legend, which I now saw to be a myth based on auto-intoxication.

Rows and rows of bottles of hock marched through lunch, like gleaming blond soldiers. I took the afternoon quietly, digesting a heavy meal with the help of a dark and Whiggish fluid called port. I found it pleasant, but somewhat cloying to the palate, so to clarify it for dinner I settled on some Castle beers with lime. I had had enough experience of these things to know they were harmless. When the aperitifs came round, however, I did not wish to be a wet blanket and felt obliged to dispose of half a dozen sherries.

I felt no pain, though as my wineglass was emptied and refilled at dinner people began looking at me as if I were the original iron man. A regiment of redcoats was cleared away as dead men. I felt indestructible. Obviously like Rasputin I had a stomach-lining impervious to alcohol. In his case it had enabled him to survive poison, so there was no reason for me to make heavy weather of a few brandies, so to top off an excellent day I took them.

Then I became aware that there was a fault somewhere in the system. I found myself moving about from group to group like a ball on a pin-table, asking in exquisitely polite and cultured tones if 'anybody present could gen me up with the landmarks and fixes needed to strafe a bathroom'. I made it, locked the door and sank into an attitude of prayer over the bowl. Nobody was ever more senseless. When they came for me two hours later they thought I'd died and smashed the door down to get in. I was set on my feet outside the hotel and pointed towards Belvedere camp. I stalked there in a straight line through the pouring rain, sometimes in the middle of the road and sometimes in the ditches. I woke up next day more than ever amazed that people tortured themselves with alcohol.

I went to the Mazoe Dam and Marandelas. I toured the Wankie game reserve. I visited Zimbabwe, built before the Pyramids, the oldest ruins of the man-made world. War is hell, said Sherman – but not as waged by a planeless pilot in the heart of a hospitable country. I thought I should do something constructive for my keep, and put in an application to join the Intelligence section. My initiative was greeted with acclaim. Shortly after, to my amazement, I was seconded into the Rhodesian Police Force. To be specific, I was posted to Salisbury Prison, as a warder.

Granted that I was spare, and that there had to be a better way of getting rid of me than going to the expense of having a plane shot down with me in it, this was still a wholly unexpected development. Considering my conduct at Caesar's Camp three years before, it was a reversal of roles for me now to be playing the heavy to a crowd of deserters. It was interesting, though, to discover that so many deserters, far from being the neurasthenic weeds beloved of film analyses, were desperadoes who looked well able to sort out a pool room or a pillbox single-handed.

In particular there was a quartet under my immediate charge whose mere appearance gave me the willies. Not all the prisoners were deserters, though some doubled desertion with other crimes. These four had been convicted of rape, breaking and entering, burning a house down, and grievous bodily harm. One who looked like a larger, tougher version of Charles Bronson showed me my first pornographic photograph. In answer to my questions he said that he had no idea how well the man and woman knew each other and that that was beside the point.

Oddly enough, this was the beginnings of *their* becoming nervous of *me*. Following a day on a road gang, where they were doing manual labour with pickaxes, they put in a bitter complaint to the chief warder. They said I was a lunatic. They said they went in constant fear of their lives. They said I had my hand on my gun all the time and that I was obviously only looking for an excuse to use it. To counter this charge I let it be understood that there was nothing personal in my demeanour, and that I would be equally ready to shoot *any*body in the compound who gave signs of wanting to clear a way to freedom with his pick.

While this was going on I had yet another first. I witnessed a flogging for the first time, soon to become a familiar spectacle. The victims were all Africans, and I can't say whether whites were subject to the same penalties. With hindsight, I should guess not.

Not so much because of my personal experience as a victim, but on account of the reading I'd done as a consequence of it, I prided myself on being an expert in this matter. It was a great surprise to me when the first African was brought forward, and trussed for a dose of the sjambok, to see that he was not protected in any way. In British prisons the neck and kidneys were protected and there was always a doctor on the spot.

Here the unit went into the native quarter, the police read out the sentence and the local headman ordered punishment there and then. The sjambok was rhino hide and laid the victim's flesh open from the first stroke, like a razor. Tied to a pole the African was very soon a hideous sight. When we carried out the sentence in the prisons it did not seem to me that the arrangements were much less primitive. In sum it was a new dimension of cruelty. I felt sure Rhodes would have been against it. If this had been part of my idol's vision of Rhodesia, there must have been a flaw in *his* optic nerve.

Blood, Honey and Sand

My service with the Rhodesian police was rewarded by promotion to leading aircraftman. I was retired to the beaches of Durban. I should be sorry to think that the severance was due to the bleats of my charges who said I was too harsh to be a warder. As every member of the force I had met had the hardness of seasoned teak, I doubt if they were believed. My time with them had been an odd sort of bonus.

Every day I trotted into the centre of Durban from the YMCA where I stayed to see if my number had come up in the tombola of postings at HQ, wherever that might be. Sometimes I imagined that the little cardboard cutout that represented me in the Ops Room somewhere had been knocked off the chart and ground under somebody's heel. If I had deserted, would anybody ever have known? My recent duty in Salisbury Prison had alerted a nerve in me which said that in the long run they always did.

Then the *New Amsterdam* came into the harbour and I was suddenly told to get on it. It was 35,000 tons, some three times the capacity of the troopship which had sailed with us from Liverpool. I steeled myself for a trip wedged in with at least ten thousand servicemen. In fact there were forty. We proceeded to what turned out to be Suez in maximum comfort. The entire passenger list was then jammed into one three-ton truck which set off for Kasfarit, a vast staging camp in the Canal Zone dedicated to killing time.

That whole area by the Bitter Lakes, full of dispersal camps like Fayyid, Kasfarit and Shallufa, was like a giant poultice into which noxious foreign bodies of every description were draining. Morale was very low. There was nothing on the programme but drill, and no distractions from nothing. There were fights that lasted for hours, reminiscent of the encounters between eighteenth-century bruisers that ended when one contestant or both dropped out of sheer fatigue.

We arrived in a sandstorm. I was at once deeply offended by the sleeping arrangements made for the Other Ranks, in which six or eight men kipped in one hole with sandbags holding down their bivvies. I drew the attention of my mate Angus Blunt to the impossibility of doing a fair day's work after sleeping in these degrading conditions, and suggested that we find more suitable accommodation. So I hauled him off to the Officers' Lines, and he had to acknowledge that these were much better for us. Each tent was properly dug out and wide enough to take two camp beds with a groundsheet underneath.

Perhaps it was because we had sneaked in during a storm, and seemed to be a fixture by the time the sand settled, that Angus and I were never prised out of our canvas citadel. We attended the same parades, guard duties, messes and bollockings as the ORs, but when the hour came for the sandfly to take nourishment we were served up *à la carte*. The sandflies came up with the bedbugs that lurked in the wooden supports. Their bites itched and when scratched became sore and left scars. And they gave me sandfly fever, which is like malaria in a minor way. Then as a legacy of the mosquito jamboree round Victoria Falls, I went down with malaria proper, for the first of seven times.

Between bouts of one fever or another, yellowed with mepacrine and congratulating myself on staving off jaundice and crab lice, I pondered the possibility that too many antimalarial tablets were disturbing the mental balance of our warrant officers. Some people, however, are inherently bastards, and in Kasfarit there were two inherent bastards, whose behaviour cannot be excused by mepacrine.

The first called for twelve volunteers for guard duty. It was a loathsome duty out in the sand by the barbed-wire perimeter. From hundreds and hundreds of men he had no takers at all. He declared that he would drill the lot of us till volunteers came forth. He did so. He had us up and down and to and fro, jig-time, quick time and deadly 'ush. Right and left we fainted. Most outrageous of all, the adjutant stood by, smirking, while this unspeakable little Hitler did his worst. More men fell. Nobody volunteered. I was proud of us. Soon there were so many men prone that a halt had to be called, or there wouldn't be enough left to do guard duty. He made his selections sullenly. That night he was done up and on the following day invalided home. I wasn't present when he was filled in. Had I been, I would have adopted the role of the adjutant, and looked on.

The second worked off his bile on me alone. While I was in the ranks he was one of the very, very few who objected in principle to my having been to a public school. When he put me to scour a mountain of greasy pans with sand and my bare hands, which were raw before I was through, he told me that it was a penance for my days in clover. He lost no chance of hounding me and as one ranker had to accompany the Arabs on the honeywagon, he appointed me as that man. Since I wasn't officer material, he said, I might as well make myself useful in some other way.

The honeywagon was the open three-tonner that emptied the latrines. We manhandled rows of brimming great drums on to the truck and drove off into the desert to tip them out, to the accompaniment of catcalls and ironic cheers. The stench in the heat was enough to kill you. The job was like slave labour in a mobile poison-gas factory. It may be, as the philosopher said, that those who study revenge keep their own wounds green, but in the case of that warrant officer I decided that I would not forget the face.

Almost anything, I felt, would be an improvement on this, so I was delirious with joy at being posted as a dogsbody to Ismailia. The new position had a vague connection with my application for intelligence work, inasmuch as I was given access to a great many maps said to be top secret, and collected phoney pound notes made by the Germans with Arabic inscriptions stamped on them warning the people not to take British bribes.

After I had been working through most of one night, an Arab jumped me in an alley near the office. I saw him as he sprang out of the shadows and moved just in time as his knife came down. It sliced into my neck, without doing me a serious injury. He soon vanished down the dim narrow streets and with the blood pouring down my shirt I was not eager to pursue him. More experienced heads than mine decided the attack was neither personal nor connected with my work, but motivated by a general irritation at the intrusion of so many sorts of foreigner into Egypt.

My programme of tourism was not neglected. I assiduously cultivated the friendship of pilots who could give me a lift, and guides who would show me what was what. I crossed the Sinai into what was then Palestine. I absorbed the conventional biblical sights, and saw the supposed birthplace of Christ underground in rock under a church, and no doubt rather changed in aspect over two thousand years from being the manger of an inn.

In Tel Aviv a polyglot Lithuanian Jew called Metz put me up in his house in Shalom Aleichem Street. He could interpret in fifteen languages, though he was absent-minded in some of them. In his enthusiasm he looked like an amiable frog. In his enthusiasm, too, he sometimes got carried away. On one occasion he started driving me about the town expounding this and that, when a stream of strange-looking people came out on the streets, all wearing black caftans and long beards and black velvet hats. They were throwing anything that came to hand at us, from stones to washing-up cloths. It seemed we had strayed into a sector of the most orthodox Hasidic Jews, and blasphemously on the Sabbath.

The journey to Cairo, however, was to the RAF hospital in Abbassia, on account of the recurrence of malaria. The finger-pricking test to see if victims had the malignant form wasn't good enough for them there. They went in for sternal punctures. There was an orderly who specialized in holding the patient's legs down while the doctor got to work, which he did with as much zest as if he'd invented sternal punctures. The doctor who performed mine was a Goliath who flattened me by leaning on me. He pierced my breastbone with an instrument like a bradawl, which he then screwed round until he was deep enough in to suck the blood out. This vampirish action, he said, was the only sure way of establishing that one had malaria. If it was anywhere, the bradawl thing would winkle it out. He thought I'd be satisfied to learn that I was playing host to a genuine AI parasite.

By way of convalescence I climbed the Pyramids and shot duck in the salt marshes of Al Fayyum. And as an act of filial piety I took a trip on a camel across the country round Mina, where father had licked his Aussies into shape in the previous war. Then, lean and yellow and cured as a strip of chammy leather, I homed in on the Pam-Pam Club in Cairo, and had my first fight – with an Aussie.

It was more of a beer hall than a club, and was by no means exclusive. The proprietor would have been wiser to chain the furniture down, because few of the cosmopolitan crowd of servicemen who got in there had heard of the Queensberry rules, nor cared about them if they had. As a regular thing patrons of the Pam-Pam with a skinful would leave the hall in search of further amusement and light on the gharris waiting outside. These were horse-drawn taxis. They would take the animal out of the shafts, put the driver into his own gharri and pull him round the streets.

The provocation I gave to this son of the Australian outback was to stand between him and some other man he wanted to thump. It wasn't my intention to be a peacemaker. I simply crossed his path in the most literal sense. He switched all his animus to me and rushed at me with a chair. Despite some quick footwork on my part which kept me out of trouble for a minute it seemed likely that he would brain me if he continued swinging. As he came for me the third time I dived under the nearest table. The chair smashed down on it. The legs gave way, the table collapsed on me, nearly rendering me unconscious, while a Niagara of beer poured all over me. I crawled out of the wreckage to learn that my opponent was stretched out cold, having tripped on my leg as he went by and run his head into the bar counter with the momentum of his own blow.

By contrast my relations with the Axis were gentlemanly. I was attached to 205 Group, consisting of Wellingtons, and in them made some missions over enemy territory. We flew out from airstrips near Alexandria and dropped leaflets over Benghazi and other points of Italian interest, recommending that they surrender. As the Afrika Korps in its last advance had reached a line not far from Alexandria, dropping these bits of paper appeared to me to be a form of whistling in the dark. Nevertheless it was nice to be doing something different and to breathe the same air as the men of the 37th Squadron at El Daba. From there I went up before a Commissions Board, which included the AOC, Air Commodore Ritchie, and a marvellous old hero of the peacetime London-to-Melbourne races, Group Captain Oswald Gayford.

For no reason that anybody could see, they made me a pilot officer. I was told to take a week's leave and report with my kit to 260 Squadron as intelligence officer. I was dumbfounded. I had got completely out of the habit of thinking any such thing could happen.

The war had been going on for three years. For half that time I had in theory been taking an active part in it. I'd not actually contributed to the discomfort of the enemy in any way save by begging them to surrender in pamphlets somewhat lacking in credibility. Now at last I had a real job. I was about to join an operational squadron. I had a strong sense that it was the end of another phase in my life.

At the end of every other phase my guardian angel had pushed forward somebody or something to further my sexual education. This time the fates deputed a splendid American Air Force captain to be my mentor. I met him in Alexandria and he insisted I come with him to Mary's, in Sister Street. I had been sitting in the place for some little while, chatting gracefully to a beautiful Russian girl with lovely white skin and jet-black hair, and telling her about the Mazirovs and the reasons for the decline and fall of the czarist regime, when it percolated through to me that Mary's was a very superior brothel. Until then, such was the luxury of the appointments, I had assumed it was a branch of Claridge's hotel.

My American friend had disappeared and the Russian girl was

beginning to show signs of regret that she had not gone with him instead of leaving the Circassian to take charge of him. She said that it was absolutely within the laws of the place to have a drink in private instead of clinging to the bar as if welded there. I was very much in a cleft stick. I'd no wish to be uncivil. At the same time I was saturated with propaganda making a parallel between the glamour of the fly-trap and the radiance of the unaccompanied woman in a theatre of war. Also, they shoved bromide in our tea.

In spite of it all, she was making a very good speech in favour of privacy and I was weakening. I was about ready to publish the banns when I spied my friend tottering downstairs. One look told me that for all his broad smile this was the mere shell of a man. I leaped off the barstool to help him home, having first showered the Russian with apologies and counterfeit German money. I said they were waiting for us and were in a terrible hurry.

This was up to a point true. When I reported to Osgood Villiers Hanbury, CO of 260 Squadron, the whole line was just beginning to move forward from El Alamein.

Spy

'Put one foot wrong, my son, and you're *out*!' was my squadron leader's greeting. In the next breath he said, 'Right, let's go and get pissed.'

He led me into the mess at El Amriyah to reduce me horizontal, with the connivance of a fearsome cast. I use the word advisedly, not only because of the way special characters flourished in the Desert Air Force, but because I was replacing one of them, a much-loved 'Spy' who'd just been raised to chief intelligence officer for all 239 Wing.

As the new Spy I found myself like an actor taking on a part in a long-running play. Except that here, the actors were obliged for their lives to depend on me: I must dovetail without delay.

To speed up the process and drive blind into intimacy, the newcomer went through an initiation ritual. I was debagged and had my shirt-tails set on fire, and was plied with every sort of rotgut, on a base of sticky Marsala, to float the evening. As it washed by, I got fragments of gen on the squadron and some of the men who in the coming months I would cleave to as lifelong friends. Some fell out of the sky and made their funeral pyre on impact. Some baled out behind enemy lines. Some went back to the various continents they'd sprung from. Some grew stout and sleek and sober in Britain. And some were unable to find anything in peacetime as real and exciting as the campaigns against Rommel and von Arnim and Kesselring, not forgetting the Italian General 'Electric Whiskers' Bergonzoli. But whatever they one day became, they were always my friends.

Hawkeye Edwards had eleven and a half confirmed kills. My Canadian namesake Hawkeye Lee was another phenomenal shot and I would have said nerveless until the weird circumstance of his being court-martialled for failing to report for duty because it was Friday the thirteenth. The aircrew included South Africans and Canadians, a Belgian, several

Aussies and Kiwis, and a Texan who was more nervous in the mess than in the air. He was known as Ah Phuckett-ah because he had a fund of droll tales but his terrible stammer interlarded the narrative with 'Aaaagh . . . aaagh . . . fuck it . . . mean t-t-to say . . . aaaagh aaaagh *fuck it*!' Sparkey Black was a Welshman who'd just joined the squadron after the singular experience of being shot down over Vichy-controlled Syria and being made a prisoner of the French.

These and many others gathered me in, pulled my leg all over North Africa and across the *mare nostrum* but accepted me. There is no shame in fear; rather it's those who have none who are exceptional and in the instance of the leader of 260, Pedro Hanbury, awesomely so. He looked like a caricature of an RAF type, with his big pop eyes and his propeller moustache and no chin. But he could do more than lower the jar. He was a great ace. He terrified me but he was a lovely man. His hatred of the Hun embraced everything that breathed and could give the enemy comfort.

It was part of my business to debrief the birdmen, as soon as they were back in the nest, on what they'd seen and what they'd done and Pedro once remarked that he'd 'knocked out two or three trucks and horse-drawn vehicles, and put a couple of nuns out of commission'. To my astonished request that he repeat the list as I wasn't sure I'd heard right, he said testily, 'Naturally. They were pregnant nuns.' This went through on my official intelligence report. Ever afterwards, occasional enquiries came to me asking what tally 260 had reached on pregnant nuns strafed.

Once the advance began to roll, we were hardly ever on any one airstrip for more than two or three days in succession. There were times when the pilots and their planes, the P-40s and Kittyhawks, were the fixed objects in my mind, while the airfields flew by: Daba, LG 09, Maaten Bagush, Fuka Bagush and through to Mersa Matruh. We were lending close support to the forces on the ground, making the bomb strikes the Army wanted and using the rest of the petrol time in strafing. We settled into the gait of the leapfrog, moving in as soon as the advance patrols had found us our next launching pad. The difference between an airstrip and the rest of the desert was that the sappers had cleared the mines, and the stones and the scrub had been swept into a neat pile.

Broadly speaking, I was expected to know everything, and to get the rest from chats with the Army and what I could glean from our own boys as soon as they set down. For this purpose I had a trailer, in which I was swathed in bumf and maps of all scales from Panama to Kamchatka. With this and a fifteen-cwt truck driven by 'Taxi' Sturgeon, I tried to race the flights of 260 Squadron to be waiting for them with some nice fresh co-ordinations when they came down again on a new bit of sandy deck. In all the shambles and fatigue they still had the strength to tease me, to tell me I'd given them the wrong maps, or drawn the bomb line at a point where they were bound to knock out our own HQ, and to rib me for always locating my trailer at the furthest point on the runway from the German artillery.

The feeling was that of being a very lithe and free-wheeling leapfrog. All the way to Tobruk there was virtually nothing to bump into and knock over, save people and tanks. And beyond that was another freeway, dotted about with charred and burning vehicles, clear to Benghazi. There was only some risk of our tripping over our own feet. We arrived at such incontinent speed at Marble Arch, in the wake of the Kiwis, and the enemy had done such a thoroughgoing job with mines and booby traps, that all personnel had to turn out to help with the disinfestation. Regulations were quite clear that this was poaching on the preserves of the sappers, but apparently this was no time to be pedantic. My respect for sappers was multiplied by two thousand, the number of devices exploded. As, too, the Germans were extremely ingenious with their booby traps, I never thereafter picked up an Iron Cross as a souvenir unless there was somebody still breathing who was wearing it.

We bounced and skipped along westward, and the wind came in off the Med and made a constant rippling change of the sand sea. The shifting patterns were fascinating. Sand gave way to scrub and that to boulders, then all three would dance round one another in the heat haze. Some men in the scorching heat went sandhappy, or as the Arabs said, *magnoun*. But then, just as one felt a little disorientated too, the landscape would brisk up with big escarpments rising, the ravines and wadis carved by centuries of wind. Desert flowers bloomed in extraordinary places. Inland, sandstorms of great violence, the *khamsins* and *ghiblis*, were whipped up as if out of nowhere. They came forward like charging curtains hundreds of feet high, flaying any exposed flesh and cramming grit into any unprotected plane. At night, sleeping in tents or ruins, there was the unparalleled clarity of the desert sky. One felt that if one made the effort one could pluck the stars down off their hooks on the indigo ceiling.

It was a haunting backdrop, even if we were too busy to paint it. All the way across Libya, through El Agheila, Homs and Tripoli, we averaged five missions a day. The P-40s were tough, versatile fighter-bombers, modified to carry six 40-pound bombs in wing racks, or one 500-pounder under the fuselage, or a 250-pounder under each wing, plus a gun load of six .5 machine guns. They could be used for strikes, cover, or as artillery, taking out positions annoying the Army.

The Luftwaffe opposition lessened all the time; their Me-109s were being saved for elsewhere. Typically, Hawkeye Edwards was the first in the Wing to encounter a Focke-Wulff 190, and he swooped on it with the joy of a lepidopterist swinging his net on a rare butterfly. The Luftwaffe was now playing almost entirely a buffer role, so their rare attacks were viewed by us almost as *lèse majesté*. I got my comeuppance for discounting the Messerschmitts shortly after we had hopped into Tunisia, and the Germans were digging themselves in at the Mareth Line.

When the first loud noise sounded I was standing on the edge of an airstrip with my back to a large gaggle of aircraft of all types and nationalities. I was staring into the distance trying to distinguish between nothingness and remoteness. I spun round and saw a sheet of flame and a vast amount of black smoke. I was astounded. My first thought was that a plane had crashed. The second was that the Americans had made a mistake. These random theories were corrected by the sight of four Me-109s diving. Their bombs were actually visible in the air! People were so little used to this that they were waving rattles, which were meant only for gas attacks. Our ack-ack was shooting back, though it was nowhere near being in position. When some bombs landed a hundred and fifty yards away I began running like hell, hoping for a slit trench or something, left over from a previous campaign.

In fact a small vehicle appeared before me. I plunged beneath it. Unfortunately three other men also plunged, and we all banged in together like creatures in a cartoon. There wasn't room for more than two, so I pulled out and began running for another one. And another bomb landed. The grit and muck and sand from the blast caught me smack in the bottom. It was like being hit with a shotgun from thirty yards. The stuff penetrated and stitched my trousers to my buttocks.

The attack was over in ten minutes, but for me personally there was worse to come. I saw the MO, who patched me up and said brightly, 'Oh, it's a bit of a mess, but we'll soon put that right. Changing your trousers will repair half the damage straight away.' As it transpired, he was wrong about this, but I was standing for the nonce by a truck wondering if I would ever sit down again when, to my horror, two senior officers came out of it and made straight for me. One was the commander of 239 Wing, Group Captain Billy Burton. With him was the Air Officer Commanding in the Mediterranean, Air Marshal Tedder.

I produced a huge salute. Tedder didn't even bother to acknowledge it. He was one of your more intimidating pygmies.

'What's all this bloody nonsense going on here?' he rapped out. I opened my mouth to speak but he answered his own question, 'There's been an aerial attack.'

I managed to get out, 'Certainly has, sir.'

Billy Burton jumped in with, 'Tell the AOC about it, Christopher.'

Being called Christopher only made me more tense – I'd never met the Group Captain before. Anyway, I mumbled a report of sorts. Tedder never took his eyes off me. 'Then what happened?' he asked.

'Then they turned back, sir,' I said, 'and went off towards the sea.'

'Did they, indeed?' he said in a severe tone. I thought he was about to ask me why I hadn't reached up and pulled them down, but he focused on my role during the earlier part of the action.

'And what were *you* doing while this was going on?'

I told him I'd tried to take cover.

'Where?' he barked.

'There.' I pointed helplessly. I felt that the opening gambits had been made in my court-martial for cowardice.

'Kept them off, did it?' he asked.

'No, sir, I stopped a bit of blast.'

'Oh? Where?'

'In my backside, sir.'

He laughed. 'That was bad luck,' he remarked. 'Stop you sitting about for a day or two.'

He got bored with that and went back to the failure of the ack-ack to shoot any planes down. I found myself laying out a string of lame excuses for them, ending up with the surprise factor. Tedder snorted. 'Surprise factor,' he said, and cut me short. 'Come on, Billy,' he said, dashing for his jeep, 'before we get any more deeply involved in the surprise factor.'

Afterwards in the mess, Pedro Hanbury commiserated. 'Did he make you feel as if you were entirely responsible?' he asked.

'I caused the whole war,' I said.

'Up to you to win it then,' he said.

I advanced towards the enemy's last redoubt in North Africa with my arse on fire.

Operation Plonk

In hilly Tunisia, the camouflage changed. In their brown and green transport, the armies toned in nicely with the new settings, incidentally reflecting our standard diet of bully beef and two veg. We were more conspicuous in our sand-coloured trucks. We perched at Medenine, Neffatia and the huge Roman amphitheatre at El Djem. Right up close, our strips took a regular pounding from German 88-mm shells. At Neffatia, enemy patrols actually captured some of our ground crew, while we flew out of the other end of the strip.

Otherwise, where possible, it was up to me to route the motorized pilots away from the knocked-out villages and scenes of carnage, so the corpses of their own strikes shouldn't weigh too heavily on their imagination.

That couldn't be done at the pass through El Hamma, where the last great tank battle was fought in North Africa. It had been a model of ground/air co-operation. We came through a dense array of stricken machines and men, still smouldering, and while I'd become used to wreckage and death, the smell that hung over this devastation was a real wrench in the guts.

Beyond it, once the Army had cracked the Mareth Line, we were through to our terminal airfield at Kairouan. The enemy held an area of Bou Ficha, Garci and Zaghouan, and the Young Fascists in particular defended it with ferocity and great bravery, offsetting some of the stories that the Italians had never had any heart for the fight.

We knew we were home, though, and were certainly very dry. Among my many unofficial duties was the liberation of booze for the squadron. While it wasn't my fault in the desert, I was aware that beers and wines had been scarce and a raging thirst was building up among all units which it would be my task to slake. Furthermore, after the tensions of the long chase, the last throes were setting the pilots' teeth on edge.

They had to prevent as many as possible of the German soldiers from being evacuated into Europe. The Afrika Korps was to have no Dunkirk. But with obstinate heroism, and no fighter cover, a stream of Ju-52s persisted in trying. They were lumbering, corrugated-iron aerial coffins. Every one of the pilots, as he told me the story of his latest sortie against them, expressed revulsion for the simple task of splitting them open, with the bodies spilling out in the sea. There was no more comeback than if they'd been shelling peas.

Similar scenes could surely be detailed right across the board. Even so, when von Arnim finally surrendered his army, and the triumph was complete, the circus of jubilation was something more than downing a few drinks and cheering on a girl dancing on a table. It was an almost incredible outbreak, combining the elements of a show for the Emperor Nero, a big event at Brand's Hatch, and the Blitz.

In all innocence the Navy triggered it off, firing salvoes in the bay of Tunis. The Army ack-ack cordially picked up the rhythm. The Air Force made its own bizarre contribution. The South Africans jacked up the tails of their Spitfires, pressed the tit and blazed away in the general direction of the mountains. Small arms and Verey lights began erupting at all points of the compass. Near me, one squadron leader picked up a tommy gun and shot at the central pole of the mess tent of a rival squadron, who returned the fire at his central pole.

It was like being in the eye of a communal brainstorm. I saw pilots drink Brasso and Milton and paraffin. I saw our boys burning their silhouettes in the walls of the marquee mess with lighted paraffin. I saw the canvases of other messes collapsing on their occupants. Trucks and jeeps were driving over the muddle. There were people behaving like cowboys on all sides. I saw a man hit in the chest and his inside burned out by a Verey light. It was madder than anything in the campaign whose closure it signalled. The local people must have thought they were worse off than before.

Somebody had the notion that it would be jolly for the RAF to have a tank battle. In the absence of tanks, we deployed our own trucks. I found myself at the wheel of one, with Pedro at my shoulder urging me to go faster, his face alight with a kind of desperate mischief. As we careered to and fro, taking potshots at our dearest friends, it flickered through my mind that I had come a long way merely to be done in by my own comrades in a piss-up. However, if it was a question of pretending a three-tonner was a tank, and therefore of not giving way to another one coming straight at us, even if it too thought it was a tank, then this was no time to let the CO think I was chicken. Now only does it occur to me to wonder if he was motivated by a similar compulsion.

How we survived with nothing worse than torn mudguards must remain the secret of those angels who guard children and drunks. Sadly, Pedro did not survive for very long. His elated face in the Tunis twilight remained the last impression I had of him. Immediately afterwards, he flew to England. Returning in a flight of Hudsons with Billy Burton and the new AOC, Harry Broadhurst, they were spotted by an Me-110 over the Bay of Biscay and finished in the drink. There must have been a tip-off though the AOC's plane was not hit. It was a tremendous shock. We thought of these men as irreplaceable. They were instantly replaced. The new Group Captain was Jackie Darwin, who flew in hunting pink. Our new leader of 260 was a South African, Major Peter Saville.

A great man for priorities, he straight away noticed how parched the outfit was. He came to me and told me he was detaching me for a plonk recce. He said he'd heard there was a cache or two on the other side of the Atlas Mountains. I was to take Bobby Brown, a pilot, and Taxi and see what I could scrounge, without actually invading Ike's HQ. It was a great many leagues to travel, round hairpin bends with precipices on both sides, demanding more effort than a gourmet would reckon Algerian plonk was worth. But, as the armourer and the engineer daily complained, we were due for a total refit. We might as well start as we meant to go on and get some wine in.

A day later we came out of Constantine with a good load on the lorry, and the idea of coming back another way, via Bône, to avoid the dizzy heights of the outward journey. And suddenly Bobby remarked, 'There's a Yank!' He passed us on his motorbike, but he kept looking back at us. Then some more Americans swept past, this time in a jeep, and they all kept looking at us over their shoulders. Fifteen miles on there was a road-block of sandbags, bristling with machine guns and manned by Americans. The armament was all being pointed straight at us.

'Do you think these are Yanks, guv,' asked Taxi, 'or are they Huns?'

'The only way to find out is to drive on, cock,' I replied. But it was impracticable to drive on, the block was solid. We got out and had machine guns thrust in our bellies. We thought they were Germans masquerading as Americans. They saw our sand-coloured truck with the albatross of the Air Force on it and mistook it for a German eagle. They took in our blue uniforms and our peaked caps and assumed we were Luftwaffe. An American officer rushed at me and started jabbering in German.

I said, 'You don't have to speak German, you know, I'm fairly capable of understanding English, since that's what I am.'

'You're escaped Luftwaffe prisoners,' he retorted.

We were very nervous, being outnumbered five to one, and not very fast with about three tons of wine on board. I grew very excited. '*You're* the Luftwaffe prisoners,' I roared, 'and I order you to lay down your arms in the name of His Majesty King George VI!'

They withdrew for a conference. But their guns remained level. I was wild with frustration, thinking that by now the squadron would certainly have liberated some eggs and chickens, and be basting the fowls in the happy expectation of wine to wash it down. Then, inexplicably, a British naval commander appeared out of nowhere, by himself, presumably getting his land legs with a stroll through the mountains. There was no reason that I could see why our captors shouldn't take him for a Luftwaffe man in disguise too, but either his manner or his white knees convinced them that he was the genuine article. He appointed himself arbiter.

After establishing to his own satisfaction that they were Americans, he came over to our side and said to us, 'It'll be all right, just answer their questions.'

So the American officer asked Taxi, 'What make of truck is this?'

Still brimming over, I leaped in like a know-all and said, 'It's a Dodge.' And it wasn't. The commander became a little bit surprised.

'What's the engine number?' the American officer asked Taxi.

'I'm fucked if I know,' said Taxi. 'I'm not supposed to know the engine number of the bloody truck!'

After these negative replies they went into a huddle again. The naval commander managed to persuade them that Taxi's vernacular was for our present purposes more satisfactory than the right engine number would have been and after about an hour's wrangle they declared us British allies. And then nothing was too good for us. They took us to their camp and dosed us to the gills with drink, and sent us home with the truck bursting with rations and beer.

I also scrounged a Great Dane–Alsatian puppy and called her Vodka. She went everywhere with me, first of all to Zuara near Tripoli, 260's jumping-off point for Malta and Sicily. At Zuara there was mail from home and all-round rehabilitation and people lying under trucks repairing them while crying their eyes out as Vera Lynn sang on the radio.

Among the unofficial roles the Spy also inherited was that of being a sort of father confessor. I was never a cosy person and God knows I had no answer to their emotional difficulties and I could only offer an awkward sympathy when I was told someone's wife at home had run off with another bloke. But I was supposed to know everything about the war, and anyway I censored the mail. The trailer was a convenient spot to talk about grudges, and worries about birdmen who were unreliable and when a posting should be applied for, so I let people talk if they wanted. And in Zuara I officially reached man's estate. On my twenty-first birthday I woke as they let the guy ropes down and the tent collapsed on top of me. It was an all-day piss-up, a good excuse for one more celebration before we tackled Europe.

Red Alert

In July a halt was called to the nightly crash of cufflinks in the cots of Malta, Captain Caruana's bar was cleared, and the Wing was ordered to move in on Pachino on the south-eastern tip of Sicily and support the invasion by the Eighth Army in the east, and the American Fifth Army to our left. We had perfect weather for the trip, though the gliders had the bad luck to run into a high wind, plus the bitterness of being stricken by 'friendly fire', and were decimated all over the sea. It was thought to be a soft proposition, and I took Vodka and a motorbike along to see the sights.

An American landing craft took us to the beach. People were debarking in the shallows when I observed a familiar face under a peaked cap regarding me with suspicion and disbelief. I recognized straight away my old persecutor of the honeywagon from the Canal Zone a year back. Noticing simultaneously that in their eagerness to be ashore a number of our chaps had left their rifles behind, I ordered him to make good the oversight and heft the whole bloody lot ashore by himself, and deliver them dry to their owners. It so happened that, enjoying every step of his progress to the beach, I missed *my* step on the slippery ramp and measured my length in the water, but on the whole I was pleased with my arrival in Europe.

On account of the puritanical habits of the American Navy, we arrived as dry as a newt in a curtain rod, but Sicily wasn't quite the piece of cake that rumour had predicted. We had to wait for some days before establishing a decent cellar. And then it was only through a lucky break that we made a start, when a wizened little Sicilian peasant was dragged before me under suspicion of espionage. To my great embarrassment he threw himself on his knees and begged for his life. By dint of patient interrogation and research I was able to discover and verify his story. This was that he had come forward to sell us his stock of Marsala before some more unscrupulous unit should take it over as part of the spoils of war. It was viscous, sickly stuff, but on the whole we were lucky to have spared him.

We weren't long at Pachino before moving forward to take up permanent residence at Agnone. The strip was in an area normally of no interest to anybody, being reclaimed marsh. It lay below a steep hill at the top of which we camped. To sleep on the field itself would have been suicide. The grass was over knee-high, and on every blade of it were mosquitoes. They infested the place in billions. We didn't even dare pee down there. They were the curse and major hazard of the campaign. Yet in a roundabout way they saved many lives.

We were peacefully asleep on the heights, with no thought of a night attack, when the Luftwaffe unleashed the most severe onslaught 239 Wing had ever suffered. Some thirty Ju-88s suddenly roared in from the sea, bombing and strafing the airfield. My first thought was that Mount Etna, nearby, had erupted. But then I had the extraordinary sensation of seeing the attackers coming straight in, almost level with our eyes on the heights where we bivouacked. It was like a grandstand view of a set-piece battle, with the earth spouting from the great plain below, and oily flames gushing from the planes on the ground.

The aesthetic mood was spoilt by Jackie Darwin on my blower. 'Get as many bods as you can down the hill,' he said, 'and shift the untouched kites to another dispersal before the whole lot burns. And try to pick spots clear of delayed action bombs.' So we hurtled down the narrow paths to a very touchy game. I found it disagreeable in the extreme to be leading plane after plane out of the mess of the airfield, with the propeller roaring just behind my ear, while flashing a torch about anxiously for anti-personnel devices and other marvels of Teutonic engineering. And the mosquitoes resented me fiercely. But it was even more disagreeable for the armourer, Flight Lieutenant Sixty Hill, because over the next few days he had to defuse every bomb we found. I wouldn't have traded for his job if a marshal's baton had gone with it.

The action round Catania became as heated as the volcano itself. The Italians threw in the sponge at this point, and it became from then on a great nuisance to me trying to distinguish truth from fiction in the matter of suspect personages claiming they had been on our side from birth. The Germans seemed unmoved by the defection. Some of the cream was fighting an orderly rearguard action back over the narrow Straits of Messina. And there we lost some planes in a most eccentric fashion. To avoid the ack-ack, the boys were flying in so low over the waves that, as they said, their airspeed gauges read in knots. To counteract this the Germans directed their artillery on the water itself, and scored a number of hits in a peculiar ducks-and-drakes style from ricochets.

The main show was the Eighth Army's last great tank battle, there on the plain. It was in many ways a replica of El Hamma, with an even grislier display of dead sprawled about the charred wrecks. There was a new young Canadian pilot on our strength who insisted I take him along for a close view of some of his handiwork, and then wished with all his heart that he hadn't. This did appear to wrap it up for Sicily though, and Peter Saville put it to me that I might link up with the Army to do a liberation recce, before the machine-gunned chickens became too gamey.

Accordingly I took an open three-tonner and some men through to Adrano, on the slopes of Etna. The brown jobs were mopping up and shouted after us, 'Here come the Brylcreem boys now it's all over, after the pickings' and a lot more banter of this kind, including waves and cheers and gestures. Until, suddenly, all this subsided, and we found ourselves bowling along on an empty road, with first crack at any buckshee provender that might be lying about. Rocketing up behind us, though, came a purple-faced captain shouting at us to 'Get back, you silly buggers, the enemy's dug in right ahead of us!' And sure enough, sticking out like a dog's paws from a house at the end of the road was a brace of German weapons.

We screamed round in a U-turn. 'Quick smart, like a ferret!' snapped my NCO and we scorched back and round into a side street. And there facing us, like a reward for virtue, was a beautifully ruined house positively strewn with desirable commodities, if not exactly gift-wrapped, at least ready for the oven as soon as the grime of battle had been washed off. The lads leaped lightly over the side giving glad cries, when to our astonishment another purple-faced officer in a black beret drew up and began uttering purple orders. The gist was that if he ever caught us looting again, we'd be up before a firing squad, as per military regulations. It was an aspect of the situation that had never hitherto crossed our minds. We withdrew, slightly aggrieved, feeling that to be threatened with summary execution both by the enemy and our own people within the space of a quarter of an hour placed too much stress on the nerves. Had it not been for the more accommodating manner of the brown jobs in the neighbouring town of Paterno, we should have gone back to base in a chastened state.

The whole Sicilian bloodbath lasted little more than a month. It felt longer. Never was there such a pleasure in watching the dust settle. I was serenely focusing my mind on obedience trials for Vodka, when for the sixth time in a year I went down with malaria. This time, however, brandy and a blanket weren't enough to sweat it off. The mosquitoes of Agnone had their revenge. I was found babbling and paid no attention when spoken to. They flew me over the water to the hospital in Carthage.

I returned quite chipper in late August to catch the buzz about Italy. The mood in the squadron was unusually tetchy. Aircrew and ground staff were restless. There was a lot of moaning. There'd been no mail. There was no beer. There were many other more petty niggles. There was a high crop of disciplinary actions. There was no doubt everyone was on edge.

Nevertheless I was amazed, waking early one morning, to see red flags sprouting on the airmen's bivouacs. I thought it must be a joke. A Welsh corporal, very experienced in the making of pretexts on his own behalf, now came to me on everybody's behalf, saying, 'The lads have decided they want to talk to you on an official matter.' I said that he knew that if it was an official complaint he should be addressing himself to another quarter. He said, 'The lads was wanting an officer out of the ranks, sir, and with all respects, you was an erk yourself, sir.' I said, 'Is it to do with the red flags, corp?' and he replied, 'Some of them are getting a bit unruly, to tell the truth, sir, not what you might call controllable.' I said I'd see what I could do.

The adjutant grew very excited and shouted out 'Mutiny!' and the word soon ran round the Wing: '260 has a mutiny on its hands.' The CO said that I'd better go down and see what it was all about. The adjutant wanted me to wear a gun, but I didn't think that was a very helpful suggestion. More red bunting had appeared, scarves and handkerchiefs and flags. It looked like May Day in Moscow. Then I went along and gathered them all together under one roof.

The heart of their grievance was that they felt they were left out of the picture. They had no mail, they had no beer, and worst of all, nobody told them anything. They wanted to know, for instance, what was going on in Russia. Was Stalin a monster or a hero? What about the trials and purges? Who were the current commanders? What were they doing? How were they grouped? Was it true the Russian women rolled naked in the snow?

All this was meat and drink to me. I'd been mugging the stuff up without an outlet for months, if not years. For a couple of hours I let them have it, with pictures. I saturated them with facts and figures. They may by the end have wished that I'd never got started. But they said it was what they wanted. We sang 'The Red Flag' and the decorations came down. After that I could do no wrong in the CO's eyes. He said he'd heard of many ways of quelling a mutiny, but to filibuster one into the ground was a novel expedient.

The Old Country

Foggia in midwinter was another planet. It reversed every quality of the desert. A claustrophobic complex of airfields near Italy's Adriatic coast, it was usually under ten-tenths cloud cover. It was rare for anything to get airborne. The army ground wretchedly on through icy mud, while we took the brunt of the bitter winds off the sea.

Termoli was little better. On New Year's Day half the squadron woke to find itself floating out to sea in floods of blinding rain, and waves breaking in the cockpits. We met our first Russians there, come down in leather and sables, to see how we operated. Then we inched northwards a bit further to operate Cutella on the Trigno River. Monty's HQ was up on Vasto bluff near us.

There the squadron got delivery of the latest Mustang, the P-51. Our new CO, South African Major Peter Venter, was so overwhelmed by the beauty of the fabulous new machine that he couldn't wait to show it off to his friends in 7S AAF just the other side of the Trigno. He rocketed over the river and pranged it directly. He lived, but he was in poor shape. G. B. Johns took over as squadron leader.

Then my Aussie friend Bruce Page had *his* nastiest moment. One of his 500-pounders stayed clamped to the wing when already armed. Nothing he could do would dislodge it. He dived and looped and twisted, all to no avail. Eventually he ran out of juice and had to land with the thing ready to go off at the slightest knock. He made it perfectly, and brought the plane to rest a few feet away from my trailer. He said he didn't feel strong enough to walk far for his debriefing.

It was somehow all of a piece with this splintery mood that when I took my turn in the officers' swap scheme, and reported for a short stay with the Army to learn their pretty ways, the first commander I met should be called Colonel Neurosis. If he was putting me on, he never corrected my impression of his name. He led the 17th Calgary seated outside his tank: perhaps he was living down his name. So far he'd collected two DSOs. Out ahead of him there was the legendary SAS commander Paddy Mayne, with a DSO and three bars, an Irish rugby international reputed to be fearless in every field of human endeavour. I knew him while on several attachments to the SAS, as an RAF liaison officer, through the Sicilian and Italian campaigns. What we all knew of Paddy was that, rather like a kettle just before it boils, he became completely quiet before erupting, and this was the moment to move towards the nearest exit.

Most of my Army time was spent with the Gurkhas. It was the 8th Indian Division. I knew about enough Hindi to ask the time but not to understand the answer. My CO's parting words had been to forbid me to go out on patrol. Naturally my hosts instantly invited me out on patrol, as a treat, and waited for me to say I wasn't allowed to. So I had to accept.

They took me along and pointed out the Germans in Lanciano village, on a rock pinnacle. Then a Gurkha courteously enquired if I'd like to make my own personal, private attack. I was encircled by polite brown faces, looking at me hopefully. I thought, My God, can they mean it? Must I go out all on my own with a machine gun through the minefields and scale that bloody crag? And with no air support? I said, 'Well, yes, if you think it wise.'

They said, 'There's a lull. It'll be safe.'

Actually they merely required me to fire a shell from a 25-pounder. This I did. And for the first time in weeks the Germans took umbrage at this break with the rules. A perfect holocaust of shells fell about us in return. I got some dark looks from people in the vicinity who'd grown used to peace and quiet. Take that, I thought, for trying to show me up.

They weren't done yet. A couple of days later we strolled out on patrol across the fields, in total view of every sniper within miles. After a bit the officer drew my attention to a burnt-out armoured car we were passing. 'That's the aiming point for the German guns, they take their range from that.'

I said, 'Then perhaps it's a mistake to stand right beside it.'

'Don't worry,' he said in a dismissive tone, 'they don't shoot at this time of year. Might get a few mortars, that's all. See that farmhouse? About three hundred yards over there? That changes hands every night by mutual arrangement.'

I said, 'In a minute you'll have us lunching with the German divisional commander.'

He shook his head and chuckled, 'Not at this time of year.'

That second, the mortars opened up, from about a quarter of a mile away. I wheeled round and stared in sheer blank disbelief. I was incensed, as if somebody had gone shooting in advance of the grouse season. When I turned around casually to express my distaste for this contravention of the rules, the Gurkhas had vanished – under blades of grass, stones and twigs. Anything above the size of a mouse would hide a Gurkha.

The same day the major said he'd heard I enjoyed patrols and took me out in his jeep to see a 'site of special interest'. As we tooled merrily along an open road, he said, 'You might like to know this is known always as the Mad Mile.'

I'd begun to have serious doubts about the Army. 'What do you mean?' I asked warily.

He said, 'It's exactly parallel with the German lines and they're permanently zeroed in on it. All they have to do is pull the trigger.'

I said, 'But I had some of that this morning!'

'As a matter of fact,' he went on, 'we shouldn't be driving along here, but I thought it would be a great experience for you to tell your boys.'

He was a portly individual, not my idea of a dashing hero. But he was evidently cool to the point of absolute zero. At the far end he turned and began driving back. Then suddenly the engine cut out. We stopped. He swore and wrestled with the gears. His orderly went over the side like a rabbit. I was unable to move. Outwardly abject fear and marvellous cool may be indistinguishable, and on this occasion I was totally and utterly paralysed with fright.

That night I dossed down in a ruined farmhouse with an airborne unit. I ate like a python after so much panic and slept like one. In the morning they woke me and said, 'You missed a real party last night, but you didn't seem to be bothered so we left you.' A German attack had come within fifty yards.

It was, I suppose, as a last desperate throw to crack the composure of a Brylcreem boy that, running me back to base in a light truck, their driver took us off the edge of a narrow bridge into a tiny ravine. He was a bit mauled about, so I had to drive him back for some plaster before returning to my unit. I was unscathed. I hoped the Gurkhas had concluded from all this that the RAF had supernatural powers.

Naturally, after this excitement I was due a spot of leave and decided to hitch a lift with an ENSA entertainment party from Termoli over to Naples. We used DC-3s for these jobs. The weather was murky, but the Kiwi pilot decided he could make it through the Foggia Gap. At least, he decided that I could make it. For, without any previous indications of fatigue, he suddenly declared that he was getting tired of holding the damn plane and he needed to get some shuteye. 'I want some rest,' he said, 'you'd better take it.' And he rose from his seat and left the controls to me.

'I can't,' I said hoarsely.

'Too bad,' he said, 'I'm going to lie down.' I heard him flop down in the belly of the aircraft.

I'd sometimes flown on ops to get the feel and see the targets for myself, and also because it was hard for me to pump them for details after risking their lives if they felt I always stayed behind in the warm. These trips as supercargo were officially frowned on, but I felt they had to be done. Once I had to scramble out of a burning Boston on landing and skulk quickly into the shadows to avoid getting a worse rocket from the AOC. But I'd never usurped the role of pilot.

The poor things in the back, who included Leslie Henson and Prudence Hyman, Kenway and Young, David Hutcheson and many others, were terribly, terribly sick, but at least they could put it down to the weather and had no idea their pilot wasn't supposed to fly. Perhaps I had a charmed life. Perhaps it was the Devil looking after his own.

In Naples I climbed Vesuvius and thought the gooey hot orange look of the lava we trod was good enough to eat. I was hardly down again before the thing erupted three days later and covered every airfield round Naples with ash ten feet deep. And I made a trip to Capri with Colonel Wilmot of the SAAF and a terrible storm blew up on our return trip and I was bound to admit to him that the water didn't like me. And one of the bravest men in the Desert Air Force went down on his knees in the bottom boards of the awful little fishing boat and prayed . . .

San Angelo, our station for the assault on Monte Cassino, sounds the right name for prayer. But somehow the prayers were mislaid. A Canadian flight sergeant came off the perforated track and one wing caught the ground as he was taking off, and he spun off into a dell at the side, where there was an Army Post Office. One of his 500-pounders flew off and exploded in the air. The plane caught fire and the other bomb lay sizzling in the grass. I'd never seen carnage like it, and all around the blaze floated the ash of thousands of letters from a mail truck that had just arrived. I dashed for Doc Kenyon in my jeep. When he saw the havoc and the bodies miniaturized by blast, and the pilots crowding to the rim of the crater, he yelled at me to get them away from the scene before they took in the effect of one of their bombs. At that moment I nearly tripped over the red-hot bomb in the grass and the threat of it going off gave me a pretext to shift them all.

The 'soft underbelly' of Europe had a damned tough corset on. The worst hour of the war for me came with the assault on Monte Cassino – not quite as the battles for that stronghold might suggest, though. On this particular occasion the target was an isolated farmhouse very close to our front line. The normal routine for operations designed to pick off very precise obstacles in the way of the Army's advance was for me to brief the pilots in the company of the Army liaison officer, to reduce the risk of our giving a bad time to our own troops. And I forgot. I sent a dozen men, led by Captain Davis, of the SAAF, off to pulverize a piece of masonry less than two hundred yards from our own front line, without an Army briefing.

For nearly three days and nights I'd gone without sleep, because of the unbroken chain of raids, connecting night bombers and fighters and day bombers and fighters with the typical cosmopolitan range of Allied units in Italy, while dishing out all the usual paraphernalia of escape routes and fun articles like silk scarves doubling as maps, and compasses inside buttons and pens with magnetic compasses, not forgetting the potions to make salt water drinkable – and, to put it mildly, I was pooped. I knew that wasn't an excuse, though, and when the Army's Captain Tom Pearce came on the line wondering where my 'chaps had got to', I could only say 'Somewhere over the target by now, I should think' and start sweating as he began shouting the odds against a happy outcome. Long as they were, however, it was all right. Thanks to Captain Davis, smack on. (I can't write 'Thank God' because there were men in the farmhouse, albeit Huns.)

When at last that heap of rubble was taken, and we'd gone through it past the immense litter of corpses lying in scummy water, I had the sense of having reached the nadir. We came to airfields outside Rome, just about steeped in lurid visions. It was a strange aftermath to be entering the capital itself, relatively untouched, on the day after it fell, and to pick my way through the ambivalent streets looking for the address of my relatives.

All through Italy I had to put up with a lot of badinage from the mess on account of my middle name, Carandini, and the squadron said 'our Spy's a double agent'. While this was pretty superficial, it was none the less a great relief to me to meet my mother's cousin, Niccolò Carandini, and establish that he was an authentic Resistance fighter. Indeed, after the war his enemies called him Il Conte Rosso, the Red Count. He was actually a great liberal, a disciple of Benedetto Croce, and soon to be a minister in Bonomi's government.

He was a fine scholar and a translator of Seneca. And Senecan terms apply to him. He kept up his hopes of freedom and reconstruction at a time when 'merely to live was an act of courage'. It was a peculiar meeting. It was just on a hundred years since my ancestor had fled Rome, but I felt very close to Niccolò. He was fifty at that time, but there was no doubt from our looks of our blood tie. He was charming. Italy and Britain might have been at peace for fifty years.

For my pleasure and that of some of my brother officers, he asked the curator to open the Vatican Museum. It was the first time it had been so opened since the beginning of the war. We went to St Peter's and walked alone under the roof of the Sistine Chapel and while ground-sheets hung ghostly over many items, there was Leonardo da Vinci's St Jerome, and the Raphaels. It was an extraordinary experience and, so soon after Cassino, literally revivifying.

Bangs and Whimpers

Promotion saddened me. The rank of flight lieutenant was nothing to brag about, and in November 1944 it took me away from Iesi and 260 Squadron. I was faintly indignant. I'd shuffled along with them from El Alamein to the Gothic Line, and thought myself a fixture. With victory imminent, it seemed inconsiderate to spoil my chance of a piss-up with them on the terminal airstrip.

Taking what I regarded as premature leave, over a jar, of Peter Blomfield and my oldest friend George Black, last survivors of the strength when I'd joined, we looked back nostalgically on events which had not all been 100 per cent enjoyable, though the cause of much laughter at the time.

There had been George's nastiest moment. This was at Cutella, bright and early, when he was about to take off. Suddenly three American P-47 Thunderbolts materialized out of the murk. It seemed that their navigation had gone to hell and that their aircraft recognition had never been good. They shot us up, with no one able to lift a finger. I stood on the end of the runway with bullets flying round me, unable to move because by now I was sure I was doomed to die at the hand of one of my own side and was as usual paralysed with fright. George, in command of the flight, would have moved if he could, but he was strapped in and his mechanic had dived for cover. The Thunderbolts made two runs, hospitalized the pilot of the Walrus air-sea rescue plane and flew off to be court-martialled. George, whose ring hadn't twitched since Gazala, said that these American manoeuvres caused him to be very, very alarmed for his personal safety.

At Iesi itself we'd only just had the most grotesque pile-up. Someone miscalculated the running time of a show over Germany, involving the obliteration of a ball-bearings factory. It was a massive combined op, and the bombers all ran out of juice together. Accordingly they all tried to land together, which was just not on. There were planes tipped up, crash-landed and burning on the runway everywhere, and more of every species of bomber coming down to plough into them every minute.

A softer run had been the anti-flak excursion from Rosignano protecting the invasion of southern France. For this I'd gone down to Livorno in advance, clutching to my bosom a package which felt practically red-hot. It consisted of the invasion plans, with a detailed programme of every mission to be flown. One moment I feared they were genuine and that enemy espionage would murder me to get the truth. The next moment I feared they were false, and that I was a decoy duck whose presence would be leaked to the enemy. Either way it was a nervous business. I spent most of the fortnight stitched into my tent.

There'd been many fine companions, plus friends from adjacent squadrons. From Bari onwards we'd had a strong liaison with the Balkan Air Force, and made a great many attacks supporting Tito's Yugoslav Partisans. In this direction Lieutenant Veitch had distinguished himself by being fished out of the drink twice near the Yugoslavian coast while a German patrolboat circled him trying to shoot him, and was named Commodore of the Desert Air Force Yacht Club.

The honours for bursting the Pescara Dam in May went to Flight Sergeant Duguid. The squadron had picked up twenty-seven gongs. It had knocked out 131 planes and enough locomotives and rolling stock to stretch from Berlin to Rome. And liberated as many eggs. So we said in our cups and made jokes about our colleague who asked for permission to finish off a train because it was already smoking, to be told that the smoke was from Chicago pianos . . . and the CO 'left alone on the telephone' one day over Mostar . . . and Gremlin Twineame the Kiwi who must have been born without teeth . . . and Snake Rattle . . . and Harry Curno, Nick Nichols and Hawkeye . . . and the fool who killed himself doing a barrel victory roll over the aerodrome . . . and Brian Kingcome, Duncan Smith, Neville Duke, Barney Beresford, all natural leaders . . . and Vodka, run over by a truck, but who had produced eleven pups which were growing up black and baleful as so many slavering hounds of the Baskervilles . . .

My last consortium op was over the Po. Again, I was entrusted with the plans, but I didn't enjoy it. I'd lost my incentive. I had a fairly good idea that my new posting at Air Force HQ to 'plan forward missions' was a euphemism for decay at a desk job, and by now I had a nice balance worked out between war and tourism. But before going to HQ I made one special expedition to Florence. On family business.

My splendid reception by the Carandinis of Rome had inspired in me a wish to know more of this far-flung dynasty. So I looked out the Palazzo Carandini in Florence and introduced myself to the two elderly Contessas who lived in it. The cordiality of Rome was not repeated here. My two relatives were by no means keen to acknowledge me as sharing the same blood. I thought at one point that I would be frog-marched out of the courtyard as a vagrant looter. Even when, after an exhaustive examination, my credentials were established to the sisters' satisfaction, they remained on terms of distant politeness. They gave me cake and light wine, but took none themselves. They nodded assent when I gave them news of the family, but they vouchsafed none in return. It had been said of them that they saw nobody, so perhaps my seeing them at all was an expression of their overwhelming curiosity. There were priests all over the *palazzo*, fulfilling all functions including meditation and idleness. I could see that there were some grounds for the general family suspicion that these two Contessas, custodians of the largest share of the Carandini wealth, meant to leave it to the Church.

Forward planning and liaison, in the spring of 1945 and after the gunfire ended, was as dotty as I'd expected. We had made immense contingency plans against a twilight of the Nazi gods in Bavaria, but it never happened. We had watched for a vast tonnage of bullion, but no doubt it went into Lake Töplitz for we never saw it. We had chatted to Tito in Yugoslavia, and assured his mountain Partisans that the war was indeed over. But it was clear the only credible voice in that land was Tito. We passed the time of day with Popski and his men. The first time, I came to his presence past a Corsican sharpening a bayonet, but the mood relaxed – in 'time! We met Colonel Valerio, who executed Mussolini. We had played host to Marshal Tolbukhin, Russian commander on the 3rd Ukrainian Front. We had organized the surrender of a German division in Austria. We had noted Cossacks who'd fought with the Germans waiting behind 20-foot wire for transport to Russia – some elderly czarist officers in tattered uniforms, many Serbs too, and a number of priests in Orthodox stovepipe hats; a multitude altogether that included many women. What we had been seeing, though we did not know it, was a most shameful episode in the history of our armies, because these people, at the behest of Stalin and Tito, were being carried back over their borders for execution.

It was still the same rope, but it was somehow slack in our hands. I was actually playing netball in Udine when the cease-fire was announced, and we finished the game before going to the bar. I trotted round Venice that summer and thought it wonderful. I patronized the Silver Slipper which led to an invitation to hunt near Vienna, with horses from the Hungarian cavalry. In Pörtschach village on the Wörther See I was billeted in the house where Brahms wrote part of a symphony. I found nothing in the Dolomites to disturb my tranquillity. And then back on duty there was a silly day when we liberated the enormous Mercedes which had belonged to the Gauleiter. There were about six of us in it and as we excitedly prompted our driver to high speed, the personal standard in metal of the Gauleiter clicked upright and a siren started. The klaxon soon brought us an escort of military police.

Over the months my service career drew to a close and there is only one part of it that has left me with a residue of tension. For a time before catching my boat from Naples for demobilization in Britain, I served with the Central Registry of War Crimes and Security Suspects, or Field Security Sections (the Americans called these mixed groups of British, Russian, French, American and Palestinian investigators 'Counter Intelligence Corps'). Starting in Austria, we had dossiers on men and women wanted for interrogation and orders to arrest them on suspicion, and this took me to a number of concentration camps which had only just been cleaned up, and some that hadn't. When I visited Auschwitz and Birkenau fifty years later, the impact of those dread places came back to me as fiercely as when my underlying preoccupation was delivery from all kinds of military activity.

But that another phase was ending was clear enough. And inevitably the Furies clustered round with another graphic illustration of the antics of the sexual world. Among the captured German vehicles was a trailer, not unlike my own in bulk and scope, which I went to inspect. It proved inside to be wholly different from my snug vehicle wallpapered in maps. It was a sort of porno-parlour on wheels. It was covered in pictures of pin-ups and nudes, with rubber goods and materials for drag. Like the *Marie Celeste*, it had obviously been abandoned in a great hurry: there were a lot of women's make-up articles open and in use, and two or three small cubicles with a shop-soiled look, like tatty miniature boudoirs. The whores' parts had evidently all been played by men. We were amazed at the efficiency of a nation that could include this amenity among its front-line rolling stock. It was one final reason for respecting the technology of our vanquished foe.

The medium of course is the message. As to that in its more blatant and obvious sense, one can never be sure just what feelings I stored up behind my official intelligence reports. It possibly had more effect on me than I realized at the time. Some while later I was in London where, after being greeted by my sister with a bully-beef treat, I roamed about getting used to my own country again. And in an arcade off Bond Street a smooth young fellow begged a light from me and followed it up with a suggestion so startling and terrifying to me that I shoved him away, with great violence, so that he went through a plate-glass window. It was a great misfortune to him that I should have so over-reacted. The noise brought a crowd of officious people on the scene, and some unforgiving policemen. It wouldn't have helped matters to tell them about military porno-parlours on wheels. People wanted, as soon as possible, to forget the war.

The 'Red Count' Moves

People can be found to disparage lunching out, saying that it is a severe break in the day's main business. They have reason on their side. If it is a good lunch, the afternoon can only be an anticlimax. If it is a bad one, you work on with a sense of injustice. In the latter part of 1946, however, the main business of my day was done after nightfall, spending my demob gratuity unwisely, while pondering a future which had no shape whatsoever. Invitations to all lunches, good or bad, came to me alike.

While embassy catering is much of a muchness, wherever you go, a personal invitation to lunch from an ambassador is not to be sneezed at, especially as in this case the ambassador was cousin Niccolò, Italy's first envoy to the Court of St James since the fall of Il Duce. I hadn't seen him since we met in his home by the Quirinale the day after Rome fell, but I knew that the grace and skill with which he was tackling an extremely ticklish mission were winning him friends on all sides.

Beecham's had kindly offered me my old job back, at six pounds a week. Posters everywhere showed famous sportsmen like Denis Compton oozing Brylcreem, but while it was nice to see the old firm on the up-and-up, I couldn't think myself back into the office frame of mind. Academe was another alternative: the Forces were sending their veterans to the ancient universities. But my Latin was rusted and I didn't care for the tales I heard of Colonels and Wing Commanders being disciplined by College authorities for taking a beer in a pub after curfew. My prospects were otherwise skinny – I could see few obvious slots for men whose sole expertise was filling in the picture for crews of assault aircraft. I was, in two words, an unemployment statistic.

Most of the time I was walking around literally in dead men's clothes, some of them none too good a fit, borrowed by my mother from her friends whose menfolk had not survived the war. However, for occasions when it was necessary for me to look half-way presentable, such as lunch with the cousin who parleyed for our defeated enemy, I had my one suit, blue with a white pinstripe, which had been issued to me on demobilization parade.

It was one of the good lunches. We swapped stories about the doings of the Carandini clan, beavering towards fame in many lands, and I heard of his wife Elena and her family who set up the *Corriere della Sera* newspaper in Milan, and of their five children and how Guido was administering the Torre in Pietra estate outside Rome, supplying most of the capital's yoghurt and ice-cream.

In return I told him how marvellously mother and Xandra had come through – Xandra at the Admiralty as a 'Secret Lady' with Ian Fleming in Ultra, the system that cracked the German Enigma code, and Mother who had changed houses so often that when I came home I had got off at the wrong station with my ammunition boxes and been unable to find her. It was always said of Mother that unless she had problems she was utterly miserable, so now I was home again bringing problems and she would be all right again.

Niccolò said he had heard I had been ill myself. I told him that it had been nothing more than my seventh and, I hoped, final bout of malaria. The delay in the RAF hospital had been caused because they decided while they were about it to deal with the other legacies of the war. There was the wound in my rump which had festered and plagued me for three years, and had left each of my buttocks with more tiny craters than the surface of the moon. I'd had a penicillin drip every three hours – very sore, but effective. At the conclusion of the course, a doctor had shoved an excruciatingly painful glass contraption up me as a probe, and with the classic comment, 'Perfectly normal mucosa', passed me fit for civilian life.

In the midst of this graphic account of my sufferings, and my imitations of people who had persecuted me along the vale of tears, Niccolò suddenly said, 'Why don't you become an actor, Christopher?' Between the Chianti and the persuasive tones of a man whose very nature was designed to make the solutions to complex questions merely a matter of will power, I immediately exclaimed, 'What a wonderful idea! I'd love to be.'

So that was that. It was settled that I was to be rich and famous, and we passed on to other matters. The fact that in a quarter of a century my sole contacts with acting had been two plays at my prep school, a skit at my next school and the role of acting pilot to an ENSA troupe through the Foggia Gap in wartime, was never even discussed. A typically Carandini decision had been made.

Nor did I spend long considering the mechanics of entry into the profession. There was nothing for me to consider. I knew nothing about it. The one great hazard, I supposed, would be Mother. I guessed right. She was violently opposed to the whole mad idea. We had a furious row. She said acting was *infra dig*, only for people with no morals, and in her more heated moments traduced the character of Sir Henry Irving, Gerald Du Maurier and Caruso. In the end I was able to bring her round to a position of rumbling neutrality only by playing my trump card: the record of the Carandinis in Australia. (I have since been joined in the acting profession by my sister's daughter, Harriet Walter, now one of our most distinguished actresses.)

Niccolò very soon followed up his suggestion by giving me an introduction to an Italian friend, a former lawyer called Filippo del Giudice who was now head of Two Cities Films with the Rank Organization. I went to see him at his Hanover Square office. He looked me up and down, waxed effusive about Niccolò, concluded that I was just what the industry had been looking for, and sent me down the corridor to see Josef Somlo about a contract. Joe looked me up and down, too, taking rather longer over it. 'Why on earth is Filippo wasting my time with someone like you? You're much too tall to be an actor.' And he sent me to see David Henley and Olive Dodds at Rank's South Street office. They already had seventy or so amateurs signed up, and the Rank Charm School to turn them into pros, so one more addition was neither here nor there. I was put on a seven-year contract, with options, starting at ten pounds a week.

That seemed a good brisk way to start 1947. It was enough regular pay for beer if not skittles. I took a basement flat in Chelsea, handy for the tube that would convey me every day to the studio. I shared it with an eccentric fellow – a former Indian Army colonel called Patrick Miller who was a walking *Almanach de Gotha*, usually in love with the Empress Frederick or someone at that level, and whose time was much taken up with the St Petersburg Club which he founded for Russian émigrés. These were poor sad groups of people standing around talking about their dear Czar. Patrick had two umbrellas, called 'the Bishop' and 'the Curate', and he always took one of them out with him. The Curate was for use, when it rained, but the Bishop was always neatly furled. If he made a mistake in his weather predictions and took the Bishop out and was met by a cloudburst, he came home wet.

Having paved the way to success, I waited. And nothing happened.

My career appeared to be over. Along with many other Rank 'starlets', I was under contract, but most of the directors were not such fools as to want to use us. I was told I should have gone in with Korda, because Rank's scriptwriters weren't writing stories *that* tall.

My first part in a film, when it came at last, was in Terence Young's *Corridor of Mirrors*. He was directing his first film, and he got round the difficulty of my being so tall by using me in a scene where I sat down at a table in a night-club. I was Charles, without a surname, who sat with four other nondescripts played by Lois Maxwell, Mavis Villiers, Hugh Latimer and John Penrose, and my sole contribution was to comment on Eric Portman when he made his entrance. My solitary line was a satirical shaft meant to qualify the lead's bravura – 'Take a look, standing in the entrance – Lord Byron.'

This took place at the Pathé Studios at Buttes-Chaumont in Paris. It was bitterly cold, inside and out, for all the charcoal braziers. Nobody had wised me up to the usual dodge of wearing a pullover beneath a shirt. For the sake of the film, not my comfort, the director lent me his dinner jacket.

Off the set Terence gently deflated one or two ideas of mine, which had percolated in through the Charm School, which was strong on the Method. I delivered a discourse on the brilliance of Eisenstein and Pudovkin, with supporting material, as we walked the cobbled streets to the studio. Time enough to consider Stanislavsky's Fourth Wall, said Terence, when I had the experience to walk about the set without bumping into the other three.

Something Rank and Gross . . .

Another crumb dropped off Terence Young's table in the same year. This time it was so minute as to be almost invisible. It was in *One Night with You,* which he made at Denham. I did not have a name of my own, but was called simply 'Pirelli's assistant' and I opened my mouth once only, to say 'Yes'. Otherwise I did a lot of nodding, in unison with other members of Charles Goldner's entourage. He was very funny and made the journey to Denham before dawn worthwhile.

My next was also a one-word part, but the film itself had some prestige, being *Hamlet,* directed by Laurence Olivier. I was heard, but I was not seen, because I shouted out 'Lights!' while standing in the dark. I was determined to get a word in somehow – even anonymously. I thought that they could have spared the expense of dressing me in a soldier's uniform and giving me a spear, but then I told myself that being in low-budget films like my previous two was no excuse for getting into parsimonious habits of mind.

Olivier never spoke to me, but I had time to see him work and to study many other box-office draws deploying their techniques before the cameras. This was because I was travelling to Pinewood, Ealing, Denham, Teddington – every studio in the southern counties seemed to be going full blast – to be used as a stand-in for world-famous stars when tests were being made for the actresses who would play opposite them. Some, I noticed with acute interest, were almost as tall as me, like Stewart Granger, Chips Rafferty, Burt Lancaster . . . Stewart Granger showed me an unforgettable courtesy by driving me back from the studio in his own car.

When lucky enough to be mixed up with a film, I got up at 4.30 and after coffee and a bun (and a bath was vital to me even if I was going to spend the day in grease and rags) I plodded off. I would ride a couple of buses and the Underground, plus a train for Shepperton or Beaconsfield, to reach the studio by 7 a.m. We, the meaningless specks, had to be got rid of to frowst in the canteen before the stars arrived at 7.45. No one left the set all day. I spent a lot of time with the stunt men. I felt at ease with them. And I read volumes about opera, because for the first time in my life I had discovered music and was becoming passionately interested in turbulent billows of sound.

Doing tests for Granger actually led to a part in one of his films, an unexpected bonus. Basil Dearden, directing *Saraband for Dead Lovers*, gave me the part of Duke Anthony von Wolfenbuttel, whose job it was to smile sweetly, from a horse receding into the distance, at Joan Greenwood. At the last moment before the cameras turned, it was decided that I might look a little too much like Stewart Granger. So I was given a blond wig and put on a white horse, on Christmas Eve. Alas, Granger and I must still have looked as if we'd been hatched from the same egg, because the sequence was cut from the film.

I was learning about eyelines, and getting used to the cameras which in those days were enormous boxes painted greenish blue and rather alarming to see dancing down on you. Oddly enough, cameras were missing from the Charm School, where Rank was making a valiant effort to convert all its geese into swans. We envied the instant swans, like Dirk Bogarde, James Mason, John Mills and Margaret Lockwood. If they were dragged into a get-together under the auspices of J. Arthur himself, we cowered away in the shadows and hadn't the nerve to speak.

The Charm School at Highbury was a brave idea, even a good idea. Learning acting techniques takes at least ten years, and most of it can't be taught, but that's no reason why a school shouldn't make a start. Molly Terraine, who ran it with artificial fruit hanging from her picture hats and bobbing hypnotically in front of her eyes, was both firm and charming. She was terrifying, but her blue eyes twinkled. She was a more precise Paula Strasberg of her day. The Method acting was amazing. Each in turn we'd hurl ourselves through a doorway and register horror, rage, love or resignation at the sight of a pair of spectacles in an otherwise bare room, simultaneously declaiming 'That is a *red* cash register' or '*That* is a red cash register.' The permutations were infinite. Molly took no impertinence, nor idleness, and she was a great elocution coach.

Most usefully I learned a great deal about fencing on film from a first-class performer, Patrick Crehan. He had some help from an ex-sergeant of the Guards called Ricky who went protesting into a film called *Song for Tomorrow*, directed by Terence Fisher, in which I had another minuscule role as a night-club MC. They had no choice here but to allow me to stand on my two feet, but poor Ricky collared all the attention in a leopard skin and his Guards moustache playing Samson while the heroine sang 'Softly Awakes my Heart' to him.

Despite some useful lessons in this area and that, my instincts told me that extracurricular work would be needed if I were to get anywhere. On the other hand I declined absolutely to walk about with a book on my head in deportment class, as if our goal was to be models in a department store. There were a number of other superfluous classes, including one on the strict rotation of the letters of the alphabet.

Yet the experience we truly needed, that is to say minor roles in films with good directors, was not to be had. The obstinate among us punted around for what we could pick up. And sometimes we asked to be lent out. What we actually got was a truly grisly free-for-all, as in *Penny and the Pownall Case*.

This, like *Song for Tomorrow*, was an Ivory Production. Ivory was an exotic name for the Charm School's own home movies. Only the technicians, working with grim self-control, were pros in the proper sense. Every other function, from direction to walk-on parts, was vitually up for grabs. In *Penny and the Pownall Case* the short straw for direction had fallen to Slim Hand. And a slim hand was a fair description of the cards he was dealt on that occasion. Normally he was a production manager at Ealing.

Here, instead of productively getting on with a bit part in a good film, I was a lead in a B feature, though Z feature would describe it more accurately. As the wicked Jonathan Blair in this thriller I was very saucy and madly attractive. In line with this concept I wore a camel-hair coat which some friend of my mother had given me. It had a series of cigarette burns right across it, but I thought it flash and never took it off throughout the film if I could help it.

For the first time, I died on celluloid. I was shot by Ralph Michael. As the moment approached I realized nobody had told me what was expected of me. 'I'll shout Bang,' said Slim, 'then I want to catch you dying in the revolver smoke. From the gun behind the camera.' The sound would be added later. We put the plan into effect. I wore an ancient brown leather raincoat which might have been worn by Tree playing Fagin, and waited for the *coup de grâce*. 'Bang,' remarked Slim, almost inaudibly. Guessing from the movement of his lips that the bullet was on its way, I gave a convulsive start. The prop man put down enough smoke to cover a whole platoon going in to the attack. There was a long pause while I was enveloped in fog and the entire scene disappeared from my view. When it cleared I could see them all peering in anxiously, wondering if I would still be there.

Very, very slowly and with immense dignity, and no expression at all on my features, I sank to my knees, like a telescope into itself. Disgust and disbelief were writ large on the faces of the technicians. Those actors who had some delicacy of feeling turned their heads away so I shouldn't see their expressions. Then I keeled over and lay still. The revolver smoke lay thick about my nostrils. There was a suspenseful silence. Eventually Slim broke it. 'I think we'd better do another one, Christopher,' he said, 'because that didn't fool anybody.'

I felt I knew about people dying, and objected. 'I've seen people shot,' I said. 'They don't, very often, get hurled backwards. Unless it's, say, a .45 at close range. Or a howitzer. They very often *do* slowly but surely topple over.'

He replied drily, 'They may topple. But there's toppling and toppling. Oblige us with another sort of topple, do.'

I toppled once again and the topple was printed. Not because anybody was convinced by it, but because we hadn't the time nor money for repeated takes. From their sidelong glances I detected a need to polish up my dying. There were no rushes. Ivory films were shown to us all in one piece for the first time on the Saturday morning that followed the last takes. So the première at the Odeon in the Tottenham Court Road became the equivalent of the rushes. I wasn't specially keen to see my Jonathan Blair. There was no option, though. We were forced to attend these showings. I wished that a crevice might have opened in the stalls and that I might topple into it. It was plain to me that there was one great fault in all the deaths I'd witnessed in the real world. The people who died were all novices. They'd had no practice.

Having a Bash

In the years after the war, there was a great surge of popular interest in classical music. Some of this may have been due to returning servicemen whose ideas had been shaken up by their life abroad. Whatever the reason, it was a generation which queued all night for places in the gods at Covent Garden and the Albert Hall. Before the war, my sister had had to drag me to opera and ballet. Now, most nights, I was there on the little stools. We could see that we'd been born too late for the golden age of composers, but we sensed a golden age of conductors and soloists.

The country itself was drab, but music opened another world of colour and beauty, excitement and romance. I'd seen Tito Gobbi in a couple of operas in Naples, and now I wanted to see everything that had ever been written. The sounds of Verdi's *Otello* overwhelmed me like an avalanche. I was enchanted in turn by Mendelssohn, Berlioz, Wagner, Rossini, Puccini, Tchaikovsky, Sibelius. I haunted the second-hand record shops of the Charing Cross Road, and spent all my money on a towering heap of 78s. In my bedsitter I cranked a hand gramophone into the small hours.

I never did get to understand music back into the time of Palestrina and Monteverdi. I never did come forward to enjoy atonal compositions. My bracket opened with the death of Haydn and closed with the best of Stravinsky, Richard Strauss and Sibelius. Beethoven, to me, was the voice of God. And rather like the Lord's butcher boy, I committed every one of his nine symphonies to memory, movement by movement, without being able to read a note, and whistled them. I developed a kind of Beethoven whistlelogue which identified me before I came round the corner. My passion for listening to majestic performances was so devouring that there was no part of me left for any other passion to take hold. Indeed, even the frail argosies of new relationships often foundered right there and then in the concert hall when I found that the girl I'd treated to a ticket was not in tune with my enthusiasm for whatever we were hearing.

Either because this made a joke for the gossips at Rank, or because somebody heard me at a sing-song round a joanna, and genuinely thought I had a voice, David Henley sent me off for some singing lessons at our patron's expense. I went to an Italian signor who sang tenor in opera and taught Ian Wallace, who said my voice was possible if I spent all day every day practising. And I had an audition with the great *Lieder* singer Elena Gerhardt. Rank obviously wasn't willing to fork out to that extent. Then I went to an Austrian madame whose windows gave out on Lord's cricket ground, who also thought I was possible, if she could turn me into a tenor.

Her grandmother and daughter sat in on every lesson, enchanted by the incredible contortions of my uvula as I tried to produce a tenor ring. I had a very fast vibrato, which they declared was not unattractive, if I would try not to slow down into a wobble. Hard as we all tried though, to whoops of encouragement from the attendant family, I would not turn into a tenor. What they produced was a voice that could not make up its mind, and when my basso profondo reached the 'bridge' from bass to baritone, it pirouetted over the parapet into a tenor baritone timbre. Unusual and distinctive, but inconvenient.

None the less, once the idea I could sing was implanted, it took root. It was furthermore watered by thoughts of great-aunts Tem, Rosie, Fanny, Bella and Lizzie, and their parents, who'd been such a nest of nightingales in the ears of Australia. So I persevered. I went for another opinion to a professor at the Royal College of Music, hoping he might say, 'Better late than never.' But it was no use. I was too tall to be an actor, and too old to be a singer. He heard me, and he said, 'You *should* have been a singer, but we can't take you at your age.'

Still, learning by doing had become my philosophy. At a period when I was looking too tall and too foreign to be cast, even sitting down with my back to the camera, in any British film, I saw a notice for an audition for the Noël Coward musical of *Lady Windermere's Fan,* retitled *After the Ball.* I turned up at the theatre on a bitter wintry night, wearing a blue Melton overcoat. With my pale face and the notion that I would freeze to death on the walk home, I was looking and feeling slightly lugubrious.

There was a crowd in the stalls round Coward, including Robert Helpmann, Michael Benthall and John Perry of Tennant's. The mob was rustling and shifting about restlessly. They had the look of people who'd already heard enough people. I was up for the role of Lord Windermere.

'What are you going to sing for us?' asked Coward.

As soon as he asked me I felt the song I'd chosen was inappropriate for Lord Windermere. I hesitated. 'I really don't know, Mr Coward,' I replied.

'We shall guess as you go along, then,' said Coward amiably, and sat down.

I said, 'I thought I'd sing the Serenade from *Don Giovanni*.' There was an outburst of giggling from the back of the stalls and I distinctly heard a voice say, 'Looks like an undertaker.'

I thought, This is pretty bloody, and became even more determined to sing the Serenade. 'Oh?' said Coward when I announced my intention. 'Well. Splendid, splendid, splendid.' I apologized. I said it was the only music I'd been trained on. He said, 'Never mind. Have a *bash*.' I had a bash. Naturally, after the provocation from the back of the stalls it echoed in the vaults of the theatre more like a call to arms than a seductive love offering.

Coward came down to me at the end and said in friendly tones, 'Do you know, you have a voice? It has a baritone quality. You might even turn into a tenor.'

I saw several meanings behind that remark and said nervously, 'Oh, really? That would be good, wouldn't it?'

'Oh,' he said, putting his head back and staring at me in a puzzled way. 'Why?'

'They always get the best parts,' I replied.

'Ah,' he said, 'true.' Half-way back up the aisle, he turned and looked back at me. 'But not this time,' he said with a smile.

Later people told me the part had already been cast before I arrived and would be sung by Peter Graves. They said this by way of consolation, thinking that performers better than me would see no shame in trailing behind such a beautiful voice. It only increased my embarrassment. On the other side, it was a lesson that no actor can have too soon: that there is no logic in the manoeuvres of casting.

A couple more films went swiftly by with me on the running board. There was *Trottie True*, in which I made the acquaintance of Roger Moore, Jean Kent and Michael Medwin, and was so besotted by Natasha Parry that in the canteen I behaved like a character in a two-reeler and asked her to have tea while pouring it meantime wide of the cup. This in direct contrast to the *savoir-faire* I had to show in the film as a stage-door Johnnie. Then Alfred Roome directed *My Brother's Keeper* for

119

Gainsborough. He was one of the top cutters in the industry. One of the things he cut from that footage was my appearance as a policeman. It was, they said, no reflection on my performance. It was simply that I had stood in one corner under the wall, and they'd had to tilt the camera so much to include my helmet that they'd included the gantry as well, and all the arcs and spots on it.

All these jovial remarks about my height left their scars. It occurred to me that there might be a conspiracy of runts among the leading men not to have me in their dwarfish vicinity. I was having to whistle a lot of Beethoven to keep my spirits up.

Savoy Fayre

After these trials, it was like Christmas in Technicolor to be given a speaking part with a name in the credits. I had to represent the Australian Bernard Day who was in charge of the motor sleighs in the Polar expedition in *Scott of the Antarctic*. I missed Norway, where they doubled me, but I had the intense satisfaction of working for Charles Frend in a major film at Ealing, where at that time some of the best pictures ever made in Britain were being turned out.

The set was a full-sized ship leaving a harbour in New Zealand. Among many curiosities was James Robertson Justice as Petty Officer Evans, without a beard because he had to regrow it en route to the Pole. Jack Cardiff did the lighting and the enormous banks of carbon arcs made an unbearable heat as we trotted to and fro in furs from head to foot. Then the blizzards came along to choke us, being made of salt and acrylic resin, minced in a sieve and blown across the set by an aeroplane engine.

It disappointed me that I was one of the few left behind when they went to Norway. Had I gone, though, I would not have improved my acquaintance with a young skier from the pistes of Savoy, called Jacqueline, who'd been brought in as one of a great army of technical experts who knew all about snow and how to get about in it. It had amused Jacqueline to see me dash out of winter quarters and be unable to speak my lines for acrylic resin, and the director go into a towering rage because, literally, I'd dried. It was nice to show off my French, too, and before parting she said she'd like to go dancing.

It was a good idea. Her auburn locks thatched a frame that rose nearly five foot nine from the dance floor of the Milroy, my favourite night-club, where they let me keep a bottle of gin with my name on it. She was one of the few partners I'd ever had whose nose job didn't instantly click into my navel. She looked very lithe and brown in her white halter-neck.

We danced all evening to Edmundo Ros and contrasted the world of acrylic resin with that of real snow, and felt sorry for those in Norway. It was downhill all the way.

Except that I didn't realize it. When she went on her tiptoes and breathed in my ear something that sounded like 'V***+=**zsh?' I had no idea what she was driving at and could only ask her to repeat it. Then I twigged. We made two complete circuits of the dance floor in silence, concentrating on the steps of the rumba. I weighed up the logistics of the problem. I was twenty-five. I recognized that I could not go on indefinitely treating women as if they were a separate species. Besides, the bromides in the tea had long since been diluted in the bloodstream. She struck me as a good-looking girl. And as to the old cautions about health, it would be flying in the face of nature to consider them. Jacqueline was obviously the healthiest creature on two legs and a pair of ski sticks.

All the same, I havered. She was staying at the Savoy. It was a place that I might conceivably want to use one day for ordinary social intercourse. Quite possibly these large hotels would frown if a girl brought a man in after eleven o'clock. I was not the size of man who could easily creep in below the level of the desks in the lobby. As a child I'd often been taken to the Ritz for lunch, but I'd never been to the Savoy. I dearly longed to. I hoped my first visit would be an auspicious occasion. With my arm round the waist of this pliable girl, I nearly gave way to temptation. But I had to say, 'No, Jacqueline. Not tonight.'

The problem, as I explained to her, was that at that particular period I shared a flat near the Edgware Road with a very difficult individual who tended to come into my bedroom and threaten to shoot himself. He was a first-rate cook, which was surprising, because he was totally possessed by one thought. This thought was: rogering, and the rogering to follow it. When I had moved in, his introductory remark had been to warn me to pay no attention to anything whatsoever that I might hear through the walls. I tried to pay no attention, but that wasn't easy. Once he came down to breakfast with his lower lip bitten through, whether by himself or someone else he didn't say. More recently he'd flung my door open, turned all the lights on, flounced in with a revolver and said, 'I can't stand it any longer, I'm going to end it all,' and whirled the gun round by the trigger guard, preparatory to pointing it at his temple. The last time, partly through terror and partly through irritation at being woken, I'd snapped, 'For Chrissakes get on with it, then, if you're going to!' But he'd only put the weapon down with a look of outrage on his face and said, 'Well, you're a fine friend!' I said I was thinking of removing myself shortly. It certainly was not the place for romance, I said, not realizing all the implications of romance.

Jacqueline laughed. 'Come to the Savoy tomorrow at three in the afternoon,' she said. Here was a girl for a schuss! My heart thumped painfully. I still hesitated, though. I wished there might have been a way to test her soul at the Albert Hall. But there would be no time for that. She would soon be leaving the Savoy Hotel for the Province of Savoy. I might grow into an old man without ever having known Woman, in a biblical sense. The unworthy thought crossed my mind that she might have invited me before lunch and not after, and then I realized that might take some explaining when presented for payment to the film company. I saw how very lucky I was to have fallen into such discreet hands. 'I'll come tomorrow,' I promised. 'At three o'clock, by the side door.'

The side door of the Savoy, called the River Entrance, was under observation from scarcely fewer members of the hotel staff than the main entrance. I felt they all could see my intentions and despised me. But though their eyes bored into my back, none of them detained me. I skulked along down endless thick-carpeted corridors, jumping at every puff of wind, like a man skirmishing in a beleaguered city.

I hadn't slept very well; I lunched on a rusk; I wondered vaguely if we would talk French; and if so, whether that would make it a superior experience. It was a wonder that I reached her suite. I was taken aback when she flung the door open wearing a peignoir, and nothing else, as was obvious as it billowed open with her welcoming gestures. I was appalled by the thought of the impression this would have made on any passing waiter.

She hung a little sign from the outside door handle which asked for no disturbances. I feared it might seem the most blatant advertisement. But I was in no position to say a word. I was extremely gratified by the appointments in the Savoy, and fascinated by the little touches she'd added herself – orange juice, Gauloises and ashtray on either side of the bed. As a bedroom set it was totally convincing, right down to a cupboard large enough for somebody to hide in. At any moment I expected to hear the words 'Lights, camera, action!'

Nothing and no one disturbed us, not even a gust of acrylic resin. I *had* been lucky, I *had* fallen into good hands, though I soon became aware that discretion is by no means everything. She evinced no displeasure at the discovery that I had reached such a mature age with nil experience. It may well have spurred her on to greater effort. It set at rest for ever my fear that sex outside marriage was accompanied by immediate moral and physical disintegration. At the same time I was amazed by the amount of energy consumed. For a girl with a good figure I thought her remarkably fit – more than once I fell right off the bed. It was a lovely day. We became prodigiously hungry and walked – via the River Entrance – down the Embankment in the twilight to a restaurant in the King's Road. It had been the nicest possible introduction to the Savoy. And while I couldn't be sure that this latest illustration of the sexual world marked the end of another phase in my life, I did feel that it was like a benediction on my choice of profession.

The Living Proof

The sharpest prong in the trident with which Rank chivvied us towards perfection was really the best. This was to send us down for two, and sometimes several, weeks at a time to a theatre in the coastal resort of Worthing for some real live stage experience. There, it was thought, we would be out of harm's way, would be learning something, and would have a shop window to show off our fledgeling talents to wretched producers trundled down for that purpose. Also, since the cinema has always had a semi-mystical view of the stage, they saw it as the authentic initiation rite, on the lines of the vigil kept by the squire before he could be dubbed a knight.

Naturally, the proven stars were spared this ordeal, and showed up only on gala occasions. The theatre was the Connaught, one of the best half-dozen stock repertories in the regions. Miraculously, the resident company showed no resentment at having a troupe of Flash Harries and Harriets regularly foisted on them. In lives more arduous than those of widows who take in laundry, they took us and everything else in their stride.

All in all, I went through my paces with them twenty-seven times. Many of these plays I began to forget as soon as I stepped into the wings. Some were seared in my mind indelibly. There was never any reason to forget the company itself, with people like Bill Waddy and Alan Robinson and Charles Morgan, with their computer memories, their tolerance and their jokes. Once only did Bill show signs of impatience with me, as we sat together in the dressing-room and he realized I hadn't the slightest idea how to make up.

They sweated on a treadmill, and they stayed upright. They always had one play on the stage, another rehearsing and a third being learned. It seemed to me like the logistics of war all over again, with a faithful but demanding audience sitting out there missing nothing.

This fantasy of being under fire once more was reinforced in my billet, which was owned by an actor, Clifton James. Of all actors, his war was the most idiosyncratic, since he so closely resembled Montgomery that he had been his double in real life. It was like being back with my old Supremo again, and finding he preferred theatre to war.

Worthing had the reputation of being a place where retired people could spend a tranquil evening to their lives. Not all of our audiences were elderly, though. The Connaught seemed to be the central drainage point for the cultural aspirations of every school south of London. Until an actor has performed Shakespeare before schoolchildren, all of whom turn the pages of the book in their laps, and has heard the gasps of indrawn breath when he gets a word wrong, he has never acted.

A great deal of cant has been spoken about The Theatre by actors in the cinema. There are surely many revitalizing influences in it and, in Charlton Heston's phrase, an actor is glad sometimes to 'renew his visas'. But it would be sentimental of me to pretend that the warm blood and hectic pulse of the legit theatre ever made me think of transferring my allegiance. I knew that I wasn't right for it, that I would never survive. Over-stimulation would kill me in rep if the audiences didn't; in a long run boredom would finish me off.

The first time I trod the boards at the Connaught was as Roberto the butler in *The Constant Nymph*. I went on believing that to be an actor you had to act. All the time. Non-stop. I buttled unrelentingly, and stressed the Italianate nature of the character at every opportunity, throwing in some outbursts of 'Madonna!' not in the script. I acted everybody else's part as well as my own, and endorsed all their emotions. If someone shed a furtive tear, I wept into my handkerchief, if someone else laughed, I held my sides and bellowed till I was puce. I upstaged everybody and all but ruined the play.

In the interval the producer came round to the dressing-room. He was livid. He obviously didn't know what to do with his hands and was holding on to his jacket to keep calm. 'Christopher,' he said, 'would you be good enough to finish the play on your own? As you're playing every part, the rest of the cast can go home.' I was very hurt. It was like a cold shower. I'd had no idea I'd offended. 'Let me give you a word of advice,' he said. Then his control went. It was a toss-up whether he burst into tears or laughter. He laughed. The critics said that I'd given a remarkable performance as Roberto the butler, and that it had been welcome light relief. An odd sort of thing to say about a comedy.

In *As You Like it* I played the furtive and unnamed forester who sings 'Who is he that killed the deer?' As the only singer there with a smidgen of a voice, I drowned everybody. In *Libel*, a court-room melodrama written by a lawyer called Wool, I was never off stage as the Junior Counsel. I was never really properly on, either, because Alan Robinson sent me up a whole series of legal notes, with coarse jokes about the audience that cracked me up. After a bit, the Judge himself was chortling. A song was demanded of me as a sort of fisherman/pimp in *See Naples and Die*. 'Funiculi' went down well the first night, and 'Santa Lucia' the second. Greatly daring, I varied it the third night with 'La Donna è mobile', started in the right tenor key but couldn't sustain it, and on the ringing high notes my voice cracked almost without stopping. It was a sequence of desperate strangled shrieks. There were people rolling in the aisles, crying.

In *By Candlelight* the role was humble enough, as a servant with little to say. But I was given more bits of business carrying dishes about than any servant before or since. It had all to be synchronized with the lines of the other characters, who deliberately changed their timing each evening to catch me on the hop. 'Would you care for a little more wine?' one would say to the other, when I had my hands full of soup tureens. Every night I worked out everything carefully in advance on a vast sideboard with enough for a state banquet on it, for a mere two people. 'Roast or boiled?' Each potato was in a different dish. I rocketed to and fro with tureens, salvers, dishes galore, toast and butter, countless bottles, sauce-boats and condiments. Always they made me so nervous that I got everything out of order, spilt the wine and served the pudding in place of fish.

Gradually with practice I disgraced myself less frequently. I was the Devil in *Man and Superman*. We did the entire thing, lasting five hours, including Don Juan in Hell. I was Undershaft in *Major Barbara*, and Iago to a rather small *Othello*. I was beginning to give something faintly resembling a performance when my great moment came – the lead in a Welsh play by Eynon Evans called *The Wishing Well*.

It is a very fey play, about a bizarre Welsh family, and full of characters like Evans the Post. My Welsh accent sounded like a cross between a Norwegian sailor and a Chinese opium smuggler. The story required me, as a cripple, to spend some part of the play under a rug in a wheelchair being sorry for myself.

The plot hinges on the family's belief that this paralysis is merely hysterical. They plan a shock cure. One of them would go upstairs and pretend to assault my great love, Delith, whose piercing screams would bring me instantly to my feet, cured. At the great dramatic climax I cried, 'I'm coming, Delith, I'll save you, girl,' or words to that effect. I had to spring out of the wheelchair, totter forwards like a lunatic robot, and collapse in a welter of tears. Not a dry eye anywhere. Curtain.

It didn't work out quite like that. I mustered a plausible Oriental Norse and Welsh accent. I mastered the wheelchair. This was in itself an achievement. It was hand-propelled by the rims of its bicycle-type wheels, but the rake of the Connaught stage towards the orchestra pit was so steep that I had to remember to act in profile throughout, for fear of moving downstage rather fast.

The first night we got through all right, and I toppled through to a triumph. I was so pleased by the effect on the audience that I threw in a couple of encore topples. My Welsh cousin, the eminent actor Clifford Evans, was present and said kind things about my Oriental Norse. I thought that, after all, this theatre lark was no worse than Purgatory. But the trouble with the theatre is that you can't just put a good take in the can and use it ever after. On the second night several things happened.

Alan Robinson as Amos the gardener had to push me on to the stage when the curtain went up. He decided his make-up wanted a little more brio. He promised to astound us. He certainly did. I was sitting in my chair waiting behind the door to be pushed through, having not seen Alan all evening as he prepared his surprise, when I heard his voice behind me ask quietly, 'What do you think of this?' I turned round and nearly went straight out of my wheelchair. He looked like the Abominable Snowman. He'd decided that Amos, to paraphrase Esau, was a hairy man, and had festooned himself from head to foot in grey hair. Nothing of him was to be seen except two distant pinpricks of light, which were his eyes. His face was swamped in tendrils, like a Kansas wheatfield.

'B-b-but,' I quavered, 'you *can't*. You can't go on . . . like *that*.'

'What's the matter with it?' he said abruptly. 'It's a very interesting make-up.'

'But you can't go *on* in it,' I repeated hoarsely, 'you can't, you must do something about it.' I became very agitated when he still showed no signs of repentance and snatched at it. 'Here,' I said, 'let's have some of it off.'

'Get away!' he said more loudly, in outraged tones. I moved towards him, bent on removing some of the growth. 'Get back in your chair,' he hissed at me. Meantime the curtain had gone up, and Alan was interlarding his remarks with the off-stage dialogue of the play: 'Get you back on your feet in no time, boy . . . *siddown*,' to which I replied, 'Thank you, Amos, *take it off*.'

Along with the confused muttering of this altercation, the audience then saw a wheelchair come half-way through the doorway and stop. Alan had somehow contrived to wedge the thing in the doorway. Already heated by my startled reaction to his appearance, his language became saltier than anything I'd heard since Monte Cassino. He quite forgot the audience. '*Fucking* thing!' he stormed at it, and to me, '*Get through the bloody door yourself. Help me, you stupid idiot, for Chrissakes* . . . Ah, you'll be all right, boyo.' I could see, bent double in the far wings, my love Delith and Charles Morgan, waiting to come on when Amos and I had our brief natter.

It was an appalling situation. Half on the stage, I was gabbling like some lunatic ventriloquist, 'Well, look you, Amos, I'm in and I'm out; trouble, have you, stuck it in the door, have you? Have to give it a bit of a push then, won't you, Amos?' And the disembodied voice was replying, 'You'll be all right, boyo, when I get this *fucking* chair through here, bugger the sodding thing!'

Just as I was resigning myself to playing the first act from the garden, there was a tearing, splitting noise and he got me through the door, taking a foot and a half of the flat with him. A piece of the scenery came on to the stage, hotly pursued by us. With the momentum we crossed the stage into the main room of the little Welsh cottage at a rate of knots, with me getting blister burns from trying to put a brake on our progress.

Alan was ad-libbing through his forest of hair. The lines composed by Eynon Evans had gone totally out of my head. I had a stone-shattering dry, lasting all of ten seconds, then shouted at the top of my lungs, 'Delith! Delith! Where are you, Delith?' She was standing two yards away. A great roar of applause and cries of 'You'll be all right, boyo,' went up from our normally respectful audience.

The next night was the crowner. I could see the front row of the stalls after being wheeled on: everybody was in a wheelchair! All the local wheelchair people had come to see it *en masse*. Somebody then managed to get me facing down the rake. Off we went, careering towards the pit. There was no way I could stop it. With a wild cry I abandoned ship. I leaped out of it two acts early, thereby completely ruining the great climax of the third act. The chair tipped over the edge. The curtain came down and draped itself over it in a forlorn sort of way.

I said I wasn't going on with the play. Bill Waddy poked his head in front of the curtain and said, 'I'm afraid there's been a slight technical hitch . . .' His words were drowned in a roar of applause. After a bit I was persuaded to get under the blanket again and continue with the play. Every time I opened my mouth the audience erupted.

All I ever wished thereafter of *The Wishing Well* was that the curtain would come down and stay down.

Open and Shut

That my final curtain did not fall in Worthing, but in the full glare of interest in the West End in London, was due to the Under 30 Group. I was asked to appear at the Whitehall Theatre, as a member of this group, in a Sunday-night experiment called *The Flat Next Door*, a story much dependent on hallucinatory experiences. It was a part that demanded my presence on stage all the time, bar about five minutes, the kind of thing which was naturally offered to Nicol Williamson, and which Nicol Williamson naturally turned to good advantage. There are not many Nicol Williamsons, and I was never one of those few.

What chances I might have had were scuppered early on in the rehearsals because I had simultaneously to be making a film at Pinewood. It was not a very important film – *Prelude to Fame* – and my part in it was almost the least important part about it, a reporter who has to sit in the front row at a concert waiting to interview Guy Rolfe as a brilliant conductor. But just as the play needed me on stage all the time, the shooting of the film presumed my continuous, albeit silent, attendance beneath Rolfe's baton.

In this tug-of-war, the film was the heavyweight, and the wretched producer at the Whitehall, Colin Gordon, tore his hair as he went through rehearsal after rehearsal without his leading man. At least he could hide somewhere on the opening night. For me it was an utter disaster. I had been able to come to the theatre perhaps half a dozen times in all, for a three-act play. When the curtain went up I was so badly under-rehearsed that I shook with fright, and the newspaper I was discovered reading fluttered in my hand with the noise of a cavalry charge. I had my first dry after five minutes, and in the course of the evening in which I played a kind of suave bastard who gets his comeuppance at the end, I had nine or ten altogether. It was the actor's recurrent nightmare come true: that he is pushed on the stage not knowing what he's doing, what the play is about or what his lines are.

Everybody was there who mattered to me, including a complete range of coaches and most of my relatives and, to cap it all, with an expression of acute distaste the President of the Under 30 Group, Alec Guinness.* As in the second act I slowly began to gather the reins into my palsied hands, I happened to point out to the garden through the French windows and elicited a roar of delight from the audience. I couldn't understand what had caused it, until I realized I had put my hand through a frame where there should have been glass.

That one night was the full stretch of my career on the London stage. But there were other forms of live torture being geared and soon Rank was pitching me into a television thing called *Kaleidoscope* that went out from Alexandra Palace. This had all the hazards of live theatre, without any of the professional aids, such as proper exits and entrances for the actors. For some reason best known to themselves, the designers of the set for *Kaleidoscope* put the office of the Commissaire de Police (myself as a mix of Fernandel and Chevalier) directly off the corridor that runs behind the stages. This corridor was used by every single person who visited Alexandra Palace – administrators, window cleaners with buckets, technicians, tourists, harlots, people in the wrong building and ladies with tea trolleys. From it I had to peep through a tiny spyhole in the door, without being able to hear what was said on the set, and gauge the timing of my entrance from some bit of business enacted by my Inspector of Police, the Mallorcan actor Richard Molinas. A splendid, debonair personality out of hours, he was, like everybody else in live television, exceedingly nervous at work.

As his tall and intimidating boss, I had to spring through the door, upbraid him for being slow with his investigation of a case, and haul him over the coals. I did so. He looked abashed. As well he might – for he'd let loose, as I spoke, a thunderous fart, a prince of farts. Nor was he finished. Hardly had its echoes ceased reverberating across the set than he followed it up, out of sheer fright, with a rival for a higher decibel count. I had done more than knock the wind out of his sails, I'd deflated him absolutely.

We played a ten-minute scene without once looking at each other. And he never stopped farting. It was like fifty rounds rapid. The celebrated Pétomane of Paris himself would have been impressed.

---

* Years later I reminded Sir Alec of it. He said, 'Yes, you really were terrible. After a quarter of an hour I realized why, and felt sorry for you. I knew nobody in the world could be quite so bad without a very good reason.'

People behind the camera were rolling in agony, but there was nothing they could do to help us. The glory and the confusion were all ours. I racked my brains unavailingly for a way to let the viewers know that the credit should all go to Richard. It was hopeless. We were on our own, with the scene to ourselves, indissolubly bound by our predicament.

Like the noble lord of Drake's day who farted when presented to the first Queen Elizabeth, and sailed away for seven years so people should forget the fart, I kicked the dust of Ally Pally off my shoes and never did live television again until I hosted *Saturday Night Live* in America in 1978. Radio, of which I did a fair amount, was also often live, but somehow less fraught. Its more peculiar moments were to do with sudden surges of naturalism, and I had once to caper about the studio with Roger Delgado, using actual foils in a duel.

I couldn't sail three times round the bottom of the world, but I did get a trip to Germany with the faithful Terence Young, who'd been the first to take me out of the purdah of the Rank Charm School three years earlier. This time it was to play an officer in the Guards (when will their glory fade? They put a high value on tall men) in a mawkish film about Allied co-operation called *They Were Not Divided*, in 1950. The closing shot had the Stars and Stripes and the Union Jack in home-made versions twining about each other in a storm above the lonely grave of the protagonists, like rambling briars. There was gush to make anyone cringe. But it was work, and it increased my debt to Terence.

Edward Underdown and Ralph Clanton were the British and American handshake. Helen Cherry wifed, and RSM Brittain came in as himself, on secondment to the Welsh Guards from his own outfit. I was a tank commander who smoked a large number of cigars supposedly given him by Eisenhower. A great many regular soldiers took part, playing themselves, thereby constantly underlining the point that it is better to let somebody like Harry Andrews do it for you. On the other hand they stood the buffets incidental to the story without complaining.

These included explosive charges on the turrets fixed on by the German technicians and covered with branches and petroleum jelly, which we had to set off by ducking down and connecting wires up. They invariably went up in a sheet of flame, and concussed everybody inside the vehicle. It was uncertain how much real animus lingered on five years after the war. Of course we heard torrents of abuse poured on the Nazi party from all sides, and had to assume that 99 per cent of the population had been rootedly opposed to it. I personally still felt uneasy, and unable to suppress the old feelings. Against my better judgement, I found myself addressing the Germans only in an abrupt and laconic way.

It was strange, because already at home I was tired of people who relived the war and refused to come down from 15,000 feet. Perhaps it was the proximity of Gmünd-Eifel, where we shot some of our tank scenes. It was still strewn with live mines, which made filming an interesting exercise, but it wasn't this so much that got under my skin. Perhaps it was the proximity of the SS stud farms, where the privileged had gone to pass on their genes through the Thousand Year Reich.

On the other hand I idled up the Rhine on days off, and took wine and strawberries while expecting a sight of the Lorelei, and wrote a ream to my mother about a trip to Beethoven's birthplace in Bonn, and how the sight of his reinforced piano and ear-trumpets had made me weep. I could also report to her with truth that I had not indulged in the heavy drinking at the hunting lodge on Lüneburg Heath.

One night when the cast and crew had all got in there and I wasn't in the mood to stay, I walked back to our camp in Soltau alone across the heath in the moonlight. It took me most of the night and was rather spooky, conjuring up visions of Montgomery taking the surrender there. Deep in these poignant reflections I was startled out of my skin, like a child who finds that a book of spells after all works, when a sudden commotion took place in the undergrowth at my feet. I stood petrified, waiting for a phantom Panzer Division to settle my hash. But it was not the Wehrmacht back from Tartarus, only a family of wild boar trotting across the road in the gloom. They could be nasty enough, in all conscience, but they gave me the benefit of the doubt, and vanished at a very polite speed.

On returning to London I was told by the Organization that it would be difficult to place me in another film soon, because I was too tall, too foreign-looking, and hadn't made a name. All these tiresome things I had been told before, *ad nauseam*, but on this occasion they were said in italics. To show that they meant what they said, they declined to renew my contract.

Hole in None

Niccolò had gone back to Rome, to be president of his country's national airline, Alitalia. Xandra, perpetually crossed in love, had finally married her original choice, Roderick Walter, whose family had founded *The Times*: they lived in Spain. Mother would have been glad to help, if I gave up acting, but no longer knew everybody. She thought me a fool for throwing in my lot with an enterprise whose boss was a miller, albeit a God-fearing miller. I only knew that the mills of both God and his miller ground exceeding small. Mother said she'd always said acting was precarious. I said everybody had always said that. Our discussions were acrimonious.

I set off, an independent, to fend for myself. Immediately luck hopped on my shoulder; I got a part in a film, after being interviewed for it in a corridor at Denham, by the American Raoul Walsh. Walsh was short one eye, after being struck by a stone which flew up from the road when he was driving. Two-eyed, he'd been a Hollywood leading man in the Fairbanks mould. One-eyed, he was still a tough hombre. He asked me two questions – 'Speak Spanish?' and 'Can you use a sword?' I said 'Yes' to both. He said, 'OK, you've got the job.' I thought this promised well.

It proved to be a false dawn. But, for the time being, I was content. The film was the Warner Bros production of *Captain Horatio Hornblower, RN*. A ship was built at Denham and soon Jock Easton and all the stunt men in England swarmed about the rigging. As a Spanish captain who was outclassed by Hornblower but refused to strike his colours, I had little to say, and that little was in Spanish, but I did have a duel with the hero.

The hero was Gregory Peck. He was a star, a big star, a big American star. I'd never had to fight for my life against one before. It was not his sword that left the profound impression, though (it was his first screen duel, too), but the fact that he and his mate, Robert Beatty, automatically stood on either side of the camera to give me an eyeline for my close shot. (Here and there leads are to be found who neglect this natural etiquette, and sit at the back of the set reading a paper, but luckily it's rare.)

The attention Walsh paid to the unimportant characters – who included Stanley Baker as the boatswain's mate – gave me a glimpse of an endemic difference between American and British films which overall gave the former a superior gloss. The Americans always homed in on their secondary characters, gave them their moment, insisted that their weight be used in the picture. The British didn't. Even in those days they hadn't the time. We weren't there to be definite characters, we were set dressing. We got not so much direction, as indirections, to interpret as best we might.

This had led to some curious stresses. I formed the impression early on that the camera was not a very supple tool. Somebody said to me, 'You must tone everything down for a close-up. You mustn't move too much, either, or you'll go out of focus. And if you go sideways you go out of frame.' Because of these inhibiting warnings I had a natural affinity for the long shot, and never dared come close. When I did, I played as if encased in liquid steel. I was so scared of moving any part that it looked as if I had locked into position.

After this liberating experience at Denham, business once again became torpid. I had ample time to reflect on Peck's retort when I asked him if the autograph hunters weren't a worry to him – that he'd be more worried when they stopped. As an autograph, I was still a virgin. It looked as if I might remain one. Certainly to Mother. I was hopeful that things might improve, if not optimistic, but she said I should leave acting and smarten myself up. As a temporary tactic, to pay the rent, I did so. I got a job as a floor-walker in a tailoring and outfitters' emporium called Simpson's, in Piccadilly.

For this situation, pure unadulterated charisma, I'd been interviewed by Dr Sam Simpson over eighteen holes on the golf links which spread away from Mother's house at Sunningdale. I'd taken this game up at about the same time as I took up acting. One of its great merits is that you can play it by yourself. Acting had given me a lot of time by myself. As an actor, I was a rapidly improving golfer.

From the first, I was a fanatic, one of those who play in driving snow with a red ball and sleep with their clubs by their side. I had an unmatched set gleaned from various donors, in an old bag. For years I was able to afford neither caddies nor lessons, but I did my best to hearken to the advice given by the professional Ted Ray to someone who asked how he should make the ball go further – 'hit it a fucking sight harder, mate'.

Height is no great advantage in this respect, in fact the bigger arc multiplies the errors. It seemed to me at the beginning that not all my clubs were long enough to reach the ball, though this proved to be an illusion. Tall, light people, I found, have special problems in a high wind, which bends them like a bow. Few golfers of my shape had been really good – George Archer and George Bayer were the exceptions. (Nowadays, Tom Weiskopf, Johnny Miller and the newest phenomenon, Tiger Woods, are three more.)

My large hands and long fingers appeared to cover most of the shaft when I held the club in my 'baseball' grip. Archie Compston, the craggy giant narrowly beaten by Walter Hagen in the final of the British Open, saw me practising in the garden of a house near Wentworth while having a drink and exclaimed irritably, 'Goddle-mighty, boy, don't you know how to play?' 'Not really,' I said. He showed me the conventional grip.

I read everything I could lay my hands on, but ultimately that proved to be not such a clever idea. The legends and lives and anecdotes were well enough, but with technique there was always a risk of being submerged. In the end you come to need trigonometry to draw the club back, and you can't bring it down once it's there. I began to notice that the swings of the masters were not consistent with one another, and that everyone should go his own way *sans peur et sans reproche*. As Henry Longhurst said of Ben Hogan's – 'a master's swing might carry *him* through to a full finish, and anybody else to the infirmary'. I often tried to do the ball a most terrible injury and, while I sent it a long way, I often landed on my back in the process.

Fiercely intolerant of my own performance, I had the most appalling manners. I only did not break my clubs because I hadn't the money for new ones. I frequently threw them round the course. My self-control stayed behind in the clubhouse. I broke rules oblivious of the way I infuriated people. My friend and mentor, the wonderful golfing writer Bernard Darwin, was always preaching self-control, sweetness and light in his column, but on the course had a terrible temper. Tested beyond endurance by the perversities of the game, he would raise his hands to heaven, crying, 'Why *do* I play this bloody game? I hate it so.' Of course, as a disciple of Wodehouse, I knew that it was understandable for a saintly man to lose his temper on the golf course. Tommy Bolt used to explode into shouts of rage; Ky Laffoon's language was unbelievable, and he often hit himself on the head with his clubs.

On the other hand, my partners and fellow members at Sunningdale gradually led me to understand that the 'wee ice man' Hogan, and Lloyd Mangrum who went round with no more expression than a Mississippi gambler, were better models if I wanted people to be willing to walk round with me. It was lucky for me that, playing in midweek when other people were at work, I was able to learn from a great many elderly and sweetly patient golfers at Sunningdale. Their game wasn't always great, but their manners were impeccable.

I actually once went round Walton Heath with the legendary James Braid, who at seventy-eight returned a card of seventy-three. Another time when I was quietly putting in solitude, the caddie master, Jim Sheridan, came up and said he would introduce me to another golfer for a game, if I would mind my p's and q's and behave myself. He took me up to the Duke of Windsor and said, 'Here's yer man, sir, that'll gi' ye a game. He's no' bad. Talks a lot.' The Duke went round at a terrific speed, and *he* talked incessantly, most of it blue.

There were other splendid old men with purely local reputations. Tiny Clive Meares looked on the verge of falling into an open grave in his bow tie, button-down cuffs and battered hat. Appearances were deceptive. He would make a bet on the outcome, on condition you or he would take a glass of kümmel on every tee. The winner of the previous hole would have that honour, and he would craftily lose the first few holes. Over the years his system was so inured to the intake that he always walked a straight course into the bar from the eighteenth, as the winner.

John Morison played a very good game, and it might have been better yet if he would have left off his old overcoat, tied up with string. When I somehow beat him I offered him a drink. He said, 'I'll have a pint.' 'Mild or bitter?' I asked. 'No,' he said, 'sherry.' But the formidable Brigadier 'Critch' was inconsolable. And Lord Charlie Chelsea astonished us by breaking a leg trying to play out of a ditch.

I played a lot at Sunningdale with the racing driver Wolf 'Babe' Barnato, grandson of the diamond king; with my London neighbour Air Commodore Lionel Stubbs, who'd joined the RAF at sixteen in the First World War; with the club's eagle-faced captain, Arnold Read; at Muirfield, later with the former head of Loretto School, Forbes Mackintosh, who used to say to me 'don't jog back' and quite rightly tried to convince me that it was no good replaying the shot you've just foozled; and with Major Guy Bennett, a sometime club secretary, who did more than anyone to tone me down and get me to feel that if I'd gone into a sand-trap it was worth waiting to see if my opponent might too.

It's very satisfying for anyone who finds it hard work to keep himself in check when he sees another, more eminent person losing control. One day at Swinley Forest, Lord Derby's delightful and exclusive private club, where I'd been taken by Lionel Stubbs, we played a four-ball with the classical scholar Oliver Hobhouse and Sir James Barnes, the Under-Secretary for Air. Oliver at the short seventeenth performed the first hole-in-one I'd ever seen. As he had a stroke on the hole, he did it in 'none'. Sir James took this as a personal affront. He was a pussycat, but he belonged to the large sector of pussycats who are upset by golf. 'That's no way to win a hole!' he said. 'I can't think of a better one,' I replied. He was apoplectic. 'Outrageous fluke!' he barked and stormed on to the last hole. On the left of the fairway was a large garden, where a monkey was kept in a cage. Its hideous noises sounded like a commentary on the tee shots.

Amid these turbulent air waves, I played a round with the owner of Simpson's. He was sorry to hear that I was having a struggle with the cinema, and said I could come to him for a job whenever I wanted one to tide me over. And so I came to be one of his floor-walkers. It was a bewildering world but my colleagues were nice to me, and it was my business to be nice to the customers. The niceness led emphatically nowhere. The feeling grew in me over the weeks at Simpson's that I was not ideally suited to this kind of merchandising, and that I ought to have another pitch at getting my name in lights.

Pleasure

Few people can have paid their dues to the talents of others by queuing for the box-office more assiduously than I did during my apprentice years. I never let a conductor nor a soloist of note pass through London if I could help it without bending an ear to their virtuosity. It was marvellous to be an actor during the golden age of the British cinema, and it would have been more marvellous still if I could have made a contribution to the films with the good scripts. I watched boxers and cricketers and golfers of the first calibre. I even gave points to Billy Graham at Harringay. Had a university fan club been founded, I could have been its first president.

If it were possible to become famous through sheer osmosis, my constant proximity to so many stars would have soon resolved one of the producers' perennial doubts about me – that I hadn't been heard of. The man who made it possible for me to gaze at so many celebrities and enjoy a huge variety of spectacle, in spite of my slender income, was Walter Carandini Wilson. Like Niccolò, he was my mother's cousin, and the son of Great-Aunt Tem by her first husband. I called him Uncle.

As a child I'd seen him briefly at Shiplake and other riparian junkets, looking stunning in blazer and white flannels. As an erk in the RAF I'd had to snap to attention when he passed by as a Group Captain. He was fifty-four when he joined the Air Force at the outbreak of war, after a previous life in the Army. But he was in his sixties when I knew him well. Finding that my progress towards my goal was continuous but crabwise and full of holes into which I vanished entirely, he adopted an avuncular attitude. Without pushing it or interfering, he cheered up my weekends.

In America, I gathered, he was nicknamed 'Pleasure' Wilson. No doubt he'd earned it in more ways than one, but I heard one story in which, being engaged to three women at once, he had extricated himself from tedious explanations by naming the date by telegram to all three simultaneously, and leaving it to them to upbraid one another over his triple breach of promise. His own gratifications apart, Uncle Walter renewed his claim to the nickname every week by the pleasure he gave other people.

Oddly enough the long list of his achievements in *Who's Who*, which included playing rugby for England in 1910, and countless tokens of his gallantry as a soldier, made no mention of the position that I chiefly associate with him through personal contact. It was obvious enough on the licence plate of his car: GRA 1, letters which stood for the administrator of the Greyhound Racing Association. He was a humane and decent man who was appalled at having to associate with the infamous Black and Tans in 1921. He took seriously the £1,000 tag that had, quite unjustly, been put on his head, but went back to Eire in the time I knew him to make his peace.

It was a relief when he got the big black car and the chauffeur, named Tate, with whom I sat up in front and swapped stories, while Uncle Walter tapped on the glass whenever he deduced laughter and wanted to have the story repeated. Until he had someone to drive him, his protective role was a debatable asset. He drove an Alvis himself, with a jockey in his own racing colours mounted as a mascot on the bonnet, and behaved as if a stop light were put there only to tease the imagination. And he had the extraordinary habit, when he drank, of downing the whole glass at one swallow, whether it held vodka, wine, water, beer or gin.

He roped me into various clubs (and paid the subscriptions) like Buck's, founded by his friend Buckmaster in a shell-hole in 1917, and he occasionally gave me the money to buy a bottle. But generally he was careful not to patronize. The usual routine was for him to call me and ask casually, 'What are you doing Saturday, young feller? If you've nothing on I'll come by about six with young Sale and pick you up and we'll pop off to the White City.' Young Sale was his girlfriend Betty. (At seventy-two he was married for the first time, and to Betty.)

Ushered up to the Directors' Box, with the best food in London, at one of the two or three small tables behind plate glass, and with a pound to put on the dogs, I had for a few hours a haven from myself and my ridiculous occupation. At the White City and at Harringay, I heard Melchior and Flagstad sing, Billy Graham preach, saw England take on the All Blacks at rugger, Randolph Turpin take the title off Sugar Ray Robinson, and Chataway pip the Russian sailor Kuts in the five thousand metres.

Uncle Walter had himself been a formidable amateur boxer. With him

I met Jack Solomons the promoter, and through him Freddie Mills and through him his great friends the Crazy Gang. And that in turn led to further meetings on the links because they were great golfers. I met boxers of all sizes, from Don Cockell to Jimmy Wilde, 'the ghost with a hammer in his hand'. I met Joe Baksi, Lee Savold, Joey Maxim, Jack Doyle, Len Harvey, and Bombardier Billy Wells who became a film extra. Uncle Walter asked nothing of me except that I spend the time with him cheerfully. He was well named 'Pleasure' and, I came to think, between his energy and his looks and his fair dealing was perhaps the most remarkable Carandini of them all.

The cinema was outside his ken. There was nothing he could do for me directly. There again, for the fourth time, I was helped out by Terence Young. True to form, the role was insignificant, but the film was *Valley of the Eagles*, whose setting by definition was Sweden. I went with the unit to Sweden and began a long love affair with the country.

By contrast with the rest of Europe, Sweden had then a high standard of living. Their neighbours killed each other; Swedes killed only themselves. Their women were famous not only for their beauty but for using it to attract men. Their people so loved drink that it was rationed. All this and other glamorous differences were a mere five hours' flight from London.

The key sequence showing Lapps hunting wolves with eagles was borrowed from the National Geographic Society. Otherwise a cast headed by John McCallum and Nadia Gray had plenty of fun in Stockholm. Jack Warner played a Swedish detective, and I played his sidekick. Being winter, it was unconscionably cold, and my bit had to do with running round the corner of a building and stopping dead on the ice, the kind of instruction scriptwriters put in without thinking of the problems involved. I became fascinated by a factory on the edge of a frozen lake whose function was to cut the lake up in cubes and sell it to restaurants, and I went out with one of the machines, a thing like a lawn-mower with a saw attachment.

In the evenings with our Swedes we drank as an excuse for singing, and sang as an excuse for drinking. At one of these extended outbursts there was a Swedish drinking song that I happened to know. For some reason connected with the schnapps I suddenly cut loose and was just making the ornaments vibrate when I heard a thrilling voice joining in behind me. I turned, by the group round the piano, and recognized the rather short singer as the great tenor Jussi Björling. I stopped at once. 'No, no,' he said, 'go on, it's good.'

I was embarrassed. 'I don't know any more,' I said.

'Let's think of something else, then,' he said. 'How about opera?'

By then the others were silent and listening. 'I know only Italian,' I said awkwardly.

'Fine.' He spoke to the pianist and I found myself singing tenor-baritone duets with Björling. Ad-libs and schnapps mingled with our songs. He pressed me to visit him next day at the Opera House and sing to the Intendant. When the morning came I went to the opera thinking all the time that he couldn't have meant it, that it was the cordiality of the quaffed drinking-horn.

He was there inside the austere building, however, punctually on the hour with Joel Berglund. As soon as they asked me to sing, every note of music I'd ever heard passed out of my head without previous contact with my vocal chords. I launched into a few phrases of *The Flying Dutchman* after staring at them, then realized that they had come into my mind because I was staring at one of the world's leading interpreters of the part, Berglund himself. But he said at the end that if I could keep myself in Stockholm they'd consider enrolling me in the Swedish Opera. It was out of the question. They were sympathetic and told me to contact them again if ever the chance arose. I walked back to the film-makers not knowing whether to feel downcast or elated, but fired anew with a desire to be chiefly known as a singer.

Determined to return in some guise, I punted about for openings in Scandinavia. I extracted promises for the following year of a stint as an English radio announcer and also of some parts in a series of television films called *The Hans Andersen Fairy Stories*. Going with the bounce of the ball I floated back to England, beat the British Open Champion in a golf postal match organized by a newspaper that spring, along with dozens of other people, and shot back over the net to Sweden in the summer to fulfil my obligations.

A Norwegian company made the films. I was in five altogether, over two seasons. My parts were all different. In one I was an ancient, playing chess with a very young boy. In another, a student helping a lovely but consumptive girl: Bohème style. In a third I was the peasant husband of a beauty, played by Signe Hasso. No sets were necessary because the Skansen Park reproduces houses in different styles over the centuries. And nobody said a word about my being too English, too tall or too unknown, even if they thought it.

For a TV half-hour the production of Andersen's story of *The Nightingale* was magnificent. Elsa Marianne von Rosen led the dancers of the Swedish Ballet in a sequence of the death of the Emperor of China, with Death sitting on his chest, when only the voice of the real nightingale can bring him back from the shadows. Death was Julius Mengarelli, one of the two tiny brothers who choreographed it all. And I was the Emperor.

There was another sequence in which I was perambulating with a totally bald head, which is inevitably murder, and reflecting in my sorry Chinese way about the nightingale of jewelled clockwork which they'd given me to replace the real one. There were no Chinese gardens in the Skansen Park, so they had to find me one to perambulate on. They hit on just the thing half an hour's drive from the capital, in the lovely castle of Drottningholm, one of the royal residences. Gustavus VI Adolf was an authority on porcelain, and kept his own collection in a Chinese pavilion there. Naturally they'd Chinesed the garden round it. I found it congenial for rumination.

At the third or fourth ruminating take, I was disturbed by a general stoppage of the cameras. On to the set came His Majesty and the Queen, disposed to refresh themselves with a draught of pure porcelain. We the intruders were immediately mustered in a line for a handshake. Reaching me at last as the Right Marker, the King raised his hat and said, 'Interesting matter of protocol – who should bow first, the Emperor of China or the King of Sweden?' Bowing from the waist, I thought what a nice king he must be. I was tempted to suggest a round of golf to him. Several royals had their handicaps down to single figures and could be relied on for a decent game. But I let the opportunity slip. I was afraid that my ragged assortment of clubs might let down the image of the Emperor of China.

Trollsaga

As this golden age of the cinema unfurled, I had to get used to the idea that for me the fifties would have to be the thrifties. It was always obvious that in the way of directors and scriptwriters there wasn't enough to go round, and that some of us would have to make do with silver and bronze, not forgetting lead, but gradually a crisis in the British industry developed in which even the base metals were in short supply. Quite apart from the strivers on the outskirts of the crowd scenes, there were many actors of talent who couldn't get work.

Acting is survival, as Vincent Price would say, and those with successes behind them were admitted to the charmed circles around the few fires still alight, like people huddled together against the night noises of the forest. It was natural, it was understandable, it was even cosy for them. One wished one might have been one of them. In the long run, though, it was bound to lead to habits of repetition and insularity which would be to the detriment of the local British product.

As early as that in my career, I think, I began to rationalize my predicament as that of an actor who wasn't sufficiently typical of his own country's images to confine himself to the home market; in order to be known at all I would have to convert myself into an international figure. I never seriously calculated just how long a haul this would prove. In the rather uncertain range of my skills, the one department where I had a solid foundation was in languages. It's also the area in which anyone can improve almost regardless of his funds. And if he has the luck to go on foreign locations, a small part will give him all the more time to chew the fat with the citizens. I worked at this, and made sure everybody knew I did.

I was getting some films. Whether Mickey Mouse operations or with money behind them, I took what was offered. As Sir Felix Raybourne in *Paul Temple Returns* I was correctly suspected of villainy in a thriller spun off a well-known radio personage invented by Francis Durbridge. I was a slave dealer in *Babes of Baghdad* shot by the Danziger Brothers with John Boles, Paulette Goddard and Gypsy Rose Lee, and in Spain, where I met some stars of the bull ring. And from there I went to be aide-de-camp to Baron Gruda in *The Crimson Pirate*, most of it made out to sea off Ischia. The cameras turned as soon as land was out of sight. It was Otto Heller's first essay in colour and despite the discomfort of wearing green velvet under the Mediterranean sun, I was delighted to come up resplendent as the waves.

We had a great time. There was a moment when from beneath a heap of brawling bodies the voice of Georgie Woodbridge came forth: 'I always knew my Old Vic training would come in useful one day.' The script started life as serious, nay solemn, but Robert Siodmak, the director, with all the sure touch of real tension behind him in *The Killers* and *The Spiral Staircase*, took stock of the material in forty-eight hours and turned it into a comedy. It was like a *Boy's Own Paper* adventure, except that Eva Bartok was in it.

Burt Lancaster was the star and lived dangerously, having got the habit in his circus days. He taught me a lot about screen fighting, and how to make something of a duel so that it is not just a flurry of movement; how to cheat, exaggerate the sweeps and time the pauses. I asked him if he went out to meet the public and he replied, 'No. Never let them get too close, Christopher.' He said it tautly. I felt that anyone who insisted would be disembowelled.

After Spain and Italy, France. 'Just be yourself,' John Huston advised me, playing the painter Seurat in his *Moulin Rouge* in Paris. Seurat invented pointillism, but in my scene at the Deux Magots café he was not called on to expound the process nor, indeed, anything else very much. The season was on and American tourists rolled like a wave bearing cameras on the crest to within a few feet of where we sat swigging absinthe. I came to know Toulouse Lautrec/José Ferrer well, and took him to see a relative who'd married into the Murat family, because they had a room full of paintings for which the Louvre had offered a million pounds. It was fascinating. It was also another little pinprick reminder of how well Carandinis were doing, by and large, in other professions.

As a nice economy, the same company, Romulus, kept me in Paris to play Lieutenant Whitlock, a feeble and fussy officer in charge of a Marine band, in *Innocents in Paris*. We had the real band over from Chatham and marched our boots off. Those tourists who already had me in their albums as part of the French art scene must have been taken aback to see me striding out in front of the band in the Avenue Foch.

Then a long, long interval elapsed in which nothing came my way. The whole medium gave the impression of being on the skids, with young TV champing on the bones of its dad. In theory there was time for all sorts of things. Xandra, for instance, took us all to Spain to see her new home and I astonished my mother, on her first flight, by being airsick for the first and only time in my life because of my experienced observation of the dangers to which the Spanish pilots were exposing us.

At a concert I met the oil millionaire Paul Getty, and the acquaintance grew into a friendship. Since there was nothing I appeared to want of him except an audience for my remarks on the cascades of sound of Romantic Opera, he invited me to Sutton Place. One day he handed me one hundred pounds to furnish him with a record library, which gave me the opportunity to spend days in the large stores hearing them all through before giving them my sanction. And then of course I played them all over again with him.

Once he loosened up, he was a good story-teller, which contradicted the impression of his character other people had given me. He never gushed like his wells, but he occasionally got into a fairly free flow. He talked about his parents and his early days and his wildcatting. One weekend he described to me, all alone at the end of a long refectory table which had belonged to Henry VIII or some other magnifico, how he had once fought Jack Dempsey. And he pushed back his chair and went dancing round and round this immense thing, punching and dodging and ducking to show me how he'd knocked out the heavyweight champion. Mother was very envious of my good luck in staying at Sutton Place: she remembered it from being a guest there before the First World War, when the owner was the Duke of Sutherland. She didn't mind me buying records for Paul, but she looked down her nose when I told her he'd left it to me to go round the tailors collecting swatches of tweed from which he could have a range of country suits made up.

My time off was increasingly given to Scandinavia. This was due not only to our modern versions of Hans Andersen and the places they opened up for me, and the bits and pieces of work that floated in orbit round the series, but my wonderful discovery that the tiny communes among the birches and pines of Sweden, Norway and Finland were well served by operatic societies and itinerant professional companies. The lure of practice with them was very strong. I realized there would be nothing to compare with Björling, nor flukes to match my experience with the Royal Opera. None the less I felt that the woods were alive with the sound of music and that I must personally contribute a few kroners' worth.

Accordingly I'd descend on some unsuspecting company, or cultural nexus, like a troll on a bicycle, as they readied *The Barber* or *Don Carlos* or *The Magic Flute*, or perhaps a mixture of all three, and tell them Francesco Sarzano was willing to join in. Sometimes, unless they were singing *The Flying Dutchman*, I'd tell them my name was Hendrik van der Decken, instead. Usually, having got over their surprise at this warbling apparition from the hinterland, they would add Francesco or Hendrik to their playbills, or maybe just A Guest. I'd do my stage trolling, take a few jars with them by the *dansplats*, leap back on my boneshaker and trundle off to the railhead, or the next knot of performers. In the end this *sub rosa* operatic career notched me up a dozen or more shows. I was frequently paid: that made me a pro. If that was a fantasy, it had some very good melodies.

More than a bicycle was wanted to get on the London stage. I had an audition at the Prince of Wales Theatre for the part of the Latin gigolo in *Diamond Lil*. The leading lady, Mae West, then asked me to come and see her in her suite at the Savoy. I kept the appointment. The Savoy had been good for me last time, but I went in some trepidation. An elderly buster ushered me in, rather crossly, to her bedroom.

She showed me albums of herself in famous roles, and a painting of herself in the nude which she said was famous, and I agreed was entitled to be. Then she said, in a perfectly detached and proper way, that if I had any pretensions to playing opposite her, I must learn how to hold her. 'There are going to be scenes in which we're close together,' she said, 'so I'll show you how to stand.' She pulled me to a full-length mirror and instructed me to stand behind her, and tuck my right knee into the back of hers. Then I must crane over her right shoulder to gaze at her, while she half turned her head back towards me. It made a pretty enough picture in the mirror, and she declared that I was technically acceptable, but I couldn't help feeling that if this was the next scene in my life course in erotic studies, it had somehow got out of sequence. Anyway, other factors to do with work out of town intervened and Bruno Barnabé got the part. No doubt I should have been grateful to him, but there were times in the next few months when I regretted that I was not him.

In that slack time for the film business, my only way forward was through television. A blush still mantled my cheek when I thought of my live scene with Richard Molinas at Alexandra Palace, and my other television credits were not in the forefront of anybody's mind, though Orson Welles had directed one, and Joseph Losey another. These, and the first of all, which was called *The Mirror and Markheim*, were movies for television, though so far as I had been able to see, the one made by Welles had not been made for showing on British screens.

This was a pity. The Losey movie – credited to a certain John Dillion and produced by Carl Foreman – was shot at Walton-on-Thames, had the improbable title of *The Adventures of Aggie* and was not the kind of show an actor would mention in his showcase. *The Mirror and Markheim* was based on a pungent story by R. L. Stevenson but had pretty well passed out of the minds of all but Philip Saville, who was the lead, Arthur Lowe as the murdered pawnbroker, and myself as the Visitant or Devil. And while the Welles movie was undoubtedly a work of genius, nobody had seen it.

It was based on his theatre production of *Moby Dick* with the Mercury Players. The notion was of a play within a play, in which a repertory company step in and out of their roles in the story of Moby Dick. He shot it as a movie in three London theatres, notably the Hackney Empire, where in the evening we had to give way to the regular bill, led by Sid Milward and his Nitwits. Welles had taken a place near me in Belgravia, and since he drove everywhere and would have taken a taxi to Land's End, I was deputed to drive him to and fro in a minuscule vehicle with my head touching the roof and his vast bulk under a heap of scripts threatening to burst the whole machine asunder.

He called us, as he'd probably called every other company he'd worked with, 'the most talented company I ever worked with'. It actually included a number of talented newcomers like Joan Plowright and Kenneth Williams in small parts. Patrick McGoohan was the Mate, I played Mr Flask the second mate and Welles himself played Ahab – in Rome, all by himself, and presumably in close-up. We had a lot of mime to perform, drinking from nonexistent cups and flinging nonexistent harpoons, and staggering about the stage while he tilted the camera. It was a great challenge, but when I made an extra special effort his booming voice would reach out to me in chuckling irony, 'There you go again, with that fi-i-i-ne brush!' And when all went well, it was 'Print – with enthusiasm!'

As it was done for the American Broadcasting Company, it caused no ripple of recognition when I spoke of it to TV casting directors. On the whole I was lucky, when the lean time came, that I'd stirred my stilty stumps in Scandinavia. The opportunity when it came was given me by Douglas Fairbanks Jr and his two associates, Peter Marriott and Lionel

Grose. The *Douglas Fairbanks Presents* series was indifferent to purely local frets and inhibitions. Their stories included Americans, Chinese, Japanese, Germans, Russians, Swedes and Italians and almost by default, a few Englishmen.

My peculiar accent as an Italian on a desert island made Douglas laugh in the read-through and opened the gate for me. It led to the kind of experience actors dream about. They were half-hour movies made – each in about ten days – in the British National Studios at Boreham Wood. I was successively a Swedish circus proprietor, a Russian lion-tamer with a clawed face, an American leading people to safety through the lines in the war, a Moroccan pimp, a half-witted Yugoslav soldier in a Dalmatian Laurel-and-Hardy act, a Mongol of the People's Army and many other descendants of Babel.

Of the twenty in which I appeared, moving gradually from support to lead parts, Douglas himself was in four or five. One of the first was *The Triangle*. Here I fought in the duelling ritual of the Mensur, as practised by the students in old Heidelberg, who coveted scars on their cheeks to create fear in men and lust in women. It was very formal and stately, our bodies padded up like ice-hockey goalkeepers, while we chanted in unison, '*Ein, zwei, drei – zurück*' and repeated it, our swords clashing in time. For the sake of the acting experience, I'd have fought a duel with pins in a flea circus.

Father Figure

Victor Borge once described the entrance of a man who sang all the parts of a song as 'coming on in a single file'. As a dubber I often came on in a single file. If I had very few lines of my own to speak, I had at least the consolation when everybody else had gone home or off to other pictures of respeaking their lines in English.

Sometimes they had first spoken the lines in some other language deliberately, with the full backing of the producer and all the other actors who also spoke that language. Those were the times familiar to all dubbers when, as nearly as possible, they fit the translations they're given to the movements of lips mouthing an original with a vastly different number of syllables. Sometimes all the dubbers were me, and I came on in a single file. On more than one translation I was so much in a single file that I even had to dub a woman.

The most widely known film for which C. Lee Dubbing Inc. was in action for the English rendering was Jacques Tati's delightful *Monsieur Hulot's Holiday*. Luckily for me there wasn't a great deal of dialogue in the whole of *Hulot*, but there were some testing moments, notably when an elderly couple potter through the shallows on the beach: the old lady picks up shells muttering enthusiastically, while her bored husband accepts them with a Gallic grunt and discards them contemptuously behind her back.

It was very useful to me that the Douglas Fairbanks enterprise was so cosmopolitan in its story make-up, because almost always after the cast was disbanded, and the film was run through, it was discovered that several extreme accents were not entirely intelligible, and a few were totally obscure. I dubbed in Malay pidgin, and Japanese English, and Soho Italian, and Detroit Swedish, to my heart's content. It was good value, and while not exactly the same as post-synching a film, which is done for a variety of reasons, especially anachronistic sounds from outside breaking in on location shooting, it made post-synching much easier for me when I came to do a lot of it.

Altogether it's impossible for me to overestimate the help that the Douglas Fairbanks jobs gave to my professional grammar. They led directly to only one role in films, that of a dog handler frightened of dogs in *Police Dog*, a Fairbanks production, but the overall confidence from being thought not only usable but actually wanted helped me survive many a lonely vigil by a silent telephone in later times.

All this was not allowed to interfere with my golf. Against all the odds of an explosive temperament, a tendency to press as well as hook, plus being the wrong height for golf and all that, my game was coming together. I was reeling off some quite low scores in a *sub rosa* way. I was playing off six, which was too generous a handicap, and I thought it would only be fair to the world at large to have it taken down a stroke or two. The committee at my club thought differently and said there would be time enough to adjust when I won something.

A couple of vivid events with frosty overtones then followed in short order. In a qualifying round of the annual *Evening News* competition I played at Sudbrook Park, a lovely course between Kingston and Richmond with a beautiful Georgian clubhouse, and turned in what remained for ever my lowest score. Coming home I met our club secretary Arthur Lucas, who had a habit of disbelieving some of the scores like seventy-five and seventy-six that I'd been reporting recently, and he sang out ironically, 'What was it this time, Christopher, sixty-nine?'

'Not sixty-nine,' I replied, '*fifty*-nine.' I had of course actually taken sixty-five strokes, but with a six handicap fifty-nine was the net.

All the same, the handicap still stood at six. My game was having its ups and downs. In the next round of the *Evening News* tournament I played at Wentworth with a delightful young man with a wooden leg, and he beat me. And so matters stood when we came to the Medal play championship at my own club. Those larding the earth included some tip-top persons of the golfing fraternity, among them Walker Cup men like Laddie Lucas, Gerald Micklem and Leonard Crawley. It so happened that my seventy-one was good enough to win the Gross, and as I had six to come off that I was more or less bound to collect the Medal for Net as well, which made the size of my handicap somewhat conspicuous and a lot of people were going around asking how such things could be. While nobody actually refused to take a drink with me, my success brought with it a distinct chill of unpopularity. The committee promptly chopped my handicap all the way down to two, in the heat of the moment. I began to consider myself nearly quite good and got into the groove firmly enough so that for some years, even after a lay-off brought on by inconsiderate film schedules, I could generally rely on something in the low seventies.

Bringing my temperament down to scratch was another matter. It let me down badly in the English Amateur Open. I reached the third round and then came up against Keith Tate of Northumberland at Walton Heath. He was in the rough all the time and I was hitting straight down the middle. I thought, time and again, that I had the hole sewn up only to find that it all came unstitched again. Again and again I was complacently looking at a good lie in the midst of the fairway while my opponent was off in the jungle. But his powers of recovery were phenomenal. A clump of heather would fly into the air and the ball would rocket on to the green. Having the cup dashed from my lips, repeatedly, frayed my nerves and I began missing easy putts. I managed to avoid blowing up personally, but my game certainly went to pieces. I had many years to go before I got myself in hand for the big occasion.

It's a mark of my esteem and affection for Father Eric Cheetham that for him, and for nobody else ever, I gave up golf on a Sunday. For a period until his death (which he would have been the first to say was the feeblest excuse for a lapse) I became an Anglo-Catholic and acted as a server at St Stephen's, Gloucester Road, the heart of Father Cheetham's parish. He was a wonderful jolly priest, the kind I always supposed G. K. Chesterton would have loved, who not only was a passionate theatre-goer, but had quite a theatrical flair himself. He had a miniature motor-bike to make his rounds, and used to say wistfully that he only wished he might have ridden it up the aisle, only the Church would frown on him dispensing blessings from a Corgi.

The great poet T. S. Eliot was a verger at St Stephen's and often after the service, when Father Cheetham had delivered one of his sermons conjuring alternately visions of fire and brimstone and suppressed giggles from the nuns in the congregation, Eliot was in the company at lunch in the Father's flat in Clarehill Court. I was very much influenced by the Father's capacity to come forward and mix with his flock on their own terms, admit the power of temptation and his own difficulties in resisting it. I loved his humour and the twinkling eyes when he admonished himself with a loud sibilant 'Sssshhhh!' following some outrageous admission of his own failings. He had a marvellous loving kindness and took endless trouble and patience in explaining to me the ideals of discipline of the Church, while at the same time drawing parallels between its deep need for ritual and the ritual framework of the theatre.

Indeed his own approach to his services had a theatrical flavour. In the vestry he'd be chatting with me and suddenly say, 'Must break off now and go and put my make-up on,' or, 'I see we're just about sold out for the second house tonight.'

Nothing was ever dull with him. There was a pointed subtlety even in his drolleries, as when he'd say to me, 'I'm sure the Lord will forgive me if I say you really must be more precise when you come to confession.' Yet, perversely, I found it extraordinarily difficult to recall some backslidings with any great precision. I had no trouble at all giving a blow-by-blow account of my developing hatred of a golfer whom I suspected of using 'the leather five-iron' (a quick kick at the ball in a bad lie) against me, but when it came to explaining the cynicism about women with which I had become imbued, I discovered that in my mind the various causes had merged together. Father Cheetham was concerned; he criticized my behaviour as ruthless.

There was some measure of justice in his view. Yet the causes were not so very numerous, nor was any affair of mine ever protracted so much as a month. Like gusts of wind from the land on a calm sea, they vanished as suddenly as they came. I was willing, indeed eager, to share my bed with a diverse selection of girls, especially if they were tall redheads devoted to the music of the late nineteenth century, but I was opposed to sharing a kitchen and a washing line. If the girls elected to stay: I was thrilled. When they opted not to continue to stay: I was well suited. I was willing to underwrite a weekend at some exotic watering place – my time and funds did not stretch to a week. I doubted that any of them wept when our brief encounters were over. If they did they wept, very sensibly, alone. I was a long way from contemplating marriage – the length of a bank manager's face.

Father Cheetham had a little rhyme about a greedy lad who 'Of buns and tarts ate his fill, and made himself extremely ill', and adapted it to my case. This was not quite exact. I was no carnal glutton, but it was true that I had an old-fashioned sentiment about women which was shocked by evidence of appetite. When I took them off the pedestal I could see nothing to break their fall except a mattress. So no durable relationship was woven. There was another obstacle too, which Father Cheetham no doubt perceived with that extraordinary empathy he had for acting people – I was more than half in love with myself and intolerant of rivals for my esteem. Since an actor's only stock in trade is himself, it behoves him (and her) to devote time and care to this one asset.

Enter Boris

No less lovable than my father in God was Boris Karloff, whose name was a byword for monstrous things that reach out from the cinematic murk and grab you, to a perfect earthquake of shudders. With his gentle manners and quiet, humorous disposition he was as much loved by everyone who worked with him as he was respected for the tremendous distinction of his screen style. I liked him from the first and in the last years of his life, when we were neighbours in a London square, became deeply attached to him.

When I first met him, at Southall Studios, he was in his middle sixties and had been famous for a quarter of a century as the creator of festering souls in hideous shape, from the Monster in *Frankenstein*, made in 1931, onwards. It did not bother him that he had become typecast. Types, he said, are continually in work. If they weren't types they wouldn't be popular. I wasn't myself desirous of being a type, though I could see the force of his argument.

Nor was I in any way eager to emulate him and become a type in the field of horror. I soon learned not to call it horror. It was a description he disliked intensely, even for the failures and second-rate projections. 'Macabre' and 'fantasy' were the words that he always used. I'd always enjoyed his work, and those of actors like Peter Lorre and Bela Lugosi who often featured with him, but the great era of the macabre fantasy struck me as being essentially in the twenties and early thirties, and hardly relevant to my own prospects.

There was a lot, however, to be learned from Boris in the way of sheer technique, and his observations on how to survive under heavy monster make-up were extremely interesting. He also persuaded me to possess my soul in patience. Because before he settled his direction for good, and had his big chance with the Monster, he had something like three score bit parts in adventures and serials, villains and victims. The big part when it comes, he says, is a fluke. 'Uncle' Carl Laemmle, the producer, used to say that the formula for success was simply 'the right actor in the right part', but Boris said bringing them together was rather a matter of the right actor in the right place at the right time. For his own part, he said, the official story of his being cast as the Monster was that the director of *Frankenstein*, James Whale, had taken note of him in the Howard Hawks production *The Criminal Code*. In this Boris was a convict who acted as butler to the prison warden and knocked off a stool pigeon in a grisly sequence. In reality, said Boris, James Whale had noticed him when he was doing nothing more sinister than impaling a cutlet when they were lunching at adjacent restaurant tables.

There was no reason for Boris to take note of me at Southall, but he was extremely kind. If I had a type at that time, I was cast right against it, in the character of a fruitily effeminate French designer. He very kindly did not discuss my performance in this. But he said to me that an actor must never be faceless, even when that face is obscured by bandages. On the set then his face was only partially obscured, by an eyepatch. This was for his part as the Colonel in the television series *Colonel March of Scotland Yard*. I was in only one of that series, *All Cats are Grey at Night*, but when I met him again we had quite a lot in common.

All the television work that I did was in series, usually making just one or two appearances before moving on to the next one. Fairbanks was the one who gave me the full flush of opportunities and in addition to working with Douglas himself there was the great occasion when Buster Keaton flew from America to Britain to do Gogol's *Overcoat* with us. In a later series called *One Step Beyond* I was cast as a Nazi officer in the story of *The Sorcerer*. It was a far-fetched story about me as a far-fetched murderer, literally magicked eighty miles or so through thick walls, providing the perfect alibi, but much less painful than most of the crashing through walls that melodrama usually demands.

Looking right in a Nazi uniform, plus periodic outbursts of praise spoken by me about Conrad Veidt, may have had something to do with my playing a swine who would make even practised heavies feel squeamish: a ruthless SS leader modelled on the Butcher of Czechoslovakia, Reinhard Heydrich. As a wartime intelligence officer I happened to have learned a good deal about the sadistic lecher whom Hitler described as 'a man with a heart of iron'. It hadn't seemed at the time to have any likely practical application, but now I was very glad to have at my fingertips a great amount of detail about the Gestapo and the way that a man could have at once a passion for chamber music and also for the stews, fly some ninety missions with the Luftwaffe and have not a fleck of nobility in his make-up.

That was in *OSS*, whose regular hero was the Australian Ron Randell. Naturally I could only expect a bloody ending in that. And likewise when I came up against Rhodes Reason, the regular hero of *White Hunter*, where as an unethical rival in league with slave traders I was bowled over by a huge stuffed lion and after writhing about for a few seconds was pronounced dead. I grumbled a bit about the violence with which this thing was thrown at me and how I'd been badly bruised and almost suffocated by its massive weight and of course everybody present was put in a high good humour by my discomfort. Fate gave me some of my own back when the real lion got loose, and the gantry and rig on the seat at Twickenham were laden with people who'd scrambled up for safety.

Disturbing echoes of daybreak in Paris just before the war came to me when at the British National Studios I played Monsieur de Paris, the public executioner Sanson, who dispatched Louis XVI on the guillotine. The executioner Webb Miller had taken me to watch was Henri Desfourneaux, a member of another of the families who made that job a hereditary perquisite, but I thought that the Sansons or, to give them their true name, the Longvals would have retained a grander style about them even into the Terror. So in *The Scarlet Pimpernel*, whose regular hero was Marius Goring, I played Longval as more aristo than the aristos, more Catholic than the Pope. Some others of his family were neither so dignified nor lordly, but he was by no means a butchering slob. I thought then as I think now that the Devil should be given his due by an actor, in whatever guise he pops up, and audiences like a cultivated air in a killer.

Also at the National I was another sort of aristocratic killer in *William Tell*, where the twenty-three-stone Willoughby Goddard made a monumental Gessler. My portion as Duke Erik was to hunt people with hounds, like Zaroff in *The Most Dangerous Game*. Having provoked a certain meed of hatred from the audience, Mad Duke Erik ended his wicked career by stopping a bolt from Tell's crossbow. There were no complaints from viewers, but actually they missed the best of the tumultuous action.

As an example of this, it was the first and by no means the last time that I flatly refused to deliver a line, to the great astonishment of my fellow actor Scott Finch, who said he had not realized till then that actors could do that. It was at a time when everyone was obsessed by the need for 'mid-Atlantic speech' and when I came to the mid-Atlantic gem

'Tell, this time I'll get you for sure' I absolutely declined to deliver it, and chaos reigned.

Tit for tat, the producers got their own back on me through the agency of the Mad Duke's slavering hounds. These were actually bassets, shorter in the leg than the average canine terror. Even made up, they still looked no more likely to tear your throat out than a couple of amiable beagles. But they were extraordinarily strong. At one point in our helter-skelter chase they veered off course – off my course anyway – and before I could check them they'd hauled me through a bush and a hedge. I hadn't the presence of mind to let go until it was too late and emerged the other side cut and bruised and my thighs as full of sharp spines as a pincushion.

Increasingly often now bits of me snapped or bent or gave way. It had never occurred to me when I gaily agreed with cousin Niccolò that, 'hey-diddle-dee-dee, an actor's life for me', danger money ought to form part of it.

Swashing Machines

Terence Young almost did for me altogether. He who got me out of trouble so often almost polished me off. In a film – *That Lady* – and with the help of water. Perhaps I should have mentioned my superstition to him.

The film was made in Segovia, the lovely old university town of Salamanca, and Madrid, especially the banks of the Guadalquivir. According to my contract, I was to 'play The Captain of the Guard *and other parts*'. The phrase in italics kept me busy from dawn till dusk practically every day I was in Spain.

I was masked assassins lurking in the Salamancan night, devious grooms in Segovia, and mad riders on Arab horses going at full tilt by the river. I fought with swords against the Spanish Olympic sabre champion and also against Gilbert Roland, who said to me, 'Careful, *amigo*! I see nothing without my glasses.' I fell back in the water in full armour. The horse I was on had never worked before a camera and shied me off. I nearly drowned. When I surfaced, still masked and iron-clad with sludge all over me, like a monster of the deep, the first words I overheard were from Terence enthusiastically telling the unit, 'Do anything for me, that boy!'

I even played my own part, as ADC to Philip II of Spain, who was one of the greatest stage actors of our time in his first film, Paul Scofield. He wasn't vastly enamoured of films for himself and said so. The Lady of the title was Olivia de Havilland. I had a long scene with her letting her know that the King had no more use for her as his mistress. It was shot on me, with her reacting. What came out on the screen was the back of my head and a full treatment of her reacting. That was my big scene out of the window. But I was too thankful to be alive to weep over such paltry vanities. On the only day off that I can remember, Gilbert Roland took me to see the grave of his father, a bullfighter buried in Spain.

And then, in *The Dark Avenger*, I was savaged by Errol Flynn. It was the first time I'd met him, and I don't think there was anything personal in it. In that film I was an officer in charge of French soldiers, required to interfere with Errol's plans. We had enormous broadswords, but he was encased in gloves and I had bare hands. It was a four-and-a-half-minute duel, in which I mainly fought his double, the British Olympic sabre champion Raymond Paul, falling in the fireplace, up and down stairs, breaking up the furniture and getting some of it back in my face.

Rupert Davies and Yvonne Furneaux looked on as Errol threw himself into the fray like a giant refreshed, as indeed he was since he'd only been looking on up to the last take, but he slipped and with the maximum possible zing struck me a shrewd blow on the little finger of my right hand, and nearly cut through it. 'Oh, fuck!' exclaimed Errol, as it bled like a fountain. 'Quite,' I said. The finger was bound up and we set to again, but it remained bent, for ever.

Not long afterwards we had a rematch at Bray Studios in a television film for *The Errol Flynn Theatre*. This time we had rapiers. As soon as he saw me draw mine, he recalled the devastation of my finger, and a shadow crossed his face. 'Now watch it, sport,' he said, 'don't forget, it was an accident, so none of your tricks here.' He was a French aristocrat, while I was a sort of Heydrich of the Revolution, Robespierre and Fouquier Tinville and Camille Desmoulins *and* Danton, all rolled into one. He represented the old nobility, dashing and debonair, with habits rather like the Pimpernel's. The only thing that marred his style was his insistence on a moustache, a very modern one which looked incongruous with his white wig. No doubt he had uses for it off the set.

He lived in an enormous, luxurious caravan in the grounds, from which he'd depart on forays, laying waste the countryside. Not that there can have been much to lay waste in the Bray area, I should think. I liked him for his honesty, and without envying him, I found myself enjoying his stories about girls. One remark in particular stuck in my mind and came back to me later on when, for once in my life, I was in the kind of situation that confronted him almost every week.

But that was not yet. In the meantime I was advancing on him with my rapier while he surveyed me narrowly, wondering if I meant to take revenge for my hacked finger. In the first rehearsal I had to do something virtually impossible. That was to cut at his head and, when he ducked, pass my sword through all six flames lit on a candelabra behind him in such a way as to make them all go out. In a big movie the special effects people would have done this. I actually had to do it. And in fact, through some miracle far harder to perform than spoon-bending, I sideswiped the branched candlestick with complete success. The only trouble was that on the take I removed his wig at the same time. He rose slowly to his feet and stalked away, looking back over his shoulder at me reproachfully. It took half an hour to persuade him that I'd forgiven him for the finger. And this time we had our fight and I was duly vanquished.

I was getting my fill of duels. I reckoned by now to have had more fencing experience than my father had, in his different way. They found duels for me and killed me in them even in stories which originally made no provision for such a thing. In another *Flynn Theatre* story, the whole series being based on classic stories, they altered the end of the Maupassant story in which a husband bricks up a cupboard when his wife's lover is hiding and she watches, powerless to prevent it without revealing him and incidentally staining her honour. But in our version John van Eyssen as the lover crashed out through the bricks with a great roar and lo, we were once more straight into swordplay.

Fighting with Christian Marquand was something else again. Not only was he left-handed, and revelled in his southpaw dexterity with great smoothness in rehearsal, but he was taken over by another personality altogether as soon as the director cried 'Take One – Action!' It was then the real thing. He interspersed the blows he'd agreed to in rehearsal with a few delivered from capricious directions on his own selection. It was like fighting a human windmill, and literally fighting for one's life in front of the camera.

I stopped in the middle, pointed the sword at him and said, 'Look, you're going to get hurt.' This was meant to be a stern warning of what might happen to him *accidentally*, and to me too, but he supposed I meant to run him through. As he was the regular hero of *The Gay Cavalier* this possibility caused alarm and despondency in the circle around us but, as I said to them, I was opposed to unscripted cuts and sweeps and by my periwig, I believe I would have genuinely pinked him if he had gone on that way.

We were using claymores, in *Ivanhoe*, when I was brought in as a sort of medieval hit man, a massive German knight swathed in chainmail, to destroy the regular hero Roger Moore. We hacked away with broadswords in a field for hours on end, under a hot sun. Different routines and workouts went with different weapons. And the fights, vicious or elegant or swashing or buckling or whatever, were choreographed in a great variety of ways. We got counsel and help from sword-masters like Charles Alexis, a *maître d'armes*, and Peter Diamond, another experienced fencer.

It was a very strenuous, physical life. Even some of the speeches were strenuous. One of the exhausting days was in *Foreign Legion*, produced by old Air Force friends Brian Kingcome and Tony Bartley, who'd married Deborah Kerr. In one of those tales I was a homicidal French gardener with a large walrus moustache and a limp who tended graves in a churchyard. In another I played an officer of the Foreign Legion as I'd met them myself in the desert, in *Sailor of Fortune* with Lorne Greene. That brought me a rare plum in the form of a commendation from the critic Billy Moss, who in another life had kidnapped General Kreipe from Crete as a comrade of Patrick Leigh Fermor. And in another, rather less cosily, I had to do a five-minute rant, full of fanaticism and foam, working up to a screaming climax, as a mad Arab who meant to be another Muhammad. At the end I collapsed against the tentpole from sheer exhaustion. That was at Beaconsfield, with desert by courtesy of Egham sandpits. I came to know those sandpits better than any child does those in his playground. I made innumerable films in them.

The duelling and the stunts were arduous but exhilarating. It was fascinating to feel the surge of adrenalin when the director called 'Action' – enough to make oneself capable of throwing somebody forty feet over a house. Except when that somebody had a rush of blood and wanted to prove he was Hercules, the duels were straightforward affairs, only requiring infinite patience and practice. There was great satisfaction in getting them right. Even the swashers must work in the end with a machine-like precision.

With the horses I had a slight problem because of my size. Ideally they ought to have been at least seventeen hands. Otherwise I'd stand there with my legs wide apart and the horse could walk quietly between them without touching on either side. And indeed sometimes they were too small and in some heroic or heavy part I looked more like Don Quixote on his mule.

And then Western horses were trained in a specific way, what was called 'even gait'. That meant that there was no posting, no rising in the stirrups. It took a long time to learn to ride Western style in a hard leather saddle, even padded with a sheepskin as the Household Cavalry have them. The long leg ride, almost straight in the stirrup, makes posting virtually impossible anyway. And without posting, I tended to crash along, bruising ego and bum, till I got the hang of it. A helpful American who watched me said, 'Remember one thing, kid, just *screw* that saddle!'

That was good advice and a pleasant image as a distraction. But American horses were trained to a different gait, with less bounce than the European. And often we could not have the right saddle for screwing because it interfered with the period of the story we were acting in. We might just have to make do with a period saddle with very hard back and front pieces and a flat part between. Hard to screw; hard to ride in. Especially in armour. I just never believed that the old medieval robber barons ever screwed their saddles.

Suspended Sentence

After a couple of seasons of near drought in the way of film parts, albeit irrigated by a steady flow from telly, there was a sudden inundation of mini-offers from the cinema. The word must have got around that I had a head for junk. In a year I sucked on the teat of no fewer than ten films. By a curious coincidence it was also the year when two very kind friends decided that I was doing sweet Fanny Adams and, ignoring all the work coming to me in the pipeline, tried to give me a chance to do myself a bit of good in a social way at top level.

Some of these acting engagements, films like *Police Dog* and *Crossroads*, passed with as little trace as the third dream between midnight and cockcrow. *Crossroads* gave me an uneasy spasm, because I was reported to Equity for misbehaviour and sent home in the middle of shooting. My offence was to have laughed hysterically at a joke told me by Ferdy Mayne. For all I know I was also punished by obliteration from the final cut of the film. I wouldn't have known: I rarely saw any of these films when they were finished.

Other engagements stayed in my mind more for the drama and portentousness off the set than in the script, or because of some wayward quirk of the director or location. It was nice to work with Joe Ferrer again, not only with him but for him since he was director and actor. It was rather strange to play a scene with him and suddenly have him interrupt, step out of character and cry 'Cut!'

No one can be sure if he himself earns his corn as an actor – in that I was a submarine commander – but I reckon to have done so by being photographed for the publicity of the film with Joe for the *Tatler*. The magazine missed a blue-blood coup, because ex-King Umberto came to visit us off Cascais near Estoril in Portugal, where the film was mainly shot. We had the technical advice of Blondie Hasler and the submarines of the Portuguese Navy, the only ones still in commission which were antiquated enough to suit the period of the film. For this reason we went to Portugal. Also, of course, because everybody enjoyed Portugal, the food, the *fados* and the sea.

The setting for *Port Afrique* was Ceuta in Spanish Morocco – sordid, verging on squalid. Again my direct contribution to the story was slight. As Franz Vermes the artist, an innocent suspect of a murder charge, I was required to paint a picture in my lovely house on the hill overlooking the harbour. There was a howling gale at the time which made painting impossible, and we reshot the scene in a different ambience. We went to the capital Tetouan, where it transpired that the Swedish star of *Zarak Khan* had just set the Muslim community by the ears when she sunbathed nude on the roof of her hotel. This was only the tip of the Ekberg, however, because this was the height of the terrorist troubles, and Arab political and religious murders were daily occurrences.

We were queasy about our reception, and once, on the way to Tangier, I was in a car surrounded by a mob that made way for us only with agonizing slowness. Nothing serious happened but people were naturally none too keen to wander off into the Arab quarter. I did my bit for the film by going into it every morning to winkle one of the cast out of a brothel. I came back from one of these missions one morning to find my room-mate Anthony Newley singing unconcernedly in the shower. On the spur of the moment I played a cruel practical joke on him, pretending to be two Arab voices whispering in the room. The singing stopped, his quavering voice told me he was suffering. The incident left, I believe, an indelible impression. And luckily for me, a kinder impression of some scripted acting was left on George Marshall, the veteran Hollywood director, who happened to visit the set for the few scenes that we shot in the MGM studio in England.

And in *Private's Progress* my only strong moment as a German officer awaiting trial for war crimes was when I took cyanide and cheated the gallows. It was the director, John Boulting, who made my journey worthwhile by dashing to the piano to relieve his feelings with a quick burst of Chopin or Liszt when he felt the pressure too much.

The rest could only be mentioned in whispers. They were made mainly under the direction of David MacDonald and his henchman Ernest Morris for the Danziger Brothers. It would have been physically possible, if the spirit hadn't weakened, to make a hundred and twenty films in a year for Harry Lee and Edward J. Danziger, because any film they made that lasted more than three days began to run over budget. That year alone I appeared in the Danzigers' *Final Column, Man in*

Demand, Stranglehold and *Alias John Preston.* In the last of these I had what was technically my first leading role, as a mad businessman who goes off his chump, beginning at the top of a table and finishing over a tombstone. For this I was paid the handsome and by no means atypical Danziger fee of seventy-five pounds.

They made countless films and almost all but the top stars were induced at one time or another to work for them. They even had their own outfit, New Elstree Studios, and I worked with Donald Wolfit on the first film ever made there, *The Traitor,* and introduced him to Tolkien's work *The Hobbit* as a much-needed distraction from the water pouring down the cement walls, the duckboards between the stages traversing a sea of mud, the lights that didn't work, the absence of windows in the dressing-rooms and the economies made on paint.

I was fully occupied in surviving this sado-masochistic switchback of a film career when an old chum of my sister, Cynthia Monteith, whom I had known since I was in short trousers with deckle edges, asked me to dinner. There would be four of us, she said, including her husband Ben, the son of Sumner Welles the American Secretary of State, and A. N. Other. I was amazed when A. N. Other walked in on the night she had chosen for our intimate supper and revealed himself to be Sir Alexander Korda.

He had an office by Apsley House on Hyde Park Corner, known as Hyde Park Korda. He had a huge house in Kensington Palace Gardens. I had never seen him, let alone met him. I wasn't on any sort of terms with any sort of executives, who rarely ventured out of their palatial suites in the Old House at Denham or the Old House at Shepperton. If they did and saw me, they hurried past muttering, 'Too tall, too foreign, too unnoticed.'

Korda was one of the greats. I would compare him in stature with Mayer, Laski, De Mille, Fox, Zanuck. With his brothers Zoltan and Vincent he had been responsible for a tremendous mileage of glamorous celluloid, from *Four Feathers* and *Elephant Boy* to *The Elusive Pimpernel; The Thief of Baghdad* to *The Third Man.* He was *the* British impresario of that Golden Age whose flavour I could just about catch through the cigar smoke.

During dinner he asked me all sorts of questions about the cinema which were purely rhetorical, since he knew all the answers. And since I knew none, for once I had the sense to keep my trap shut. He addressed me as Lee, talked at very great speed in a flowery Hungarian way, presenting me with a miniature crate which contained a cigar, about three feet long, from Havana. They were made specially for him, with

A.K. stamped on the sandalwood box, on the individual box for the cigar itself, and on the greaseproof paper inside, leaving in its original state, for some mysterious reason, only the band on the cigar. I was a smoker, but I hadn't the nerve to light up such a cigar and burn it away to ash. I carefully folded it up and stowed it away in its crate and preserved the lot.

He asked me about my family but very little about the films I'd been in. Nor did he make any reference at all to the kind of parts I'd played in them. But late on in the evening he suddenly asked, 'And what are you doing now, Lee?' Before I could stop myself, I'd told the truth: 'I'm making a film with the Danziger Brothers.' A great hush fell.

After a long and aching pause, his magnificent Hungarian voice recovered its sonority. 'You know,' he remarked, 'once these boys came to see me and Zolly. You know Zolly?' I stammered nervously, 'Oh, yes, yes, yeees', though I'd never met Zoltan in my life. 'These boys, they come to see me – they're brothers, did you know that?'

'Yes, Sir Alex.'

'Yes? You knew that? Well now, Lee, my boy, they come like jacks-in-the-boxes, they're jumping up and down and they talk and they talk and after they've left the office I say to Zolly, "What do you think of those boys?" and do you know what Zolly replies?'

'No, Sir Alex, I don't know what he said he thought.' I felt somehow that my future hung upon Zolly's opinion of the Danziger Brothers.

'He says to me, "Alex, they are almost absolutely—"'

I was half out of my chair with my cigar like a torpedo waiting for ignition, and I almost fell out of it when, at that moment, the bell rang. Korda's chauffeur, punctual. He rose. He beamed at me. He left the sentence hanging in mid-air. He made his farewells and surged out. I never found out what Zolly's opinion of the Danzigers had been. And I never saw Sir Alex again. He died very soon after.

But oddly, without any prompting from Sir Alex, Zolly did direct me that year in *Storm over the Nile*, with Terence Young at his side. It was a remake of *The Four Feathers* and in it I played an ex-governor of the Sudan, Karaga Pasha. It was another peak in the sado-masochistic graph. I arrived every day shaved and washed and delicious and would immediately be plastered in every kind of filth and rubbish to look unattractive and foul before being chained up for the entire day in a horrible prison (at Shepperton, I never went to the Sudan) in the company of Anthony Steel and Ronald Lewis. Periodically crowds of Cypriots, presumably high on hashish, would come in and lay about us with rifle butts and whips in an altogether too realistic way.

Zolly would arrive every day with his beautiful blue suit rumpled, his handmade shoes all scratched, with a dented porkpie hat and a weekend's worth of beard. He was often in great pain from some spinal injury and worked in the cutting-room with a rope round his neck to pull it and alleviate his discomfort. When directing he always carried a baton like a sergeant-major's and made extraordinary mangled-English remarks. He was fluent but not always accurate. He once instructed Ian Carmichael to 'play the scene with butter on your head', a literal translation for the German phrase which means 'oily/charming'.

Another direction was, 'In this scene you're unhoppy. You mus' sank down in this chair into a glum.' One morning he happened unfortunately to notice a packet of Player's cigarettes sticking out of the top pocket of one of us prisoners. He flung his baton down. He tore the pack loose and threw it on the floor. For the only time in my life I saw somebody actually dance with rage, on this pack of cigarettes. 'You barstuds!' he yelled. 'You're troying to rhuin my picksher!'

Somehow the moment never seemed opportune to ask him his real opinion of the Danzigers.

Crock v. Croc

There's a lot to be said for making an asset of your failings. Like the lad who offered a sight of his sore thumb in exchange for a bite of his friend's apple, I began to make a shop window of my foreignness, height and cold expression. In return I was frequently employed to be shot, poisoned or cut to ribbons and hardly ever played an Englishman.

In *The Battle of the River Plate* I spoke nothing but Spanish as the owner of a waterfront café in Montevideo, though of course the only salt I tasted was in the canteen at Pinewood. In *Ill Met by Moonlight* I spoke only German, to Dirk Bogarde in a dentist's chair, and was penalized for being a German SS officer by being shot at his feet and also, perhaps, by being cut from some versions of the film. In *Fortune is a Woman* I was an idiot Welsh opera singer suspected of murder. I sang – or rather, mimed to a record, which was rather wounding – the *largo al factotum* from *The Barber of Seville*.

In *Truth About Women* I had a damn good cameo as the cuckold in a French farce sequence with Eva Gabor as my wife, and Laurence Harvey as the lover whom I interrupt after doing callisthenics on the veranda, for which I was penalized by being shot in a duel. That was a Betty Box comedy which I enjoyed, though the only whiff of Paris that came to me was from the *pommes frites* in the Shepperton canteen. And as a German Jewish doctor in *The Traitor* I felt that the rubble of Germany would have been more comfortable than the new Danziger studios at Elstree. But it was interesting to work for Michael McCarthy, young and brilliant and soon to die. Had he lived he would have been one of the great directors.

If that was lacking in creature comforts, *Bitter Victory* was utter chaos, though made by another brilliant director, Nicholas Ray. The story was about a commando unit being parachuted behind the lines in the desert.

169

Though I wasn't told before I got there what part I was to play, I was greatly attracted by the invitation to work in Libya and the chance to see again the fantastic changing beauties of the sands.

When the cast, which included such distinguished actors as Richard Burton, Curt Jurgens and Raymond Pellegrin, reached Tripoli, we were ferried out to the Marcus Aurelius ruins and there the dramatis personae were apportioned with the same casual optimism by the director as if the clock had been turned back fifteen years and we'd all been in fact doing a skit for the camp entertainment. All but the stars took part in this lottery. Everybody got a part they either did not want, or somebody else coveted more than they did.

The producer never visited Libya because, being Jewish, he was quite rationally afraid of being kidnapped. We lived in the Hotel Mehari, which was previously a brothel, in rooms barely large enough to contain the beds. Not that we saw much of them: we never got in till ten at night, and had to be out again at four. In one sense a wartime entertainment would have been more professional – there would have been no Frenchmen and Germans in the same show hating one another.

Raymond Pellegrin was in a rage because he'd drawn the short straw in the casting and had only four lines as an Arab guide. I was in none too agreeable a mood after being told, as Sergeant Barney of the Guards, 'not to bring all this British Army nonsense into it', which I thought was an odd direction in a story supposed to be about the British Army. The cameraman broke his collarbone. My all too brief slumbers were interrupted because one of our number had cut his wrists. He did it for private domestic reasons, bad news from home, but as I said to him rather tartly, we all of us had plenty of good justification for suicide in the circumstances all around us. He lived. We all did, and parted after six weeks in the certain knowledge of having shared in a failure. Usually this is hidden from actors till later, when they're otherwise occupied. Fortunately. Otherwise only a very few films would ever be finished.

Another film that took me to Africa – Kenya – raised the highest hopes in me of a personal breakthrough. George Marshall, who'd wandered on to the set when I was making *Port Afrique*, gave me my first big part, as a white hunter, in *Beyond Mombasa*. George Marshall had made about four hundred films – more, surely, than any other living human being – but his zest for work and life were undiminished. In the river that flows near Mombasa he disported himself like a dolphin, and did backflips among the sharks and rays like an acrobat.

I was fairly exhilarated too. I took my golf clubs and played with George and Leo Genn on some of the wildest courses I'd ever seen. The greens were called 'browns' and there was a great pressure on us to drive straight down the fairways, as the caddies declined to go into the rough on account of snakes. And just as I'd crushed Anthony Newley with my little joke in *Port Afrique*, I was suddenly inspired to put the fear of God into my good friend Ron Randell. Since this was the period shortly after the Mau Mau uprisings, I woke him urgently one night, where we bunked in huts in the grounds of the hotel where the stars slept, and warned him hoarsely that I could see torches and hear whispers, and that the Mau Mau were on us. 'Quick, for your life!' I hissed. 'We're being attacked.' He was instantly convinced and leaped to escape, became enmeshed in the mosquito net and brought the whole apparatus crashing down. For a time he was surly with me about this jape, which puzzled me.

However, he had the laugh on me when I was called upon to do a full fall into an opencast mine. The only double they could find for me tall enough was a Kenyan policeman who flatly refused to do it. It wasn't a sheer drop, but there was a slide of forty feet or so. The plot had me get shot in the back with a poison dart, and slither and tumble to perdition. In the excitement of doing it at all, I forgot to mime the moment of receiving the dart, and George had me do it again. On the second take, I ripped myself from wrist to shoulder on a jutting outcrop of quartz.

Taking the rough with the smooth, though, it was an enjoyable picture to make. I was sure I was going to get somewhere with it. The mere sight of American stars wafted by American money, like Cornel Wilde and Donna Reed, made me bless my good fortune and be hopeful the picture would be seen in every corner of the globe illuminated by the art and public relations resources of Columbia Pictures. It was nice too, to work near Malindi, where a ruined Arab slave-trading city had survived with a strange and eerie beauty, but essentially I was there to crock myself up to get a better future.

I was willing to do practically anything for this prospect, and damaged myself quite a bit. In one scene in the river, in which I was shot, I had a temperature of 103 degrees from a spasm of malaria. When the tide came in, the sharks and crocs and rays came with it, but mysteriously the raft bearing the camera and Freddie Young went the opposite way, leaving me still swimming bravely and calling feebly in my French accent, just in case the sound was still functioning. And after it all, when I went home in a terrible crocked state, I had still to confront a mechanical crocodile in the studios of MGM. It was programmed in its vicious metal innards to behave just as nastily as its saurian comrades out near Mombasa. The wretched thing churned along at such a pace that it knocked me to the bottom of the tank, and carved me up with its wires and nuts and bolts and tin flippers.

The film was not the success I had hoped. It didn't get the send-off nor the attention I had somehow persuaded myself were built into it. It was all a grievous disappointment to me. But one thing of value that came out of it was the friendship of George. And there was an odd epilogue to our golf near Mombasa.

George was as crazily addicted to golf as I was. He asked me one day in London if I could play him at a club he'd heard mentioned, called Swinley Forest. I said it was possible, though it was an exclusive club and I wasn't a member. The food was delicious. The members were nice, though obliquely they'd made it plain that there was no point in any actor putting himself forward for membership. But I had only to ring up and somebody would sign me in. As I said to George, I'd once met Clark Gable there as the guest of the Earl of Portarlington so it would probably be all right. George laughed. He, with Bill Graf, turned up in a siren suit and baseball cap. With his battered eagle visage I thought he looked splendid. But members in moth-eaten sweaters and stained flannel trousers thought it was an infamy on my part to have brought such an American along. I felt more inclined to apologize to him than to them.

A Taste of Blood

As a rule by the age of thirty-five the men of my family had become cardinals or colonels, chairmen or ambassadors. As I turned this marker and girded my ill-treated sinews for the long voyage home, I could hardly claim to have left any significant impression behind me on the outward journey. I had gone into acting without a natural gift for it; after ten years in the cinema I was as tall and as foreign and almost as unknown as when I started. But I could fairly claim to have learned by doing and to have scorned nothing as beneath me. I had fought to the death countless times, and the death by definition of the script was usually mine. Outside the cinema I had not yet learned to live, but within it I had most certainly learned to die. I could die for you in every way known to man, and in a few ways known only to scriptwriters. I could see now that provided I remained fit, the future held many more deaths yet. I could only hope that they would serve some purpose, and that perhaps a reputation might come in the same way as a coral formation, which is made up of a deposit of countless tiny corpses.

It seemed merely like one more indignity on a grander scale when my agent John Redway told me that he'd heard Hammer Films meant to do a remake of *Frankenstein*, in colour, and that he'd been asked to suggest someone to play the Creature – what about it? I hesitated only briefly. It was self-evident that this was not the path to glory, but I'd seen the 1931 Karloff film and it was equally obvious that purely technically it was a tremendous challenge. Besides, my visions of glamour in the business were by now totally blown. I told John that I'd have a go, saw producer Tony Hinds and director Terence Fisher and was given the job. A decade had passed since Terence directed me in *Song for Tomorrow* and I wondered if he would be influenced by that dread memory. But he'd either repressed it or thought I'd been so grotesque as the MC that I'd be just right for the Creature.

After some preliminary limbering-up in their *Quatermass* successes, the make-up and effects men at Hammer were fully into their stride. Phil Leakey did a marvellous job on me, all the more so since he was always working against the clock. Copyright prevented us from imitating Karloff's robot look (despite which he'd moved brilliantly fast) and we made numerous tests on make-ups which didn't work. I wound up looking like a madman's picture of a circus freak, or Elephant Man or Pig Man. I said to Phil desperately, 'I ought to look more like a human being, but a mess.' We got it more or less human, which after all was what the Creature Mary Shelley invented was, but we overdid the mess in our hurry. Eventually someone wrote, 'Christopher Lee looked like a road accident.'

From the first time we met on the set of *The Curse of Frankenstein* at Bray, Peter Cushing and I were friends. Our very first encounter began with me storming into his dressing-room and announcing in petulant tones, 'I haven't got any lines!' He looked up, his mouth twitched, and he said drily, 'You're lucky. I've read the script.' It was a typical wry comment. I soon found Peter was the great perfectionist, who learned not only his own lines but everybody else's as well, but withal had a gentle humour which made it quite impossible for anybody to be pompous in his company.

His dressing-room was more comfortable than mine. I had no chair to sit on, and if I wanted to relax had to put some cushions in the bath and lie on them. Generally when I was fully encased in bandages I preferred to go in and harass Peter, singing opera to him through the crevices, and performing soft-shoe shuffles with him before the blank screen while we all waited for the rushes to come up. The whole set was very small, a tiny grotto under the office of the producer, my dear friend Tony Nelson-Keys. When the red light was on, nobody could scratch himself or light a cigarette without the sound being magnified a thousand times.

The atmosphere of the unit was the happiest I'd ever worked in. Even the food was out of this world. Alas for Mrs Thompson's delicious cooking, my make-up made it very hard for me to eat it. I had to subsist on mash and mince and spinach and drink through a straw. And nobody was keen to eat with me, because the sight of me put them off their food. Hazel Court and Valerie Gaunt did so only under pressure from the publicity department.

Playing the Creature taught me to appreciate just how great the skill was that Boris had used in creating his Monster. And perhaps, in a way, that helped me to adjust to the very notion of working in the horror genre. It was a case of inventing a being who was neither oneself nor anybody else, but a composite of pieces of other people, mostly dead. Terry couldn't very well tell me what to do, but only tell me 'Wrong' and 'Wrong again' and 'Wrong again' until he could say, 'Right. We'll go for a take.' I decided that my hands must have an independent life, and that my movements must be sudden and unbalanced.

It was absorbing work. I was never so content. The five weeks of the schedule flowed by, plus a sixth because the sensation had grown at Hammer that we were on to something and the ship mustn't be spoilt for a ha'p'orth of tar. Naturally disaster-prone, I had those crises which make an insurance company blench. In the first of these the Creature was shot in the eye. I had blood in the palm of my hand, the viscous, acrid stuff Hammer facetiously called Kensington Gore, and had to smack it up in my face and then take my hand away. It got into my eye. It was excruciating. I shrieked with the shock and the pain of it. I couldn't see anything. For an hour I thought I'd lost my sight, until with bathing the pain subsided.

The film was made in the dead of winter, and there was snow on the ground. In one scene I had to appear as if I had just climbed out of an acid bath, with my bandages fuming. That meant steam and the only way to produce that effect was to ladle hot water over me in the crisp, cold air. They poured it on and poured it on and never stopped pouring for three or four hours. As it percolated through to my skin it got colder and colder, and I started to freeze. It would have broken Mary Shelley's heart to see how the poor old Creature's teeth chattered. Tony Nelson-Keys brought me a bottle of brandy and I drank most of it. I might as well have poured it on with the water for all the good it did.

I survived. We all survived to go on to yet more horrid things. Before any further projects could be realized, however, there was an unexpectedly horrid experience for all of us, when the press saw it and gave it a venomous reception. 'Disgusting' and 'Grand Guignol' were two of the milder epithets from that quarter of the entertainment world which is hardly famous for keeping its own nose clean. However, the wounds they caused had the appearance of being dealt in private, because nobody heeded them and the crowds flocked to the picture in millions.

To offset the bemusingly sudden identification with horror, I sought and obtained a part in the remake of another classic, *A Tale of Two Cities*. This was a top-level swank villain, the Marquis de St Evrémonde, who was offhand and ruthless with peasants and paid for his sins with a knife in his chest while sleeping. Having stepped into the shoes of Boris Karloff, I was here exchanging them for those of Basil Rathbone. It was an undemanding part, but a magnificent showcase. It was shot in

Bourges and had everything in it but the kitchen sink (a fashionably growing genre with no use for my services). The cast was solid gold: Dirk Bogarde, Dorothy Tutin, Paul Guers, Rosalie Crutchley, Donald Pleasance, Athene Seyler, Freda Jackson . . . I even had a relative in it – my elderly cousin Nicholas Hannen. And a neighbour, the photographer Tony Armstrong-Jones, took some mesmerizing glossy stills of me in the course of a magazine assignment. The gentlemen of the press condescended to like it. As well they might: there is nothing to beat a strong story well made.

In this my *annus mirabilis*, or *annus horribilis* perhaps, my third strong story, my third classic remake, my third pair of second-hand shoes, was *Dracula*. It was the one that made the difference. It brought me a name, a fan club and a second-hand car, for all of which I was grateful. It also, if I may be forgiven for saying so, brought me the blessing of Lucifer, the third and final nail in my coffin. Count Dracula might escape, but not the actors who play him.

'Beware of your fantasies, for you may become them,' said that great clowning fantasist Kurt Vonnegut. There is no question but that when an actor's fantasy collides with a certain fated role, there's a relocation of the atoms of his professional life, akin to a change of state in chemistry. The simple explanation of why I was chosen as the noble leech of Transylvania was that I'd done a competent job as the Creature. But had I all along really been asking for it? I'd seen Karloff as the Monster and Rathbone as Evrémonde, but in this instance I'd not seen the original, Bela Lugosi's *Dracula* of 1930. I deliberately chose not to, to avoid being influenced. I didn't even know at that time that the legend was based on a real and horrendous historical personage, Vlad Tsepesh, known as the Impaler. I decided that my source would be Bram Stoker's novel, and I read it twice. It was about a vampire not at all like me in physical character, but there were aspects of him with which I could readily identify – his extraordinary stillness, punctuated by bouts of manic energy with feats of strength belying his appearance; his power complex; the quality of being done for but undead; and by no means least the fact that he was an embarrassing member of a great and noble family.

Naturally, we did not follow the book exactly. That was never done, neither by *Nosferatu* nor the Lugosi version, though both used bits of it. We hadn't the money. The whole thing cost eighty-two thousand pounds which would not stretch, for instance, to a shipwreck. And there are chunks of turgid disquisition in Stoker which could never be film. Some omissions disappointed me, though. They could have been both inexpensive and good film. A detail that might, for instance, have gone in, would have been John van Eyssen as Harker shaving, cutting himself and then turning, on hearing an indrawn hiss, to find Dracula, whose image had not been reflected by the mirror.

This little touch would have been deeply satisfying to the pedantry of the Demon Incarnate buffs, whom I discovered from the mail, within a year, to be legion. Try as we might to get accuracy, someone always popped up to reproach us with an oversight. One fan for instance grumbled because I cast a shadow. In a perfect world it could have been erased by painting it out on every single frame, but the deeper truth would be that sometimes compromise is not a bad thing dramatically, and the shadow of Dracula at the stairhead before he made his bodily appearance was just the article to get the adrenalin going in the front stalls.

When I did see Lugosi, I was surprised. He had tremendous presence but the direction seemed vague. According to Boris he had trouble with the language and had to do it phonetically, which in turn tightened him up. But there were some gorgeous things in Stoker we should have borrowed, like the time when the woman is crying in the courtyard and Dracula ascends the battlements to summon the wolves and you hear the harsh metallic voice while the beasts stream forward. Insuperable stuff!

On the other hand there were additions. Stoker made no mention of a cape. I accepted that, black on both sides. My sticking point came when the suggestion was mooted of evening dress with an Order, which struck me as unlikely in a castle in the middle of Transylvania. Stylization is all very well, but if it goes over the top you're left with camp. In the end I was allowed to wear a black suit with cravat and pearl tiepin. We held out against ruby tiepins and cufflinks, and scarlet lining to the cloak, until the sequel.

The same wonderful back-up Hammer team officiated: Albert on the grips, Jack on the electrics, Monty on the hairdrier, Tommy on the props, Jack and Len on the camera and Jimmy on the till. And the real star of the picture, who could make sow's ears out of silk purses and vice versa, was the art director, Bernard Robinson.

On this occasion my mishaps were the consequence of the contact lenses designed to give a blood-red effect. They irritated my eyes so that I wept copiously, which was utterly out of character for the heartless Count. Furthermore they hindered me from seeing where I was going, so that I was constantly crashing into people and falling over things. Poor Valerie Gaunt, who was splendid, was terrified by the sight of me hurtling towards her with my fangs bared and my eyes flashing, with the added terror of knowing that I would only pull up when I felt myself safe in her neck.

All good things come to an end, and the final sequence was a contrivance of genius by the writer Jimmy Sangster, brilliantly shot in one day by Jack Asher. Flapping about like a bat, pinned by a shaft of sunlight, I disintegrated into dust. There were many stages in the process. The first thing to go was my foot, and I had to do a Lon Chaney, almost dislocating my foot and tucking it under me. Then a hand, likewise. Then the other coming up over the face, and the face crumbling . . . Clever fellows! It was almost an honour to be so ably pulverized.

We interrupted the making of *Doctor of Seven Dials*, in which Francis de Wolff and I played a kind of Burke and Hare pair robbing graves, for a fortnight to attend the New York première of *Dracula*. It was my first trip to America and I flew over with a severe knee injury contracted when, after having acid thrown in my face and stabbing Boris to death on a bed, I crashed blindly into an iron stove.

I didn't care a fig for such paltry injuries. It was spring, and Peter went with me. As his birthday was the day before mine, we celebrated it together on the peak of the Empire State Building, which gave me vertigo, and again at a party given by Universal when I launched myself on the cake with its thirty-six candles and stabbed it to the heart. There was a picture of me several storeys high – some fifty feet of bloodthirsty Count holding a girl in his/my arms – on a building beside the cinema in Times Square.

The midnight screening for the profession and the media had me worried. Not a few of that exuberant audience were well tanked up and greeted each new character with a Bronx cheer and a fusillade of cracks and laughs. Someone even fired a gun. When the silhouette showed at the head of the stairs the roof was like to have been lifted off. But the ordinary conversational tone of the Count switched them off like a knob being turned on the radio. From then on there was only direct reaction. The Count tamed them. Then at two in the morning Peter and I sat in the foyer and signed our wrists stiff. At last I knew what it was like to taste blood.

My pay for that film was £750. Better than a blow in the carotid artery and higher than most people got for six weeks' work. I was able to afford a Mercedes which hadn't too many thousand miles on the clock. The film is said eventually to have grossed something like twenty-five million dollars. Universal's president Al Daff told me it pulled the company free of bankruptcy. The profit/cost ratio was higher than for any other British picture ever made. So we were not overpaid. Jimmy Carreras, Hammer's founder, came with us and Tony Hinds to New York. Answering a question about plans for the future he said, 'You're the public. We make films for you. If you want Strauss waltzes I'll make them.'

Nobody spoke up for Strauss. Apparently they all liked waltzing with death. Hammer Horror had its dance card full.

A Matter of Form

Boris was above all things graceful. In the domain into which I'd recently stumbled and poached a couple of triumphs, he was king. When I returned from the heady whirl of the New York opening to finish off *Corridors of Blood* (as it came to be called), he never condescended to nor patronized me. He avoided any implication of my intrusion into the business and in fact we discussed everything save that. But he had a kind of running gag, a sort of oblique comment, whereby he made himself out to be on the discard heap.

'I'm only a feeble worn-out old wreck, it'th plain to thee,' he would lisp. 'What am I here for? Jutht to *thweep* up the odd jobth left behind.'

It gave him a great kick to pour this on. It was plain to see from his performance in the lead that he was anything but *passé*. But, 'All I'm fit for ith to thweep up the lawnth at night when the thet is detherted and the playerth have all gone home!' During the party at the end of the picture the unit gave him a broom. He loved that.

It's a paradox of success that when it comes one often begins to wish it had taken some other form. I was more than happy to borrow the shoes of Chaney and Lugosi and Karloff and Rathbone and Veidt, considering the mileage of which they were capable and my fervid conviction that without exception these five men were among the most outstanding entertainment artists. At the same time, I didn't want the shoes to wear me. I wanted perhaps to run a kind of three-legged race, with the spare foot keeping up in some other rut. This yearning has never left me, and accounts for 90 per cent of the irritation I have ever since felt. I began by contracting straight away my next two parts as Kharis, another bandaged juggernaut, in *The Mummy*, and as the fine upstanding public-school figure of Sir Henry Baskerville in *The Hound of the Baskervilles*. I hoped one would balance the other.

I had a weird kind of fame growing with many dotty side effects.

Among the least expected of the possibilities that came in its train was my sudden freedom to marry. It was as if the trigger which all these years had been on 'Safe' was now in the firing position. I knew almost as soon as I saw her that I must marry Henriette von Rosen.

We met, almost peradventure, at the night-club called Riche in Stockholm. This was the first such place to be opened in Sweden, and got its licence to celebrate the seventh centenary of the capital, and was much used by opera and ballet people. I'd been a regular through most of a decade of time off in Sweden, mainly because, in high summer when the night shrank away to nothing, it was the one place I could find some dim light.

It was in both senses, then, a blind date, after Henriette had been praised to me by a Swedish girl in London, though I had known her cousin of the Royal Opera, Elsa Marianne von Rosen. She came in a blaze of red hair in the dim lighting, with green eyes and the sweetest smile, all of nineteen. To say that I was struck dumb would not be literally accurate – I have never been bereft of the power of speech – but my liver changed place with my heart, and the great seal of the Carandini ring felt too tight.

I then embarked on a fortnight high, with no other thought but to impress and obtain Henriette. We walked as if in a dream through boundless acres of fir and pine and birch and I chattered like one demented to her of the films I'd been recently making which, due to the strictness of the Swedish censorship laws regarding horror films, she had been unable to see. And of course my head was full of *The Mummy* which I'd just been making, and the impossibility of such a poor old monster having a love life, owing to the bandages and his mouth being sewn up.

And how one could only breathe through the holes in the eyes. And what a dear man Peter Cushing was and how fortunate I was to be teamed with him, how he was the only actor I'd ever known to keep eighteen props in action at once, the despair of actors like myself who hated them, who could tear off a piece of paper, light his pipe, look out of a window and remove his shoes, all while reeling off his lines.

And how I thought of Dracula as rather human, with a terrible solitude of Evil, whereas the Mummy wasn't a living being and obviously the director didn't think so either. Because I'd been most horribly bruised and battered and bashed on this film, bursting through real glass windows, and a door that someone had bolted from the inside without telling me so that I'd almost dislocated my shoulder, and had had explosive charges detonated on plates set within my bandages, to give the illusion of my being peppered with a shotgun. And I told her how the muscles of my shoulder had become torn through carrying Yvonne Furneaux eighty-seven paces through a swamp at night, three times, with my arms fully extended because these lovelies were unable to put their arms around my neck, having fainted from the horror of being within my embrace. I could add to that an incident in *Dracula*, where the unexpected weight of a tubby stunt double I had to cast into an open grave had caused me to tumble in after her.

All this, and more, Henriette sweetly and sympathetically hearkened to and, after forty-eight hours of romantic communication, agreed to be my bride. This made me feel my fairy godmother really had the bit between her teeth, as a girl of the great von Rosen family could fairly have been expected to be united to something grand and ancient and respected and rich. Henriette immediately hastened off to let her family know she had plighted her troth in the woods to a tall, dark and alien actor.

Her mother and her excellent brother Otto took the news in good part. Her father, Fritz von Rosen, did not. He called for photographs. In the normal way I never carried images of myself around, as singers did their sheet music. On this occasion I had bundles of them with me, since I hoped to gouge some contracts out of Sweden and Germany during my travels. I passed these on to Henriette, for Papa to case.

This may have been unwise. They included Dracula dripping blood, necrophilic studies of Resurrection Joe, plus the Creature from *Frankenstein* and the Mummy going berserk. They did not further my suit with Henriette's father. He must have asked himself what his grandchildren would look like.

He summoned me. Well, the castle turned out to be a small house in the forest nearby, and we went by tram. But I'm sure that in his imagination it was a castle. Most of the branches of the von Rosens had one or more. Alas for Fritz, his father had lost some gross amount like eight million kronor in the Kreuger débâcle, obliging Fritz to live more modestly than the rest of his blood. It did not prevent him from being fully conscious of the pecking order of the aristos, and he did not disguise his feeling that Count Dracula was not enough of a handle to earn his goodwill as a prospective father-in-law. He cheered up a bit when I mentioned the Carandini connection, and the Countess was at all times charming and nice. I sprinkled noble names around as if I had been hosing the garden with them, from my sister's godfather Lord Carisbrooke to George VI when he'd inspected us in the desert. He so far relented as to ask me if I would wait for a year.

This was agreed. Like a jinnee squeezing itself back into its bottle I vanished back into the cinema studios. Henriette and I corresponded, and once she made a lightning visit to England and met my mother, who was ill in bed and inclined to think I was far too young to marry. But when she was introduced to Henriette she thought our engagement was the only sensible thing I had ever managed. So that was all right.

When Henriette had gone home again I became aware of something extraordinary developing all around me. A senior executive of Decca Records, called Jimmy Gray, invited me to the Caledonian Club for lunch and quizzed me about my life. Then another businessman invited me to lunch saying, 'Fritz von Rosen wants us to meet.' They came at me from all sides to report back on my doings and curriculum vitae to Fritz von Rosen. They were very civil but some were rather dull and uninteresting and a considerable waste of my time. I suspected most felt foolish doing it.

Then I was dogged by a rash of private detectives, checking up on the account of myself I'd given to Fritz von Rosen. There were absurd mix-ups. I happened to have mentioned to von Rosen that I occasionally played golf with Marshal of the RAF Sir William Dickson, and the next I knew on the topic was a phone call from my tearful fiancée saying, 'Daddy says you're not in the RAF. Daddy got a message from one of his friends saying there's no trace of Flight Lieutenant Lee in the Air Force List. And Daddy went "Aha!" and showed it to me!' and I had to say, 'But my dear love, that was practically twenty years ago and some boiled brain he's hired in London doesn't know the Air Force List only records *serving* officers.'

Having seen this wave of attackers shot down, he tried a new tactic. As if I were entering domestic service, he asked me to furnish references. Staunch to my love, I swallowed my pride and asked some of my friends to put down a few words about my character. Douglas Fairbanks gave me a very nice boost, John Boulting wrote a masterpiece of courtesy which sent Fritz von Rosen into transports of rage, which began, 'You must realize, dear Count von Rosen, that actors are no longer rogues and vagabonds', and the third was from my old friend Joe Jackson, who sent me two with a covering letter saying, 'Here is something for your apparently idiot father-in-law.' One was signed Nasser, and testified to my being a confirmed rapist and sodomite and the other was orthodox, and signed with his true title, R. L. Jackson, Assistant Commissioner CID.

I got on quietly with a raft of sleazy characters in the cinema for *The Man Who Could Cheat Death*, *Hot Money Girls* and *Beat Girl* and was burned to death in a monk's robe as a Satanist in an American Gothic with a Lovecraftian flavour called *City of the Dead*. Then I rose like a phoenix from it all and went off to spend Christmas and my next trial of strength with the autocrat of the von Rosen family.

This was followed by the great etiquette marathon, when I was taken on a round of the great houses and castles of Sweden. I already had a decade of familiarity with the punctilious observance of eating, drinking and friendship rituals in Sweden, the angle at which the glass is tilted for the toast, the length of time the eyes are locked with those of the interlocutor, the interval between toasts, the age and rank engaged in them and the tactful routines used to establish who has precedence in the offer of a toast. And much, much more besides. The pattern was set straight away for me by a visit to the castle of Örbyhus, outside Uppsala, an amazing structure where they still kept fresh and serviceable the dungeons in which mad king Eric XIV was imprisoned. At Örbyhus I was paraded for inspection before the assembled von Rosens and their retainers.

As a preliminary piece of treachery, Fritz advised me to wear a tweed suit. This proved to be entirely wrong for a snow-laden Sunday in the country. The family were uniformly in dark suits with stiff collars and dark ties. The women likewise, ancient and modern. Faithful retainers rustled about in black. It might have been a wake, not the engagement which had just been announced in the papers. In my light English tweeds and bumfreezer I looked like something out of H. G. Wells breaking in on the world of Thackeray.

Innumerable speeches were made, to which I was obliged to make innumerable answers. It was a nice point whether I should reply in English, since the whole of the upper crust in Scandinavia is fluent in at least ten languages, or in Swedish, thus cutting in the flunkeys. As we repeated the business in half a dozen castles, attended by every great name in Sweden, I was able to try both approaches. At Örbyhus the drawing-room was full of white Marie Antoinette furniture and I made a great gaffe by sitting down in one of the chairs.

The servants wore white gloves to hand around the aquavit and beer and scowled at me when at the end of the meal I failed to roll up my napkin and insert it in its ring. This was quite new to me. In England it would have been bad form, but here when I flopped my napkin down, long lines of heads turned and stared – it was like a Buñuel film.

In the absence of Fritz everybody was charming, within the limitations imposed by all this formality. We went to Gothenburg for a few days, and Henriette and I were never given a moment alone. We stayed a time in the lovely province of Skåne, at the fantastic castle called Trolleholm, which belonged to Fritz's brother-in-law Carl. We shot and we drank and it was nice. The endless stream of footmen in kneebreeches was wearing, though, and Henriette was being got at. They were killing me with cream. After vodka in a hothouse of flowers, we'd confront about a hundred dishes in some gigantic hall, stagger away from that to be told that dinner would be ready shortly. Then we'd troop into a cellar, with renovated dungeons leading off, where I expected any moment Boris to loom up in his full cinema regalia to welcome us to the feast.

After one of these we tottered into a library and Fritz prepared the *coup de grâce*, running to a massive tome and saying playfully, 'This is interesting, Christopher, let's look up your family on your mother's side.' His tone conveyed that he expected to find they were butchers in the Boer War. And then to his intense chagrin it was revealed that the Carandinis were hundreds of years older than the von Rosens. He was as mortified as a melted candle. All the sports among the vons began teasing him by saying things like, 'Of course, to a *nouveau riche* family like the von Rosens . . .'

So, coming to the eighteenth, I appeared to be dormy one. I had only to ask permission of the King. And lo and behold, who should the incumbent be but the delightful monarch I had last met when I was Emperor of China! He gave me not only his blessing but a pair of cufflinks with three Swedish crowns on them, which I always treasured. So there was a birdie on that hole.

The wedding was on. Once again the completion of a phase in my life had been saluted by my angels with an erotic ceremonial. Henriette travelled to London for the run in. At this point there was a hitch. It was demonstrated that Fritz von Rosen had tackled the problem from the wrong angle. It was seeing Henriette in London that brought reality into the fairy-tale.

She showed not the slightest sign of pique that the English were totally uninterested in feudal estates and the people who owned them, nor did she give the most minute intimation of nervousness at the idea of exchanging a life of comfort and great style for the insecurity of being an actor's wife. She was an utterly sweet young lady. And it occurred to me that the person who had shown me the barren nature of my disaffected relations with women deserved better of me than to be married to me and pitched into the dishevelled world of an actor.

So one day in my second-hand Mercedes parked in Eaton Square I told her that it was off. She was startled and upset but she was a clever girl and I felt sure she understood. We parted then and there and I never saw her again. She went back to Sweden, and married a gentleman farmer with a large estate. They had three children and lived happily ever after. Which is just the way a fairy-tale should end.

Fall-out

The fall-out of the Catherine wheel leaves no lasting scars. When one goes off with your name on it, it's practically irresistible to fool about with it. From whizz to fizz I had sundry gratifications from mine. Immediately the sparks had gone out, I forgot the pattern. Except for one or two that flared eccentrically.

The ones I liked the most came in the shape of a golf ball. In the centenary year of Wellington College (1957) I was asked for the first time to play for the Old Boys' Golfing Society in the prestigious Halford Hewitt Cup. Wellington had never won that. But then, to be fair to the committee, I had to own that my game had only recently settled down enough to justify a handicap of one at Royal Ashdown. We played, we won.

It was an actor's putt that got us into the final. On the green of the last hole, with a thirty-foot putt to sink to get us through, some spirit of madness prompted me to tell the caddie to remove the pin from the hole. I heard our captain say, 'That man will never play for Wellington again.' I remembered how as a boy I had talked a great game and not been able to deliver. Now at last the rub of the green was with me. The hole swallowed my putt like a Hoover. We went on to bring home our first victory in the Cup. I was invited to play the next year.

Altogether the orbits of my acting and golfing were getting much closer. An offer came of a film about a human golfing robot who could declare his shots and place the ball on every occasion exactly where he said. The film was never made, which was a pity because it was a good idea and apart from the risk of losing my amateur status I'd have been glad to do it. But I did play with some of the nearest creatures to human golfing machines when I entered my first Pro-Am.

My partner was Bobby Locke. He had a delightful and whimsical humour, always called his partner 'master' and punctuated every round with a stream of quaint aphorisms, such as 'I'm hitting the ball beautifully and more often', and 'the most important club is the fifteenth, the one that holds your hat on', and 'You took a divot with that putt'. It was the first of many, many rounds. He became a firm friend. That time out at Sunningdale in the Bowmaker Pro-Am, drawn with the Open Champion, I was paralysed with nerves. I'd played a few times in the English Amateur, never getting further than the fifth round, but I'd never seen crowds like this.

My first shot went down the middle about four feet from the ground. I'd supposed Bobby to be aloof and indifferent, but he was wonderfully encouraging. He played as I'd never seen golf before, went round in sixty-two and won the Professionals' score. After a shaky start I turned in seventy-one, which for me was good. Though as a combination we were beaten, it was Bobby Locke's attitude to me that day that gave me the taste for Pro-Ams.

As a vehicle, *Dracula* was by no means a bad model, but there was always a danger of vampire overdrive. Eventually I made too many and long after I had become fed up with them gossip writers couldn't resist inventing daft quotes for me like 'Lee says he means to make *Dracula* every year'. The press always thought we were easy meat and made jokes about us going over the top, without ever noticing the beam in their own prose style: journalists were inclined to write about my eyes as bolt holes into hell, and compare my teeth with a row of tombstones.

In the flurry of vampire offers, the first off the mark were the Italians. Being Italians, their idea was to make a slavish parody of a success. This has always been the essential juice of their industry. In the case of *Tempi Duri per i Vampiri* I had no reason to wish it otherwise, and the result was fairly jolly. The pint-sized Italian comedian Renato Rascel was with me, and the contrast between us was very amusing.

It was directed by Steno in the castle of the blond giant Prince Livio Odescalchi on Lake Bracciano. I declined to be Dracula, but played a baron vampire in similar apparel – played him straight in comic situations. The hinge of the story was that I turned Rascel into a vampire, with the object of being able to lie down at last and get everlasting peace, and died quietly with delight. Then he, happy little vampire, dashed about after all the girls. Then the twist; one of them, chaste and pure, kissed him with love, reversed the process and I had to return with curses to the undead condition. It went down very well, in Italy.

It's a commonplace that vampirish characters, notably Dracula, have a powerful erotic appeal for audiences. Inevitably some of my mail betrayed this. Contrary to the general supposition, though, the letters were not obscene, unless an offer to make French love came under that heading. In the era that was even then stripping for action, I thought this one might be termed rather a billet-doux.

A couple of responses that were more overtly disconcerting were claims to have made love already with the dreaded Transylvanian. One letter from a cinema manager in the north of England reported that an usherette of his had said she was pregnant by Dracula, presumably from seeing him five times a day for a week, and that I ought to do the decent thing. That one, I felt, I could safely ignore.

The other was nearer at hand and came in person. She caused some trouble, because she was a true carnal acquaintance of recent date. She also wanted me to do the decent thing. In this case the interpretation of decent thing was that I should pay up, or she would slap a paternity suit on me. According to the specialist I consulted, a pregnancy as advanced as hers, eight days after intimacy, would create medical history, and he thought it more than likely somebody else was responsible. The many words of wisdom spoken to me by Errol Flynn then rushed to my consciousness. I quoted him to the girl and her protector, saying in his words that 'the pregnancy would either abate or abort' without my connivance and that if they pressed me further I would mention the matter to my friend Joe Jackson, CID. They then went off to work the old college try on some other mark.

Dracula and Co. did not have a monopoly of the response. I was more than pleased to trawl in a following with Sir Henry Baskerville, a different sort of fellow altogether. He was not even a villain. He was Romantic, while at the same time a bit cross, with a dickey heart.

The Hound of the Baskervilles was one of Hammer's best money-spinners. As Sherlock Holmes, Peter Cushing was wonderful. There was villainy from the Hammer regular villain, Francis de Wolff, and comic relief from the regular Hammer comic, Miles Malleson. Conan Doyle had also stipulated two horripilating beasts, a slavering hound the size of a donkey, and a mean spider. These Hammer duly furnished.

Spiders head my list of fearsome things. This one was a ghastly bird-eating spider from South America. It was brought to the set by its guardian in a plastic box. He said that it wouldn't kill a man, only give him a nasty bite. I observed that its legs were hairy and about the thickness of my fingers. It was not at ease in the studio and shed its entire skin on the floor. When it walked towards them the intrepid people round the camera fled for their lives, led by our director Terence Fisher. None the less he stated that the plot required me to take it on my neck, after it had crawled out of a boot. I said I hated the thing. I wouldn't have it on my neck. A compromise was agreed whereby it only strolled on my arm and shoulder. This was enough to turn me green with nausea. The realism of my performance was universally commended.

The dog was not at all realistic. He was real, but his behaviour made a nonsense of the story. He was a Great Dane called Colonel. After he had been on the set six weeks, he was so acclimatized, so amiable and stuffed to the gunnels with chocolate, that he was a non-starter as a hound of hell. When the time finally came for him to attack and savage me, the entire team had to get together to prod Colonel into action. He stood a great deal of vexatious treatment from everybody without a bleat until suddenly, when I'd relaxed and given up, he lost his cool and hurled himself on me. He bit me through the arm.

The aspect of the film which caught the eye of an enthusiast in America was something much more glossy and smooth – the sheer Englishness of Sir Henry Baskerville. This lady rang me from New York to say that she had been very impressed by my Englishness and wished to fly over straight away and discuss the matter with me personally. This was a turn-up for the book, after being reviled so long for being un-English, and when she hinted that there was a chance of money in it for me, I did not discourage her from making the flight.

She was very small, under five foot tall, but what there was of her was very elegant. I thought I was prepared for almost anything, but the proposition she made me was truly astounding. She wanted me to go home with her and impersonate an English solicitor in negotiations with her father.

The scenario she sketched was of an immensely rich Sicilian father who would not let her marry, under pain of disinheritance, the man she loved. According to her, the father had an Achilles heel: an idolatrous respect for the English, the word of an Englishman and suchlike paraphernalia, including the integrity of English justice.

I would tell this hoary old bandit, who presumably never looked at television, that I was a London lawyer. I would make a great courtroom oration, quoting the Bill of Rights, the Declaration of Independence, the Book of Isaiah and Rex v. Blackstone, disenchanting him with his plan to disinherit his child and evoking his blessing for her union with her lover.

'Your father is presumably not a stupid man?' I asked.

'Oh no,' she replied, 'very smart.'

'Fairly good businessman, I'd think?'

'Tough as nails,' she agreed.

'You're asking me to pass myself off as an English gentleman, legal division, without his checking on my firm or finding out I am an actor? The possibilities emanating from this scheme are so frightening that I find myself blenching right here in front of you. He'd throw me down all the stairs in New York and then not be satisfied till I wore a concrete tuxedo at the bottom of the river!'

I was sorry to disappoint her, but I could see from her determined little chin when she left that love would find a way. I mentioned to Joe Jackson that she had offered me $10,000 for this charade, and wondered aloud if I would have got it. He said he thought I would have got about ten years.

The Greatest Actor

Television films had been good for me, but now that I was gathering blooms in a minefield of terrible cinema offers, I could give less time to them. When I could sneak one in, I did, between things like *Too Hot to Handle*, which was made with an alternative version for those who preferred Jayne Mansfield with her nipples painted out, and *Two Faces of Dr Jekyll*, in which I was a cad strangled by a python, and *Terror of the Tongs*, where I tended to limit myself to speaking Cantonese.

Increasingly the films I was making had their base on the European mainland and it was in the midst of some travel of this sort that I had the chance to appear in a new television series being shot in Munich by a Kirk Douglas company. Called *Tales of the Vikings*, it was a spin-off from his massive film success. I had two good reasons for quitting wonderful Copenhagen and signing up for a spell with the Vikings. One was the chance of secretly meeting a young Austrian von there whose father thought I was twice the age I should be and only half Catholic enough to associate with his daughter. And the other was the prospect of working with the greatest actor in the world.

I swept in on a Caravelle jet to bands playing in Munich – for the Mayor as it happened who was on the same flight – and with my young Austrian friend travelled about a hundred yards before encountering her mother, which was a great test of aplomb on all sides. But really my mind was entirely filled with the imminent arrival of the greatest actor in the world.

Our tale was *The Bull*. The background of it was that William the Conqueror wanted an alliance with Norway. As a symbol of it he not only sent one of his nobles to marry a Norse maiden but also this prize bull to mate with a Norse cow. The point of the tale was that the Saxon serf ordered by the Norman tyrant to dispatch the bull had formerly been a great chief, and now after years of slavery had reached the end of his tether. I was the Norman tyrant, while the Saxon was to be played by the greatest actor in the world.

There was no argument among the people I knew as to who was the greatest actor in the world. It was Wilfrid Lawson. As soon as I knew that I was going to work with Wilfrid Lawson I went around telling people and briefing them on his record. He was on a plane apart – he was a genius – he was the original Doolittle of *Pygmalion* – he had the divine madness – and a lot more besides. He really was an inspired and idiosyncratic performer and when the unit had tired of hearing me say so, I repeated to anyone who cared to listen in the Hotel Schottenhamel that Munich would shortly be receiving England's greatest actor.

The tension built up over three days, chiefly spent on my snarling at three Vikings who'd come to the court to take over the bull. My character prescribed that I be beastly to all, and whenever the action slackened I strode on to order floggings or thumbscrews. We did this under the direction of Elmo Williams, a talented and resourceful man. All that could be done without Wilfrid Lawson had been done when we had the telegram giving his flight number and expected time of arrival.

All keyed up, at 8 p.m., I was pacing to and fro in the Schottenhamel lobby when a distraught German assistant burst in from the road and cried, 'Herr Lawson is not!' which I took to mean, after a pause for reflection, that he had not come off the plane. Indeed, he had not. There was panic. His scenes were scheduled to begin with the first light next day. Cables were sent. I withdrew to the bar, and knocked them back with dwindling hope for a couple of hours. I was all over despondent when suddenly the doors flew open and an unmistakably English figure surged into the lobby, in an ancient mac and a hat pulled down over one eye, and meandered about with a suitcase. I shot over to him.

'Mr Lawson?' 'Ye-es.' He had a deep voice like Magoo. I found myself looking down into a red scarred face with a wonderful infectious grin. I rattled on, 'I'm Christopher Lee. Thrilled to be working with you.' 'Uhuhuh, ye-es, my deah boy.' 'Great moment for me.' 'Hah kind, hah kind. Where's my room?' 'Care for a drink, while the boy takes your things up?' Again his seraphic smile flashed. 'Dullighted, deah boy.'

He was dullighted. I guessed that causes for dullight had been fairly frequent. We took a few more on board. He was rather pleased with himself. He had been on the plane and fooled them all. For some mysterious private reason he'd hidden himself somehow at the airport and given the welcoming committee the slip. Before going up to his room, he turned a puzzled face to me from the door and said, 'Have you read this story? *Most* peculiar! It's all about a *bull*!'

Came the dawn of the great day. We were all kitted up, but no Saxon chief. The first assistant said, 'Herr Lawson is not.' Chaos again. They beat on his door. A voice within called, 'Go away. I know you not.' After much shouting and coaxing he was persuaded to come out and join us.

He arrived, but not to work. The assortment of clothing hung about him made him look like a fugitive from a flea market. He said, 'A little nap, I think,' and went straight off to sleep on an adjacent set. Again they wheedled him. 'Why are you bothering me? Who are you? Where's the beer?' he grumbled.

Eventually, with the help of a few beers, he was channelled through make-up and emerged in a sort of cowl and russet jerkin and hose, looking right for a mix of *A Midsummer Night's Dream* and *Treasure Island*. I was already up on my charger in a surcoat of chainmail, while the American actor Ryan O'Neal, who played the Saxon's son, leaned negligently on his hoe and would continue to do so while the scene was shot.

What we needed was a long shot of me galloping up to the pair of them, to establish all three, then a close shot of me ranting and calling him a Saxon dog with dire threats if the bull wasn't ready and combed by 4 p.m. – then a reverse on Wilfrid for his big defiant reply. In this he would remember his previous dignities and greatness and assert himself. In rehearsal it went without a hitch, though I thought I detected Wilfrid's lips at one point moving to mutter, 'What am I doing here?'

They did my Saxon dog bit. Wilfrid looked at me without a flicker of an expression. I was moved nearly to tears at finding myself working with the greatest actor in the world. Occasionally he would give me a sweet smile from behind the camera as the scene progressed, and rip off his lines with no effort at all. Elmo said, 'Right, now we'll reverse on you, Wilfrid.'

He shook himself like a man coming up from a reverie and said, 'Eh?'

'Yes, yes, on you, Wilfrid. Reverse on you.'

He beamed at Elmo. 'I see,' he said, 'splendid, splendid. Well, how about a beer?'

Elmo then said to me in a stage whisper, 'I'm going to put in a new magazine and keep running, no matter what Wilfrid says.' What he actually had to say was not all that long, being composed mainly of defiance with a few grunts and glares and beetling looks, plus the classic line, 'I, I who fought with Ogier the one-eyed Dane, will not bow the knee.'

Like the legendary Charles Macklin of Drury Lane, Wilfrid had a Grand Pause, a Medium Pause and a Little Pause. He was soon giving us the benefit of all three.

Action, gallop, Saxon dog bit – deathly silence from Wilfrid. 'You Saxon dog!' I insisted, more loudly.

'I beg your pardon?' said Wilfrid.

'Can we start again, Wilfrid?'

'Eh? Of course, my dear fellow. Hadn't realized . . .'

The camera continued to shoot while they all worked out their positions anew. 'Ah yes, yes, you've said all that already,' said Wilfrid. 'Well, *I'm* ready.' The blond American leaned on his hoe and nodded rhythmically, like a car mascot.

'Now what was it again?' asked Wilfrid. 'No, no, I will not . . . no, no, no . . . is that right? no, no, no, will not . . .' Grand pause '. . . will not bow, will not, bow the knee, the knee no, to, to, to . . .' Medium pause '. . . to you. No, never. Is that all right?' 'Yes, Wilfrid, fine,' said Elmo, 'go on.' 'Go on? But I've finished.'

'You remember the business where you talk about the battles,' Elmo patiently prodded.

'Ah, the *battles*!' Little pause. 'What battles?'

'The battles where you fought with the Danes and were a great Saxon chief.'

'A Saxon? Oh yes, would not bow, yes. Saxons will never bow the knee. I, I, am a Saxon and consequently will never bow the knee to you, you Saxon dog, I beg your pardon, Norman dog.' Grand pause. 'Do you think you've got another bottle of beer nearby, dear fellow? . . .

'Cue me, dear boy, Saxon dog, I'm quite ready. I *fought*, that's right, isn't it, Elmo, did fight with Aggie the one-eyed Dame. Really only one eye?'

'What the script says, roughly.'

'*What* script? Ah . . . said that bit . . . Doesn't this boy say anything at all? Nothing? Don't *you* say anything more? Said it? I who fought with Ogier the one-eyed Dane will never, never help you more.'

'Great, Wilfrid!'

'Have I finished now?'

'That's it, Wilfrid.'

'*When is the next plane?*' he cried.

Cut.

Gitte

y wife does not care for golf and she cannot hold a tune. All the same, without golf and music we should never have met. The chain of causes which led to my marriage began with my friend Lionel Stubbs. We often went round the course together, and even more often I dropped into his flat next door to chat about golf and what the RAF was up to. One evening Lionel had a Danish friend with him who like himself was 'in hides and skins'. When the topic of tanners and trappers had given out, the Dane and I discovered a common passion in music.

Harry Rabinowitz (namesake of the conductor) had an encyclopaedic knowledge of music – in fact he wrote an encyclopaedia. I cannot fathom the technicalities. If somebody talks about the magnificent bowing and fingerwork, it is lost on me. Triple tonguing and pedal work are closed books to me. But Harry was uncanny. He not only knew all that but he could recognize any singer and give you his name, the label on the record and its number. He'd published a catalogue of pre-electric recordings. I used to test him on obscure Romanian tenors and so forth. We sat for hours together, engrossed, and soon had a rapport so close that his Brooklyn-born wife Sandy ironically suggested we ought to get married.

I replied that there was no bar in my case, since I was single. They both stared at me as if they had thought I had a secret wife. 'You're *not* married?' they exclaimed in unison. Married people cannot bear anybody to remain in a single state. In no time they were snowing me with comments on a dazzling Dane they knew who was the one person in the world for me. She was twenty-five and they couldn't bear her being single either. Her name was Birgit Kroencke and everyone knew her as Gitte. She was a daughter of the director of the Tuborg brewery in Copenhagen. She was a painter. She was a model who'd worked for

Balmain, Balenciaga and Dior. They showed me radiant pictures to prove it. The red hair, the green eyes, the feline elegance, all haunted me. I avowed a half-wish to meet this paragon.

Having softened me up, they busily snowed Gitte, telling her the one person in the world for her was dying to meet her, and extolled me as a noble, kind genius. They showed her a non-Hammer photograph and she said indifferently, 'That's a reasonably normal-looking man,' and tried to get on with her life. They gave her my address and number in London, and when she flew over for a dance told me I must wait in for her call. I did what I had never done for any woman – I gave up my golf that Sunday and waited by the phone. The call never came. I said loudly, '*That's that!*' Then I added, '*I've finished with this woman and never want to meet her again.*'

The romance was ended and I consoled myself by making quite a good picture in which I had a marvellous part as a night-club magician who blackmails a strangler. *The Hands of Orlac* was made in English and French. We'd do a scene in English, and then the cry '*Version française*' would go up and we'd do it again in French and with rather more expression. It was like making two films for the price of one. It was the first of many times that I made a film in two languages. I was coached for my magic tricks by Billy McComb. Even without him they would not have been hard for me as they were rigged, but I was made a member of the Magic Circle. That was a pleasant perk at the English end, and from the French studio in Nice I was able to go round Mont Agel golf course near Monte Carlo, with Nigel Green, in sixty-three. The film was a remake of a well-tried German tale whose previous versions starred in turn Conrad Veidt and Peter Lorre. It concerned a pianist who had the hands of a murderer grafted on after losing his own in an accident.

So that set me up in a good mood to take a holiday, and I opted for Christmas in Copenhagen with the Rabinowitzes. It was like some old melody when Sandy began wangling a drink with Gitte at the Angleterre. We both glumly agreed. I trailed along till I heard 'Hello' and there was a very beautiful girl in fur coat and hat. I thought, Oh, my God! She really, she truly, she actually is, a stunner. We all talked at once, and shut up at once, as in a film. Gitte and I got on a track of saying how little we each had wanted to meet the other, and I boringly went on about giving up golf that Sunday. She said, 'Well, I was told if ever we did meet, you'd either shoot me or ask me to marry you.'

I wasn't carrying a gun. I said nothing. After hearing about her experience of England with a miner's family in Barnsley and life in New York as a mannequin, I set up a row of invitations, whereby she lunched and dined with me without a break for the next three days. In the second, over schnapps in her flat in the brewery, I said I couldn't live without her, asked her to be my mistress in London and, without giving her time to reply, topped it with an offer of marriage.

She gave no answer, but showed me some paintings she had made of New York. She was very entertaining, even about the German occupation when she was a child. She was never any respecter of persons. I kept on at her to marry me for the next couple of days. She said I should meet her father. This was encouraging, but alarming too when I recalled my Swedish engagement. But Richard Kroencke was utterly unperturbed. He only said jovially, 'You know, Gitte, I thought you were never going to be married!'

I rushed home to the Rabinowitzes and was delighted to find my mother's engagement ring was still in my cufflinks box, where I'd shoved it after Henriette returned it. It looked none the worse for this cavalier treatment. That night the Rabinowitzes gave a dinner for six, the four of us plus Hans Raaschou and his wife, ideal guests since Hans was not only head of the Magasin du Nord, with a great esteem for models, but president of the Danish Golf Union. When Gitte showed the ring to Mie Raaschou in the girls' room that made the engagement public as well as official.

Gitte and I solemnized the momentous event by staying overnight together in her flat in the brewery. It was like a drunkard's dream. The refrigerator was crammed with beer. Wherever I looked the horizon was bounded by lagers. The flat was on the third floor and I had the illusion of being on a raft afloat on fifty fathoms of beer.

We were woken from sleep by a thunderous crash on the window. To my horror I could see a man crouching on the window-sill. His features were contorted with rage and he banged furiously at the window. I had no idea who this human fly could be, until Gitte focused on him and said, 'This is ridiculous, it's Rosenqvist!'

Rosenqvist was a gnomelike janitor and handyman at the brewery who helped look after Richard Kroencke. My first reaction was that after all she had a nutty father, who had sent him to get me. 'Go away, Rosenqvist, go away!' shouted Gitte. But he wouldn't go away. He just hung there on a six-inch ledge, a middle-aged man in overcoat and boots, looking very annoyed. Perhaps going away was not feasible. It was impossible to imagine how he had got there in the first place.

In a towering state of indignation Gitte rose from our couch, assumed a robe and opened the window. In an equally transcendental state of rage Rosenqvist hurtled into the room. He yelled at her, 'You locked me out! I couldn't get in.' He was too het up to pay any attention to me, as I lay cowering with the sheet pulled up as far as my height would allow. He was almost weeping. 'I tried Herr Kroencke's room, but could not get in, so I had to come up the wall here.' Then he shrugged irritably and clumped off in a dudgeon.

Gitte's father thought it very funny and told everybody in Copenhagen.

With my previous experience of being engaged, I decided that this time it would not be for long. I had just one film to make first, and thought we could squeeze the marriage in between that and the really busy time that began in the spring. The date was set for 17 March 1961, a little before my thirty-ninth birthday.

In anticipation there were some Danish celebrations. We stayed at Nakkebølle Castle on Fyn, between Jutland and Zeeland, with Preben Philipsen, who named the biggest cinema distribution system in Germany after his father, Constantine. Every meal was wilder than the one before, and I woke every morning looking like potted death.

The film was *Taste of Fear*, directed by Seth Holt, ex-cutter and one of the best British directors ever. The film was nearly Hammer's best, though not up to Holt's *Never Give Sweets to a Stranger*, in which I didn't appear. Jimmy Sangster wrote a strong story for *Taste of Fear* and I had a goody's part, as a family doctor with a French accent.

And in a twinkling there was Gitte walking up the aisle at St Michael's, Chester Square, beautiful in beige and a fur hat. There was my best man Michael Henderson, all his life 'in drink', having started by cleaning vats and risen to direct the firm that makes Vat 69. We had a quiet wedding and a noisy reception. Vast numbers of people came to the latter, in a very good mood because they had not been obliged to go first to church. My mother had barely recovered from her initial shock, and was on tenterhooks till the last moment in case I let the bride down. 'Let's talk about something else,' she had said when I told her I meant to marry Gitte, but the ceremony convinced her of my good intentions.

There was no time for a regular, full-scale, Niagara-Falls-or-its-equivalent honeymoon. We had only a weekend before I had to start work Monday at dawn on *The Devil's Daffodil*. We resolved on a serial honeymoon through the year between pictures, and to start by taking our weekend at Brighton.

The staff at the Royal Albion Hotel behaved oddly. They ran the Union Jack up and down the pole outside our room every half-hour. When they were not doing that they were coming to the door to offer a shoeshine, a newspaper, room service, laundry, valeting, drinks, the menu for dinner. This seemed to us to go on round the clock. It was as if it were not the done thing for a couple to be married when they went to Brighton for a weekend.

It was very inconvenient. I had my lines to learn, in English and German, for *The Devil's Daffodil*. My part was a Chinese detective called Ling Chu in this thriller by Edgar Wallace, who was having a great vogue in Germany. Contriving a Chinese accent when I spoke the German lines was a new problem. Being fluent in German, Gitte was able to hearken to me, though naturally the Chinese aspect was new to her as well.

Our wedding day had been sunshine all the way; on the morrow it rained. We played some golf on the Downs. Gitte went round in a hundred and eighty-four. We called on Jimmy Carreras, our Hammer godfather, at his house near Roedean. He was startled by the sight of us on his doorstep and said, 'You're not supposed to be here. You're married.' We said, 'We know our lines, we've played our golf, it's raining, we don't want to sit around Brighton doing nothing all day, we dropped in to say hello.' The consequence was that we spent the next two nights with Jimmy Carreras, his wife Vera and his mother, near Roedean.

It was the start of what show business calls a 'miraculous marriage', because it has lasted from that day to this.

Sweets for the Bride

As Mother turned seventy, and I came up to forty, she began to accept the improbability of my changing horses and becoming a diplomat. She never entirely forgave me for becoming an actor, but my marriage to Gitte did much to mitigate the offence. My circle of honorary uncles, Walter Wilson, Joe Jackson and Paul Getty, were all delighted with her.

Like Jimmy Carreras, Uncle Walter had settled on the south coast, at Hove. I'd given him such a severe fright on one occasion recently that I was lucky to have him around still, in his late seventies, to bless the bride. In the course of a no-account picture called *The Battle of the V1*, made near Brighton, I'd played the part of an SS officer, an out-and-out baddie who has his head crushed by the hero with a rock, and had swaggered about a good deal in the full fig of an oppressor. This uniform caused great alarm to the citizens of Hove who apparently still had a conditioned reflex to the traumas of the war.

This was proved to me when the director gave me a lift while wearing this rig, and crashed his bubble car into a hulking Daimler at a crossroads. In the aftermath, as I staggered about getting my bearings, everyone hid behind trees and generally made themselves scarce, until a clergyman was sent for, possibly to exorcise me. This gave me the idea of a jape on Uncle Walter.

Still in my uniform I bounded in on him as he snoozed quietly in his retirement, yelling at the top of my voice, 'Hands up, this is the German Navy!' His wife Betty fell to the floor behind the sofa and Uncle Walter lifted about two feet off the cushions. After a shaky interval he laughed, and told me that I had run a serious risk of his having an assegai handy. However, as he proved to Gitte, he was still in great shape with a cocktail mixer and we all went round the golf course and he lashed into the ball regardless of its destination. As a putter, age made no difference

201

to him: he always putted like a contortionist with a square implement he had specially made entirely of wood. He had the 'yips' and, as Henry Longhurst said, 'once you've had 'em, you've got 'em'. Yips are twitches. You can't get the putter back, and when it finally moves, the ball travels at ninety.

As a mark of special esteem, Joe Jackson invited Gitte to look round the Black Museum at Scotland Yard. As president of Interpol he had asked me, as a favour to him, if I would keep my ears open on my travels for hints of drug trafficking and other illicit contraband in the entertainment world. Seeing it through his eyes it was a reasonable request, but even if one is sure of the facts one does not like to peach on one's colleagues. Life would become intolerable on location if one got an international name as a copper's nark. I tried not to hear any hints, and had nothing to report, except on non-actors.

The Black Museum grew as a memorial to every kind of criminal twist. I warned Gitte, having made the tour three or four times already, that the twists became more devious with each successive room. Beginning with gentle articles like con men's tricks, forgery and the cheques of Jim the Penman, it progressed through murderers' weapons and Himmler's death mask, to a more vividly grim repository of relics from the Heath and Christie murders, and at last to the world of harnesses for riding people round the room with, flogging triangles, rubber suits and spools of kinky film.

Gitte was undismayed. She wanted to see everything. She sailed through the first two rooms. In the third she was hot and wanted a glass of water. While a sergeant fetched it, she sat on the edge of a bath. A policeman said, 'Don't sit there, madam, it's a bath used by George Joseph Smith, who drowned three brides.' Water proved inadequate and we skipped the fourth room for a strong drink in Joe's office. He was pleased with the impact of his little sideshow.

All Paul Getty's establishments were showplaces, except the little room under the eaves at the Ritz, where he did most of his work. We stayed with him for another small chunk of honeymoon after making *Pirates of Blood River*. It was one of the top ten money-spinners of the year. Visiting Paul was a salutary reminder that wealth is relative.

Pirates was a fearsome film to work on. Gitte could well have been widowed. Tarted up with palms and banana trees to resemble the Caribbean, Black Park near Pinewood looked most appetizing. It was a cruel deception. In the middle of the park was a lake more stagnant and polluted than anything in Poe and through this filth and the hazards of sharp underwater obstacles I, as the pirate captain La Roche, had to lead my piratical stars and a cohort of piratical stunt men. The ooze and the sludge and the stench were appalling. Poor Oliver Reed's eyes were so badly affected that he had to be treated in hospital. The lake, without outlets, was in fact condemned. Anyone under six foot was in constant danger of drowning, which meant most of them, and I had a slight advantage there over my shipmates. This was offset by seaboots which filled and made walking right across an immense muscle-racking strain. Where there's muck there's brass. The film did very good business, and Gitte had a touching gift from an admiring stunt man, formerly a notorious tearaway, who personally made her a set of dinner mats as a tribute to her beauty.

With my hips so strained that I could hardly drag myself about, I took Gitte to stay with Paul. The last time I'd stayed at Sutton Place was the previous year when he'd opened it up to a public event for the first time, well described by the press as 'the Battle of Gettysburg'. It had afforded me a great deal of amusement to ensconce myself in a little balcony on the private side, with the photographer brother of Robert Capa, and look down at café society (or Nescafé society perhaps) trooping in for the millionaire's handshake. The party was thrown to celebrate the coming-out of some girl with a military painter name like Constable or Sargent, but she, poor flotsam, was ignored as the celebrants made sure of being photographed for the gossip columns. They went round and round to repeat the handshakes, like ten soldiers in a film instructed to be an army.

Now the place was utterly quiet. Gitte made a huge impression on Paul because she pulled his leg – asked him for the key of the drinks cupboard, wore a fur coat to indicate the rooms were too cold, and borrowed change from him to make him say that he never carried money about. All this was fine, but Paul had one serious weakness – he was a terrible hypochondriac and terrified of any sort of germ. When on the second morning Gitte woke up with a rash that looked like German measles, I feared we should be expelled or at least put in the kennels. For two days I had to keep her in hiding and pretend she was suffering from migraine and nervous exhaustion.

We had fragments of honeymoon also in Rome, Hamburg, Dublin and Estoril. The first three were tied up with films. Only the week in Portugal had no strings. We went to Rome to make *Ercole al Centro della Terra*, with Reg 'Mr Universe' Park as Hercules, and myself as the Satanic monarch of the earth's core, Lico of Ecalia, who turned to flame at the end and disappeared. The posters billed me with Dracula fangs, borrowed by the artist from some other film I'd been in, not unconnected with vampires. That was wrong. But it was an unserious film, widely liked by the Italians, had pretty Leonora Ruffo in it and Mario Bava for director, who looked like Toto and mugged before the camera before saying 'Cut!'

The only sour note of the year came in Hamburg with the completely German, Edgar Wallace-based *Das Rätsel der Roten Orchidee*. I was an FBI agent hunting gangs moved from America to London and fell out with the director openly (which I'd sworn never to do with any director) because he struck me as a throwback to the manners of the totalitarian state. Furthermore he criticized my American-German accent.

The Irish venture had German money behind it, was made in English, included Peter Cushing in the cast (though I never once met him), was called *The Devil's Agent*, used me as a Krupp-like industrialist, put the cast up in a delightful hotel whose suites were all named after Irish writers, and staggered from crisis to crisis as it was never certain whether the money would be coming for the next reel.

What most people would call a honeymoon took place in Portugal. We were the guests in Estoril of the banker Duarte Espirito Santo e Silva, whom I knew through golf. Duarte and I played in Portugal with the pretender to the Spanish throne, Don Juan, Count of Barcelona. It was bizarre to hear people say, 'Good shot, Barcelona!' He was not the best of the royals – that had been Leopold of Belgium, who played off one – but he was pretty good.

It seemed to me that all was for the best in the best of all possible worlds. All kinds of childish pleasures came back in my memory. One day Duarte took Gitte and me to the fabulous Guincho beach, where we bought lobster from a little tin shack which in later years became a gigantic costly hotel renowned for its seafood. We climbed up the rocks of the cliff towards Duarte's house. I reached the top first and looked exultantly down at the two of them down below still climbing. And out of sheer good spirits I selected some well-rounded rocks and bombarded them, dropping each missile a few feet short of them, just to amuse myself. Gitte was cross when she reached the top and said this was the only honeymoon she'd been on where the husband tried to kill his wife. It took me a long while to explain that when I was a boy my chief happiness was throwing things near people, and that I did it in a quite impersonal way.

Swiss Time

A saving on tax was only one of the attractions in our list of reasons for making a home in Switzerland. It struck us that Switzerland was exceptionally beautiful, exceptionally well ordered and exceptionally well placed to be a hub for my expanding commitment to continental films.

We settled on the French-speaking part, and chose a site near Vevey on the northern shore of Lake Geneva. It seemed to us that even if none of Switzerland's huge population of tax exiles ever spoke to us, we could still savour the propinquity of our own kind. We could watch Charlie Chaplin buy a newspaper down the road, and we had hardly installed ourselves before Noël Coward and Marlene Dietrich burst in on me while I was having my hair cut, under the mistaken impression that they would find the director David Lean under the drier. Deborah Kerr was at Mürren, David Niven at Chateau d'Oex, the Burtons at Gstaad, James Mason at Corseaux, George Sanders near Lausanne, William Holden and Yul Brynner in the town, and Brian Aherne a near neighbour at Vevey. And that was without even beginning on the racing drivers.

The Swiss themselves pay high taxes. People who maintained castles and a large establishment of serfs were mulcted, whereas those like ourselves with a small bungalow and an unreliable daily were not hit very hard. Our bungalow, thrown together hurriedly during the building boom for foreign visitors, had cellars and looked pretty, and did not reveal its defects till the winter, when a sort of loggia started to leave the rest of the house, cracks appeared in the walls, the cellar exhaled a chill mist and as the ground subsided we had the impression the whole package would at any time slide down the hill into Lake Geneva.

We had a small garden. Being on a slope with stony, mountainous soil it was not easy to cultivate. Nevertheless a gardener called Bürki came with it, who deserved better than our wretched plot. Commenting on his countrymen's fanatical adherence to rules and regulations he made the only native joke that we heard in three years' sojourn in Switzerland: '*Tout ce qui n'est pas strictement défendu, est formellement interdit.*' (Everything not forbidden is formally banned.) It was the literal truth, treated as a joke. The Swiss made up for only having one joke by repeating it at every opportunity.

We had two cars – a large tourer and a little one with chains on the wheels for local hauls. And we acquired a dog. We called him Bongo, from the Congo, a dog without a bark, from the strange race of the Basenjis. I was devoted to him, and allowed him to become a total tyrant. He was the only talking point of frontier guards wherever we crossed from one country to another.

The very first journey was into East Germany for *Sherlock Holmes und das Halsband des Todes,* based on *Valley of Fear.* It was made in Spandau, with some location shots in Ireland, and it seemed fortune was smiling on our plans. Terence Fisher was over to direct, and a brilliant replica of 221B Baker Street was made on a German stage with everything so much in its place that Holmes's redoubtable housekeeper wouldn't have been able to fault it. Thorley Walters made an excellent Watson, and for Holmes there was me. I looked like him. And I was naturally brusque. We were backed by many eminent German actors. And the sum of it all was a mess.

The sound was unusable. Instead of bringing us back to post-synch it, they dubbed even the English version. The music was awful, a jazzed-up anachronism. I made a Holmesish discovery myself when I had to do a sequence down a sewer with Leon Askin. We thought the smell was a bit stiff even for a sewer and persevered with our enquiries till we found that the place had been used in the war to make poison gas. A superstitious person – like an actor – might have said it had always been an unlucky place.

With Bongo for passport, Gitte and I drove through a foggy night to the dawn ferry to Denmark. Off the autobahns the loneliness was intense. Russian soldiers more than once loomed out of the murk to detain us and argue among themselves whether the speed limit was eighty kph. or only eight.

We surged back from old friends in Denmark for a year of thrills and spills. For once the old public-relations cliché is precise. *Devil Ship Pirates*, directed by the Australian Don Sharp, was the perfect example. My Swiss residence obliged me to ration my English ventures. What time I had, I gave mostly to Hammer. On this pirate lark it was understood my boots stayed dry. I was Captain Robeles, a satanic privateer with no redeeming features.

A full-sized galleon was mounted on sub-surface cast-iron blocks in the reservoir by Egham sandpits. Stepped platforms were rigged on the hidden side for communication between water and deck. The mighty vessel rode there proudly until the launching of the tea-boat. As this came alongside with its trolley and glad cargo, all hands flocked for their cuppa. Their combined weight, added to the trolley, capsized the ship. As she turned, the cables and electricians, the camera and its crew, the technicians and carpenters were hurled into the scummy, inky water. Stunt men and producers alike thrashed about among the wreckage. As the captain I surveyed the disaster from the poop, and thinking that it was my duty to be last off the ship, and that there was no danger money in my contract this time, clung to the shrouds. Twenty years earlier I might have considered saving somebody's life, but experience had given me a new set of priorities. I saved the most valuable article possible: the continuity girl's typewriter. The whole structure took several days to right, so that it could be blown up at the end in a glorious holocaust. I died nastily, shot dead among flaming rigging, and as a bonus my wig caught fire.

Only one other English film could be fitted in before my allocation of time ran out. This was *The Gorgon*. A fine cast made it a promising proposition, and I was a saintly Einstein figure. Alas, like the amiable hound of hell who was meant to fray the nerves of the Baskervilles, the Gorgon in question wouldn't have thrown a scare into anyone. When she came on, through no fault of the actress, she was a sad anticlimax. Patently the snakes in her wig were being run by a remote hand with an electrical kit.

My Swiss time became overwhelmingly Italian. Very weird some of these Italian projects were. It was back to the Odescalchi Castle and Lake Bracciano near Rome and characters spawned by Dracula. *Katarsis* was very hard for those involved to follow. It seemed to be about drop-outs who find an old man in a castle, who turns into the Devil and seizes them, but no one was ever sure. In its efforts to find itself, the film forked into two films, the sequel being *Faust '63*. I was Faust in the first and Mephistopheles in the other, which must have confused the people with the strength to see both.

Then back to wonderful Mario Bava and *La Frusta e il Corpo*. The thrills here depended largely on white flesh and whips and the uses made of them by me, as the Byronic Kurt Menliff, in the imagination of the astonishingly lovely Daliah Lavi. Without leaving that studio, hardly pausing for breath or to collect my pay, I plunged into the character of a scarred SS man in *La Vergine de Norimberga*, where the leading female presence was of the Iron Maiden. As my adored master, a tortured SS general who'd been turned into a living skull, the Yugoslav Mirco Valentin went through extraordinary tortures in make-up. It was quite relaxing, for once, to be able to look at somebody else getting the sticky end of the wedge.

We moved down to a Gothic pile in southern Italy to make *Maledizione dei Karnstein*, a confection of elements of Le Fanu's *Carmilla*, and here it was my pleasure to be Count Ludwig von Karnstein, the noble father of a brood of lesbian vampires. And from there we retraced our steps for a bonne-bouche in the shape of producer Paul Maslansky and his *Castello dei Morti Vivi*. It was my first meeting with Maslansky, who had just got going and had settled straight away into a speed of 145 mph for everything, which pace he kept up for ever after.

Another newcomer to the scene was the Canadian Donald Sutherland, who in the same film was at once very funny as a policeman and very scary as a witch. Fellini's cameraman Tonti was there, waving his stick at everybody. The doomed and clever young Michael Reeves was all the assistants from first to fifth. I was something called Count Drago and we spent much of our working time in a shivery garden replete with statues of gods and demons. I'd liked Maslansky enormously and looked forward to coming back to Rome for the post-synch. He was not only a man in a great hurry but very efficient with it, and it is always reassuring to an actor to know that his own voice will be heard on the screen, because that is the way the producer wants it.

On the trip home I had a disconcerting experience. Late at night between Milan and Stresa we had a tyre blow. Already at this time the fanzines – the fan-club bulletins – in America were carrying the news in their own special argot that 'Christopher and Gitte Lee are infanticipating'. With difficulty I slewed the car to a stop just off the road, put out the warning triangle and walked round to Gitte's window to tell her to stay put with Bongo while I went for help. As I did so, I vanished.

A cutting for a new road ran right beside us. I slid twenty feet down in sand and mud, then clawed my way back up to warn her not to follow my example. Rounding up now to the term of her pregnancy, she went and stood by the triangle, and waved the torch and her silhouette at passing cars. They all ignored her. I made off in the dark towards some lights about half a mile away, back down into the cutting, stumbled through cement and rubbish on the road under construction, tottered through a field of turnips and many other unidentified growing things and fetched up panting by a building near a telephone pole. An Alsatian appeared in the window and let loose a volley of disapproval. A voice shouted '*Chi è là?*' I shouted out my predicament and asked to use the phone.

After a pause the door was unlocked. As I advanced into the doorway I saw a man before me, goggling. I realized that I must look strange, a tall thin man covered in muck from head to foot, but I wasn't prepared for his extreme reaction. He uttered a piercing shriek, cried '*È lui!*' and fainted. The dog leaped in and straddled him, ready to defend him against the apparition, and his wife entered in a great state. It turned out that only the previous night they had seen me as the dreaded Count in *Dracula*.

With this alarum passed, and further excursions in the close neighbourhood of Vevey, I returned alone to Rome for the post-synch. I turned up at the dubbing theatre and found Maslansky and his wife Ninki already there. Paul's demeanour struck me as shifty. He was avoiding my eye, which was unusual in a man who was never taciturn. As soon as I sat down he said, 'Good morning. Roll it!'

As the lights went down and those on the screen came up, I detected him slinking along the seats to the aisle. I had to bend my attention on the job, though. And I found I could not hear myself, either through the cans or in reality. There was no sound. I said, 'Tell him nothing's coming through.'

There was silence. Then the slightly uncertain voice of Paul came out of the darkness, Oh, I was going to mention that.'

As in Hamlet, I shouted, 'Lights!'

When they came on, I said, 'I don't believe it.'

Paul said, 'We have a problem.'

I said, '*You* have a problem.'

'*We* have a problem,' he said fawningly, 'we lost the sound.'

I thought, Oh well, there's always a first time, and said eventually, 'We'd better have the continuity sheets then.'

'As a matter of fact,' said Paul, 'we've lost the continuity girl, and, as I understand it, she'd already lost the sheets before we lost her. Furthermore she didn't speak good English, we never told you that, she wrote nothing down.'

I started to soar towards the ceiling. Up near the lights I looked down at him and roared, 'How *dare* you? Never, ever, ever, ever, in all my long career, have I heard of such a bog-up!'

And just as I was getting into my stride, a glint came to his eye and he interrupted me. '*Listen!*' he yelled. 'I'll have you know I am not just any odd asshole that's rolled in off the street. I'm a producer!'

This great line, better than anything in the picture, convulsed me. Ever after I would do anything for Paul Maslansky, even post-synch an entire picture to a dead screen.

Christina

In Switzerland they say, 'It happens!' When something happens, whatever its nature, they think you should say so. It happened that on the day I drove Gitte, ten days overdue, to the clinic in Lausanne where she booked in for the birth, President Kennedy was shot.

I knew nothing about it. I had flu, and a broken rib from grappling with Bongo. I was preoccupied with Gitte's situation. I phoned the gynaecologist, a charming man from Lausanne, to say we were on our way and was confounded at the door of the clinic, when the woman who opened it said, '*Oh, Monsieur! Oh, Madame! M. le Président est mort!*' and burst into tears. I had no idea what she was talking about, and assumed she must mean the president of the clinic. '*M. Kennedy – assassiné!*' she added.

There was no disputing that this was tragic news. On the other hand it had happened on the other side of the world and we were an emergency on her doorstep. The staff at the clinic was thrown into total disarray by the events in Dallas. I asked for the matron and was told she was watching television. I asked for the gynaecologist and was told he'd given instructions to prepare the delivery room. Everything was ready, except that the anaesthetist was not to be found.

Gitte was taken to the nurses' quarters. They sat her on a hard chair among a cluster of girls watching the story of Kennedy's murder on television. Evidently they had forgotten what kind of place it was and why people went there. They absent-mindedly put a meal in front of her. I protested to the matron, who replied, 'But M. Lee, it's happened.' I had been used to getting the same reply when I protested to the woman who had given Gitte exercises for natural childbirth and at the same time filled her head with stories of rupture and failure. It had all happened.

There was a flurry of movement. The gynaecologist. 'Ah, madame! How are you? Everything will be fine.' We all went upstairs, save for the dog which was left to watch a few reprises of Kennedy's assassination with the nurses. I was left, reeking of flu, to wheel Gitte myself into the anteroom to the delivery theatre. The gynaecologist put his stethoscope to work and said to me, 'That's not going to play.' Gitte said nothing. 'The waters are green,' he said.

'What does that mean?' I asked.

He said, 'That means maybe the child emptied its bowels and might be suffocating. There is a danger the child might die – and your wife.' I looked at him in amazement. He saw no reason not to say these things in her hearing. They had happened.

I went away fuming, and waited, and fumed some more. Then suddenly the theatre nurse dashed down the stairs, poked her head in the door, said to me, 'You have a lovely daughter!' and wheeled about to go back up. I said, 'Oh yes, thank you, and what about my wife?'

She hesitated. 'Oh, she's all right . . . for the present.'

'What do you mean?' I asked. 'For the *present*?'

The nurse said, 'Oh, Monsieur, don't disturb yourself,' and shot back upstairs. But one way and another I was disturbed, very disturbed. I passed a long time with a pleasant American couple whose ordeal was over, when without warning the lift doors opened and a stretcher came out bearing Gitte, all blood and bandages and moaning deeply.

'What's all this?' I cried.

'An operation, an operation,' they said impatiently. After all, the anaesthetist had been found, annoyed because he'd been watching football, and they'd gone ahead as soon as he arrived. I waited by Gitte's bed for her to come out of the anaesthetic, and gradually I was able to tell her that we had a daughter.

This was just sinking in when a nurse came in and said the doctor would like to see me. I stood up and found the surgeon in my way. He said, 'Because the child was relatively large for the size of the womb, and one doesn't X-ray for fear of killing the foetus, she had her feet, instead of being planted against the wall, tucked under her . . .'

I finally grasped what he was telling me. The baby had her feet turned at right angles, almost backwards. I was dizzy with the successive shocks. I had to leave the hospital. I was getting iller by the minute and obviously I wasn't entitled to stay even if there had been any object in it. I drove back not knowing whether to break down or blow up. Out of sheer misery I drank too much and got out of bed next morning feeling that my nervous system was on the point of disintegration.

One look at Gitte's face told me that someone had been before me to speak to her. She said a doctor she didn't know had come in and said to her directly, 'You know, Madame Lee, that your child has been born deformed?'

Hearing this, I went straight up in the air. I lost control. I became hysterical. This was the final straw. I rushed out to find this man and literally screamed at him. They must have heard me blocks away. 'How *could* you?' I shouted. 'Have you no sensitivity *at all*?' The other man came in. I said, 'How dare you just walk in and blurt it out like that?' And he replied stolidly, 'It's true. The truth must be told.' It had happened.

It so happened also that my confidence was severely dented by all this and a week later I took our baby, Christina, to London, having alerted our own doctor, Kenneth Newton. He enlisted the help of a great Australian specialist, Sir Dennis Brown. When he heard Christina's legs were in plaster he said, 'I'm sure that's wrong, but bring her over and we'll see.'

Gitte wasn't well enough to travel. I took the child in a cot. Sir Dennis took the plaster off. He looked at her feet for a while without moving. Then suddenly, with two quick movements, he wrenched her feet round to point in the opposite direction. Christina gave a single, piercing cry, and was quiet again. The girl who came with us went white. 'Nothing so drastic again,' said Sir Dennis, 'but we'll have to give her some aids.'

With the aids, and to some extent relieved by Sir Dennis's prognosis of continuing improvement, I took Christina back to Gitte and our home in Switzerland. For the first year of Christina's life she was permanently in splints, which were connected by a rigid bar, with her feet turned out. The second year she still had the splints but could move her legs up and down, though not outward. In the third year she had them on at night, but could remove them during the day. Gradually she learned to walk, and by infinitesimal stages discarded the splints altogether. She fell over constantly. She was always covered with bruises. But she had the courage of a lion cub, and no hazard deterred her.

By one of those freaks of bad timing which are incidental to an actor's life, the offer to do a Hitchcock television movie for the first time in Hollywood came in the midst of this crisis. My feelings rotated like a whirlpool, of happiness at the birth of our daughter, and anxiety about Gitte and the unexpected complications with which she had to cope. I would at any time have been nervous about my first visit to Hollywood and now I felt petrified. I longed to go, but not to be there. It was horrible to leave Gitte and the twelve-week-old baby behind, but we both felt I should not let the opportunity slide.

I got on the plane. High as it flew, my psyche never got above the clouds. I was a prey to strange imaginings, that I would never see Gitte and Christina again, that the plane would ditch with everything still to do. I'd flown a great deal, quite apart from my RAF days, without any serious worries, but now I was filled with an absolute horror of flying. I was gripped by a phobia which was never to leave me again, despite the experience of flying umpteen thousand miles. It was not the thought of dying that choked me, as I flew towards Hollywood. We must all do that and there was no point in being frightened. It was rather the thought that I would miss seeing Christina conquer and blossom. And I sat there saying to myself, 'So many things I have to do, must do, should do, ought to do, will do. I shan't go. I *won't!*'

But I was already aboard. We were airborne, over the Pole to Montreal. I was met in California by a large car and a man who told me they had booked a room for me in a hotel very handy for work. I'd heard of the great hotels in Los Angeles where stars lazed by the pool for days on end while the film was set up for them. My hotel was a motel, still being built, directly across the street from the gate of Universal. There was a pool but a man my height would have had to fold his arms before diving.

A Slight Hitch

If the pool was tiny, the restaurant of the motel had not yet come into being. I took my meals in a Chinese restaurant alongside. It was a good one, with a hundred dishes to choose from. In the course of twenty-four meals during my Hollywood stay, I ate my way right through them. By the end I could have eaten Hollywood itself with soya sauce.

After an orthodox chow mein start, I tucked up in my first-ever kingsize bed to see what Hollywood was watching on television. The very first image to stare at me from the set in my room was my own. I was just thinking that I should be in a larger hotel, when the phone rang and I heard an English voice I knew, the actor Bob Douglas who was often a heavy in remakes in the *Prisoner of Zenda* class. I was surprised. The last I'd seen of him was golfing at Sunningdale years before.

He said we'd be seeing a lot of each other in the next two weeks. I was even more surprised. Then he explained, 'I'm directing the film.'

'Isn't Alfred Hitchcock directing it?' I asked.

'Good heavens, no!' laughed Bob, as if I'd suggested Winnie-the-Pooh or the Flying Dutchman would be in charge. 'He's only the host. He tops and tails. He never directs. He has a staff of directors, and I'm one.'

After the immediate pang, I thought this would be fine, and never had cause to reverse my opinion. I went to his house and met the female lead playing opposite me, Gia Scala.

I was tremendously excited, and to avoid any chance of an eccentricity on my first day of work in Hollywood, I was up betimes to report on the dot to Bud Westmore in make-up. It was there that I met one of my idols, Groucho Marx. Seeing me in the make-up chair with a high black wig, chin beard and dark clothes, he remarked, 'I bet you played Abe Lincoln many times.' I wanted to chase after him for his autograph, but

Bud Westmore said, 'Forget it. He's not known as Groucho for nothing.'

The studio was literally fifty yards away, across the road from the motel. The gate was like a fortified camp, guarded by armed policemen. Two men peered at me out of a glass booth. I wished I'd had Bongo with me, remembering his success with the frontier guards at East Berlin. In a very ripe Scots accent one of the men said, 'Guid morning. What can ah do for ye?' I said, 'Well, I've come to work here.' He said, 'What d'ye doo?' 'I'm an actor,' I replied. He obviously found this hard to believe. 'What are ye working *in*?' he enquired. *'The Alfred Hitchcock Hour.'* He considered this. 'What's yer name?' he asked. 'Christopher Lee.' He shook his head. 'You don't look like him.' 'I've been told that before,' I said. He thought of another objection. 'Christopher Lee has parking facilities.' Then he peered right into my face. 'Aye. You could be him. Yes, you are. My apologies. In all my years at this studio I never saw an actor arrive except in a car.'

So I was allowed in. Scotty hunted out my parking space, outside Gregory Peck's offices, put up a board with my name on it, and lent me a bicycle. And I went into make-up . . .

There was a Chinese-box effect about my position vis-à-vis this tale. It was by the author of *Psycho*, Robert Bloch. It was filmed as *The Sign of Satan*, based on his story *Return to the Sabbath*. It was about an American producer in search of an actor to play in a macabre film. One day he sees the man he wants in a piece of film about a Black Mass. So he tells his henchmen to get him over to play the lead. They get the actor, but the fellow won't collaborate on publicity. Every day he comes to work, and at the end disappears again to hole up incognito. The reason is that the Black Mass clip was the genuine article and the coven are after his blood.

With the exception of an outing at Bel-Air at the weekend, when I lost eight of Ray Milland's golf balls, two of them in Hitchcock's garden, I behaved a bit like the actor I played in Bloch's story. For radically different reasons. To make an hour-long film in two weeks leaves no time for mistakes, and I wanted to be back punctually with Gitte and Christina.

It was surprising to me on that film that the Americans seemed to include all kinds of routine falls and fights as stunts and when I maintained that I saw nothing arduous in throwing a man over my head, or falling over a chair, Bob Douglas told me that I would have to make good my comments. After I had obliged, my own double remarked that when I had thrown the chair at the window, it had actually gone through the glass. I wondered if he had thought the British had become too effete with the devaluation of the pound and the loss of India to break a pane of glass.

He was a very, very strong young man. Outside the script there were things he could do that I could never have imitated. One day, when we were shooting, an extra 10K light was wanted on the rig. In the great range of lamps used on a film set, from light pups and little inky-dinks, key lights for facial highlights, and bashers on the camera itself, the two-, five- and ten-kilowatts are the last that can be manhandled before getting into the carbons, the arcs and brutes. So when the 10K was called for I expected to see a chain hoist attached and everybody on the floor heave on a pulley to raise it to the cakewalk where the electricians worked. My double took it up a ladder himself in one hand, and placed its spike in the waiting socket.

'Any more parlour tricks?' I asked. 'Karate tricks, yeah,' he said. 'Smash a board with your bare hand?' I suggested. 'If you like,' he replied. I'd not seen it done, but was willing to take it on trust, after his exhibition with the 10K light, which he'd hefted like a bricklayer his hod. Not so my coven, composed of Austrians, who surrounded him like dogs baiting a bear. When he saw he'd have to demonstrate for this gaggle of bit-part Teutons, he was willing to do it for free, but I made him bet each of them a lunch. Then he went through the board like an axe, and lunched free all week.

This was a good chance for me to speak at some length to the Teutons on the subject of karate, and I let them know that the cry he had given had been known to kill a bird in flight, and was designed to paralyse an opponent's reflexes. This finished them off. After that we didn't hear a peep out of them. Shortly after, as I was cycling from the stage to the commissary a large black Cadillac went by, and behind its tinted glass I could see Hitchcock, looking neither left nor right. He was real. That was all I needed to know. Altogether, that was a good day.

I'd had Marlon Brando's dressing-room, the size of a house, I'd played golf at Bel-Air, I knew Chinese food from noodles to Precious Duck, I'd seen Hitch, and we finished the job on schedule. I'd got used to the standard practice of having busloads of matrons come on to the set and watch every move. Best of all, I'd been on a wavelength with the technicians. I could not meet Bloch, but I did meet Ray Bradbury at work in his basement, and he said he wanted me to play Mr Dark, in *Something Wicked This Way Comes*. That never came about, but I did get *Leviathan 99* – his SF version of *Moby Dick*, on to the radio airwaves, and played the Ahab figure in it.

*

There was plenty to talk about in, and from, Switzerland, but as the months passed the talk did not lead to action. Gitte and I were increasingly unhappy there. We had to recognize that we were suffering a defeat. In spite of a row of Italian films, we were not getting the pan-European spread for which we had hoped. On a trip to England I made *Dr Terror's House of Horrors*. It was directed by a first-rate cameraman, Freddie Francis, but we had to admit that a role in a portmanteau film of four stories was no way to keep a name before the public.

It appeared to me that what little I had gained was being thrown away by the restrictions on my freedom to work. I was going through a form of nervous breakdown, without the luxury of men in white coats to beat me up and give me injections. Everything about us seemed heavy, depressing and dull. The Swiss spoke with acumen about work and money, but we were in need of other topics. Everything was tight and buttoned up. Gitte had been through a devastating experience. We fretted all the time about the best course to take with Christina. It was plain that if she couldn't walk very well at the best of times, on our awkward slopes it would be always harder still for her. And when the ice of winter clamped down . . . ?

I brooded savagely. I tried to write, and found myself producing an account of an execution with a guillotine. I walked miles. The snowy slopes seemed to jeer at me – I didn't dare ski in case I broke something and should be unfit for work if it was suddenly offered. Even golf seemed to provide absurd little sour incidents, as when I fell out with an American who insisted on applying the letter of law and penalized me, quite rightly, two strokes for picking up a branch which had fallen over my ball in a sand trap.

Switzerland was no less beautiful than it had always been. The people were industrious and honest. Everything ran on time. The jonquils came out in the spring and the edelweiss too if you cared to hang by your toes from a ledge to look for it. The autumn was lovely with its golds and yellows. But you must be fit to withstand the humid föhn, the undertakers' wind. The comments of the disenchanted came to our minds, especially Van Johnson's, that it's lovely to look out of your bedroom windows and see the mountains, but when they get to the foot of the bed it's time to leave. They had reached the foot of my bed.

We said goodbye to our sunny outlook on Lake Geneva, the great Massif and the Valley of the Rhône as seen from the patio, the Dent du Midi and most of the land between Vevey and Geneva. We needed to reconnect and get a fire going in the abandoned hearth. We fled to a flat in a quiet London square, within a mile of the places where I'd been born, married and had Christina named.

It was on the level of the tops of the plane trees. Not for the first time, the nearby King's Road was becoming notorious, but we hardly felt the vibrations of that. It was very peaceful. We made the walls apple green and came through gold curtains to face the sun. Our immediate neighbour was the delightful, soothing Boris Karloff. In the mews behind lived an owl.

As a fillip to my chronically enervated outlook, the best cure seemed to be a streak of films. I got the part of Ayesha's high priest, Billali, in Robert Day's *She* for the old gang, Hammer. *She* was a perfectly happy film, Ursula Andress was charming, but I carried my burden on to the set with me. I was afflicted by a hangover from my recent experiences, and the sense of personal shambles that goes with them.

There was a scene on an extremely large set of a throne room where I stood while Roman soldiers, obedient to the tyrant, flung endless quantities of victims through a hole in the floor to the flames beneath. I felt totally hemmed in. The sensation was utterly unexpected, the unfamiliar horror of claustrophobia. I actually ran off the set, without pausing to make any excuse.

I rushed into my dressing-room and sank down. Immediately the walls started closing in. Hurriedly I shoved the window open. A wet, grey day slapped me in the face. The sky started to come down. I ran outside and walked about in the freezing rain, still in my priest's robes. After some fifteen minutes the hideous threat dissolved in the downpour and I returned, drenched, to the set.

The relief when the feeling had evaporated made everything else in that film seem like child's play. I had a violent fight with John Richardson in the story, and he thrust a torch into my face, causing me to look like Al Jolson. I felt my old self returning. I had thereafter to make a bid for immortality by stepping into the flames but 'She' transfixed me with a spear before I could make it. I died to the best of my ability. It was like old times.

Hammer and Tongs

The remake of a classic may be worth everybody's while. The sequels rarely are. I never had any sense of embarrassment over the first *Dracula* nor *The Face of Fu Manchu*, where I featured as Sax Rohmer's arch-villain and deadliest of yellow perils. Alas, in the follow-ups to both there was much to make me look shifty and suck my paws. Knowing this, I nevertheless repeated each character many times over. I did so because they were my livelihood. And each time that I convinced myself I should don the Transylvanian mantle or the Oriental robe, I told myself that while you stay on your feet, you can always win the fight. Hope went fifteen rounds with experience, won them all on points, and was knocked out in the last.

Between 1965 and 1968 I was Fu Manchu five times. I was lucky at the crucial bridging time of my return to London to fall so soon into such decisive hands as those of Don Sharp. I was desperately in need of a sure direction, and he was just the man to provide it. As a rule I believed in approaching a new picture with the idea of the script as no more than a guideline, partly because it will be changed and I'd seen actors who were word-perfect completely floored by the differences, and partly because there must be some room for good ideas to sprout spontaneously, but with Don there was no uncertainty. He'd spent a couple of years on a script and when he called the opening shot he had the whole thing worked out to his own satisfaction. He wanted every word on the page spoken and in the same order.

We went to Ireland for *The Face of Fu Manchu*. The author's widow went too, and told me I exactly resembled the man her husband had seen one night in foggy Limehouse, a tall and imposing Oriental, getting out of a Rolls with an elegant half-caste girl, who had given him the idea for the book. North of Beijing, I was told, the Chinese are often as tall as Texans.

The conditions were execrable. The weather was bleak and miserable. Everyone on the unit was croaking under the impact of flu. The elderly German actor Walter Rilla almost died. We worked in a number of ramshackle, dilapidated dwellings abandoned by their occupants and the water ran all the time down the walls.

We worked also in Kilmainham Gaol, which had once housed the Irish martyrs before their execution. I had to make an entrance for my own execution in the film from the condemned cell, and there was concern and agitation from the Irish people that we should not defile the sacred places of this historic site, especially after the tactless use of chickens and goats. I lay in thin robes on the freezing ground with my throat upturned, to give an extra frisson. And to add to the grues of our sensations, just down the road the funeral passed of the patriot-called-traitor, Sir Roger Casement.

The make-up for Fu Manchu was extremely complicated. It took two and a half hours to put on and left me extremely uncomfortable. My features were rendered immobile – I had only my eyes left with which to act. And at that, my eyelids were fixed and I was unable to blink. But I was not disposed to grumble at any of it. My own equilibrium was coming back with my confidence in the picture.

It was a justified confidence. The picture did well. In America it was called *Chop-suey Bond*. Once again tall posters of me appeared on the walls in New York. Nor were they used only to promote the film. It was the time of an election and a number of them were run off by people disaffected with politics and plastered up with the recommendation, 'Fu Manchu for Mayor'. On polling day, Fu Manchu scored a considerable write-in vote.

Fu Manchu at the end of the film had his citadel blown to smithereens. He did not himself die. The echo of his voice, barely anticipating the credits, warned the world that 'The world shall hear from me again'. And the world did. Unfortunately. None of the rest lived up to the pioneer.

Brides of Fu Manchu was tosh, in which an extravagant publicity stunt almost sank the picture. At the instigation of producer Harry Alan Towers, who took an enthusiastic part, and heavily chaperoned by Gitte, I toured European countries choosing from each the winner of a national beauty competition whose prize was a part in the film. They tittuped and titted about the set, draped themselves about pillars in Fu Manchu's great stone den, and between takes some draped themselves about members of the unit. They had careers to advance and beauty is too ephemeral to waste any opportunities. But they could not show themselves off to best advantage because they were not members of Equity and therefore they had not a line to speak between the whole dozen.

The Vengeance of Fu Manchu took me to Hong Kong for some excellent golf, more excruciating make-up and, as an economy measure while there, we simultaneously made *Five Golden Dragons*. Three of my fellow dragons were great adventure stalwarts: George Raft, Dan Duryea and Brian Donlevy. This syndicate of crime had little to do except fly in from all over the world and look like Raft, Duryea, Donlevy and Lee round a table. To liven things up and jerk some expression into all our faces, Raft without warning fired a gun under the table. Later, waiting in his hotel room for his plane home, he talked to me for six hours about his early life. A film of that would have been better value.

Castle of Fu Manchu introduced me to golf in Barcelona, and some spectacular courses in Brazil fell to me with *Fu Manchu and the Kiss of Death*. Never was a picture more aptly named. It was the last. Fundamentally the weakness of the series was lack of trust in Sax Rohmer. The blame did not attach to the directors who took over from Don Sharp. It's always a mistake – the Dracula films reiterated the proof endlessly – to take a plot and try to graft in an extraneous character just because he has box-office appeal. The character must give rise to the story, so it's only logical to go back to the original author for the stories.

Many fine actors contributed to the Fu Manchu business, and even while I sighed over the end results of the productions, I could never dismiss them from my mind as reasons for doing another. Especially there was the little Chinese actress Tsai Chin, Fu Manchu's deadly whelp, who could walk under a five-foot bar and provided a stark contrast as she walked beside me. As we travelled on location it got me many astonished and speculative looks as she addressed me as Daddy. She helped me with the Chinese bits, and reassured me when news came from distant lands of Chinese communities offended by my portrayal of the dreaded Tong leader of fiction. Tsai Chin was the daughter of a very eminent Chinese actor, and her brother was Mr Chow of worldwide restaurant fame, but if one moment more than any other comes back to me it's the sight of her, helpless with laughter one afternoon on the set, after an entire day of failures to say the phrase 'the Essex marshes'. It came out as 'the sex's arses' or 'the messy arches' and other broken fragments, until the scene had to be postponed.

At the time of the first essay in Tong rapacity, I made one after the other, two more Hammer successes, *Rasputin the Mad Monk* and *Dracula, Prince of Darkness*. The first deserved to be a success. They were made back to back. So much so that fans wrote to me recognizing Rasputin's quarters in Dracula's castle and vice versa. Healer and rapist, peasant and seer, Rasputin was a legendary enigma, a real actor's part, one of the best I'd had. From a mass of conflicting evidence, I tried to convey inspired wisdom and grotesque appetites. And I had a long-drawn-out, exquisite death to get my teeth into. We couldn't actually do the death we wanted to, because Prince Yusupoff, that same man that I'd met as a child when my mother woke me to see Rasputin's enemy, would never permit it. Surely it is unique in an actor's life to have met Rasputin's assassins as a boy, to have played the part on screen in 1965, and to have met Rasputin's daughter Maria in 1976 (who said I had his 'expression'). Finally, in 1997, I visited the Yusupoff palace on the Moika canal in St Petersburg, and went down to the actual basement room where the murder took place.

Much gore had flowed under the bridge in eight years since we'd made the original *Dracula*. In this new one I never said a word. I hissed, I spat, I snarled, but no word escaped my ruby lips. I was determined none should. I had read the script. I realized that it was impossible for anybody to write convincing lines for me. Rather than say the lines written down, I said nothing. Occasionally I remarked that Stoker had written some good lines for Dracula, and in subsequent pictures I made a point of borrowing a few from the book to interject when I thought the moment propitious. It was interesting in the aftermath, always, to find that the fans had recognized them.

The death prescribed for me in this one was less imaginative than the first but in the event it was still a memorable piece of shooting. It was based on the superstition that vampires expire if they try to cross running water. Here my own fated ill luck with water affected the outcome. I had to slide down a piece of wood on a hinge, painted white to look like ice, and disappear through the crack into a watery grave. But there was a malfunction. I got stuck, and my stunt double Eddie Powell was trapped under the ice when the hinge swung back, and nearly drowned. That would have been a very serious disaster for me too, as well as Eddie, because he was a double with me on many pictures and a good actor in his own persona. I'd known him from the early Hammer days, when he married the wardrobe mistress Rosemary Burrowes, who called me Nasty and sometimes Green Mould. The camaraderie of Hammer was special, and at times a consolation.

In this hammer and tongs fashion I made film after film to get my momentum going. All actors are unhappy while 'resting'. I had to recognize that the accidents of the life which I've chronicled had made me a compulsive worker. I always looked for some redeeming feature in any script I was offered, and contrived to find one if I possibly could. Anything but hang about. So I made *Theatre of Death* for Sam Gallu, and as he'd once sung tenor with Toscanini we howled snatches of opera at one another between takes. In that I was a theatrical producer drowned for severity by one of his actors.

Then I made *Circus of Fear* at Billy Smart's Circus at Winkfield. I was a lion-tamer and since we dealt in real lions the only double I could have was the real lion-tamer. He gained my great respect when he told me he was terrified of lions. All the shots of him had to be close-ups because he was half my height and they couldn't show him full length unless they wanted to make the point that he'd shrunk through sheer terror. The story was fatuous and I was disguised for nine-tenths of the movie in a black mask.

So, too, I made *The Face of Eve* in Spain, as an explorer reduced to a wheelchair, and died of natural causes. And then I made *The Skull*, based on a better story because it was by Robert Bloch. My lines were few, however, and not Bloch's. Those few Patrick Wymark, with impish humour and his usual impeccable timing, sneezed away in an auction-room scene of rival bidders. Even while wistful at my loss, I had to recognize they were well-chosen sneezes . . .

Storm in a Tee-cup

In spite of all temptations to belong to other nations I had remained, like the fellow W. S. Gilbert sent up, an Englishman. With some alien qualifications, of course, obstinately clung to. I had righted myself, after being blown off course and nearly scuppered. We established a pattern to our lives which was fairly flexible.

Gitte painted, had an exhibition on Madison Avenue in New York, travelled with me on location whenever possible, and generally refused to let anybody in her vast and always expanding circle of acquaintance stand on his dignity. But we agreed never to fly in the same plane. If one ditched, there'd always be a survivor to look after Christina. The element of those born under the sign of Gemini is the air, but I hadn't enough faith in the zodiac to overcome my brooding unease when airborne. Sometimes I came to alarming conclusions about the planes I was travelling in, and got off at the first opportunity. Bringing Gitte and Christina back from a Christmas holiday in Jamaica, after paying a fortune in order that I could play golf for three weeks there in driving rain, I became sure the plane would not make it back to London. I insisted we all get off on Bermuda, and even burrowed into the hold of the aircraft myself to extricate our luggage. It was thought that my reason was an overwhelming desire to taste the pleasures of golf on Bermuda, and I certainly indulged, but the truth was that I was terrified.

To the world at large I was an image made to inspire terror, not to feel it. If the word appeared in the title of a film it was an instinctive reaction of producers to consider me for it. This may have been the explanation for my being invited to narrate *Victims of Terror*, a nice, sensible, erudite documentary on the relics of Pompeii and Herculaneum.

Inevitably, audiences expected me to expire in exquisite pain, or at the least make an ambiguous exit. If I survived, the watchers had the hideous frisson of knowing that like a wounded animal in a cane brake, I was bound to be more ferocious than before when they came up with me. It had the makings of a cult for buffs to see in how many ingenious new ways I could dissolve, disintegrate, evaporate or turn to talcum before their eyes.

In *Blood Demon*, a perfectly dreadful composite of *The House of Legends, Eternal Life, The Hunchback of Notre Dame* and *The Pit and the Pendulum,* I was chastised by having a gold mask driven into my face with spikes attached to it, so that my features resembled a green at the end of a major tournament. I was also torn asunder by four horses, but joined up again to wreak undead havoc. The conclusion, when I vanished like a pantomime king in a cloud of green smoke, can hardly have persuaded the audience that I was dead enough to stay away from their jugular veins when they put the cat out for the night.

The Lord Lieutenant of Buckinghamshire, who presented Hammer with the Queen's Award for Industry, came on the set with it during *Dracula's Risen from the Grave* and stayed on to see me hurtling about with a cross in me, uttering unearthly cries and streaming blood, and remarked to his wife, 'Do you know, my dear, that man's a member of my club!'

Dying as Dracula was usually worse than having a tooth out. Being struck by lightning was the least of my discomforts. The worst was the time they discovered that vampires cannot abide hawthorns. I thought the religious connotation in dubious taste, but a film studio is not the ideal setting to thrash out a theological issue. I had to crash through a tangle of hawthorn bushes with a crown of thorns on my head, with Peter Cushing on the further side waiting to impale me with a stake snatched from a fence. They lacked the foresight to provide a dummy tree and I had to tear a way through vegetation with spines two inches long, emerging for the *coup de grâce* shedding genuine Lee blood like a garden sprinkler.

Bullets, daggers, paper-knives, stakes, darts and lances were embedded in me. Poison, heart failure and old age attacked me from within. I became dust – red, green or sooty. I was drowned, asphyxiated and incinerated, and three times when I was burnt, the barn or studio went up too. I always came back for more. Through clouds of nuclear waste I intoned, 'The world shall hear of me again.' As she grew, my daughter greeted each fresh contract with, 'How do you die this time, Daddy?'

It was not all shot in the same vein, though, as the junky said. The terror merchants came to me, and I put out feelers for variety. This brought in one-offs, sports and windfalls. Like the little science fantasy *Night of the Big Heat.* It dealt with the invasion of Earth by alien protoplasm. Looking like fried eggs, they ruined the climax. They were as bad a letdown as the Hound of Hell and the Gorgon's snakes. They rode in from space on a heat ray. We wanted the illusion of 115 degrees Fahrenheit so Peter, Patrick Allen and I worked in shirtsleeves, and the girls had bikinis. That was fine, except that it was the middle of the night in winter. To foster the impression of sweat we were drenched in glycerine.

After years of urging black-magic themes on Hammer, I had a breakthrough with *The Devil Rides Out*. Conservative, Hammer had always worried about the Church's reaction to the screening of the Black Mass. But we thought the charge of blasphemy would not stick if we did the thing with due attention to scholarship. I appointed myself black technical adviser, as well as playing a goody, and spent many hours in the British Museum guddling for Satanic trout, and came up with a useful catch, notably the genuine prayer of exorcism we used at the end. And I had the friendship of Dennis Wheatley, the author of the story, who lived on the other side of the square from me in Chelsea.

Charles Gray was tremendous as the Satanist, and Terence Fisher and Hammer made a superb job of it. I was delighted. It was a new venture for everybody, and it came off. It did well then, and it had a strong reprise in a cult revival. The terrible vibrations of Evil were clearly felt. It was right to scare people, to put them off the sinister dangers implicit in dabbling with black magic. A new vogue began. And out of it, when I set up my own production company – Charlemagne – to make *Nothing but the Night* with Rank, we were able to get the rights in all of Wheatley's black-magic novels. That Charlemagne effort, based on a John Blackburn story about a possessed girl, failed because it was ahead of its time.

Prancing from genre to genre, like the devil on stepping stones, I made my only Western, when I was nearly fifty, and wished there were more. It was *Hannie Caulder*. It was shot in Spain to look like Mexico, with a tumultuous shoot-out and Raquel Welch, and me as a reformed gunman, complete with cigar and straw hat. Off the picture, however, the people of Almería recognized the demon beneath the hat, hauled the children off the street as I passed, and made the sign of the evil eye.

Erotica was a genre I did not fancy. It was true that as Dr Sadismus in *The Torture Chamber of Dr S* I was surrounded by a sea of nude women, and the effluvium that rose from their bodies as the lights grew hotter was like marsh gas, but I could not believe the picture incited to erotic indulgence.

The day came when a fine-looking woman with red hair called Edna

O'Brien called at my flat in the company of the Finnish director Jörn Donner and placed in my hands a script called *Stud*, the like of which I had never seen. The script was curling at the edges and my hands as they turned the pages did likewise. The beautiful author laid her hand on my arm, gazed in my eyes and said in her delicious Irish voice, 'You have good vibrations!' That was kind, but I felt that it was rather vibrators than vibrations that the part called for; not a weapon that I could use with any dexterity. And when Just Jaeckin in his turn arrived to offer me the male lead in *The Story of O*, I was for once monosyllabic. 'O?' I said. 'No!'

In the cinema, though, an actor can never be sure what he has got himself into until it appears on the screen. I was never so badly off as the actor who was hired to play Long John Silver and then found in his contract that he had to have his leg off, but in the case of *Philosophy of the Boudoir*, I did feel that people were more secretive than past friendship warranted. I only had the part as narrator in the Marquis de Sade's tale of *Eugenic's Journey into Perversion* as a result of an emergency. It was George Sanders's role. I was scrubbing my golfing kit for the weekend when the producer rang from Spain to say that Sanders had opted out through illness, the German substitute Wolfgang Preis had arrived by air, received the news that his wife had been killed in a car smash and flown home again, and would I drop everything and help out? I dropped my clubs and went. I'd be home again on Monday.

At such short notice I did not suppose the Wardrobe could muster anything presentable for the narrator so I took the smoking jacket I'd worn as Sherlock Holmes. This was rich and plummy and was entirely acceptable for the Sade-aesthete.

My weekend was innocuous enough. I narrated away, suffused with the virtuous sense of giving a hand where it was needed. Everybody I could see kept their clothes on. There was nothing a Boy Scout could have quivered at. Little did I know that the woman on the altar behind me was naked, and that as soon as 'Cut' was called, drapery was swirled over her. Little did I know that the same scenes were reshot when I was back in London, and the actors then peeled. Little did I know of the cross-cutting from me to scenes of debauch that would take place. I first knew of it when I heard that despite being only a guest star my name figured at the very top of the credits on a cinema in Soho frequented by a phalanx of men in raincoats. I was peeved. I told the producer so. He said all the big names were doing much more. It was true. That was not, strictly speaking, relevant to my complaint. And then, to my astonishment, within a year something similar happened with *The Bloody Judge*.

Here I was the terrible Judge Jeffreys, handed down all kinds of ruthless sentences against a mild background, and when the film was completed, found myself playing to scenes of extraordinary depravity in the stews. One must shrug. There's no scope for hiring private eyes to vet what is happening in every film when one's back is turned.

That was a strange time altogether for storms in teacups. I went directly from those films to relax in a showbiz golfing event. It was the Sean Connery Pro-Am. Until he had to learn the game for *Goldfinger*, Sean knew nothing of golf. Thereafter it was hard to keep him away from it, and his application made him a fine performer in an amazingly short time. It was always a tonic to play golf in his vicinity. This one he hosted was the big one. He had all the Open Championship field bar Doug Sanders and Jack Nicklaus, and entertainers flew into Troon from all over the world. We played two rounds, and did so in groups of three. I was with Neil Coles and Buddy Greco who'd come six thousand miles. After the first round, the sea mist or fret or haar, which had been troublesome all day, dropped, and a feeling grew up among the entertainers, including Buddy Greco and Rod Laver and myself, that they'd like a practice round. And nobody said us nay. Eight or nine of us went out, making no secret of it, and ours was the only threesome to finish. As we came up the last fairway the pros were all having their dinner and saw us. And most of them peaceably downed their steaks and thought nothing of it.

But the Australian Peter Thomson lodged a formal complaint. It was his right to do so. Practice between rounds is forbidden by tournament rules. In the upshot the Tournament Committee were very much to blame for not persuading Thomson to leave it at most as a token protest. As it was, we all three had notes shoved under our bedroom doors at five next morning, advising us that we were disqualified. It was silly and petty, and caused a great deal of bad feeling. For a long time afterwards it upset me whenever an American asked me jovially, 'What rules have you broken lately?' And when on a golf course Dean Martin said to me, 'Man, you're *evil*!' it took me a minute or so before I realized with relief that he wasn't referring to golf.

Inhuman Bondage

By a kind of knight's move on the chessboard of human relationships, the author of the James Bond thrillers, Ian Fleming, was my cousin. My stepfather's sister Evelyn was Ian's mother, so we were not consanguineous, but it pleased him to call me his cousin, and it pleases me to return the compliment.

I read some of his books, and he took in some of my films. As cousins should. We had the family tree on our mental horizon, but never got too close to it. As cousins shouldn't. We talked, not too intensely, about cloak-and-dagger operations, he from the eminence of his role as assistant to the director of Naval Intelligence in the war, and I from the chilling experience of working in the aftermath with the Central Registry of War Criminals and Security Suspects. His mind was dry and cool – one might wonder if he had ever been shaken or stirred. Like the hero of his thrillers, he could sometimes seem heartless in shrugging away the praise given to able people who had served him well. And he was fourteen years my senior: surveying me quizzically with his cigarette in its tortoiseshell holder set at a slant, he could seem daunting.

However, there was one field of high endeavour where we could meet on level terms. A golf course. Specifically either Sunningdale or, more often, Royal St George's at Sandwich. There we were both members, and he borrowed it, hole for hole, for the epic match at 'Royal St Mark's' between Bond and Goldfinger, changing only the names of the pro from Albert Whiting to Alfred Blacking and of the short sixth from The Maiden to The Virgin. (The film ignored Ian's pious devotion to our club, and filmed the scene on the course at Stoke Poges.)

Long before that, before indeed any of his stories had been screened, he said to me, 'One of my books is to be filmed. Have you ever read *Dr No?* I said that was good news and, yes, I had. 'I want you to play Dr No, if you will. You'd suit the part,' he said. Well, Dr No at six foot six tops me by a couple of inches, but then he wore lifts. Dr No had steel hands, possibly inspired by the steel hands I wore in *Hands of Orlac*, and he was a sinister Oriental, as I had been often enough. So it all seemed quite logical, not merely the idle fancy of a cousin, to pick me for Dr No. 'Great,' I said, 'wonderful!' 'I've asked them to offer you the part,' he said.

I really did look forward to playing this power-crazed character who 'looked like a giant venomous worm wrapped in grey tin-foil'. It would in 1962 have been a spectacular diversion from acting in a German translation of *Valley of Fear* and an Italian one of *Carmilla*. While we were on location in Jamaica, I might have been able to visit Ian at his home there, Goldeneye. But I was to be disappointed on both counts. No call came from the company, Eon, and it turned out that while Ian had asked the producers Broccoli and Saltzman for me, and Terence Young had often directed me, they had in the meantime found Joseph Wiseman to be the slime. And he proved to be class slime. So I never did get to Goldeneye.

Bond succeeded. And Bond succeeded Bond. Nothing succeeds Bond like another Bond. And so it has gone on, beyond even the luxuriant imagination of the originators. Beyond, for that matter, the shelf of stories created by Ian, which now are neighboured by a sequence of imitations by other writers, including Kingsley Amis and John Gardner. Regarded by some across the seventies and eighties as a copper-bottomed disaster for morality, and a role model worse than *The Rake's Progress* for young men, the fantasy Ian created has been the most reliable vehicle in the story of cinema that any actor could want to carry him round the world. And I had missed my chance.

Or so I thought for another ten years, by which time my cousin was dead. But the very durability of the Bond factory led to a high wastage in heavies. Bond can come back from the dead, but his opponents are seriously terminated. And no actor, not even Sir Alec Guinness, could play two different heavies. In 1973 the pool of really offensive heavies must have been low, because I *was* given a second chance. Or perhaps, since Ian had set *The Man with the Golden Gun* also in Jamaica, it jogged the memory of Cubby Broccoli, and he acted on it. That's being a producer, though as it happened the film was switched to Thailand, and that's being a producer too.

It was the director, Guy Hamilton, who gave me the invitation, over lunch at the White Elephant in London's Curzon Street, to play the title role of a nasty piece of work called Scaramanga. Had I read the book? I had, and it dealt with Bond's mission to wipe out this loathsome hit man, whose mildest trick had been to show off his skill with a gun by shooting the pet birds of a woman in a Jamaican brothel. Ian had named him Scaramanga after a contemporary at Eton whom he had particularly disliked. Naturally I said I'd be delighted. 'Ah!' I said. And, 'Finally!' And 'At last!'

'It's a breeze,' said Guy imperturbably.

It wasn't quite that, though it was fun, and for me the winds blew kindly, with a better-written script for Scaramanga than for any other Bond heavy bar Goldfinger. Besides, it was much to their credit that they radically altered the figure Ian visualized, and replaced the lurid thug with a more diverse character, some ambivalence about his own compulsive sexuality (mysteriously linked to his third nipple, which my doctor surprised me by saying is not uncommon), an edge of humour and a sense that he is indulging himself in a great game. This was Guy Hamilton's insight, directing me to play his encounter with Bond as an exuberant child. He said, 'He's like a boy with a toy. Here is the world's most famous secret agent, and you're going to kill him because you think you're better.' I'd like to have had the chance to play against Sean Connery, with his earthy physical presence, but it was surely the right recipe against Roger Moore, with his laid-back style, his charm and wit.

Over the decade Cubby Broccoli had kept many of the same crew together. That's being a producer. Richard Malbaum was still writing the screenplays, Ted Moore was still the cameraman, the special-effects men were ever more specially effective, the stunt men were out-stunting their predecessors. You could go into these films with a virtual warranty for complete success and worldwide recognition. You knew that no expense would be spared except on your own salary, and all production values would be top line. Cubby Broccoli would turn up in a helicopter for the island scenes near Phuket, bringing us all a champagne lunch. That's being a producer.

As the heavy, you also knew that the producers would scour the planet to give you a bizarre sidekick, whose appearance generally suggested a circus background. For me, as a visual joke, they came up with a diminutive Frenchman, Hervé Villechaize. He had no great film record, nor regular engagements with other midgets or dwarfs. But he looked like a miniature Edward G. Robinson, and had the vigour of six, with the promiscuity of six for that matter, as if he wanted to make the most of every second of a life that would not be very long. The dawn sometimes saw him in terrible condition, so that I feared for his health. But, as the sun rose, so did his stature, such as it was.

Hervé gave me a melancholy explanation of his condition. His father was a famous surgeon in France, but had been powerless to save his mother, a French Resistance worker, from being tortured by the Gestapo, and she was then pregnant with him. Likewise he explained the odd regular scars on his arms as the result of being bullied as a child in New York. I didn't know whether to believe either of these stories, but obviously they would do for the purposes of our professional connection, and he was often very amusing. The film launched him into a television series called *Fantasy Island*, in which he played a similar character, but the further account is sad, because he had the reputation of a complete monster, and committed suicide. It appears to me now that those golden weeks in Thailand working with us may have been to him like a layer of honey between a sour past and bitter future.

We moved to Bangkok for the most interesting, and certainly the most dangerous, sequence in the film. In the phenomenology of Bond stunts, there's hardly a case study to match the feat of Bumps Willard in vaulting over a Bangkok klong, or canal, while the car somersaulted through 360 degrees. It was so well done that many people in the audiences still think it was fake. But every second was for real. They had the dummy figure of Bond on one side, and the dummy of the Sheriff on the other, while Bumps lay beneath the steering wheel in the middle, covered in a black outfit and mask. He was down on his stomach holding the wheel, controlling brakes and accelerator with his feet at the back, watching the speedometer so that he could hit the broken-down part of the bridge at the necessary angle, at precisely 31 mph.

It was perfect. All three cameras got it perfectly. When the car stopped, Bumps got out, with the stark face I've seen on men returning from a tough mission in the war. Guy Hamilton exclaimed, 'That was absolutely wonderful, Bumps! In fact it was so wonderful that I don't think anyone's going to believe it wasn't a trick. Would you be prepared to do it again?' And Bumps replied in his rich deep-South drawl, 'I would not. Because that is the first time I've ever done it, and I ain't going to do it again!' His support team from the Houston Astrodome under the leadership of Jay Milligan would endorse his decision. Cubby had to buy their act for a year, and at about a quarter of a million dollars he thought it worth it. That's being a producer.

The rest had been done in Pinewood Studios in England, where we did the routine Bond destruction of the entire set, doing the end of the movie first, and Scaramanga's duel with Bond, in the Fun House, which I thought was clever. What we shot, on what is now known as the James Bond island, was me looking devious as I walk towards the camera, then disappearing out of the frame. I'm actually hiding in the rocks, so Bond fashions a Molotov cocktail and lobs it into the air. But I see it and shoot it out of the sky. My last bullet! as Bond supposes. But lo! I have another in my belt buckle! Excellent scene.

And they cut it. Removed the whole sequence from the film. Well, you can't have everything.

Have Gun, Will Travel

A promotional tour on behalf of a major film such as *The Man with the Golden Gun* is harder than shovelling snow, and not so healthy. The American trip that I made with the beautiful Maud Adams and Hervé in 1975, ricocheting from city to city to city, was bound to be more about the Gun than about the Man. But *noblesse oblige*.

I had a love/hate relationship with the Gun. I should say the Guns, because there were three. One, after much practice, you could take apart and reassemble. The next was like any other gun except for the pretence of being gold, and unable to function. The third functioned, but pitifully: it was capable of firing a cap, so you got a flash from the muzzle – sufficient, in the world of make-believe, to kill the Chinese Chairman Hai Phat. (A nice change for the delightful Chinese actor Richard Loo to play a Chinese, when he was usually cast as an insidious Japanese.)

Now the number-one Gun was 100 per cent gadget. An armourer's brainstorm. It consisted of a cigarette case, a lighter, a pen and a cuff-link, all complete and workable away from the weapon. It was a cute invention, but taking them apart and putting them together again was exceedingly difficult, especially when I had to time it with what I was saying, and without looking at it. I'm not very good with my hands, except when holding a golf club or the hilt of a sword. I would drop one of the bits. Or not finish in time. Or it would get stuck. Props need to be kept in their place and this was a very important prop. The entire picture revolved about it. Now I foresaw glumly that the whole promo tour would also revolve about it.

I arrived to meet my colleagues in Los Angeles with the wretched thing in pieces in a box. Despite their innocent appearance I thought I'd better declare their true nature to customs, because customs people can be very mean if they sense that they're not being let into a secret. I opened by announcing myself as due to fly the flag on *The Johnny Carson Show* for a new film called *The Man with the Golden Gun*.

'Oh, yeah, I read about it.'

I said I wanted to make it absolutely clear, gentlemen, that I was that man, and I had the Gun with me, and furthermore it was not a real gun but a fake; it couldn't function.

'We better take a look at it.'

I said I would slowly open the box, and they could see it was all in pieces.

'We better see how these pieces add up.'

I explained the operation as painstakingly as a corporal introducing a firearm to recruits. I opened the cigarette case, flicked the lighter and demonstrated that the pen would write. I put them together and pulled the trigger, which was the cufflink, and pointed out that nothing happened.

For the same reason, I suppose, that it hooked the Johnny Carson team, they swarmed round it. They took it and wouldn't give it back. 'We've got to take a look at it. Then, maybe . . .' I protested that on *The Johnny Carson Show* they would expect me to *show* it. 'Sorry, got to take a look.' They wouldn't give it back, and who would argue? They have guns of their own.

Unarmed, and in single file, as Victor Borge would say, we went on *The Johnny Carson Show*, which was hosted that night by an acolyte called Joey Bishop. Everything that could be known about our film was set out in bite-sized portions on his cue-cards, to prompt his questions. He ignored them until I mentioned my reason for being there. 'Could we see the gun?' he asked.

'If you ask the US customs you'll find it *in bond*!' I retorted in a Pooterish way. Nobody got it.

He consulted his cards and suddenly said, 'It says here you can sing.' I wondered what that had to do with the film, but I let rip with some Iago, which drew a round of applause from the band, and a blank otherwise.

After this inauspicious beginning we left in the morning for San Francisco, arrived at noon and off at once to all the TV stations, local press, through lunch, after it, through the afternoon and back to the airport. We went from LA to San Francisco to Denver to Dallas to Atlanta . . . overnighting in every other city, and repeating the process every single day. In the lobby of the hotel in Dallas I was waylaid by a man with a suitcase, which was brimful of original posters of films I'd been in, and he had me sign every one of them, while the organizers of our tour fretted. But, never give short shrift to a fan, I felt. When he'd gone they scolded me. 'Do you realize what you've done?' 'Signed some posters,' I replied. 'They're originals,' they said. 'He can get five thousand dollars for a signed original.' I only wished I'd had the foresight to have saved a few for myself: it doesn't occur to you that a scruffy sheet of second-rate artwork will one day be worth more than the finest Turkish kilim.

In Dallas, the Gun caught up with me, and nearly precipitated my downfall. Carrying it openly and absent-mindedly down the street towards a TV studio, I heard a bellow: '*Drop it!*' I spun round to find a cop aiming at me. Without a trace of the suave and condescending manner of Scaramanga, I shouted, 'It's not a real gun! I'm an actor! I'm appearing on television. I'll show it to you, show it to you!' He looked at it and I'll say this much for him that, having studied the gold plate, he could recognize a fake at close range, and let me proceed to examination from the next talk-show host.

In Fort Worth, same process, but we had lunch in the Petroleum Club where the billionaires eat. I wanted to meet the golfer Ben Hogan in his factory nearby. They said, 'Don't be ridiculous, you're promoting a film.' Next day in Atlanta we had a day for sleeping, but I asked for and got a car and chauffeur to take me to Augusta where, for the only time in my life, I played the Masters Course. (Not a demanding course off season – they make it much harder for the championships.) Next morning, Chicago, back to the process. Then New York, same process. Leaving my room in the Sherry Netherland, I faced Billy Wilder, coming out of his room. Seeing the Gun, he cried, 'You wouldn't shoot an elderly Jew?'

I don't know what impact all this had on the box-office. I'm told that over the years Bond films have made far more money in the rest of the world than in the USA. This may be attributable to the rest of the world being much larger but it is also, I feel, because most of the characters are English, and Establishment English at that. But, for what it may not have been worth, such was the promotional process. It did not include being allowed to keep the wretched gun, though I dropped broad hints.

As a rider to this episode, I must add that *The Man with the Golden Gun* was the first Bond movie to be shown in Moscow, albeit not to the public. Cubby Broccoli put on a private showing for Soviet officials. That's being a producer. One of them came to him at the end and said, 'That man Scaramanga – interesting!' Cubby waited, while the Russian's eyes bored into him. Then the Russian added sternly, 'Inadequate training.' Because he was killed. My Russian friend can have had no idea how much training it takes to die well. It would never have happened in Department 8 of Directorate S of the First Chief Directorate of the KGB.

The Way Ye're Hitting Them

cting has been good to me. It has taken me to play golf all over the
world. Every sane production schedule fixes its location work near
a good course. Golf is the habit more actors have in common than
any other. In the words of Oliver Hardy to Stan Laurel, '*You* work it
out, *you* set it up, and you know where you can find *me*.'

On *Blood of Fu Manchu* we played at Itañanga near Copacabana, and
it took us three hours to get through nine holes. On *The Private Life of
Sherlock Holmes* we stayed at a hotel on Nairn course itself. On *Castle of
the Living Dead* we played at Olgiata near Rome with the sun on our
backs. As I grew older I played better with the sun out, especially after
injuring my back when turning round to wave goodbye in the doorway
of an aircraft. On *Nothing but the Night*, made near Dartmoor, we
played at Thurlsdon. At least, I played. Peter carried my clubs and, great
ornithologist that he was, constantly electrified me with cries of 'Look,
there's a throstle-pated gurk!' or 'A blue-cheeked sandthruster!' We
were spotted, ourselves, near the course and accused by an angry man of
trespassing. He said he would inform the landlord. We said we'd talk to
the landlord; where was he? He said, 'I don't know where he is, but his
name is Charles.' 'Charles, eh? Charles what?' 'Prince Charles.'

On *The Man with the Golden Gun* I nearly stepped on a cobra at the
seventeenth green at Nava Tanee. A snake in golf parlance is 'a loose
impediment'. One may pick it up. On *The Five Golden Dragons* we
played at the Royal Hong Kong, otherwise Fanling. That was the
qualification for the Fanlingerers Club in Edinburgh, a charity for blind
people. On *Whispering Death* we played at Elephant Hills and were up
to our waists in dangerous warthogs, a hazard taken into account by the
designer Gary Player, who named a hole after them. He also named
holes after elephants, impala, waterbuck, baboons and various other

fauna. Often in Africa the caddies carried brooms to sweep the greens flat after we'd putted.

On *The Devil's Agent* I played at the Royal Dublin against Christie O'Connor Sr. Very competitive, with a superb wristy swing, and masterly in the wind that comes off the bay. I was playing to my handicap in those days, which was one. When we got on the last tee after a tremendous battle, he was in grave danger of being beaten on his own track – he'd given me four shots. He said, 'You'll need all your poise here.' The eighteenth is a dogleg. He added, 'The pin's on the right, the line's on the left. You have to hit over the out-of-bounds area.' I unleashed an enormous drive. He said quietly, 'That's in the ditch.' I said, '*What* ditch?' He put in his tee and said, 'Oh, didn't I tell you? It turns all the line of the out-of-bounds.' He beat me by one stroke.

On dozens of films I kept myself within bounds because of my access to the local golfery. I imagined that golf helped my work, and that work helped my golf, and in both I went on marking off the milestones. My first hole in one came at the thirteenth, during the Autumn Medal of the Berkshire, when I was fifty. The second was well publicized because it happened in a Pro-Am at Dalmahoy – 181 yards with a three-iron.

And after all, via the unexpected doglegs of fate, I became an England captain. It was through the artificial business of Pro-Am showbiz for TV. Nevertheless I can claim the glory of an England captaincy. And we won, our team playing against Captain Dick Martin and the Americans.

Actors are expected to enjoy appearing before a big crowd. Many of them do, and think it was what they were born for. But it is one thing to appear in make-up and costume, with the support of a director and rehearsals, quite another when your only defence is a golf club that may very well betray you. So when in 1982 I turned out for the Million Dollar Pro-Am tournament in South Africa's Sun City – golf course by Gary Player – I was unnerved to discover the game's followers not only around the greens, but all the way there from the tees, on either side of the fairway, like an Open Championship. I remembered what Richie Benaud had once said to me as we walked to the first tee in another Pro-Am, that he felt more nervous than when going out to bat in a Test match at Lord's, but this was something of another order altogether.

I told a marshal that he should advise the crowds to watch themselves, as I might very well stray off line rather more than the brilliant professionals I was teamed with. And to prove my point I just missed one eager fan's head by a foot or so, which made them all draw back. The format here was two pros with one celebrity amateur in a three-ball. As they were playing for serious money, a million-dollar first prize, they were not likely to come in and help me, or the likes of Peter Falk or Cameron Mitchell, or even Rear Admiral Alan Shepard, famous for hitting a golf shot while on the moon, if we put one in the trees or the long grass. However, over the four days I was teamed in turn with Ray Floyd and Lee Trevino, then with Gary Player and Johnny Miller, next Seve Ballesteros and Jerry Pate, and finally Greg Norman and Jack Nicklaus. On that last day I shot 75, and ceased envying Shepard for his moonshot, or even Ray Floyd who won the million dollars by one stroke from Craig Stadler. A Pro-Am should be fun and good golf, and after the first hole it usually is.

Playing before the cameras is unnerving, because they wander all over the course and may take twenty minutes before they're happy with the way they're set up and let you get on with the shot. When you address the ball, you've already played it in your mind forty-three times, and now manage to invent a forty-fourth. You lose rhythm and concentration. Playing with Billy Casper against Doug Sanders and Henry Cooper, it took us eight and a half hours to get round the course.

However ill you may be, if you've been advertised, the crowds expect you to turn out and enjoy yourself. Once, weak as a kitten from flu, I turned out and staggered along as if stoned. In trying to blast my way out of a sand-trap I fell flat on my back. I heard a woman say with disgust to her friend, 'They're all the same, these actors.'

To preserve your amateur status you can't be paid for making a film about golf. On the other hand it's pleasant to combine work and play, as long as it doesn't become a habit. So I made a half-hour film about golf with Peter Alliss, for British Airways. They were advertising their flights to the sun in winter, and showed Alliss and Lee getting on and off planes at Marrakesh and Mount Irvine Bay in Tobago.

That, and our games, was not quite enough to hold an audience, so we had to have a story. The story was about slow play, the bane of modern golf – though we might equally well today make a repeat about fast play, in buggies. The thought was that millions of people were seeing the great players prowl about the green and line up their shots from both sides and feel they must do the same. The pro has to examine the borrow (or 'break', as they call it in the USA) and the nap, and besides makes most of his calculations en route to the ball. The amateur starts testing the wind and reading the barometer and making five practice swings when he gets there. And everybody goes mad, waiting. In a word, the film was about etiquette. That I, of all people, should be its standard bearer, speaks volumes for what the game can do in the way of mellowing a man.

The clubs I used were the ones I have taken with me everywhere since Arnold Palmer gave them to me, having had them specially made to suit my overlong, over-English and unfamiliar shape, at his factory in Chattanooga, Tennessee. Once again I struck lucky at the Savoy, when I met him there for the first time in the company of Mark McCormack. He came next day to dinner. The Everyman of golf, he became a folk hero because, though a great champion, he was capable of hitting the ball out of bounds over a railway station. We got on well, became firm friends, and he promised me a game. He kept the promise, after a trip from Scotland, even though he'd just come through a gruelling tournament. He gave me five strokes, which was just enough for me to beat him at Sunningdale, and paid up the twenty pounds of our wager, which was the highest sum I'd ever played for in my life. Then, on his own course of Bay Hill, he won it back with a vengeance, though, as I said to him, it would not have been so easy if the clubs I'd borrowed had reached the ground. And he gave me the magnificent set I treasure.

Among many memorable American courses, wonderful Bel-Air in Los Angeles was my own club. But altogether I must have walked a million miles across others. Such as Jack Nicklaus's own course at Lost Tree Village and Loxahatchee. And then Seminole, which seemed to bring out the best in me. And awe-inspiring Pine Valley, New Jersey, deliberately designed to bring out the worst in anybody. They used to bet you that you couldn't break 100, no matter what your handicap. They don't rake the bunkers, and there are bushes in them beside the green. The ninth green is prefaced by a tiny little pot bunker known as the Devil's Arsehole.

My initiation was given me by its uncrowned king, Ernie Ransom III. It was very hot and humid, and I was worn out after the struggle to coax the ball through this strange environment. You walk and walk and walk; nobody dreams of using a buggy. Staggering back into the lift at my hotel, I felt I could hardly last another minute without a shower and a drink. But I couldn't ascend until the lift had been more than filled by a stampede of Hasidic Jews in long black coats and hats and sidecurls. When I pressed the button, nothing happened. I pressed again and still nothing happened. 'Oh, what are we waiting for?' I muttered petulantly. The man on my right answered. 'The Messiah.' Perhaps He was stuck in a bunker at the eighteenth.

Of the hundreds of courses I've known, the notes of purest joy have been struck when I have played the hallowed ground of Augusta National, and my own club at Muirfield. The great gap in my experience was St Andrews. I'd been playing for quarter of a century without ever knocking divots out of the sacred turf of the home of golf. I mentioned this wistfully at dinner one night while staying at Grey Walls near Muirfield and next day a young Scot named Duncan McGregor rang to say he felt this tragedy should be rectified. He'd booked a time, seven minutes past one, and a caddie for me. 'Oh yes,' I said, overjoyed, 'I must have a caddie who knows every inch of the shrine.'

We arrived late, in a lather, and I cantered to the tee with a piece of cold pie clenched in my jaws and carrying my clubs because the caddie hadn't shown up. A starter like an angry bee stuck his head out of his sentry box on the first tee and complained to the skies, 'What about m'times, m'times?' He caught sight of me. 'Are you McGregor?' I thought I'd better be. 'Ye ... es,' I said in terrified tones. 'Well, McGregor, what about m'times?' I said I had no caddie. 'Can't help that,' he said, 'if you don't go off at the right time, you'll have to wait till seven at night. Because m'times are m'times.'

Duncan thundered up with a trolley, but no caddie. We had to drive off. Then the ground shook, I was nearly knocked over by an auburn fog of usquebaugh, the water of life, and turned to find an enormous old man, six foot two in all directions, in Army boots and a windcheater. He looked ready to fall at my feet like the oak of Avernus. The starter slammed his window down. The old man said, 'I'll just put this wee bag on m'wee trolley. Sorry ah'm late, but my bruither just died.'

He drew out my driver, pointed at the famous Swillican and said, 'Aim it left, at yon burn.' I hit a low whistling hook, heading straight for a group heading up the eighteenth fairway. The old man bellowed 'Fooare!' loud enough to be heard in Banff, and two elderly Americans and their caddies flung themselves to the ground. 'Aye,' said my caddie, 'if ye hook at St Andrews ye be all richt. If ye slice ye'll never be out of trouble.' They were true words. Gradually things returned to normal.

'Ye look at if ye'd served in the Forces,' observed my caddie. I said, 'As a matter of fact—' He cut me short. 'I was in the Indian police,' he said. 'I was a sergeant. I made the boogers jump!' I believed him. From time to time he handed me a club which I knew was at least two out, and I'd feebly protest, 'I can't get there with a seven-iron, I'd need a five.' He'd sweep this aside. 'Och! The way ye're hitting them, ye'll do it easily!' I played the whole round like that.

Every now and again the old man would vanish for 'a wee in the whins'. Plainly, from his stertorous breathing and glazing eyes, he took liquid on board simultaneously. This went on until we reached the famous Road Hole, where the hotel appears to be right in front of you. You think you have to hit right over the top of it. I actually hit the hotel with my tee shot, and the ball came to rest over the porch on a piece of netting put there for that purpose.

The old man rushed me up to the entrance and shoved a club in my hand. 'I'd have to get into somebody's bedroom to hit that,' I objected. 'Och, not the way ye're hitting them.' The manager turned up and said angrily, 'Where do you think you're going?' 'My man's going to play his shot,' said my caddie. 'He's not, you know,' said the manager, 'we'll get his ball for him, that's all.' I dropped a ball, and got a six on the hole.

And so to the eighteenth. It's enormously wide and theoretically you can't get into trouble. The green looks to be on the other side of Scotland and you think of Jack Nicklaus driving it when he played Doug Sanders in the play-off for the Open Championship. I said, 'My God, I'll really have to hit one here.' My caddie said, 'Don't hit it to the right.' On the right I saw a row of buildings including the New Clubhouse, plus a road and a lot of cars parked. I said, 'I'd have to be pretty wild to slice it *there*!'

My old caddie said, 'Well, I did once hear tell of a gentleman who sliced his drive very badly indeed. It soared over the fairway and the road, pitched on the roof of one of yon cars, bounced off to hit the New Club wall, bounced back on the roof of another car and all the way back into the middle of the fairway. The gentleman got his four.'

I then produced a replica of the gentleman's shot. It crashed on a car, hit the New Club just above the window so that all the members sprang up in alarm, clattered back over the car roofs and fetched up in the centre of the fairway. I thought of insurance. 'What do I do now?' I exclaimed.

'Ye do nothing. Look neither richt nor left,' advised my caddie, 'but march up to yon ball with a five-iron, and hit it on the green.' I did. I got my four. My card read sixty-eight. I thought that wasn't at all bad, in the circumstances.

Black Limelight

The best publicity can't be bought, nor calculated, nor even worked for. It just catches you up and gives you a ride on the magic carpet when you weren't contemplating going anywhere in particular. For me the lift came when a fan of the old mainstream macabre cropped up who'd done rather well for himself in another gory line: Muhammad Ali. A tall fellow, he could look me in the eye. Evidently he liked what he saw because I narrated and introduced his television life for him: *Muhammad Ali: Truth Victorious.*

Ali is not only the greatest, he's the most generous. Our first meeting chanced through my hearing from Jarvis Astaire that he'd like to meet me. So I took him up on it, and met him at his hotel in Cleveland in March 1975. He said, 'It really *is* you! I never thought I'd meet you. Now stand opposite me and give me that *look*.' And I said, 'What look?' 'You know,' he insisted, 'that look you give people on the screen and it chills the very marrow in their bones.' I said, 'I'm not standing opposite you giving *you* any close looks – I know what happens to people who do that.' But they got us together, literally nose to nose, and I waited for the colossal fist to end the party. Then he gave a shriek, doubled up, half laughing, half serious, saying, 'I just can't look, I can't . . . I'm going to die!' He called his entourage round, and built *me* up as 'the greatest', and offered me Chuck Wepner's scalp at the end of the World Heavyweight Championship fight about to take place. And to my astonishment he *remembered* his promise in the midst of the turmoil in the ring when his arm went up at the end. I was in Hugh Hefner's home watching on close circuit with some of the tallest (Wilt Chamberlain, basketball's 'Wilt the Stilt'), strongest (OJ, then OK), deepest (Linda Lovelace, the kissing extremist) and mostest of show business, when a journalist asked Ali, 'Any message for your fans, Champ?' and he said 'Yes, indeed I have – I won this fight for them, and for Christopher Lee, out there, watching me.' And I might as well have gone home forthwith, because one could tour a thousand whistlestops promoting a film and never get together as much promotion as Ali bestowed in five seconds.

It came at the right time to cheer me up, because although I'd just been fronting two commercial juggernauts, the roles that I was subsequently being offered did not seem to be broadening my horizon. Absurd as it may sound from a person who sees his travel agent almost as often as he does his family, I felt restless. And, I had an inkling that time was passing.

On certain days, when the telephone was silent, it appeared from the windows of our flat in London almost visibly to be passing, leaving its message in the changes in the plants in the gardens below. The silence was broken only by the sound of my daughter Christina playing records of the Osmonds. So, since underwork has always put a severe strain on my nervous system, and 'needs must when the Devil drives', and the Lord helps those who help themselves, and all that stuff, I had my own company Charlemagne organize with Rank and Hammer the production of Dennis Wheatley's *To the Devil a Daughter* (of that, more anon), which we eventually made for £350,000 with Richard Widmark and Nastassja Kinski.

And yet these were only stays in the execution of a plan that Gitte and I had gradually formulated. The people we might have talked it over with a decade earlier, the men and one woman a generation older than me who'd been my benefactors, were no longer there. In our ten years in London, beginning with Joe Jackson, all five had died. Uncle Walter struggled gamely on to eighty-three before succumbing to a long and painful illness. I had to get used to making funeral orations about Boris Karloff, whom I'd loved dearly.

Niccolò also made old bones, worked at his scholarship into his eighties and died with his Seneca translation at his bedside. Before he went, his ambassadorial instinct was exerted once more on my behalf and he arranged an audience for me with Pope John XXIII. Most men are of short stature to me, but His Holiness fell even shorter of the norm. I was nervous as I couldn't make up my mind whether to kneel or bow, and looked like a giraffe off balance. The Pope leaped at me saying, 'I hope you're not going to kneel. In the first place because it would take forever for you to get up, and in the second place people will think you're frightened of me.' He gave me a little pat. Niccolò himself, an inveterate talker, couldn't get a word in edgeways. Every time the Pope invited him to talk about the Carandinis, he'd jump on Niccolò's first phrase and launch himself on an anecdote of his own. Finally he said,

'There you are, I'm not free here, I can't do what I like. I never get a chance to talk to anybody.' He rushed off and the audience was over.

The thirteenth Marquis of Sarzano also died, and his son took over at the central hearth of the Carandinis in Parella in the Val d'Aosta. Tradition had it that all the bells of Sarzano should be rung whenever the count entered, but possibly that grand gesture in the sleepy little village had been abrogated since the Pope curtailed the privileges of the Black Nobility.

Paul Getty died in his eighties also, in 1976. It was not so long since Gitte and I had stayed at his museum of a castle called La Posta Vecchia, near Rome. Our favourite last image of him was when we dined with him at Herstmonceux Castle and someone asked him how it compared with Sutton Place. He rose in his dinner jacket to pace it out from one end to the other. He was just into the flower beds when we suddenly heard him say, 'One . . . two . . . *My God, there's a photographer!*' And he scooted back in before the press could cook up some tale that would radically alter property values.

So they had all gone, except Mother, who was still going strong, and emphatically in place, waiting to see the Silver Jubilee of Queen Elizabeth II in 1977, to compare and contrast it with the Diamond Jubilee of Queen Victoria that she'd witnessed in 1897. My sister Xandra, an equally firm monarchist, would keep her company in this, along with her second husband Dermot de Trafford, a most civilized person with genes handed almost personally to him from the Norman Conquerors, whom we can assume to have played golf on the run, since that was Dermot's style.

And Christina, our only younger generation, was at a boarding school, and liking it. We had taken a deal of criticism for sending her, but we felt that being with children her own age was the priority. She was growing up with a very winning personality. She had gone through years of being in splints and then, at the Children's Hospital in Great Ormond Street, the specialist Lloyd Roberts decided on a further operation because her heel was too high off the ground. She was in plaster afterwards for months, and Roberts said there'd be no need for any more. Her bravery was astonishing.

On her one trip to California she had had a very happy time, so when we told her that we meant to rent out our flat in London and move, lock, stock, barrel and Christina, to California, she thought she could give it a go. The feeling that I had somehow come to the head of the queue coincided with a deep wish to do something a little bit different in the cinema.

Over a period of some years, friends and colleagues in Los Angeles had insisted that I was not advancing my career by staying in Britain, where I was in danger of being typecast. Billy Wilder was one of the first to encourage me to move to America, but it was Richard Widmark who finally convinced me that this was the obvious decision to make. That is, quite simply, to become a part of the American film and TV industry, where I knew there were infinitely more opportunities for me to extend my range and versatility. The die was cast.

In at the Deep End

We took almost everything: furniture, books, pictures, Osmond records – it's amazing how much fits in a container. Leaving customs officials in Los Angeles to ponder my reasons for having so many swords, we went there via Paris, to mop up some available work. Well, I thought, it's soon going to be *adieu* to all that *marchandise*.

What we gained from renting out our flat in London was instantly annihilated by the cost of our flat in Los Angeles. You don't rent in the Wilshire Boulevard (known today as 'the Golden Mile'). You buy. Furthermore it's where all the richest and most powerful people in LA have their gigantic pads, though actually we were on the eighth floor, with a deep draught of smog directly we opened a window. There was, however, a savoury view of the Hollywood Hills draped in sunsets.

As a prologue to our life there, my agent told me that a signed contract meant nothing in Hollywood, actors were bilked and shafted wholesale on a daily and weekly basis. And we were still hanging our pictures and curtains when he came on the line again to say that Universal were 'quite interested' in having me in *Airport 77*, playing an oceanographer whose job is more interesting to him than his wife. This project was the follow-up to *Airport* and *Airport Two*, and there was no need to get into a discussion about what type of movies these are. They are what they are, disaster movies. The scenario this time was that the passengers of a jet are trapped in an air bubble when their plane ditches and submerges, a situation never imagined by actual cabin crews when they tell their charges how to behave in the event of a crash in the water. The list of famous players could be recited like a mantra: Jack Lemmon, James Stewart, Joseph Cotten, Olivia de Havilland, George Kennedy (up for a third dose of Airporting), Lee Grant (who was to be my wife in the story) – and they even squeezed in some up-and-coming young people such as Kathleen Quinlan. The very first name sold it to me: I was to have a scene with Jack Lemmon.

The producer, Bill Frye, came clean with me about this scene. 'If you accept this role, you'll notice there's a scene where you go into the hold of the 747 with the pilot, Jack Lemmon. You're fiddling around in there when the door to the hold blows and this great Niagara of water comes in, which drowns you. You're all tangled up in the canvas webbing that they put the luggage in. He's all right. He comes over to try to revive you. But you die. You do realize you'll be doing this?' I was preoccupied with the joyful thought that I'd have a scene with Jack Lemmon. And I supposed I'd be six or eight feet down, at most. 'Of course,' I replied, 'piece of cake.' Frye persisted: 'You'll need training. Are you a good swimmer?' 'Not particularly,' I said airily – and I'm not. 'Manfred Zendar will be your trainer,' Frye said.

Zendar, a German, then in his late sixties, was as legendary for his exploits as a waterman as Yakima Canutt was as a stunt man. He coached me patiently, in this enormous pool on the Universal lot, through all the things that every scuba enthusiast knows, but that I'd never heard of before. 'Are you good at holding your breath?' he enquired, and I said, 'Well, yes, what with singing and making long speeches.' Manfred said, 'Now you have a mask over your nose and you breathe through this tube we call the "regulator". Oxygen, yes? You go to the bottom of the pool and lie on your back. I will be there. In the pool with you.' I did these things for a week, and became rather hooked on it, holding my breath until I couldn't any longer, then raising my fist like an ANC salute, to be given the regulator. They were very thorough, but they overlooked one briefing that I'd have found useful.

As with the Gun, there was more than one version of the main prop – a 747. The first, a full-scale mock-up, was used in Florida, where the good weather and clear water are just right for the raising of a wrecked aircraft. It was done with huge flotation balloons by the Seals of the US Navy, ever happy to help with a movie, and backed by a Battle Wagon swanning around. It was good to be reminded on my very first job as a 'resident alien' what a great contribution the US Armed Forces make to the film industry, by contrast with Britain, where it's often impossible to get support for clearing a street. Once, in England, when we were doing a night scene a man came up from his basement and flatly refused to leave. He complained that we were keeping his dog awake. We had to move.

The interior shots for *Airport 77* were done in two separate tanks at Universal and CBS, nearly thirty feet down. In the first I had to be seen from the point of view of the horrified eyes of my wife in the plane, slowly floating up dead with my head on my shoulder, enough to put anybody off their food even if they were dining in first class. I had to present myself to the cameras in this disagreeable fashion several times, sinking to the bottom with a lead weight belted to my stomach. Then, when they bellowed 'Action!', I'd unclip the belt, take an enormous breath, pass belt, tube and mask to Freddie, and set off hoping that I would not surface truly dead. The possibility that I might not surface at all did occur to me after the first take, when I passed all my gear to Freddie and then made a hash of unclipping the belt.

However, the second phase, when I had to be blown away in the baggage compartment, alarmed me even more, because I had not expected them to build the set so far down, with no way out except sideways. So Jack and I went down with our life jackets and safety apparatus, though naturally we did not wear them because the hold is dry until the door gives way and the Niagara pours in, to blast us out on the other side. It was like a convention of stunt men and frogmen and sub-aqua experts down there behind the camera, which was operated by the underwater cameraman of *Jaws*, Rexford Metz. He asked, before we went down, 'Do you want anything written on the blackboard?' I said, 'No, I haven't got any lines.' The awkward part of the business for me was that they start in with a screen-filling close-up of me defunct and with my mouth hanging open, then gradually pull back, with no cut, to admit Jack into the shot, and he works on me unavailingly and finally tows me out. So no double could be used. The difficult detail to handle was to open my mouth and close my throat so that no bubble would give away that I was a live actor. Once I did run out of breath – and was instantly handed the oxygen bottle. It was empty. They had a spare – it was a big-budget picture. The scenes in the tanks were not quite fun, but I *was* with Jack Lemmon. We never played together again on the screen, but often did on the golf course.

And the stunt men came to me with the gift of a Stunt Men's Association belt buckle from Ted Duncan, one of their number. 'He wants you to have it,' they said. I value it more than I would an Oscar. I showed it to Jack as we sat together, soaking wet, in a small caravan. I remarked that I couldn't help wondering why we were doing this. 'Because we're fucking crazy,' said Jack.

Guest Host

Clowns are suspected of wanting to play Hamlet, the prince of dark thinkers. Nobody supposes Hamlets want to play clowns. But I did, just by way of letting a little light into the musty files held on me by casting directors and journalists. When the chance came, I did not at first recognize it, and nearly let it slip. My then agent, Keith Addis, was almost cross with me for dragging my feet. 'They've asked for you to host it. You go to New York for a week, but it's live.' After my experience with the man who couldn't stop farting, I wasn't keen. 'No, no,' I said, 'I don't want to do anything live.' He brushed aside my objection. 'They've asked for you,' he repeated. 'You've got to do it.' 'I don't want to.' 'You've *got* to. What's more, watch it this coming Saturday.'

Grudgingly, I obeyed, and switched on the next *Saturday Night Live*. The host had to talk to the audience directly, connect the sketches, and then take part in them with the resident company. But it wasn't very exciting. 'Awful,' I complained. 'You've *got* to do it,' said Keith. 'Unfunny,' I noted. '*You've got to do it!*' he barked. I sighed. 'I've got to do it,' I acknowledged.

The show that changed my life was made in Rockefeller Center, in a studio made before the war for Toscanini's recordings. So the acoustics weren't bad. It was performed by a group of people living and working in New York who were 'not yet ready for prime time'. And they weren't bad either. In fact, most of them went on to become major stars, and the programme to be probably the biggest show in American TV history. I took off for New York full of foreboding.

The hosts were always hosted at the Essex House, but I was whisked straight away to the studio. It was ten o'clock at night. They were all there, every one a stranger to me, with about fifteen writers and the producer, Lorne Michaels. With only a round of 'Good evenings' for a warm-up, we got to the business of comedy. 'Would you mind? Start reading.' We read and we read and we read. No laughs. No smiles. It was clear to me that we were en route for a catastrophe, a total derailing of the express, with me on the footplate. RIP John Belushi, Dan Aykroyd, Bill Murray, Gilda Radner, Laraine Newman, Jane Curtin and their front man, Wossisname Lee.

Then there was a scene in a sauna with the whole cast stark, and I walk in dressed in a suit – typical uptight Brit – and, while they sweat, complain it's not hot enough. Something I said, probably even more typically British, suddenly prompted a general guffaw. From that moment I felt more at ease. 'My God,' I said to myself in an astonished *sotto voce*, 'it's going to work.' (As it happened, this sketch, with its complement of nudes, was dropped from the final running order, but it had served its turn.) I wondered if Keith would be watching me. My agents very often don't. Other actors report a similar experience.

My optimism was dampened in the succeeding days, as we worked our way through sketch after sketch, only by the bad colds afflicting one or two of the men. I was terribly worried. I thought they'd be ill on the night. I'd say, 'I think you should go to a drugstore and take something for that.' They'd say, 'Why? I haven't got a – *snuffle, snuffle* – cold. At all – *snort*. Nothing the matter with me – *sneeze* – whatever.' I thought of their names in lights: 'Sneeze, Snort and Snuffle in *Saturday Night Half Dead*.' And then, with a couple of days to go, I caught on. The pressures, the regime of countless new sketches every week, with no time off, left some of them in need of resorting to 'other substances'. It had been naïve of me not to have guessed sooner. Their work was unaffected. They were brilliant. By the end I was camping up the drug scene myself in a sketch in which I played Sherlock Holmes, notoriously addicted to a 'seven per cent solution', by inhaling with a ten-dollar bill up my nostril.

'Comedy,' Jack Lemmon once said to me, 'is timing.' There was a scene in which I played Death, not often a funny character, who has taken away the puppy of a little girl – Laraine Newman, then in her thirties, in nightie and pigtails – and she settles in, cold-bloodedly, to drive Death out of his mind. 'Mr Death, I hate you,' she says. Is that a funny line? In the context of a cleverly written scene she made it so. When we did the live show, after a dummy run with an audience embittered by the knowledge that they would not themselves be shown on television, the timing through sketch after sketch was magic. It is impossible, alas, to reproduce it on the page.

Later it was announced that the percentage shares of that programme were 37, 38, 39. They seemed very pleased, but for me it needed interpreting. So I asked the producer, 'Lorne, how many people watched that show last night?' and he said, 'Between thirty and thirty-five million.' It was lucky for me that I had no idea of such an audience when I went on, so I was able to make the, for me, important discovery that with this structure you could do anything. You might be talking to the audience a few feet away while changing your costume for the next set. 'Excuse me, while I take off my trousers.'

There are few actors who would not benefit from having to take off their trousers in front of thirty million people. Most of all, he who (as a rule) plays the king.

A Choice of Nonsense

Some offers of comedy roles came in. One was from John Landis, the only director I know who directs everything in shirt and tie and suit. He was making *The Kentucky Fried Movie*, a portmanteau of coarse and funny skits, in which a number of actors were referred to in the script under their real names – thus 'Oh, look! There's Donald Sutherland!' Had there been an equivalent line for me: 'Oh, look! There's Christopher Lee!' I might well have gone for it, but it seemed I was to be recognized only as Fu Manchu, and I had no wish to be sucked back into that. So I declined, but reluctantly, because Landis is innovative and *sui generis*. And the film was dotted about with good satirical bits, so perhaps I made a mistake. If so, it was a trailer for an even bigger mistake.

A core group among the participants went on to develop a manic project called *Airplane*, and I was sent a script while working under the direction of Steven Spielberg on his comedy *1941*. It was tempting to be in a send-up of a disaster movie series in which I'd lately made my own earnest contribution, but I found it hard to make sense, or even the right kind of nonsense, from the fragment of script in my hands. Friends and colleagues gave it the thumbs down. 'You don't know who these people are,' they warned me. 'It's not a complete script and it doesn't make sense. You are now making the greatest comedy of all time, with the greatest cast ever assembled, for the number-one director in the world. Don't touch it.' The part of the doctor that I was offered was eventually touched by the comic brio of Leslie Nielsen in an all-over very funny film.

However, the description of my situation as lucky was not altogether misplaced. The 'number-one director in the world', Steven Spielberg, likes and understands actors, and has an encyclopaedic knowledge of their track record (two cheers for that), so he is always a treat to work for. And the 'greatest cast ever assembled' might well include the two actors I was most concerned with on a daily basis, the Japanese Toshiro Mifune (of *The Seven Samurai*) and the sometime rodeo clown Slim Pickens. As for the 'greatest comedy of all time', it had at least the makings of the hugest comedy of its time, based on the improbable, but true story of a Japanese submarine that opened fire on the Californian coast, killing a cow in a field near Santa Barbara, and causing a war panic.

Mifune was the Japanese commander. He was required to speak only Japanese. I was the German observer, named von Kleinschmid by the director after the dean of one of his universities. I was required to speak only German. The audience is given to understand that each actually understands the other's language very well, and is aware of the other's understanding. The outrageous things they say to annoy each other, such as, 'The Führer is right, of course. Only the Aryan race can rule the world,' make a running gag. There were no subtitles, except for the last outpourings from the Japanese commander when he uses karate on his tormentor, flings him overboard and grimly says, '*Auf Wiedersehn*', and these were translated simply as 'Sayonara'.

Now *1941* has become a cult movie, a phrase that covers a multitude of sins on the part of critics and distributors, meaning that years pass before they get the point, and the audience is given a proper chance. Once we'd all arrived in vintage 1941 cars at the Los Angeles première, *1941* had the stickiest of sticky starts. At the end of the showing there was a rare and peculiar silence. Next day the critics seized their chance to flay Steven, their golden boy. I've never seen such harsh reviews. Quite unfair. If there is a fault in the film it's the overload of banana skins, but today the consensus is that there are also some wonderful falls. At another première seven years later, of the stage show *Les Misérables*, Steven said to me, 'Would you believe it, *1941* is making money now?'

The Japanese submarine itself was a full-size mock-up built (happily for me, mostly on the surface) in a tank in Culver City. For my role as a German naval officer I had to take off my moustache, and put it back on again for the Polish scientist that I was playing, more or less simultaneously, in the film version of Alistair Maclean's thriller *Bear Island*, which was being shot in Alaska. It's a long distance for commuting, but there were some spectacular sections to enjoy at the northern end of the journey, taking a floatplane called a Goose from Prince Rupert Island to land in the sea near Stewart, where there was no airport.

The author set his story in the Arctic, but Stewart was already cold enough for us. It was said to have the heaviest snowfall in the world. We accordingly learned to walk on snowshoes, and also flat on skis, and I practised up and down the main street, finding it difficult. The cold (minus 40 at one location near a glacier) was at times intense enough to garble our speech, and Donald Sutherland once risked being impaled on my skis when he remarked of an iced-up speech of mine, 'I don't remember that line in the script.' The cast was wonderful, including also Richard Widmark and Vanessa Redgrave. My old friend Don Sharp, with twenty-five years' experience, knew as much as anybody about directing. The book was a good yarn. The snow and the ice and the mountains were, in this instance, as the Lord provided. Yet for some reason the ingredients failed to come together. That reason could have been a horrible accident at this location, which shocked and depressed us all, but I can't be sure of that.

Every day we would go pretty high up the mountain, where they'd built some huts to shelter us between takes. Two helicopters carried the Canadian crew and the equipment. On one terrible day the weary pilot of the second helicopter, returning, failed to notice the first already squatting on the pad, and landed on top, killing the second's pilot. This ghastly experience obviously affected the whole team, and the under-lying shock trembled on long after.

For the boat scenes the only ship available for hire for a month was the *Ljubov Orlova*, a Soviet vessel from Vladivostok, purpose-built for the Japanese tourist trade. This explained the very short bunks. The carpenter was summoned to make an extension of about two feet to mine. He looked at the bunk and at me, and said jovially, 'We have a problem. You are not standard.' My variance from being standard became a running joke. But the tourists evidently ate and drank well; there was some splendid Georgian wine. The Russians were very friendly, until some fool drew a moustache on the huge picture of a Soviet film star. It took days to calm them down. The most agitated Russian, however, was the captain, who was anxious lest the American pilots run his ship aground in an Alaskan fjord and the entire crew be taken prisoner.

My fate in this story was to be struck down by a sabotaged radio mast, and I returned to Pinewood studio for my death scene, reciting the creed in Polish in my delirium – where I disgraced myself. There I was, cosily pyjamaed in a lovely warm hospital bed, with the lights low, while Vanessa and Richard murmured about my chances of pulling through. I was woken by the director, saying, 'Do you mind not snoring during Miss Redgrave's dialogue?'

Character Witness

Jobbing actors who need to be in work, not only to make a living and support their nearest and dearest but also to prevent the muscles of the mind from going flabby, and who put making films ahead of making money, can reckon on a bizarre variety of experience and a switchback of triumph and despair. Taking on a promiscuity of roles is a desperate gamble. Character actors who share the opinion of the great Liverpool football manager Bill Shankly, that to waste the public's time is a criminal offence, may often feel like turning themselves in at the local police station, after some film they've worked on has gone horridly wrong. Or, since their responsibility is only partial, they may want to turn witness for the prosecution and have everybody else gaoled. And of course there are occasions when coroner, judge and jury should be sent down.

It was for the variety of work that I went into voluntary exile in America. I wanted to separate my work in future from my image as the parish's tame cannibal. Knowing that, and despite my having been in some big commercial films, those who hired me were able to mark down my fee. I did not altogether resent this, because I was aware of the risk involved in changing horses in midstream, and I was glad of any chance to show I could ride whatever beast came alongside, but there was a catch to it, which is endemic still in Hollywood practice. Contrary to any other competitive business imaginable, the most expensive candidate is the one most likely to get the job. A performer's stock-market quotation is crucial and may be the benchmark for a career of upward failure. This laid, and lays, a tiresome weight on all casting negotiations, and is a pernicious evil in the business.

In fifty years the longest period that I have been out of work was four months, and for me it was like being stretched (even further) on the rack. In Los Angeles this is made worse by their heartless habit of greeting you with the word, 'Working?' If they find you on the golf course they will say, 'Working?' as if you had just taken to golf as a profession. 'Working?' they ask in a puzzled tone when they find you with your wife and child in a restaurant, as if there should be a camera turning in the corner. Occasionally you find an actor who is more active when resting than when working: they used to say of Errol Flynn, 'He's resting, he's making a movie.' My favourite story is of Mel Brooks who, when filming at Fox, walked into the commissary where there were a lot of people in animal costumes. A friend of his, dressed head to foot as a bear, rushed up exclaiming, 'Hi, Mel, how are you? I'm Jack K—' Brooks eyed him up and down, and asked, 'Working?'

Most of the time I could cheerfully answer yes to what now seems to be the $64-million question. Even though, as I said, that sometimes led to peculiar results. For instance, in a blond wig and blond eyebrows I played the Duke of Edinburgh – they thought my request for blue contact lenses excessive – in *Charles and Diana: a Royal Love Story*, a ninety-minute TV film. My wife, Elizabeth II, was Margaret Tyzack. Would it, I wondered, be *lèse majesté* for me to impersonate the irascible Duke? Then I reflected that, after all, Peter Ustinov had been George IV and, come to that, Bela Lugosi had played Jesus. On the set in Windsor, locals asked me, 'Are you going to talk like him?' so I said I would, and gave them an imitation of his wardroom accent. But it was his salty language that interested them. Alas, it was all terribly proper: no tiger-shooting, no chastising of reporters, no gaffes and, as a result, unforgivably dull.

Then there was *Once Upon a Spy*, a pilot for a TV series I wouldn't have been in if it had matured. Ted Danson was the star, who was very good and has gone on to greater things. But it is the name of the director, Ivan Nagy, that has become a byword, owing to his association with the notorious madam Heidi Fleiss. As a director he was a real slave driver and for one scene found us still in a room in Houston at 4.30 a.m. At this point, the operator of a heavy hand-held camera quietly put it down, declaring, 'I have reached my limit.' He spoke for us all, and we went home. The incident was unique in my experience.

Another completely forgettable pilot for a TV series I would not have been in was *Massarati and the Brain*, in which I was a Nazi war criminal, and I mention it not for that but to stress that I made a policy of accepting one-off TV roles, but of declining episodic TV and sitcoms. Seemingly you must decide whether you are a movie or a TV actor, and never the twain shall meet except on special occasions.

On the positive side were *Serial* and *The Return of Captain*

Invincible. The former was introduced to me by my agent, remarking that it was 'what you read, not what you eat', and named after a book which had been a tremendous bestseller at the height of hippy life in San Francisco. But would I go along to Paramount for an audition? That actually meant reading some pages of dialogue to the director Bill Persky and Marion Dougherty, in my book the ace of Los Angeles casting directors.

Their aim was to test my capacity to speak in an American accent, which I'd said I could do in a generalized way, though not a regional specific. The character, they said, was a hard-headed businessman. So I managed the accent and got the part. I was delighted that I would be playing an American for the first time. (Itinerant actors tend to look on such 'firsts' as milestones, and to me this was an important one.) Then they added, 'Of course, there is another side to his character.' I thought, Here we go! Jack the Ripper or the Beast from a Thousand Fathoms. They said, 'At weekends, you see, he's the leader of a band of gay Hell's Angels.' My smile did not slip. 'That's tremendous,' I told them, 'I'm even more keen to do it.'

And truly, it was hilarious. The San Francisco setting had changed little since hippy days. The Hell's Angels were the genuine fireball. The language was the worst I've heard on any picture. Their motorbikes were their own bikes, big machines from the sixties. I hadn't ridden a motorbike since Malta in 1943, but I managed everything except the wheelies and the drive up some stairs in a house. The highlight for me was the dash across the Golden Bridge, in black leathers and Nazi regalia. With the summer fog rolling in and my army of Angels thundering along behind, we were actually doing 40 mph. but, with my steel helmet tipping over my eyes, it seemed more like a hundred. It was hard to see where I was riding, and the young stunt man in his purple dress sitting on the pillion was paralysed with fright. It was a comedy that won an extra laugh at the preview when this beautiful young man in the purple dress said to me, 'We love you, we love you, we love you,' and I replied, 'You say that, but are you willing to prove it?'

The Return of Captain Invincible was another off-the-wall gift, but for a different reason. It gave me a chance to sing. Now I am not exactly a *sub rosa* singer: almost every day of my life I unleash a few numbers, mostly operatic, and I may do that on location as well as domestically but, though I've made a few records, it has been a disappointment to me that I've had relatively few chances to sing on screen. In this film, shot in Australia, I was once again a Fascist Beast, playing opposite but also singing a duet with the most diversely talented performer I've ever shared a frame with, Alan Arkin. The number, 'Name Your Poison', was written specially for me by Hartley and O'Brien, the pair who wrote *The Rocky Horror Show*. It was verbally very clever, mixing the names of some thirty drinks into a barrage of temptations used by the villain to seduce the superhero back into the alcoholic ways he's given up to save the world. As Mister Midnight I failed in my wicked plan, but I like to think my song would subvert anybody but a superhero with a tin ear into cracking a bottle with me. The film, part rock, part opera, part musical comedy, had some good patches, but they didn't hang together in a seamless piece, and there have been many others I would rather drink to.

Crackerjack India

If only visitors to India could leave their stomachs behind, they would be better fixed to face the hazards and enjoy the charm of filming with Indians. It seemed on many days in and around Jaipur, during the shooting of *The Far Pavilions*, based on Molly Kaye's doorstop novel, that several people on either side of the camera were stricken with gut-rot. I was among the victims, with a bonus of asthma. The only two immune were Gitte, who flourished on curry taken three times a day, and Sir John Gielgud, by a long way the oldest person among us and playing a dashing British officer of the Raj (and perhaps therefore seasoned).

Sir John's clarinet voice, tuned to deliver every syllable perfectly understood at the back of the stalls, easily reached the far corners of the dining-room of our billet, the former palace of the Maharajah of Jaipur, which doubled as a tourist hotel, and the American tourists hung on his words. Reminiscing with me and Omar Sharif, he said, 'The last time I played Hamlet was in Cairo in 1946.' Omar said, 'But I saw you do it!' 'Really? Were you there the night Horatio had an epileptic fit in my arms? I was furious,' Sir John asked. His utterance was a continuous, even stream of words. 'No. What did you do?' Omar asked. 'I said, "Put something between his teeth and get the understudy" and of course he came on from the wrong side of the stage, so I said, "Get off! Come on from the right side."'

'Nothing like that in Julius Caesar,' I ventured, referring to the last time he and I had been in a film together, he as Caesar and I as Artemidorus. Sir John considered this observation. 'But you remember,' he said, 'when you came over to us to try to warn me when we were all on our way to the forum?' Indeed I remembered. 'I had bare feet,' I said, 'and everybody in the crowd was treading on them.' 'You remember,' he repeated, 'that Charlton Heston was Mark Antony?' 'His favourite role,' I assured him. 'So you remember,' he continued, 'that for reasons of his own he'd come straight from some athletic arena where he'd been throwing the javelin and therefore appeared practically naked, wearing only a loincloth.' I confirmed this. Sir John nodded. 'Naturally he took up his position beside me, and you'll remember that behind me there was Jason Robards as Brutus, Robert Vaughan as Casca, and Richard Johnson as Cassius.' 'Yes, stunning cast,' I agreed. He said, 'Yes, but remember Heston's superb physique, magnificent figure of a man. How could one forget it?' I said that I hadn't forgotten it. It was quite impressive. 'Yes,' said Sir John.

What I remember principally of *The Far Pavilions* was shooting on a great plain outside Jaipur, with hundreds of extras, the wedding procession of my niece, an Indian princess, played by Amy Irving in a make-up which caused one reviewer to say made her 'look as though she'd been dipped in cocoa'. The procession was led by me, flanked by Omar on one side and Ben Cross on the other, all of us on horses. Immediately behind us were the elephants, the first ridden by a man with an enormous pair of kettledrums perched either side of the beast's head. Countless camels loped enigmatically along behind, and thousands of people carrying things. There were several Indian actors determined to speak perfect English, reversing, as it were, the Peter Sellers imitation, with phrases like 'Spot on' and 'Isn't this a crackerjack day?' For a while we wandered about getting used to the horses until the director, Peter Duffell, told me, 'We're going to take a very long shot of all this. Just take your horses down there, and the parade will follow. We'll give you "Action" through a megaphone.' That was the idea.

It did not take long to discover that the horses had never seen an elephant. They were uneasy, probably because of the smell, and inclined to shy away, but without actually unseating us. We thought we'd got them close enough to the elephants and trouble-free, but when the director called 'Action!' several things happened at once. The drummer, totally carried away by the glory of it all, and inclined to believe he was performing in a Bruckner symphony, crashed on the drums on either side of the leading elephant's head. This worthy let out an outraged trumpeting shriek. Our horses leaped five feet into the air and took off at speed with us on top of them. The impeccable English of our Indian cavalry suffered a sudden change, and one horseman disappeared into the distance, crying, 'Mr Lee, Mr Lee, my horse is going absolutely bonkers!' I stayed on my horse, but perhaps I'd have been wiser to dismount, because galloping through clouds of thick dust gave me the asthma that bothered me almost throughout the film.

In the re-creation of important ceremonies such as the wedding and the *suttee* funeral service, some of the villagers who were hired for crowd scenes, despite the anxiety of the government, apparently had difficulty distinguishing between fantasy and reality. When the actress playing in the *suttee* sequence went round and round the byre intoning the traditional phrases, some villagers really believed it was all going to go up in smoke for real, and the atmosphere on the set became uncomfortable. On a more cheerful note, the wedding in the courtyard of the Pink Palace, where the Maharajah still lives, involved a real pandit, with other priests for acolytes, who recited the whole ceremony, on and on and on – remarkable breath control. He was totally serious about what he was doing, and as far as he and many of the onlookers were concerned the pair were really married. And who can be really sure that they weren't? It caused a stir.

The Far Pavilions, a film for television in three parts, ended up well as a wonderful romantic mix of the Raj and princely India. Even the Indians thought it very good. I had similar hopes for *The Bengal Lancers*. The script was exciting, and we were again in a Maharajah's palace that had been turned into a hotel, this time in Jodhpur. When Michael York and Trevor Howard and his wife Helen Cherry arrived and we'd shot some scenes, I thought it all looked splendid. But then, mysteriously, everything began to bog down.

There were sidelong looks among the crew, half-finished sentences, 'latrine rumours', and the smiles vanished from the technicians' faces. Together they spelled 'Problem'. It was formulated very simply when some of them came to me, as the member in the cast some already knew from *The Far Pavilions*, to beg me to ask management whether they would be paid or not, as there had been nothing for anybody in the last three weeks. It's not the cast's business to deal for the crew, but I thought that as we had common cause I could at least make an enquiry. I was told everything was fine. There was a captain in the Indian Navy flying all over India to collect cash to bring at any moment to pay the crew and the crowd and so on. This story made it clear that the situation was rapidly deteriorating, and indeed they had eventually to admit they hadn't the money to finish the film. It just stopped, and everybody went home lamenting.

It should not ever happen. But it happens quite often. It has happened to me that several productions were either terminated or were finished without my having been paid. The prudent actor has the money put in escrow before ever he starts, but that is more difficult for the crew and for actors who are still on the first rungs. And somehow you always imagine that nobody could be so careless as to neglect the budget.

The Longest Short Course

I never found out whether Lloyd was his first or his second name. Lloyd was my first caddie at the Bel-Air Country Club. Winter and summer he went round in an overcoat, rather stooped – whether or not he was carrying the bag – and very slowly. Though not more than middle-aged, he gave the appearance of being one of the Nibelungs in Wagner's *The Ring*. He mumbled a lot, and into his waistcoat. People thought he was a little off-centre, but he was anything but. His opening remark to me was, 'You don't want to goof off in front of the pro.' Half-way through the round he asked, in a Brando mumble, eyes blinking, 'Misterleemisterleemisterlee, c'n I askaskask a question-tion?' I innocently agreed. 'Mis-terlee, did you ever-ever-ever make a si-si-silent movie?' The pro, Eddie Merrins, waited, grinning. I said, 'Well, Lloyd, actually I have done a few in which I didn't say anything.' A few weeks later he again wanted to put a question: 'I s-s-saw one of your movie-movie-movies last night. Great-great, I liked it. Misterleemisterleemisterlee, did you ever-ever-ever make any films with Lonch-Lon Chaney – Senior?' I said, 'Lloyd, *leave* the course. I'll carry the bag myself.' Over the ten years of my membership of Bel-Air, fellow members often mischievously echoed Lloyd's questions. The course itself was difficult, never dull. The former Open champion Tom Weiskopf observed, as we finished our game, 'It's the longest short course I've ever played.' The club champion was Ted Richards. Going into the final, his opponent asked him how many times he'd won the championship. 'This'll be the fourteenth time,' said Ted.

The joining fee had been $15,000, an awful lot of money I thought at the time. Today it would be five times that, and some clubs around Los Angeles charge ten times. It's an equity, though; you sell it when you resign. The annual sub then was $5,000, plus a 'Food and Beverage' section divided up among all the members, whether or not they eat and drink there. But I never grudged a cent of it. It was five minutes from

266

our flat: when not working I could play five days a week. And it's part of the American system that you have only to turn up and they'll find you a partner, and company at the restaurant table. Bel-Air had a catholic range of members: among its five hundred were lawyers and doctors, actors and architects, musicians and sportspeople, journalists and bankers. Unlike too many American clubs, it had no bar against women or minorities: we had Jews and Britons. I went round with people who played par golf, and once was matched against a man with a handicap of thirty-six – and he needed every stroke. It was the essence of American hospitality, which never lets you feel like an outsider – except perhaps in Hollywood. I sat in the grill one evening watching the big football game on television, with Joe Namath and Tom Harmon either side, two of the great names of American football, explaining it to me as it unfolded. I'm still none the wiser, but I treasure the memory. And one other memorable occasion: playing with Ray Bolger and Fred Astaire – together.

In American golf the buggy is gradually superseding the caddie. You see groups of eight or ten buggies rocketing round like a Grand Prix. Bel-Air still had caddies, and sometimes the player would carry the bag and the caddie would ride. I'm a walking golfer. George C. Scott, on the other hand, is a buggy golfer. When we came to the tunnels – Bel-Air is unique in having some that connect a green with the next tee – he'd put his foot down, the wall an inch away, to test me. George burned with a short fuse: I once saw him fling his driver up into a tree, and it's probably still there. With George the nineteenth hole was a test too, because you never knew whether he was on or off the wagon. Primed with a beer and a stiff dose of vodka, he once told me of his dislike of acting and how he'd always wanted to be a teacher, and wondered why 'people are always so alarmed when they're around me'. But it was the same aura that made him such a powerful actor.

Jack Lemmon is the only man to have broken a finger putting a tee in, but that wasn't so much native violence as frustration with a game that he took very seriously. 'I'm dangerous today,' he'd say, 'the human hinge!' He competed every year in the Bing Crosby Tournament, yearning to make the cut. But he never did. His game would hold up well until he was in range of the cameras, then he'd disintegrate. He chomped his way round on a cigar, periodically extracting scissors from his pocket to trim the soggy end. Jack belonged also to the Jewish club Hillcrest, where I played with him and Burt Lancaster, but I couldn't afford the membership, although it was offered to me, considering the tacit understanding of an annual contribution to the United Jewish

Appeal. The comedian Lou Holz once sat down with us and said, 'I'm playing so badly they won't even allow me to throw my clubs.' The club was a regular nest of comedians. Danny Kaye and George Burns were members, and Groucho Marx, despite his famous remark that he wouldn't join any club that would have him. On a very hot day he took off his shirt while playing, and earned a rebuke from the committee. Not to bring obloquy and shame on the club, they told him, he must wear a shirt next time. So he did, and left his trousers off.

Both these clubs were ideal for actors. The usual club for killing people, I was told, is the eight-iron. In some establishments an actor might feel like using it. The LA Country Club with its wonderful course and antebellum clubhouse won't have show-business people – they turned Bing Crosby down even though he had a house on the course. The exception was Randolph Scott – after he'd retired as an actor and went into oil. Refused on the grounds of being an actor, Victor Mature said, 'I'm not an actor – and I've got thirty-odd movies to prove it.'

That's Showbiz – Unfortunately

I t was all right for me to spend my resting days on the golf course – and such a golf course – and it was all right for me on my working days to leave Los Angeles for Australia and Alaska and India and South Africa; there were even satisfactions to be had in filming behind the Iron Curtain, despite grim hotels and ghastly food that guaranteed a weight loss every time. But it was not all right for Gitte to suffocate in the cultural vacuum of Los Angeles. When I came back it was to Gitte, but not to a place either of us could call 'home'. Los Angeles is a collection of suburbs in search of a town, spread out all over hell, and strung on eight-lane freeways, compelling everyone to drive locked in at the same speed, like ball-bearings in a circuit. Contrary to our normal practice, we each had a car, a Buick Regal and a Chevrolet Camaro, and contrary to local practice we each kept it for ten years. Everyone has a car. You can't exist without one. If you went for a walk at night you'd probably be arrested, and if you had your dog as the reason, it would be arrested too as an accessory. Sometimes Gitte would come with me on location, but more often she couldn't, and she got into the habit of making long solo journeys to exotic places. She travelled independently to Peru, Ecuador, Colombia, Guatemala, islands in the Pacific, the Caribbean – places I may never visit, as producers generally give them a wide berth. Once, during the major strike of the film business, we went on a long journey together, via the deep peace of Finnish lakeland and, in the tight embrace of Intourist, to Moscow and Leningrad, with a sidetrip into the Baltic republics, flying in high-winged little planes like relics of the Second World War.

Film is only one of many products generated in Los Angeles. With cross-pollination it might seem to have a very exciting cultural potential. Unfortunately the people who work in these various trades seem to be insulated within their own communities and obsessions. Most of the film

269

colony live close by one another in similar neighbourhoods, in our case Westwood, which had palliative bookshops and restaurants, but was gradually invaded by the malaise of drugs and crime that already affected many parts of the megalopolis. You have to be a megastar such as Robert Redford or Clint Eastwood to live in another state and not be immediately available when the call comes from the studio. You find yourself attached on the basis of your income to a band of people who drive similar cars to similar restaurants to browse on a similar faddish diet, to compare similar purchases and to talk relentlessly about other people's money, which had a limited appeal to us, whether they were talking thousands or millions. For reading matter they had, exclusively, the *Hollywood Reporter* and *Variety*. The most fashionable church was Our Lady of the Cadillacs. If you went to a party – and it is an illusion that jobs grow out of the bottom of a cocktail glass – you'd be liable to find yourself in the focus of a camera. I had my escapes from this enervating social life but, for Gitte, endlessly exposed to it, it was pretty dreary.

At the risk of seeming to bite the hand that feeds me, since after all during that decade I appeared in more than forty films and had a good time professionally, proving I could survive without being typecast, I here mention some diseased aspects of the trade circuit. Chief among these is the paralysing fear that infects corporations from top to bottom, and overwhelms small businesses. It is the fear of being thrown out for having made a mistake, or for having seemed to make a mistake or, indeed, without having made a mistake, which is the most corrosive of all. It is not peculiar to America; it merely appears there in its most exaggerated forms, because there's so much more to lose and gain. As I write, the average budget for a studio picture is well over $50 million – absurd, an inflation of the order of a Baron Münchausen fantasy, hiked up by the indefensible sums allowed to leading players, from which all dependent expenses are multiplied. It's an ethos in which people prefer making deals to making films, so the deals result in quite a polished entertainment for an inner circle, but the films are not so exciting or amusing as the Byzantine intrigues that set them in motion.

At the level of the journeyman actors there's a fog of uncertainty, as to whether any more films are likely to be made, or only deals; as to whether they are really wanted or are just a stalking horse for some other performer; as to whether, having been chosen, their contract is anything more than some philosophical ideal; as to whether, having arrived on the set, they will be immediately sent home through the caprice of the leading performer; as to whether anybody in the management has enough sense of the history of the cinema to have heard, for instance, of Garbo; as to whether anybody has enough confidence in their own judgement to give a picture they claim to love a decent run after a first weekend in which the box-office figures are disappointing; as to whether performers can make a public protest about any of it, without being told they'll never work again.

The answer to this last is that this *is* what they will be told, and they will be shunned by all their acquaintance in the business, and it will be said of them that they are 'so unpopular they couldn't get arrested'. And if they stay unpopular, and some terminal disaster befalls them, everybody will say, 'Oh, well, that's show business.' Well, it shouldn't be show business. It's the most depressing phrase in show business, used by people in it to shrug off mishaps and calamities as if there were no difference between them.

This was the dark side of my feelings about working in America, present almost from the beginning, but it never became paramount, despite the accumulation of depressing detail, or we would not have lingered as long as we did. We left because we felt we had done what we came for, and when we talked it over between us, one or the other of us seemed always to be saying, 'Let us return to our roots. We are, after all, Europeans' – a notion that was becoming increasingly important to Europeans wholesale. As for Christina, she took no part in the deliberations because she had already, long before, made her own decision to go back to the school and friends she had been happy with in England, and complete her education there at boarding school. In fact she made the best of both worlds, flying across the Atlantic six times a year to take her holidays with us. For the young, California, with its horseriding, its beaches and its mountains, is paradise.

Almost the last film I made before leaving America was a comedy called *Jocks*, shot in Las Vegas with many of the scenes, inevitably, in a casino. This was functioning throughout, a nightmare for continuity, with random gamblers drifting in and out of shot. The *pièce de résistance* of my portion was a scene in which I realize that the girl I madly love, who has invited me to her room, is a man. But this was a less upsetting problem to me than the real-life situation of working every night from one o'clock in the morning to midday. My body clock couldn't understand what was happening, because there is never any light in Vegas casinos. The consolation was that a genuine crap-shooter introduced me to his game, or rather he played for me, winning $600. It was a gift. Amazing.

Out in the daylight, I felt less buoyant. And not just because I'd been working all night. At that time I often felt mysteriously tired. Walking along the road, even on the level, was a drag. The slopes on the golf course seemed like a ploughed field to climb. My beloved doctor, Maxine Ostrum, said I had the blood pressure of a man of thirty. But the heartbeat was irregular. She sent me to a specialist, Dr Dee, in Santa Monica. Tests showed that the mitral valve of the left ventricle didn't close properly. It fluttered. They gave me instruments to listen to my own heart. 'Whoosh! Whoosh!' it went, like water gushing. Dr Dee recommended that, when I was back in London, I should consult my doctor. I fancied I heard them saying in Los Angeles, 'Faulty valve? Big problem for a producer to take out insurance on an actor with a faulty valve. Oh, well, that's show business.'

Home Is Where the Heart Is

Back in London, there was our flat to be fixed up, and also my heart. For the latter I went to see my GP, Dr David Hay. He thought the time had come for a specialist. 'See one of my old friends, Dr Emanuel,' he said. This famous cardiologist ran the usual tests, and concluded that surgery was 'virtually certain. As quickly as possible.' This was April, with my sixty-third birthday imminent, and though my golf handicap was officially two, I could barely walk along the street without getting out of breath. This was private medicine, but I'd have to wait until June before the Harley Street Clinic could offer me a bed. First an angiogram must be done to check that the arteries were not blocked. Dr Emanuel passed me on, like a baton in a relay race, to Dr Donaldson.

The angiogram is a fibre-optic camera that travels up one of your arteries to photograph your heart. You have to be conscious. I'd been photographed from many angles in all sorts of light, and including underwater, but this was the first time I'd been photographed from the inside. There seemed to be a good house for the show, and lots of machinery. We could all see it on a screen. Dr Donaldson shoved a catheter into the femoral artery and started excavations. He said to the girl at my head, 'Well, talk to him. Talk to him.' She replied, 'What about?' Seeing her short of inspiration, I said, 'I'll do the talking here.' Then the catheter stalled, but eventually Dr Donaldson cleared a bit of rubbish out of the way and the catheter reached its destination. The doctor had been putting all his weight on his thumbs on the artery, because arterial blood could have hit the far wall, so when he was finally able to remove them his hands were a fine colour. 'That's all right, doctor,' I said reassuringly, 'I've seen that stuff before.'

After a while he said, 'You'll be delighted to hear your arteries are completely clear,' and I said, 'Splendid. That means I don't have to have the operation!' He dashed my nascent hopes by saying, 'You most certainly do.'

But not till June. The surgeon was to be Mr John Parker, the anchor man, as it were, of the relay team. He wouldn't know, until he'd 'had a look', whether to repair or replace. I didn't fancy a plastic valve; I'd heard of people pegging out in mid-sentence. 'Don't worry,' said Mr Parker, when I voiced my fears. 'We'd give you a pig's valve.' It is truly said of this noble creature that everything can be used except the squeal, but for a couple of months I couldn't look on pork without thinking of it being reared by cardiac units. Waiting for any serious operation for more than half an hour is a gloomy business, and I am not a good patient-in-waiting. And as part of the process I had to have a tooth out, which can make anyone resentful. An actor friend, meaning to lift my spirits, said, 'When you reach a certain age, and you wake in the morning and everything's crystal clear, and you haven't an ache or a pain, and you feel like a million dollars, and were never so well in your life, you're dead. But if you wake and creakily stretch your arms out and don't hit wood, you're OK.'

Usually when I'm obliged to rest I keep up my singing, play some golf, answer the mail, nag my agents, and polish up my collection of special-forces insignia, which I began almost by chance through discovering some of my own special-services insignia from the Second World War in an old ammunition box while filming *Safari 3000* in South Africa. Since 1981 it has grown apace, with a worldwide provenance of insignia worn by commandos, paratroopers, underwater people, anti-terrorist groups, anti-sabotage units and so forth, some of it given, some of it bought. And I read a lot, more often general books than fiction, though at that time I found the escapes that best ate up the time were my favourite detective stories by John Dickson Carr and Carter Dickson. Best of all for leaving the uncomfortable present behind is Tolkien's *Lord of the Rings*, which I read once a year and always take on location, thinking myself Gandalf.

I wandered around, realizing for the first time how much we take for granted. But despite these pastimes, thoughts of the impending operation would break through, and my knowledge that the percentage of fatalities is quite small did not save me from being scared. On the day that I went into the clinic I wrote special letters to Gitte and to Christina, just in case.

It was interestingly more complicated than a bypass. They brought my temperature right down – practically cryogenic. They sawed down the middle of my breastbone, like filleting a fish, then clamped it back, when they'd done, with steel clips, which are still there and hurt when I press them. The pig's valve remained in a side-dish, unused: when the surgeon had his look he decided he'd repair my valve instead.

Then they raised my temperature again and kept me for three days in intensive care, of which I remember only giving my heart, metaphorically, to an Irish night nurse who told me she'd never known anyone do so well, and that I'd be out in no time, an optimistic forecast but well meant: actually I was out after nine days, and then lay on a sofa at home looking like potted death.

The whole thing wasn't cheap, but my insurance helped, and it wasn't a fraction of what it would have cost in America. Besides, the Harley Street Clinic deserve credit for not giving the press an inkling. By far the worst part of the whole sequence was the daily physiotherapy from a delightful but merciless girl who made me open my arms and rotate them. There was a natural progression from that to walking eighteen holes of the golf course and trying out my putting, always an important part of my game. Finding that I was sinking a few, I felt it was time to test my stamina with some work, so I took on a role in a Channel 4 television film.

The Disputation proved fairly demanding, though the argument of the play is more vigorous than the action, and I had the congenial task of playing the liberal King James I of Aragon in a script based on a series of public disputations in Spain. Here, under the aegis of the king as judge, the Catholic and the Jewish faiths confronted one another more than two centuries before the Inquisition took centre stage.

The brunt of the dialogue was borne by Alan Dobie as the Rabbi and Bob Peck as the Jewish convert to Catholicism, while I had Bernard Hepton for confessor, Helen Lindsay as my wife and Toyah Wilcox as my mistress. Geoffrey Sax directed it on a set left over from the Welsh National Opera's production of *Ernani*. With all those candles it looked splendid, and everybody was extremely pleased with the way it had gone. Then something extraordinary happened to this film. Or, rather, didn't happen.

Normally a play of any consequence is given a build-up in the press, with perhaps a controversial essay and a rash of brief lives of participants. But there was nothing, not so much as a sniffy preview. When it finally went out, it was trailed with a repeat sign. The critics of *The Times* and *Time Out* won points for having their ears to the ground and printed heart-warming reviews, but the rest of them presumably took the repeat sign as a signal that they could look elsewhere that night for their material. It was enough to cause a man just recovering from a heart operation to have a relapse.

Three, and Four, and More

As potential sources of great costume drama the exuberant French novelists Alexandre Dumas, *père et fils*, put all other historical romancers, including Victor Hugo and Sir Walter Scott, in the shade. Of all their huge output it is *The Three Musketeers* and *The Count of Monte Cristo* that film-makers come back to again and again. The 1974 version of the former, which I was in, somehow bifurcated into two films, such was the quantity of celluloid in the can, with the second portion issued as *The Four Musketeers*. It was reasonable to do this, rather than waste the richness of the material, but there were actors and agents engaged who thought that modern skulduggery had intruded on Dumas's plot. It wasn't exactly seamless, nor were they even in quality – the *Three* is better than the *Four* – but they were High Romance and only partly an irreverent view of everything that was everything in the thirties and forties.

For me as the Comte de Rochefort heavy, and Milady's lover, it had been a major part in a major picture. It was just as well that I had brushed my teeth conscientiously for fifty-two years, because it had been a physically exhausting stream of battles with men twenty or thirty years my junior: Oliver Reed, Michael York, Richard Chamberlain. Nothing was faked; we were all quite badly knocked about. In the very first of my four duels as 'the Cardinal's living swordblade' I tore a ligament in my left knee which hindered running, jumping, fighting on ice and walking up or down stairs. I had discovered that at fifty-two I could still do it, but it took longer to recover. I had withstood a certain amount of teasing from my boisterous young colleagues. In my final duel, in the conclusion of *The Four Musketeers*, I was run through, pinned to the Bible, and died.

Or so we thought, until 1988. I was then brought back to life again and dispatched once more to Spain, to join most of the same crowd, now verging on fifty themselves, for some swashbuckling under the magnificent towers of Toledo. The story was loosely connected to the Dumas sequel *Twenty Years After*, and the film was called *The Return of the Musketeers*. I said to my not-so-young-any-longer colleagues, as I enjoyed watching them getting out of breath, 'I've done my bit, it's your turn. I don't know why you find it so difficult.' I was safely excused from sword-fights by a plot that had me coming out of the Bastille after seventeen years of no exercise.

And that's as far as I can go with a dispassionate recital. *The Return* should never have been made. They attempted the impossible, trying to shoot a twelve-week picture in eight weeks. Much worse than the failure of the film, however, was the accidental death of Roy Kinnear, one of the most loved men in the business, who came off his horse on cobblestones taking a corner, as he rode with the musketeers over a bridge from a Toledo castle. He had always been terrified of riding horses on the earlier films, and now he was fifteen years older and heavier. That very morning, walking the streets of Toledo, he had said to Gitte, 'Oh, God, this afternoon I've got to go on a horse. I'm not looking forward to that. I don't know if I can stay on.' Some of the Spanish stunt men who set the scene up, laying down straw and earth, had their doubts too. One of them said to me, 'It's all right. If you can ride.' Roy's death spread such a pall of misery that it was surprising the film was ever finished and, in truth, the world would have lost nothing much if it hadn't been.

This sad experience was the odd one out in a year of generally pleasant working episodes. While in Spain I was simultaneously performing a small part as a forger in *Honeymoon Academy*, doing a sort of eccentric waltz while bleeding to death. Kim Cattrall was similarly doubling up, as the lead in Madrid and my daughter in Toledo. I thought her very good. In Amsterdam the blossom was coming out as we shot *Murder Story*, which included a scene where I was filmed coming out of a porno shop. A photograph of my doing so appeared in the press without any acknowledgement that it was an exercise in fiction.

In America I had a more substantial role, in *Treasure Island*, directed by Fraser Heston, son of Charlton, who meshed in as Long John Silver. I was well named Blind Pugh in that, as with the overwhelming make-up of hideously scarred blind eye-sockets they gave me, I couldn't see out at all. And here was Oliver Reed again, this time as Billie Bones. In the famous scene where Pugh hands over the Black Spot to Bones, Oliver's greeting, 'Pugh! Pugh!', sounded fierce and contemptuous as if he were reacting to a bad smell. This was because for reasons of his own he'd decided to play the part with a strong Glasgow accent. I had to say, 'Gimme his hand, boy, or I'll break your arm – the Black Spot, yiss, yiss, yiss!' That was the moment Oliver chose for his heart attack. I was trying to get this vital sentence over above the incredible volume of Oliver's subterranean noises, but I doubted anyone would hear it. Oddly enough, the scene played well, I noticed, when I saw the whole film two years later in a New York hotel room, while publicizing *Gremlins II*.

There was no travel at all for me in *Around the World in 80 Days*, with my bit done in the Travellers' Club in Pall Mall (we couldn't use the Reform Club, where Jules Vernes began his tale). I had only to play whist, for which I have no talent, and lay the crucial bet. But without being a member of the Travellers' I felt *chez moi*, because I have a silver salver signed by all the club's staff, and presented to my mother's father, the Marquis of Sarzano, who, after retiring from the army, had become secretary at the Travellers'. And I dare say that we both have journeyed a league or two more than many professional travellers.

The Scaffold Is Also a Stage

When Gitte and I had talked of returning to our roots, we meant Europe, not just Britain. No place is more convenient to Britain than France, so it was bracing to be offered work near Paris. We had some roots there in the shape of a cousin by marriage, incidentally their topmost producer, with a company called Films Ariane that produced most of Belmondo's films: this was Alexander Mnouchkine.

It was our ongoing joke that he never asked me to work, though he knew I had enough French. So when he rang me with a job, I said, 'Nobody, Sarnya, can accuse you of nepotism. After forty-two years you offer me my first job with you.' He said, 'Yes, yes, and in France it will be a gigantic thing. I'm doing the French Revolution as a bicentenary celebration. And I want you in it.' I guessed right in one: 'You want me for Sanson, the public executioner.' He seemed surprised: 'How did you know?' I replied, 'I just knew.'

An actor should not shrink from getting into the skin of such a person, and Sanson was exceptionally interesting. But you learn that when you take on the persona of one on whom the fears of the community are projected, there may be knock-on effects. It's rare for headsmen or hangmen to have speaking parts, or for the vital technical details to be given more than cursory notice. So you hesitate. But by 1989 I felt I'd sufficiently expanded my repertoire not to be imprisoned in this one baleful image. And though I'd never had a professional need to study the methods of an executioner, I had picked up some special knowledge along the byways. As for instance, in the early eighties in America, I'd been given a personal tour of San Quentin penitentiary, when the then chief of the execution squad, Mike Madding, had given me a full-length account of the last hours of a condemned man and the nuts and bolts of his termination, which included me entering the 'Green Room' and actually stepping into the gas chamber, which I noticed had two chairs marked A and B. And my enduring thought was 'There, but for the grace of God . . .'

Moreover, I knew the English hangman Albert Pierrepoint very well. We'd met at the end of 1945 in connection with War Crimes Investigation. I had photocopies of excerpts of his executions book, which contained on the one hand the Belsen perpetrators, and on the other all the figures whose crimes meant anything as news or for the nature of the murder, and these he highlighted in red ink. We had some correspondence, and later he visited us in our London flat. He retired in 1959 to keep a pub – the first was called Help the Poor Struggler.

There is a right way and there are several wrong ways of doing everything, and the point about Albert was his strict observance of the correct ways of dispatching the wretched person, from the calculation of the drop to fixing the knot in the noose always under the left side of the chin – a whole sequence run off with maximum expedition, so that from the moment of his entry into the cell to the release of the trap he prided himself on taking not more than eleven seconds.

With this kind of discipline in mind I set about my research on Charles Henri Sanson, like Albert one of a dynasty of executioners, who came before and after him for two hundred years. His title was *Exécuteur des Hautes Oeuvres et des Basses*, and he insisted on its use. The conventional idea of an executioner as a sadistic thug is misplaced here, and he was up to a point fastidious. 'Simplicity and absence of noise,' he recommended, when Dr Guillotin and Tobias Schmidt, Swiss cabinet-makers, consulted him on the priorities of '*La Machine*'. Louis XVI suggested the blade would be more effective if angled rather than a crescent. 'The gentleman is right,' commented Sanson. They conducted trials on bales of straw, then sheep, then corpses, until Dr Guillotin is reputed to have said, 'All they will ever feel is a slight breeze on the back of the neck.'

I spent two weeks on a scaffold with an exact replica of their machine. It was in a disused airfield that became a sea of mud outside Paris. It was terribly cold except under the lights where I polished them off one after another. I was a staunch monarchist with the bearing of an aristo, in the long bottle-green frock coat of Charles Henri who on the eve of executing Louis went to Mass in his gloves, in order not to profane the sacrament. It was a grief to execute the King, and a shock to execute the Queen. I suggested he say, '*Courage, Madame,*' to Marie Antoinette, and Peter Ustinov (otherwise Mirabeau) said this added 'a grace note to the whole scene'. The executioners were all armed, fearing an attempt to rescue the King. The piece of cord I used to bind his wrists was given to me as a souvenir and I have it still. It reminds me of the difficult task of being dramatic without going over the top, in a serious documentary about a society which had in fact gone over the top. When it went out in France (in two three-hour parts, called *The Years of Light* and *The Years of Terror*) I was interviewed on French television news with a Sanson descendant, who gave me a copy of Charles Henri's death certificate.

The King was played by a Swiss, Jean François Balmer, the Queen by an Englishwoman, Jane Seymour. Robespierre was a Pole, Danton the Austrian Klaus Maria Brandauer; Marat an Italian, Mirabeau a Russian Englishman. And there were some parts played by French performers. Taken altogether it was a pan-European production. I kept my ears open for another French project but when it came, a bizarre story set in the sewers of Paris, it was shot at Shepperton.

In *The Rainbow Thief* Peter O'Toole was the man who lived in the sewers, Omar Sharif his visitor and I was O'Toole's uncle, raving mad in a pleasant way. Paralysed from the waist down, I careered around mounted on a cowboy's saddle on a machine like a small car, singing Wagner. As another part of my eccentricity I gave a dinner at which the guests ate dogfood while the chairs were occupied by dogs, eating food for people.

The dogs had to be Great Danes, but the usual providers of animals for films hadn't enough Great Danes so some rank amateur Great Danes had be brought in. So, as I racketed round the table belting out opera, the dogs became restive, and each had to have a handler hidden under the table hanging on to his paws. The scene took an incredibly long time to shoot, further protracted by the director's insistence on doing it at night, although it was an interior.

He was Alejandro Jodorowski, a Polish Chilean, reputedly a genius of the order of Welles and Buñuel, and actors such as Jack Nicholson were ready to give their back teeth to work with him. In my last scene I sang 'Plaisir d'Amour' instead, lying in a four-poster bed, cosseted by a dozen topless girls, and died of a heart attack. When I'd finished my stint, Alejandro confessed it was the first time he had worked with a professional cast, though this couldn't be said of all the dogs.

Alongside this, *Gremlins II* was a doddle. The script came to me in Paris from the director, Joe Dante, who subsequently became a much valued friend, and we went to Los Angeles to see him in his office, known as Dante's Inferno because of the way it's festooned with posters, curios, models and bric-à-brac of all kinds. His mind is similarly furnished. He appears to have read and seen everything and, what is more, to like and understand actors. The feeling is mutual. His father was a golf pro and author of a golfing book, which Joe gave me. We talked about my character of a mad scientist, Dr Catheter, in a futuristic lab full of eccentric genetic experiments. I supposed a Karloff make-up would be right, and he was very polite: he let me discover for myself it was wrong by looking at the lab. But really what the humans wore was of marginal interest, because the charming little Mogwai and his fiendish destructive offspring that swell in a gelatinous ooze to terrorize a building, then a city, dominate the screen with their fantastic shapes and brilliant colours. The film crackled with jokes and pastiches, a rare instance of a sequel improving on the original. It was unnerving playing a scene with a gremlin since all you see is a dot of light on a table. When you have a full-scale gremlin to react to, about three feet tall, there are four or five puppeteers hidden, controlling eyes, arms, mouth, body and legs with wires. They were amazingly convincing, so real you almost felt that actors of flesh and blood would become redundant – if not already sidelined by the departments of explosions and special effects.

The Italian Jobs

There is always a risk in Italy that my Italian blood will boil. But I love Italy and its people and their language, and their spectacular, confusing history. The prospect of working there is always irresistible, even though experience tells me that it is likely to entail psychological stress and/or financial loss. And it is usually impossible to find explanations for the loose ends that seem to hang around each picture.

There is no guarantee, for instance, that a film with an Italian financial interest will have Italian distribution. This was the case with *The Salamander* (1981), despite the authenticity of the melodramatic events in modern Italian history on which it was based. The Australian author of the originating novel, Morris West, prided himself on the extent of his research and the accuracy of his retelling. Perhaps that was the problem, that in holding up a full-length mirror to the corruption of Italian politics, and pegging it to an actual scandal, the attempted extreme right-wing coup by the Italian war hero Prince Borghese, it provoked the administration to put out a caveat. Or perhaps it was an aesthetic judgement: the novel was let down by the script.

At all events, despite my character's name being changed from Borghese to Baldassare, and a muster of actors that included Anthony Quinn in the title role, Eli Wallach as my collaborating *carabiniere* general, Franco Nero as the good person and Claudia Cardinale as the beautiful person, the film has never to this day had a showing in Italy. Now, of course, such a film would be redundant: the scandals of Italian politics have become a daily serial in the media, and a right-wing leader with the idea of making a chunk of northern Italy autonomous has achieved a fair degree of credibility.

Nothing so hot afflicted *L'Avaro*, a totally Italian rendering of Molière's play, which I appeared in ten years later in the fabulous robes

284

of a seventeenth-century cardinal, an addition to Molière's cast. It was directed by Gino Cervi's son Tonino, who was under the thumb of the most popular actor in Italy of his time, the late Alberto Sordi. The aggravations here were a barrage of pinpricks – practically everything, except the fantastic sets in real *palazzi* in and around Rome, the sort of backgrounds you couldn't buy for a million dollars. Among them was the Palazzo Farnese, where I was involved in a most curious episode, unique in my experience.

Away from the cameras I rehearsed some of the lines with Sordi, then dressed full fig as the dodgy Cardinal, sat at a splendid table and started delivering my lines. It was awkward, though, because of a strange echo. I stopped, started again, and again heard the echo. And I thought, Oh, well, it is a very high ceiling. Marbles. Mosaics. Maybe it all adds up to a kind of echo chamber. But it was a nuisance: I seemed to be hearing myself a split second late. I looked over to the sound people, Frenchmen whom I knew from a production in their country, and I indicated 'echo' to them. One shook his head and pointed behind the camera in the direction of Sordi. I said, from the script, 'I don't know what the Holy Father will say, because he had it in mind personally to bless your marriage with my sister,' and watched fascinated as Sordi said them too. He was repeating every line I spoke. He was simply incapable of doing nothing. He carried on echoing my lines, and eventually I said to the director, 'Would you mind, because I don't want to say anything to him directly.' And Tonino was evasive. 'Um, difficult,' he replied, 'because people will talk.'

They were already talking, about all kinds of things. It was not only Sordi's echo, but the whole crew was talking. In Italy people talk non-stop during a take. They smoke too, and the smoke goes wafting in front of the camera. And they move around all the time, in your eyeline. They have helicopters and fighter-bombers going past your window, and while those had to be ignored, the general commotion got to the point where I leaped to my feet and slammed my episcopal hand down on the table and yelled, 'I want absolute, total and complete silence while I'm working! Otherwise I will leave the set. Nobody moves, nobody talks, nobody does *anything*!'

There was a penetrating silence. One or two people smiled, one or two looked offended. The rest were as still as the marble of our walls. Then the make-up man bustled up to me and said, '*Bravo! Bravissimo!*' It seemed that planes were re-routed, cigarettes were extinguished, even Sordi swallowed his echo effect. There was total and complete silence. For at least twenty minutes.

But Alberto Sordi, the most popular actor in Italy, the lead in this film, its *de facto* director and editor, had doubtless put a hex on me that echoed on after the film was *finito*. I left, I'd been paid, everything was fine. Some weeks later I had a call from my Italian agent, who had seen the film and was deeply sorry to give me the news that the credits on the screen were all wrong. The contracts had me the same size with Alberto Sordi and Laura Antonelli above the title, but 'your name is in smaller letters alphabetically with the rest of the cast'. I was displeased. 'It's up to you to put it right. But couldn't you have done that at the press show?' There was a pause. 'I didn't go to the press show,' he confessed.

Only once, before cameras, have I ever forgotten my lines. It was during the filming of *L'Avaro*. I had an immensely long speech, a page at the least, to deliver in Italian, with several rather obscure phrases, and I had them hold up boards with some of these. I hated this happening, not only for the embarrassment but for the rattling distraction and awkwardness of it all. I pray that it never happens to me again. But really I have been lucky to have a mind in which lines stick, so that sometimes if I wake in the night I hear them again from long-ago half-forgotten films, and it may be that the habits of my early education have helped, drilling classical texts for recitation.

But that one experience on *L'Avaro* gives me a heartfelt sympathy for others who flounder and tend to go into a sort of coma. Some actors make little cribs by inscribing reluctant lines in the palms of their hands, or beside their wristwatch. Billy Wilder told me years ago of coping with the notoriously forgetful Marilyn Monroe in *Some Like It Hot*. Even in a scene with only one line to say she couldn't get it out, so he said to her, 'In this scene you're looking for a handkerchief and you pull open a drawer and there's your line.' Telly Savalas, when making every ten days or so a new television *Kojak* story, in which he never stopped talking, found it impossible to remember so much dialogue and worked out a plethora of such devices. He told me that he planted lines all over the set – on the side of the camera, in drawers, behind books, on a desk, and on one great occasion actually stuck a speech to the forehead of the person he was talking to. My friends' anecdotes came to my mind when I was feeling mortified after stumbling over my speech in *L'Avaro*.

About eighteen months later I went to Italy again to work on a film whose title gives no clue to its content: *Cybereden*. (They had six titles to choose from and eventually settled on the worst.) It had basically to do with an old lady (played by the sometime Baby Doll, now in her seventies, Carroll Baker) who hits on a make-up formula for making people young. I was her butler. She was a lovely person, well used to making films in

Italy, and so, naturally, was the charming male lead, famous in Italy, Adriano Celentano. The drawback was that he spoke not one word of English, nor did the little boy from *Cinema Paradiso*, but then he didn't have to.

The rest of the cast were English or American. We began by Lake Como, off-season, with the wind coming bitterly cold off the Alps or horrendously damp off the lake, with the shops closed and the hotels too. We finished in Cinecittà in Rome, another sort of nightmare, because you couldn't understand a word this delightful man said, after learning his English scenes phonetically. It was just a slur of sounds; he might as well have been speaking Inuit. We thought he would be re-voiced by an English actor, but he insisted on doing it all himself. The director was no help, because he spoke no English either, and we had the bizarre spectacle of him and his leading man having interminable discussions in Italian about how to play a scene in English. The whole thing was a nightmare, what Jimmy Durante would call a 'catastostroke'.

And how could I forget *Sorellina*? Impossible. That was an Italian film, and my blood boiled. But there was a *nuance* of difference: it was made in Slovakia, already separated from Czecho.

Faery Lands Forlorn

airy-tales suit me, as a witch does a black cat. Mystery and wonder
float just above the eyeline of the mundane. The real and the
imaginary combine in unexpected ways. That can be true not only
of the stories but in the routine of actors making them. Cast as the
sorcerer in the Grimms' tale *The Boy Who Left Home to Find Out About
the Shivers*, I was amused to find a musician playing my malevolent
hunchback retainer in the castle: the late and much lamented Frank
Zappa, in his only acting performance.

The caprice of acting tends to strike directors just the once and never
recur, like measles. Not everybody will hire them, but they're often
indulged by their fellow director John Landis, one of the few people in
Hollywood whose home is not like a film set or a department-store
window. On receiving the script of *The Stupids*, based on the popular
cartoon-strip family of Stanley Stupid, he read 'Enter the archvillain, like
Christopher Lee' and it occurred to him that nobody resembled
Christopher Lee so much as I did, so I had better take the part of the
wretch attempting to corner the American garbage market. We made it
in the summer of 1995 in a record temperature of 105 in Toronto.
There too, enjoying a busman's holiday, were directors such as Robert
Wise, Pontecorvo, Costa Gavras, David Cronenberg – about ten of them
– appearing as Petrol Pump Attendant or Man in Garden or Second
Builder.

This feeling of the blend of the real and the fantastic impressed me
strongly on an earlier occasion as I stood beside the grave of Kafka in the
Jewish cemetery on the outskirts of Prague, attempting to dispatch a
werewolf with a silver bullet. This was in *The Howling II*, produced with
the Barandow studio, in the days of Soviet control and Soviet
propaganda signs and dreadful greasy food. On the uplift side a splendid

Czech actor sang chunks of *The Bartered Bride* with me, and the Czech cast chimed in.

This venture, subtitled *Your Sister Is a Werewolf*, could not be classified as a fairy story, though the Bohemian castle gave it a family resemblance, and the wolves walking around upright did give it a children's-theatre aspect. It could hardly be dignified with the label 'horror movie' either, since it apparently wanted to send up the lycanthropic genre, but failed to frighten or amuse. The fun was unintentional, as when a group of us, fighting on the side of the angels with holy water and crosses, creep round outside the castle to surprise the evil wolves, and are ourselves surprised by an attack from a werewolf. He springs out of a hole in the ground. My Czech friend was told 'say something in English'. As his second language was German, he could think only of 'Achtung!' so his line came out as 'Attention! Werewolf!' Shooting stopped for half an hour while we all tried to compose our expressions.

As a film, *Mio, My Mio* was an authentic fairy story by the Swedish children's author Astrid Lindgren, with a great black castle surrounded by birds. As a work environment it was a horror story. Some countries use the alternative title, *The Land of Far Away*. For us the faraway land was the Soviet Union, where the food was uneatable, the sanitation unspeakable, the political people ubiquitous. From our window in our hotel, the National, we could see straight on to Red Square; the interior was less inspiring. The living-room had a huge mahogany table down the middle, where Lenin was said to have hatched up this and that, but getting to his bed must have tested his ingenuity. Gitte arrived in time for our silver wedding anniversary on 17 March, a date when I am always either in a desert or a brutally cold city with no taps in the basins.

As the mournful knight in the castle who entraps the souls of boys and girls and turns them into birds, I wore a steel hand. To don this I was whisked off to a basement in a decrepit alley. The mechanic who made it had wild, staring eyes and a mass of hair like Rasputin, in contrast to the picture of his father on the wall, in the full uniform of a Red Army general. The boy in the tale whose soul I coveted had to face not only the steel hand but a sword in it, which I had to whirl down, just missing him, and cleave a marble table in two. He didn't like it, which was understandable, seeing they'd put protective guards on the camera, but at the right moment he leaped nimbly out of the way, as I smote the table precisely along the given line. Among the other boys running around was Christian Bale, who went on soon after to make a name for himself in Spielberg's film of J. G. Ballard's novel *Empire of the Sun*. Our film wasn't in the same league, but it wasn't bad except for being a little slow and poorly edited. It was irritating work: nothing ever happened before lunch, and since it took forever to light a scene, not much after it. These were the standard frustrations of Russian film-making at that time.

Seven years later, in 1993, I was back in Moscow and a rather different Russia, though some things never change and our so-called hotel was again unspeakable, with the local pursuit of hard currency enough to get you banged up for years, and the interface between Russians and foreigners as surreal as it ever was. The film was not, however, a fairy-tale, but the next best thing, a farce.

My presence stemmed from my connection with the producer Paul Maslansky. After many excellent films which had not greatly rewarded him, he made the first of a popcorn series called *Police Academy* about a bunch of lunatic American cops in trouble, in a non-stop sequence of idiotic situations. When he realized the box-offices were under siege from an avid public, he rang us at three in the morning, chanting, 'I'm rich! I'm rich! I'm rich!' Now he was ringing to invite me to dabble in the seventh, *Mission to Moscow*. I would be an old Russian general from the Stalin days, weighted down with medals and a soup-strainer moustache. I would help Yeltsin out in his struggle to cope with his crime mafia by bringing over my American police pals. The Russian capital seemed to be at peace, so I accepted.

Like many others who'd tasted the Soviet Union before *glasnost*, I'd never dreamed of the kind of incidents I'd now be involved in. There was, for me, for instance, an exquisitely unreal moment when I stood on a rostrum, built smack in front of St Basil's Cathedral in Red Square, with Lenin's tomb on my left, dressed in the full uniform of a Russian general and bowed down with decorations, to make a speech to several hundred genuine militia men. The fairy-tale feel was not even marred when the militia band struck up 'Ta-ra-ra-boom-de-ay', followed by 'When the Saints Go Marching in'.

But this was the end of the film. We still had to make the middle and the beginning. Before we could, we had some interference from reality. On a Saturday when nobody was working, Gitte and I, with the American actor George Gaynes who played the police commandant, and his wife, were in a taxi, sightseeing. As we approached the bridge over the Moskva River that leads from Gorky Park to the Russian parliament, we saw a mob of civilians charging across the bridge, then riot shields and helmets flung into the river. We sped straight back to our regrettable hotel. We phoned the American and British embassies and

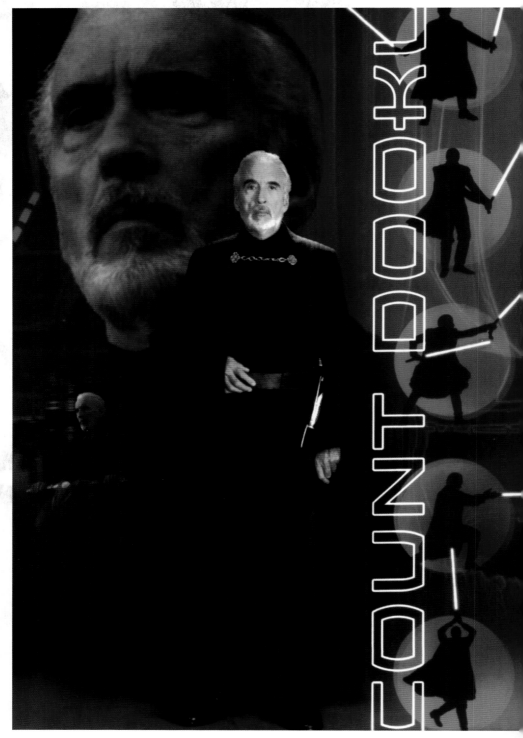

As Count Dooku in *Star Wars Episode II: Attack of the Clones*

Opposite At the World Awards in 2002

With Mikhail Gorbachev

My investiture at Buckingham Palace

CNN and a young colonel in the KGB who'd become a friend on this trip. Indeed, I'd been to his house, unthinkable on the previous occasion. They all told us: 'Stay under cover.' For four days, as it transpired.

I'd met the colonel through a London friend. He invited me to tea and came for me in the dusk in a car covered roof to hub with mud. The smell inside was worse. We rattled all over Moscow until I had no idea where I was, halting at last in a disused lot piled with bricks and planks. I thought, It's very cold for a collation al fresco. He said, 'We walk along by this wall, then through the wall.' We did that. Through the hole in the wall, we met a hedge. He said, 'We walk along the hedge, then through the hedge.' We did that. I was thinking, I should phone Gitte and let her know where I am. But I don't know where I am. Besides, there is no phone in the hedge. Through the hole in the hedge we faced the door of what looked like a derelict building. On either side was a man with a Kalashnikov. I thought, I'm a dead man. KGB. Then I thought, The KGB doesn't exist any more. But then again, although they don't exist, everybody still calls them the KGB.

The young colonel said, 'We walk through the door, and welcome.' We did that, and it was like walking into Claridge's. Cubby Broccoli, most unstinting of producers, would have eaten his heart out. Under a cosmos of chandeliers, men and women in civvies were downing caviare and champagne. Immaculate waiters moved among tables covered in damask and crystal. I thought, In a minute I shall probably see the pretender to the Russian throne. I was offered the full choice of goodies. 'Just a piece of cake,' I said. A hundredweight of cakes appeared from nowhere. 'Forgive me,' I said to my host, 'I wasn't expecting anything like this. What a place! What food! What service!' He replied nonchalantly, 'Oh, well, you know, it's KGB.'

This did not save us from having to stay under cover for several days. We had permission for some scenes at the airport, but getting there through security was a performance. Then it began to snow. The destiny of Russia hung in the balance and we worried about continuity problems. There's a scene where an idiot cop, spreadeagled on the roof of a car, rockets past the White House – there it is in shot, blackened by shell fire. Another continuity problem. (They left it in.)

For relief Gitte and I headed for the Ismailovo open-air market, where you can buy anything from a tank to a day-old chick. Closed. No crowds permitted anywhere. On the way back, we met a crowd. Our driver suddenly stopped. 'Look!' he cried. About twenty cars were slewed across the road at different angles, and beside them men with their hands in the air were being searched. They were darker than Muscovites, and called 'Caucasians', a term almost synonymous in the Russian mind with 'criminals', given their origins in Georgia, Azerbaijan, Armenia and other former republics. The troops of the Ministry of the Interior were piling them into special buses for the airport and the first available plane, no matter whither.

Finally we got through too, and filmed the arrival of our actors through customs. There in the concourse were all these unfortunate 'Caucasians' being distributed willy-nilly across the republics, while Russians crammed the check-in desks. The normal chaotic business of an airport went on, and people could see a great gaggle of American policemen with guns arriving, to be greeted by an elderly Russian general in full uniform.

In Hoops of Steel

Over the long haul, an actor can be sustained by the goodwill and asides of a regiment of colleagues, and wafted into the empyrean by the praise of a flock of luvvies, and few would deny their contribution. But there is no greater help to survival than the feeling that you have, or have had, some real friends. They're the ones unaffected by shifts in your reputation, the scale of your income, or long separations, and whose successes give you the feeling the home team has won. I'd like to claim a long list, but I'll restrict myself to four whose friendship we kept in good repair over the years. They were all older than me; they have all died; I miss them.

I first met the American writer Robert Bloch when he came to London for a science-fiction convention nearly forty years ago. Like myself, he was not very outgoing socially, and in America was never to be seen away from his home except at studios and SF conventions. SF writers, unlike authors in other genres, have shrewdly built up a tremendous fan club through conventions. Sci-cons are always full of weird and potty people who are enormously well read, so it's easy to talk about anything. Having found an affinity, Bob and I carried on talking over drinks at my flat. Later I stayed with him and his wife Ellie on my way home from filming a *Fu Manchu* with George Raft in Hong Kong. (There George poured out his entire life to me in a marathon confessional, lasting six hours; our subsequent meetings in London and Los Angeles were considerably shorter.)

Our friendship was founded squarely in the field of fantasy, and irrigated by the stream of people who came to Bob's house off Laurel Canyon in Los Angeles: among them Ray Bradbury, Fritz Leiber, Clark Ashton Smith and Fritz Lang, director of *M*, one of the most terrifying of all films. Surrounded by his library of the macabre, Bob talked in his den about H. P. Lovecraft and the mythos he'd invented, the Old Ones from outer space with unpronounceable names, and Lovecraft's odd habits, like living mainly off ice-cream and going out only at night.

Other favourites were Ambrose Bierce, Arthur Machen, Algernon Blackwood and M. R. James, when the going was good in the short-story market, and more recent writers who coped when it hasn't been so good, like Isaac Asimov and Kurt Vonnegut. Not to mention Bob himself, who could write about anything and make it chilling or hot, most famously *Psycho*, but usually with a strain of black humour. If you perform in this genre, at a desk or on film, humour is vital, though it may not be obvious in the results.

With Vincent Price it was usually pretty obvious. He was an extremely funny man. Indeed, he was a dazzling all-rounder. As a professional lecturer he toured in painting, sculpture and cookery, and bought art for Sears and Roebuck. His comic sketch of the tipsy cook demonstrating Caesar salad was a gem of television. He was as much at ease in the theatre as in the cinema, a model of versatility. We met at Shepperton for *The Oblong Box*. It was not until I was dying, with my throat cut, that my story intersected with Vincent's, so that it was a hail and farewell meeting, as I lay expiring in his arms, with him asking me, 'Which way did they go?' and I glugged in answer through a severed artery. He was swathed in a cloak like a tent, and by mistake rolled me on to it so that the camera could relish my death agony to the full, and kept hissing, 'You're lying on my train!' as I gurgled.

He could be acid and devastating, as could his wife Coral Browne, but they were never otherwise than sweet to me. It amused him to pretend that wherever he went people pestered him for an autograph, thinking he was me. 'This has got to stop!' he'd write. I remember, dining with him at Spago's in Los Angeles, a procession of people rising from their tables to greet him. He was already ill, and when driving us home – Gitte in the back with Coral – he reached across and patted my leg, saying, 'It's really wonderful to see you, dear boy, and here's to the next time.' We were shattered by the realization that there wouldn't be a next time, because always when our next meeting was mooted he'd respond with a crack, such as 'Not if I see you first!'

The closest of my friends, physically, was Boris Karloff. He lived next door. When we came out of our houses simultaneously, people expected to see body-bags dumped on the pavement. When Gitte first met him, she exclaimed, 'What a wonderful tan!' He must have been used to that, being Anglo-Indian. Of course we both knew what it was to be monsters, and in that respect I had to follow in his painful and childlike footsteps.

But he never patronized me. He told me he'd been given the opportunity only because he'd been spotted browsing in some studio canteen by James Whale, who said, 'This is the monster for me.' After twenty-four hours as 'the dear old monthter' for a day and night shoot, he told me, 'I was ready for the cemetery.' He once passed on to me Lon Chaney's advice: 'Find something other actors can't or won't do. If you succeed, you'll never be forgotten, and you'll survive.' No one else would have wanted to take his make-up for *The Mummy*. He told me that when he was all bound up, he barely dared take a breath lest the bandages break, and if he breathed out too much they'd come loose. Perforce he'd spent hours in this condition because the whole process was too complex to repeat. He also said, 'Leave it to the audience. What they imagine is more frightening than anything they see.'

There are patches of Boris's life that remain opaque and mysterious, despite the books written about him. I knew of three wives, but there may have been five. His last wife, Evie, told me she thought she was the fifth, but she couldn't be sure. His daughter Sarah Jane told me that up to a point he would talk, then she'd encounter a wall. My experience of him was similar, but I don't think he made mysteries because he had anything personal to hide – he was just naturally discreet. He was a versatile actor, like Bela Lugosi, with whom he'd often worked, and neither had the opportunity to show it. When I questioned him about Lugosi, he would only shake his head – 'Poor Bela! Poor Bela!' Lugosi's career tailed off; drugs accelerated the decline; as a last ambiguous comment he insisted on being buried in Dracula's cloak.

From his school-days Boris had been a cricket fanatic. We discussed the game a lot and watched matches at Lord's. In Hollywood he'd played in the club team founded and skippered by the tyrannical C. Aubrey Smith, known as 'Round-the-corner Smith' because of his peculiar bowling approach, emerging at the last second from behind the umpire. But Smith had also taken an England side round South Africa, and for good measure was an eminent character actor. His team, which mustered along with Boris such important cricketers as Errol Flynn, Ronald Colman, Basil Rathbone and David Niven, held him in awe. So when he commanded them, 'Stay on your toes for the next man, none of your slacking, Flynn, no dropping catches behind the wicket, Karloff, everyone smarten up in the field,' they were all shaking in their boots as they awaited this terror. And out to bat came the oldest and most decrepit fellow ever seen in bat and pads, barely able to make it to the wicket. Smith hadn't noticed that the years had passed.

Perhaps, laughing at this story, Boris hadn't either. He had become very arthritic and bowlegged and in his last years was always in pain with his legs, particularly when having to wear a brace, but he smiled and laughed and made light of it all, dealing with tremendous spirit even with the emphysema that finished him at eighty-one. We were in *Curse of the Crimson Altar* together when he was in his eightieth year, and as many as five films he'd worked on had yet to appear when he died. His photograph hangs on my wall, signed shortly after we made that film, below the legend 'Dear Christopher, many many more together, I hope.'

So, too, would Peter Cushing have gone on beyond his swan song, had someone written him a part with a wheelchair. In 1994, the year he died, also eighty-one, Peter and I were together for the narration of a Hammer archive video, *Flesh and Blood*. There was something a little bit different about Peter, waiting for the end: for twenty-three years since his beloved wife Helen died, his friends recognized that he wouldn't mind packing up on this earth to join her. Vincent once, in a phone call to me, asked, 'Is he still expecting Helen to be there to greet him?' And I said, 'And looking forward to it.' And Vincent said, 'And what if she's out?' I said, 'I shall tell him what you said, Vincent,' and when I did, Peter laughed fit to dispatch him immediately on his journey. When he'd recovered he said, 'Only Vincent could say such a thing, and only you could pass it on.'

While Helen lived I stayed with them in Whitstable, where they kept an elaborate aquarium of tropical fish, and in their house in Campden Hill in London, where he was always busy with his hands, making row upon row of lead soldiers and painting them, so you'd talk to them amid the set pieces he contrived for battles, and planes dangling from the ceiling. Or he'd make mock-ups in cardboard of theatrical productions. Although he appeared in fewer films than I did, he had a more serious career on the stage.

When Helen died he let all these craft hobbies go, though having a close friend in Edward Seago kept him painting. The Cushings had a collection of toys, but no children, so we felt it was down to us to perk him up with ridiculous stories and imitations, and the absurd postcards I sent him announcing the discovery of non-existent new birds to add to his enormous ornithological knowledge. He responded in kind with entertaining letters and satirical verses. By good fortune he had for more than thirty years an able and indefatigable secretary, Joyce Broughton, who prodded him outward and interrupted his introspection. In Whitstable he became a kind of patriarch, with a pier named after him and a regular place for his meals in the Tudor Tea Rooms.

Like Boris, he was reticent about his family life and never discussed his parents, though he wanted to know all about mine. On one occasion he told me he had a brother. 'This was forty years ago,' he added. 'Still alive?' I wondered. 'Oh, yes, yes, he farms.' 'Do you ever see him, Peter?' 'Very seldom.' I risked pushing on: 'Any reason for that? Don't you get on?' He sighed. 'We get on very well,' he replied. 'I'm quite fond of him, but you see, his wife doesn't approve of what I do.' Apparently she was one of those who consider an actor a rogue and a vagabond, not suitable company for solid citizens, an opinion not confined to starchy members of certain golf clubs.

Peter and I appeared in twenty-two films together, though not always as a pair. In the first, *Hamlet*, when he was Osric and I carried a spear and had no share of the marvellous speeches, we did not meet. In the last, *House of Long Shadows*, thirty-five years later, we had Vincent and John Carradine along too, billed by the press as the four masters of the macabre, and there wasn't a single marvellous speech to share between us. The direction was a blank, and we agreed with the critics who shredded the film. However, in between, and with varying commercial and critical success, but unvarying pleasure in working together, we knocked off a row of fantasy milestones. Most often I was the menace, and Peter was the force from academe, a savant, devoted to putting a stopper on me. As American golfers say of complementary partnerships, 'We ham-and-egged it.'

He was the most tolerant of men, expressing for instance nothing but pleasure when I sang arias to him in our dressing-rooms. Only once did he say something that brought me up short. It was on the set of *Horror Express*. The train in question was meant to be the Trans-Siberian Express, but our location was just outside Madrid, in an unspeakable studio at Daganzo. The food was deadly, salmonella the principal sauce. Peter never used the restaurant. He always ate the same meal, day after day, year after year, either because Helen liked it, or because he thought it was healthy: apple and cheese. Afterwards he would smoke a cigarette wearing white gloves, because the stain might show on the screen, and because Helen didn't like him smoking. So I found him in our so-called dressing-room. 'I can't stand this any more,' I said. 'Oh, what is that, dear fellow?' Then I went into a tirade about the food. '. . . I feel I'm going to die of this frightful food. This is a ghastly studio . . .' A massive whinge. He looked at me and peeled his apple. He just said, 'Well, there's no good belly-aching about it, you know.' That was about as severe as he could be. Coming from him, it was shattering.

He really was the gentlest and most generous of men. It could be said of him that he died because he was too good for this world.

In Search of Vlad

ad Bram Stoker been immortal, like his most famous creation, he would have been 150 in 1997 (exactly twice my age) which was the centenary of his enduring novel *Dracula*, and it behoves me to lift a glass of Romanian red to them both. I've always been Stoker's admirer. For one thing, he died of overwork, not a bad way to go. And his most popular fiction is better written than most huge bestsellers, and remains from an actor's point of view an unscaled Everest of fantasy, since no film-maker follows it all the way.

He was Irish, and clever, an invalid as a child, a civil servant as a young man and Henry Irving's theatre manager afterwards. It may seem odd that a man so steeped in theatre should choose the novel for his most dramatic idea, but of course vampires were a regular commodity of Victorian popular literature. As a civil servant he gave it the complex structure of overlapping documents; as an Irishman whose mother is said to have read endless fairy-tales to him when he was bedridden, he infused it with the sinister ethos of a waking dream.

Reading it aloud for a recording, I had to admit that it's overwritten, but compared with Mary Shelley's *Frankenstein* it's a children's primer. And at least Stoker never wrote any lines like those given to me in the script of my second Dracula film, such as 'I am the Apocalypse'. There's a story that Stoker had some of his actors on the stage of the Lyceum read passages from the manuscript, when Irving himself happened by, stopped to listen, then passed on into the wings saying, 'Dreadful.' And it is, full of dread. Had Irving lingered long enough he might have recognized some elements of himself as Mephistopheles in the physical description of Dracula's face. At all events it was immediately successful, and it's a nice thought that Queen Victoria, catching rumours of it, asked for Stoker's first book and was sent it: *The Duties of Clerks of Petty Sessions in Ireland.*

One thing Bram Stoker does seem to have got wrong. Dracula casts a very long shadow. More than thirty-five years have passed since I last played him, and the myth of the man and the undead is still regularly reused by others – with a difference now of $40 million in the production budget – but I am still identified with him. I have appeared before the cameras in well over two hundred and fifty guises, but apparently to little avail. Journalists still affect to be dismayed at the chilling, gaunt figure I cut as I come through the swing doors of some great hotel they've chosen as an arena in which to bait me.

Of course I should be grateful. And I am. The Count was the first firm footing on the ladder for me, and I don't scorn the base degrees. I am not ashamed of him, have accepted the ribbing, and never agonize over the possibility that I may be unleashing the cannibal strain among audiences, or any such nonsense. In my mind Dracula, the Mummy and Frankenstein's monster are driven figures, unable to help themselves, eventually out of control like a runaway train, and consequently very much alone. Audiences are terrified – very well, but they should also see the pathos of it. The characters have to be central to the story, not just get taken on board for the ride.

My feelings about Stoker's character never radically altered through seven films. Simply, it was aesthetically depressing to see the films step by step deteriorate, chiefly because after the verve and dash of their first decade, Hammer became complacent and careless, backed unimaginative scripts and tawdry production in the dangerously casual view that they had a captive audience that would take anything. The letters of fantasy addicts over that period read like one long cry of grief against the wickedness of slipshod practices. When I went to America to live it was quite poignant to recognize, through the appreciation by great omnivorous directors like Spielberg and De Palma and Dante and Coppola and Scorsese, how much they'd been influenced as young men by Hammer, and what an asset had been wasted.

After *Dracula* and *Dracula, Prince of Darkness*, I was in *Dracula is Risen from the Grave*, all of which still had elements to keep hope alive. Then came *Taste the Blood of Dracula*, in which three elderly gentlemen are desanguinated. It had the best cast but after an initial burst the story drooped. *Count Dracula*, made against the grain of this decline by Jess Franco in Spain, and outside the Hammer aegis, was a damn good try at doing the Count as Stoker meant him to be. It was made with the deepest of bows to the theatre manager who invented the character. In the whole vast Dracula industry it was virtually unique in that. Here the tragic, doomed Count was an old man getting younger as he imbibed the indispensable fluid. It was not only blood as the elixir of life, but the rejuvenator. It was a shadow of what it might have been, but nevertheless it had the right outlook on the protagonists. The film also benefited from Herbert Lom as Van Helsing and Klaus Kinski (who subsequently played Nosferatu) as Renfield.

Scars of Dracula was truly feeble. It was a story with Dracula popped in almost as an afterthought. Even the Hammer make-up for once was tepid. It's one thing to look like death warmed up, quite another to look unhealthy. I was a pantomime figure. Everything was over the top, especially the giant bat whose electrically motored wings flapped with slow deliberation as if it were doing morning exercises. The idea that Dracula best liked his blood served in a nubile container was gaining ground with the front office and I struggled in vain against the direction that the fangs should be seen to strike home, as against the more decorous (and more chilling) methods of shielding the sight with the Count's cloak. In the context of many modern extravagances this fussing may seem like the Victorian preference for having table legs covered.

At the age of fifty, I took the firm decision to Draculate no more. The deciding factors were *Dracula AD 1972* and *The Satanic Rites of Dracula*. The former had certain things in its favour. I was, to begin with, aghast at the plan to bring the story into modern times, but a compromise was effected whereby at least his Gothic homestead and the church were retained. I reflected that the Victorian period was arbitrary, the accident of Stoker's having lived at that time, and that after all Lon Chaney Jr as Count Alucard had erupted into a jazz ballroom. All the same, the hippy idiom used was already out of date when the film was made and the programme at large felt wrong to me.

That was just about bearable, with strong misgivings. But with the other one, originally called *Dracula is Dead but Alive and Living in London* I reached my irrevocable full stop. Thereafter I flung myself out in the snow for the wolves to gorge themselves on, leaving the thing to carry on without me. I declared that I'd never get back on board unless the story faithfully followed the book, or alternatively if the account of Henry Irving and *Dracula* were set up (which had been considered).

Even as I was coming to the realization that I couldn't suck another white shoulder in anger, a Catalonian director of avant-garde fame and Surrealist leanings, and expertise in vampirology, called Pedro Portabella, flattered me into being involved with a bewildering project called *El Umbráculo*. It was pure film, had not the slightest pretensions to being commercial, and subsequently won a prize. For all its critical nosegays it's possible that only Portabella and perhaps his mentor

Buñuel fully understood it, and for my own part I gathered only that it was the expression of his personal feelings and was a cry against the oppressive regime in his own country and the suffocation of artists.

I spoke no dialogue as such, though I recited a sizeable chunk of Poe's 'Raven', sang without music excerpts from *The Flying Dutchman* and *The Damnation of Faust*, and had a long, silent, motionless close-up of me which lasted one and a half minutes and for which I never received full credit, as people supposed it to be a still. The great Spanish painter Miró was in the film too, along with clips from *Nosferatu*, and he gave me a signed book of his work. It was all very pleasant and, most probably, excellent. So that was an upbeat note to end on, I felt.

Yet there was one more to come, to provide a gloss. Soon after the Portabella excursion, I was asked to Transylvania as protagonist in another kind of enquiry into vampires, fact and fiction. *In Search of Dracula* was a television feature by Calvin Floyd, an American living in Stockholm. We explored the whole thing, from the bat that punctures, then licks, to the monastery of Snagov where Vlad III, Knight of the Order of the Dragon, Voivode of Wallachia, known as the Impaler, who signed himself Dracula, Dracole and Dragwyla, supposedly lay in his tomb for five centuries – without a break, we devoutly hoped.

It made a very good outing to the province of Muntania in Romania, where Vlad Tsepesh was overlord. The documentary was a species of twin to a book co-written by Professor Raymond McNally and a *soi-disant* descendant of Vlad, Professor Radu Florescu. A great deal of sheer historical nastiness came out of the shadows to grimace at me – werewolves and criminal psychopaths plus the extraordinary sight of the vampire bat itself, first hypnotizing, then feeding on its prey.

There was never anything to touch the original Vlad, though. The dreaded Werewolf of Paris, Sergeant Bertrand, plus England's John George Haig, a killer who boasted of vampirism, plus the vampire of Düsseldorf, Peter Kürten, who remarked before being beheaded that he was sorry he'd miss hearing his own blood flowing, all the shocks of the criminal annals, do not match the horror of Vlad the Impaler. Or so we thought, on reading his record of pillage and torture and extortion and such tales as the time he nailed the turbans of the Turkish envoys to their foreheads because their religion forbade doffing. Thinking of Bram Stoker and Arminius Vambery, the Hungarian who is said to have regaled him with the exploits of Vlad, I wonder how closely he tied him in to the folkloric vampire myths of Transylvania.

Modern Romanians, however, regarded him as a national hero, despite the atrocities and the impaling of 50,000 Turks after one battle.

Only to be expected, apparently, by a defender of Christendom. This view was shared, we discovered, by the soldiers conducting manoeuvres while we were there. I was togged up in moustache, fur hat and flowing robes to wander about his forests and castle of Bran. The armed forces with luscious camp followers were having a mighty carousal by the castle when I emerged into their midst, and the crossings in haste in the Orthodox style by this Eastern gathering were beautiful to watch. The official line said Vlad had turned the invading Turk out of the country and was therefore its heroic benefactor. This did not stop them making the most of the cinema boom in Dracula in the Western world and, soon after, Dracula tours were instituted. (And, in a quieter way, Harrogate helps tourist pilgrims interested in Bram Stoker and his hearth there.)

The countryside was faithful to all I'd read, and beautiful beyond the book, with towering pinnacles of rock, cloud-capped peaks, mists coiling through valleys, and a strange unease and unreal cold when the moon flickered through the foliage. Calvin thought the creatures sensed my affinity with the place. When we alighted at Pojana, above Brásov, it suddenly became seven degrees colder, the moon hoisted itself over the crags for a straight stare, and a bat brushed past my face. 'They know,' said Calvin.

Sweet and Sour

Films are not made for actors. True, we're invited to premières, and sometimes go, but not so much to see as to be seen. We play the part of cinema props, like the stills, but with less flattering lighting. We arrive for the opening and are importuned for autographs, and would gladly give them, but have no time even to explain that we are commanded to be in our seats before the lights go down. I dislike premières only less than I dislike Hollywood parties, and the hundred or so minutes stretch out like so many years – it would hardly surprise me if the audience emerged looking like people on an outing from an old folks' home. The ideal situation, when a film opens, is to be working on another, preferably on a location where you're irretrievable.

The truth is that I don't like watching myself anyway. On the one hand there is this cursed voice speaking to my inner ear, reminding me how much better I should have managed this, that, or the other speech or action. On the other hand there is the disappointment of finding that scenes that seemed to have gone down well at the time of shooting have been left on the cutting-room floor. Or there is the purely professional outrage at finding yourself in a film wholly unlike the one described to you when you did your bit, with the story and the tone changed, and possibly another cast substituted for the one mentioned when you signed up. Even without the suspicion of anything underhand, many actors have only a transient sense of being part of it, which fades when they leave the set. Too much happens afterwards, they feel, and too many alien influences are at work in the shaping, to encourage their faith or interest in the result. In addition, actors are not welcome at the daily rushes, so may have only a sketchy idea of what is going on artistically.

It is not always as bad as that, but it happens that you miss seeing the films you were in at the time they come into bloom, and never pick them up again as cut flowers. I have seen only a minority of the films I have worked on, though I have a few videos scattered around in various cupboards, sent to me by studios and well-intentioned colleagues, and perhaps only Gitte has an inkling of what is where.

The films that have been most important to me – aside from those I have been working on in the last decade, which I'll come to, and with an affectionate nod to the three fantasy monsters which made me what I am not (the Mummy, the Creature, and the Vampire) – were all imperfect, but each had its own character, or furnished a coincidental link with my own sense of the past, or simply gave me something back that lifts my spirits.

Thus, for instance, *Rasputin, the Mad Monk*, not only because it was such a good part based on an extraordinary historical phenomenon, but because of the eerie sense of contact with it through my childhood meeting with his assassin. I include *The Man with the Golden Gun* because a lead role in a Bond film is the most public way to go public, from the Halls of Montezuma to a village in the Celebes, that any actor can imagine. I can incidentally correct the widespread belief that it also gives you financial security for life: the money goes to the Bonds and not to the heavies.

Of a completely different order was *The Disputation*. This I include to salute the seriousness with which Channel 4 television put it together, and because the historical conflict that generated the story appealed to me immensely, and because as a job it got me over the hump of a serious operation.

Good, bad and astonishing direction has fallen to my lot. The most succinct was from an overworked and harassed Stuart Burge on *Julius Caesar*. He clove his way through a throng of people to say to me, 'Of course, you do realize, don't you, that Artemidorus is quite, quite mad?' and passed on, without ever speaking to me again.

But my first encounter in a major role with direction as a class act was with Billy Wilder in *The Private Life of Sherlock Holmes*. I have worked with a number of great directors before and since, but performing a role for him gave me a glimpse of how to be so much better than usual. He was unimpressed by whatever image I might have as a totem of the horror industry, and unfussed by the thought of any influence that might have on the distributors of a comedy, and gave me the part of Sherlock's brother, Mycroft. It was a witty and beautiful picture. It was the nearest I had come to being in a movie where all the desirable qualities featured on both sides of the camera.

Wilder gave no evidence of his alleged capacity to cut actors off at the ankles with some devastating comment. He was a driven perfectionist and his criticisms were therefore happily accepted. Once, when I found I was getting some laughs quite easily in a scene, he said only, 'Don't *sit* on it, Christopher,' and I knew what he wanted. We made the film around and about the south shore of Loch Ness, and as we stepped out to do our first shot in Castle Urquhart, by that spooky stretch of dark water, bats came wheeling out. Billy said, 'You must feel quite at home here.' It was the only reference he made to my past, and I was profoundly grateful to him for his tact. When Gitte and I moved to Los Angeles to live and work some years later, he and Jack Lemmon surprised us with a wonderful welcome party.

Although it was made more than thirty-five years ago, *The Devil Rides Out* remains in my head as an ongoing project. Here is a case for the special effects that were beyond anybody's scope at the time. And the case for employing *me* again in a remake, in the same role of the Duc de Richleau, is that now my age more or less matches his. There is a climactic scene within a pentacle, when he says to three others with him, 'He has sent the Angel of Death. You cannot see the rider. If you look upon his face you will die.' It wasn't possible in those days to show a winged horse charge in with reins held taut by unseen hands and stirrups extended by unseen legs. Our horse's hooves slipped about on the studio floor, and though the animal did some good stuff rearing up and trying to strike away vases of holy water, it was on the whole a relatively low-key spectacle by comparison with what we could do with computer special effects today.

There is no way that I could leave out *The Wicker Man*. This I think might be the one I would take with me to a desert island. It is often described as a 'cult movie', a phrase that hints at exclusivity and maybe critical snobbery. But if it simply means that there are some like-minded enthusiasts that will save it from oblivion, I'm delighted to have ministered to a cult. Written by Anthony Shaffer, it was the best-scripted film I ever took part in, and it turned out to be a flawed masterpiece.

It is a terrifying story of the Lord of Misrule, a conflict between Christianity and paganism worked out on a Scottish island in the spring, when the people respond to the urges of the sap rising, and pay their dues to the ancient gods of fertility, for themselves and to reverse the trend of poor harvests. The virginal and puritanical policeman from the mainland, enticed into a game of cat and mouse by the islanders, and burned alive in the Wicker Man as a sacrifice to the Druids, was beautifully played by Edward Woodward as an obstinate young bullock of duty-bound energy, oblivious of the portents of his horrible fate until the great wicker totem appears before him, rearing up on a headland with the sun going down behind it.

My part was the sophisticated leader of the pagan community, Lord Summerisle, whose head in a sense is also on the line, orchestrating the movement and the meaning of the dreadful game. I think that before it was written the part was intended for me. Shaffer, fresh from the success of *Sleuth*, wrote superb dialogue; the American Paul Giovanni composed marvellous background and foreground music; the women dancing *au naturel* were quite natural. Peter Snell, managing director of British Lion, produced; Robin Hardy directed.

For a year's work Paul has said that he was paid £1,500; but the budget of £500,000 did not stretch to payments for Tony, Robin or me. (A generation later I played in a film directed by Robin's son, Justin, and I had to say to him, when it again became clear that money wouldn't be part of the package, that I really couldn't afford to go on working for the Hardy family. Though I took on this second job too, it seemed to me that I had become too senior to engage in work experience, and feared that the Spanish saying 'no two without three' might be fulfilled.)

However, with Robin Hardy off we went to Ayrshire, Kirkcudbright-shire, Newton Stewart, the Logan Botanical Gardens and Culzean Castle (where Eisenhower once kept a flat), and with these and other sites on the Scottish mainland, we stitched together a totally plausible island. Since we had to represent spring in a very cold October, flowers had to be brought in on trucks.

The great thing was that we shot the entire teasing script, the poetry as well as the prose of it, the ripening sex of it, the pretty dances and the lusty ones (*coup de théâtre* for Britt Ekland), the butcher, the baker and the candlestick-maker of it, with those lovingly observed characterizations of small traders that British cinema does so well. It is nature on the move in the spring, the whole community singing in joyful chorus as the grim ritual of sacrifice is enacted. *The Wicker Man* was in the end horrifying, but not what I call a horror film. It was about growth, not decay.

We all went our separate ways feeling pleased with each other. Some while later, during which time Peter Snell had been replaced by Michael Deeley as managing director of British Lion, I saw a private screening in a small projection theatre in the company's premises in Soho. My good cheer gradually ebbed away as I remarked that one great piece after another had gone missing. Cuts are unavoidable, but some of these seemed like amateur butchery. It wasn't merely that I personally had had some good lines shaved off, but entire parts, excellently played, had gone. The doctor. The chemist. The baker. The fishmonger. These had been created by marvellous Scottish actors in considerable scenes, not just group appearances.

Feeling that the editors had unpacked the portmanteau of talents rather carelessly, I went upstairs and met Michael Deeley.

'What did you think of the film?' he asked me.

'Very, very good,' I said (being the dutiful team player), 'and most unusual. It should have a terrific impact, do very well indeed.'

He then said, 'It's one of the ten worst films I've ever seen.'

I was dumbfounded. I said, 'I suppose you're entitled to your opinion, Michael, but I couldn't disagree more.'

I was angered by what I thought was an unfairly dismissive view, tactlessly uttered, and bothered by the idea that it did not augur well for distribution. I suggested to Robin Hardy and Tony Shaffer that the film be recut and some considerable parts be restored. They said they'd take a look at the negatives and the out-takes, and try for a rescue operation.

From the moment that decision was taken until now, the negatives have remained lost, stolen or strayed. Two versions of *The Wicker Man* eventually went out on the circuits, with twenty minutes more for America than for Europe, and when the British version went out, coupled with Daphne du Maurier's story *Don't Look Now*, there was not a squeak of publicity to be heard. I broke the rule of a lifetime and begged a number of critics to go and see it, at my expense if necessary. Some did go, paying for their own tickets, and praised it. Now I think it's mandatory for critics to know the film.

But neither version contains the material we searched for. The negatives and out-takes should have been in the vaults of British Lion. Or possibly in the labs where film is processed. Or they could have been in the catacombs of Shepperton. Every place we went to denied all knowledge. Some suggested they were in cans with wrong labels; others suspected cans with no labels.

Peter Snell spent months investigating. Finally, he ended up near Shepperton, standing by a hollow which had been filled in for the new road. At the bottom of the hole, he learned, were the cans of more than three hundred movies thought to be obsolete. Among them, he was assured, were those of *The Wicker Man*. It wouldn't surprise me.

The Great Leader

According to Viola in *Twelfth Night*, urging the poor fool Malvolio to get into exotic gear, some have greatness thrust upon them. In my case I had to wait until I was seventy-five, and furthermore had no anticipation of greatness. Indeed, my most recent engagements had been on a minor scale and hardly auspicious. In one I had played the part of a garbage entrepreneur in a film based on a series of popular American children's books. And in another, where I worked (unpaid) in a school story, with a lot of real schoolboys, in a real school that was about to be closed down, *Empire* declared, 'Nothing about it suggests that it should have been made for the big screen, so modest is its scope.'

Modest was a good word for *Feast at Midnight*. In it, the real world and fantasy were like an alternating current. Its charm harked back to some of the Ealing stories. I suppose young commentators would call it retro. The school, Hawtrey's, no longer exists. It was on the Cardigan estate and, while we had official permission to be there, we were uneasy on the first day to hear that the owner was sitting in his car at the gate with a rifle on his knees.

The film was totally English, a gentle farce produced by Yoshi Nishio who, by virtue of having been to Eton, sounds more English than I do. As a puritanical housemaster I had to be strict, while in the real world helping one of the boys with his Greek homework. Another delightful boy became so immersed in his role as the school bully that he shed tears at the hostile reaction he prompted. But he did reveal to me his ambition to be an SAS warrior. I assured him that I thought he would be, and at the end of term/end of shooting gave him my SAS regimental association tie.

Robert Hardy was the headmaster, and Edward Fox gave us a day because he so liked the script, and we three stayed in a pleasant hotel owned by the actor Richard Johnson, in the Savernake Forest. Though this had been a nice comfortable interlude, the film was not likely to reach a very wide audience, and it had not left me with any sense that the fates might be looking to thrust greatness on me.

Of course, in 1997 the press were busy with me, but it was to thrust Dracula down my throat with renewed vigour – the peg was the centenary of the first publication of Bram Stoker's novel. So it was a nice and mysterious variation to be invited to talk about something completely different at the Basil Street Hotel in Knightsbridge.

My hosts there, Dr Akbar Ahmed, head of Islamic studies at Cambridge, and film director Djamil Dehlavi, had also been stirred by an anniversary, but a far more serious one. Fifty years had passed since the foundation of Pakistan. They wanted to make a film about the founder, Mohammed Ali Jinnah.

'What do you know about Jinnah?' they asked me.

I replied that I knew he had created a new state, divided into two parts, West Pakistan and East Pakistan, now Bangladesh. I believed him to have been extraordinary, a man of determination and brilliance. That seemed to be enough.

'We'd like you to play Jinnah,' they said.

Who knows how this idea came to them? They did not seem like the kind of people who might have watched me in recent small screen performances such as the Grand Master of the Templars in *Ivanhoe*, or *The New Adventures of Robin Hood*. And I did not like to ask them: an actor invited to come aboard does not care to risk upsetting the boat. Perhaps for once my height was a help; Jinnah was quite tall and thin, and I was not much above my present weight of eighty-eight kilos, though I look more with the slight 'cascade of the waistcoat' that comes from singing. Sadly, towards the end of his life, devoured by tobacco, Jinnah was barely half that.

Just as I am happiest when a fiction script closely follows the novel, or at the least the spirit of the work, so I think that as nearly as possible actors should match the physical appearance of the historical characters they represent. Naturally this becomes an imperative when the story is that of the life of an eminent person. I would not be credible as Napoleon, nor Danny de Vito as Wellington. In due course in Pakistan I found that Jinnah's portrait is everywhere, public and private, his image an icon, and it's much to the credit of the film's make-up department that they made me look enough like him to qualify to hang on the wall.

Similarly one would like the narrative to parallel the main course of events as plausibly as records allow. I was told, 'Look, nobody has ever made a film about Quaid-e-Azam (The Great Leader), as they call him today. He has appeared in *Gandhi* as a malevolent demonic character threatening civil war, which is an appalling distortion of the truth, and a complete farrago of nonsensical film-making.' So my patrons seemed to be on the side of history.

Minded of the responsibility that I might shortly be taking on, I carried off the script to read, and borrowed several books on the subject for homework. I thought the script was a fair picture of a husband, father and brother, as well as of a visionary politician. Except that there were some painfully obvious fabrications, of his meeting Saddam Hussein and Yasser Arafat, which had to go. And they went. It was never clear why they had them in. They were totally out of the historical scene.

Having Akbar Ahmed as a scriptwriter should have been a safeguard against solecisms in the matter of the Muslim religion. As a distinguished Islamic scholar, who subsequently became High Commissioner of Pakistan in London, and is now Professor Emeritus of Islamic Studies at Princeton, he knows as much about it as anyone else on earth. Beyond the implicit importance of the faith in making an independent Muslim state, and its essentially peaceful nature, the script was not concerned with a religious message. Nevertheless there were some odd gaffes.

One of these threatened to sink the whole project. As the fulcrum of the story the famous Indian actor Shashi Kapoor, one of a whole family of famous Indian actors, would play an angel who summons me as Jinnah to account for my life on earth, while in limbo. But we soon discovered – I had to learn everything quickly – that 'angel' wouldn't do, and there's no such place as 'limbo' in the Muslim view. So these dangerous words were out too, but we kept the device, ingeniously transmogrified into a kind of celestial library full of computers, from which the Jinnah file is absent, and Shashi, now the library curator, requires me to supply my curriculum vitae.

So here was an enthusiast for Jinnah who had never produced a film in his life, with a director whom I knew only as the creator of a couple of films that had been seriously controversial in Pakistan, one of them called *Blood of Hussein*. I had the feeling they thought that once I was in the role I could make everything come right. Anyone with an inkling of the complexity of affairs on the subcontinent can imagine how I might feel on hearing, 'I don't know anything about producing films. You're an expert. You've done so many pictures. I beg of you, I beg of you, please, if there's anything you think is not functioning the way it should, in any area, before the camera, behind the camera, tell me at once!' Often I mentioned dysfunctions, but nothing was ever done.

Much about the background to this film is opaque. 'Who's financing it?' I asked. No one could give a cogent reply. 'Pakistanis living in America, possibly some living in England,' was the typically vague answer. 'The Pakistan government,' was another optimistic suggestion, meaning the Bhutto government, which had not long to go before it was replaced – it later turned out that this was the case. The budget was small – a scant £5 million.

But I'd agreed to be saddled up with a giant on my back, the father of a nation no less, so I should not complain if it proved to be an arduous journey. One lightening factor was the support of an excellent cast. Shireen Shah, a very good Pakistani actress, played Jinnah's sister, as important in her own way as Jinnah was in his. Jinnah as a young man was the British actor Richard Lintern. The Anglo-Indian Sam Dastor, with a high-pitched, slightly weak voice made a brilliant recreation of wily old Gandhi. For me, he is the definitive Gandhi. Nehru was Robert Ashby, a Bangladeshi whose father was one of the first prime ministers of Bangladesh, and there was little he did not know. The villain of the piece was Lord Mountbatten, played by James Fox, and for Lady Mountbatten first Vanessa Redgrave said she would play it, and then Patricia Hodge, but both found reasons not to, so Maria Aitken stepped in just before we were about to go, and made a fine Edwina. She wasn't likely to be scared of much.

There was actually quite a lot to be scared of. Karachi was and is a dangerous place. Apart from which there were the warnings of friends who couldn't see a happy outcome. But I could hardly back out of playing one of the great figures of the twentieth century, and in a way their pessimistic voices added fuel to my ambition.

Keeping Cool in Karachi

Karachi deserves a day or two, said the Lonely Planet guide. We spent ten weeks there, with a foray to Lahore. In that length of time a wandering backpacker could have had ample leisure to explore the bazaars, chill out on Zoroastrianism, enjoy the rare treat in Pakistan of a beach, take pictures of the wildlife in the mangrove swamps, not to mention photogenic turbans and donkey carts wholesale in the hinterland of alleys and little shoebox shops. I could never find even the day or two that Lonely Planet reckoned Karachi deserves. Besides, I was in a sense a marked man, and travelled hither and yon always within a defence of Kalashnikovs.

On the other hand, I was put up in a luxury hotel, the Pearl Continental, with my own butler and plenty of room to accommodate the troupes of journalists who formed the habit of asking me leading questions. The first thing I saw when I arrived at the hotel was an armed guard in the corridor outside our rooms.

'Is this some sort of bodyguard, or minders?' I enquired.

'Oh yes, yes. Twenty-four hours a day,' they answered.

'What? Even when I'm not there?'

They nodded confidently. 'Oh yes, no one can get in.'

Except the butler, of course.

From the first day everybody in the hotel knew who I was, and who I was pretending to be. From the second day all of the eight million in Karachi who could read a newspaper knew it too. I had a letter of welcome from the President of Pakistan thanking me for coming to play Jinnah, but the newspapers had no such courteous manners. From the start they plagued me, expressing shock, horror and outrage. They found it intolerable that a Westerner, a Christian, a man who had played Dracula and Scaramanga, etc., should be cast as the father of the nation. I could steel myself for these reactions in Karachi, but it was saddening that the British press, including a responsible broadsheet that prides itself on its arts coverage, should echo their strange arguments. As if actors are the characters they play. As if one couldn't by turns be Hitler and Nixon and a cannibal, or Charlie Bubbles and Churchill, or Richard III and Gandalf.

Well, newspapers soon get tired of their own excitement. Most of them calmed down a bit, except for *The News*, a national newspaper, which maintained a relentless barrage of attacks on the film and on me, with small-arms fire in the letters page. A Major (retired) recommended I be deported and took out a writ in the Court of Sind to that effect (it was thrown out). Someone else proposed that Shashi Kapoor be sent back to *his* own country, which left him unmoved. Another poor half-wit proposed the theory that our script had been written by Salman Rushdie. At long range the Indian press surmised that the film was a scheme to vilify Nehru.

Most eccentric was the behaviour of one editor. Though editors love to criticize politicians, they do not usually want to step into the boots of one. But apparently this man did, and had even been to audition for Jinnah. He was wholly unsuitable, both in physique (too small) and previous experience as an actor (nil).

Meanwhile we got on with the daily job, which opened with an exhilarating cavalcade through the streets of Karachi and on to the various locations. Out in front was a motorcycle outrider, leading a truck that contained four policemen with Kalashnikovs, then my car with myself beside the driver and a policeman with Kalashnikovs in the back, then the Kalashnikov sandwich completed with another truckful of police, and finally one more motorcycle. The only weakness in this design of harmony and symmetry was that the guns in the truck ahead were naturally pointing at me, and it must be admitted that it would have taken only one Kalashnikov, wielded perhaps by a crazed editor on a roof, to bring everything to a halt. However, we certainly dealt with the traffic problem.

Gitte, exploring the bazaars and visiting what sights I felt were within a safe distance of the Pearl, had to walk, though always with an armed guard at her side. Nothing exotic ever fazes her, and she could be said literally to have taken all the difficulties in her stride. Likewise Christina, spending three weeks with us, but not allowed even to cross the street to buy a newspaper without the Kalashnikov escort. At one point my back went and I had to go to the local hospital for treatment, with two armed policemen ahead and two behind. It may have looked to curious bystanders that I was about to be deported.

The real problems in making *Jinnah* were quite different. The production team was a very small unit of fifteen people, coping with hundreds of local extras who might or might not have been told what was afoot. The production and accounts people were having nightmares. We worked very long hours among poor people in formidable heat. Communication generally was pitiful. It was a personal frustration for me that telling us the truth was not an ingrained habit – though honesty was the vital premise of our film. The director was indecisive and without enough experience to communicate easily on the set. There were critical moments when he stood like a rabbit in the headlights. We had a brilliant cameraman who effectively directed many of the scenes.

And nobody could fault the performances of the cast: the charming but devious manoeuvres of Mountbatten; the court actions when Ismay, Gracie and Radcliffe testify to the orders he gave them in shifting the boundary line (an invented scene but exactly true to their eventual depositions); the subtlety of the affair between Nehru and Edwina; the confidence of Shashi Kapoor with whom I played many of the scenes . . .

For my own part I studied the minutiae of Jinnah's gait and voice wherever I could rustle up an old Movietone newsreel or radio broadcast. I imitated the flat arm gesture he used when going through crowds, and coughed a lot in tandem with his cigarette habit, which we believed to be the cause rather than the symptom of his final illness (more commonly attributed to tuberculosis). And I put on the eyeglass that he used to read, even during his speeches. I made some great speeches in the film, because they were his, just as he made them. It was interesting to discover that he always made them in English, because his Urdu was poor, to 100,000 people who understood not a word; that he had spent a great deal of time in Lincoln's Inn in London (they too have a great big picture of the icon, this time as a barrister); and that he frequented the House of Commons regularly to hear the English language spoken properly – which they may have done in those days.

I made one great speech precisely where he had made it in front of a famous mosque in Lahore, flanked by local Pakistani actors being his government officials. The crowd consisted entirely of policemen in plain clothes, who were wonderful. Only a few knew English, the heat was fierce, and nobody brought them any water, but they applauded as if all the troubles of the Sind were now resolved. I made his last great speech to the Pakistani Parliament, about the freedom to worship any religion you choose, in the former London County Hall festooned with flags, to an audience of movers and shakers and mullahs, the producer biting his nails and the director terrified I would blow it before this august assembly.

It was amazing that we were there at all, because six weeks into shooting the government suddenly pulled the plug on our finance. The Bhutto regime had gone, so the new Nawaz Sharif government had a good excuse. Or maybe they simply lost their nerve, under pressure from the press. Or they had turned up our director's earlier films and objected on political and religious grounds. Who can say why they withdrew our funds?

The producer, in a panic, had to go hurtling backwards and forwards. I did some hurtling, and reported our sad condition to the son of General Habibullah Khan, a power behind the throne. My friend expressed sympathy. Outrageous, he said. Eventually money to finish the film was found. Who can say how they were able to restore our funds?

From the outset when I visited the Jinnah mausoleum – empty but for a military guard who sprang to attention – and invoked the help of the spirit in the marble tomb, I felt a horrible degree of responsibility. Perhaps this is why, right at the end, for the first time in my life I broke down on camera, in a scene of great pathos, involving a little girl in a refugee column whose mother is among the victims of a murderous onslaught. I couldn't stop crying, and those are my real tears on film.

There was matter for tears in the aftermath. The first cut was unshowable, but with the music in and several edits in London and New York it was clearly very presentable. It was shown at the New York Festival and had wonderful reviews. And in Los Angeles, wonderful reviews. Same again at the London Festival, and Cairo . . . Best critical spread of my life. But, with the exception of Pakistan,

It. Could. Not. Get. A. Distributor.

And if it never does, through timorousness on the one hand and unquantifiable debts on the other, my consolation will be that the people who had worked with Mohammed Ali Jinnah, the man in the street, the people who made the clothes, the shopkeepers, the vendors in the bazaars, the police and the soldiers, all those extras who were normally strangers to film-making, all said the same thing.

'Thank you.'

Coming Back for More

Despite my frustration at seeing *Jinnah* driven into a cul-de-sac, I had to give over grieving and, in a phrase in vogue at the time, move on. I moved, briefly, to Lithuania, where I'd been twenty-five years before in Soviet days with Gitte when frustrated by an actors' strike in Hollywood; and I moved, again briefly, to Luxembourg, where I had also been before to make a couple of Sherlock Holmes tales: *The Leading Lady* (with Morgan Fairchild as Irene Adler) and *The Incident at Victoria Falls*, which took us to Zimbabwe as well. Neither of these can be found in an index to Conan Doyle's works, because he did not write them.

The reason for Lithuania was, believe it or not, to make *The New Adventures of Robin Hood* for television. They were dreamed up in America, and all shot where I would not have expected to find a professional studio, on the outskirts of the Lithuanian capital, Vilnius. They ran successfully, especially in America, for three or four years. The first and second Robins were both Americans. I took to the first particularly because, in addition to being very nice, he was an Italian American who had been a singer, and a good one. We would charge up and down the studio corridors blasting out the great duet in *Rigoletto*, well enough to attract an audience of other people using the studios who couldn't possibly have been actors.

British actors took the other leading roles in the *New Adventures*, but were required to speak with an American accent. I flatly refused. My part was Olwen, a benevolent wizard roaming through the forest, a kind of Merlin to Robin Hood's King Arthur. I took the precaution of having some photographs taken, as material evidence of wizardry – the beard, the robes, the staff, the omnipotent expression, and the magical aura – to lend support to my claims should wizards be required elsewhere.

From Luxembourg though, I took no souvenirs. Our film there, *Talos the Mummy*, did not justify them. And the actor in the title role probably felt the same. A man about seven feet tall, he broke his leg, poor fellow, in falling through the floor. They had me as the usual busybody archaeologist who rashly opens the tomb. The more interesting aspect was that the whole excavation, with local Asian immigrants dressed as Egyptians, took place in Luxembourg gravel pits. It looked exactly like contemporary Egypt.

Another benefit for film producers in Luxembourg is that they can arrange a tax shelter – shoot a certain number of days in the duchy, go anywhere else in the world as well and still have a tax shelter deal for Luxembourg. There was no talk of gravel pits and mocking up the waterfall for *The Incident at Victoria Falls*. Instead we went to Zimbabwe, and the genuine, awesome waterfall, at the instigation of Edward VII, with such unusual suspects as Marconi, Lily Langtry, Theodore Roosevelt and Lord Roberts. It was great fun with Richard Todd and Claude Akins and all, but there was no prospect of Holmes shooting up 'the seven per cent solution' – the American censor would have killed the film stone dead. Nor for films on TV would any of today's spouting gore be allowed: people who were shot would just gasp and fall over.

Back in Luxembourg we did the palace scenes where the King, played by Joss Ackland, briefed me on the need to rescue the great diamond, the Star of Africa. The real local royal, Jean 'Lux', the Grand Duke, visited us on the Sherlock Holmes set and, with his perfect English, it was like talking to a colonel in the Brigade of Guards. I said, 'Sir, you'll become the European Hollywood with all these companies filming here on tax shelter deals.' And, by Croesus, that is just what has happened.

The completely different event that signalled a renewal for me was the invitation from the energetic director Tim Burton to 'appear for just five minutes' in *The Legend of Sleepy Hollow*, a story by Washington Irving subtitled 'Ichabod Crane and the Headless Horseman'. Call no man happy until he's dead, but those five minutes, right at the beginning of the story, were enough in some strange way to prefigure a roll of luck that has lasted me through until the time of writing. When people in the business said, 'He's back,' they didn't mean that they'd seen me in London, but that I was getting work. A perception like that tends to lead to your getting more.

In the opening scene in the town hall my message as Burgomaster, to Johnny Depp as Constable Crane, is to proceed to a faraway town in the mountains where several people have had their heads lopped off, 'clean as dandelions', and bend his scientific intellect to resolving the mystery.

The story is comic gothic, and Johnny Depp, who became a lasting friend, made an excellent job of dealing with the weird phenomenon of the headless horseman who erupted from a tree and hunted terrified members of the Dutch community. The legend was spun around the idea of the restless corpse of a Hessian soldier left over from the Revolutionary War. Hessians apparently filed their teeth to points, as shown in the head when discovered, and this, in my view, was as alarming as the absence of a head. Christopher Walken played the grisly galloping apparition with his own head tucked out of sight.

With Christina Ricci as the leading lady, and such other outstanding actors as Michael Gambon and Miranda Richardson, not to mention the distinguished American Martin Landau who never got a credit for his performance as the frightened passenger of a coach being chased by the headless one, I was very glad to have had my token five minutes. Michael Gough, a Hammer regular a few years older than me, came out of retirement for a neat little cameo. Tim Burton paraded a fan's knowledge of Hammer productions, and finally remarked that this film was his tribute to Hammer.

We worked in a strange studio at Leavesden in Hertfordshire that had been a Rolls-Royce engine factory and was never properly soundproofed, despite which handicap it was much in demand, and many movies were made there, including James Bond, and the first in the *Star Wars* sequence, *The Phantom Menace*. Burton's enthusiasm shone through from the first reading and his eager, helpful persona behind the camera was a trait peculiar to only a few directors today.

Some of those few, however, were waiting for me not far down the line.

Filming the Unfilmable

In an earlier chapter of this memoir I wrote about *Ivanhoe*. Twenty years on I was in *Ivanhoe* again, shooting four in a sequence of six in Northumberland, Edinburgh and Durham. I used my senior citizen's railcard to make it cheaper for the BBC. It was my first time with them, with the luxury of having no ad breaks. For this *Ivanhoe*, instead of milling about among beefy, quarrelling knights I had a subtler role as the Grand Master of the Order of Templars. In Scott's bestselling historical romance this alarming figure, virtually an avatar by virtue of his powers over life and death, arrives unexpectedly at the Precentory where the lovely Rebecca is imprisoned by a lesser Templar, Bois-Gilbert, and releases her from her lascivious captor. By coincidence I am in the real world a Commander of the Order of St John of Jerusalem, a charity that goes back originally to the Templars, with the nine knights set up to protect the pilgrims of the first crusade. So I like to think of my eminence as Grand Master in this fantasy as a promotion.

Though it is not likely that many viewers cared about Scott's cavalier attitude to history (his use of hostility between Normans and Saxons as a lever to the plot is an anachronism), I nevertheless felt I should check out the authentic model for my own character. If there's material available, it is something I do. I discovered that the Templars' name derives from the place where, at the invitation of a local cleric, they stored their arms and equipment in a church directly above Solomon's temple. More strictly relevant to my character in *Ivanhoe*, who for some reason was given a different name, was the realization that the Grand Master was the most powerful man in the Western world, temporal and spiritual, with kings and emperors at his behest. In the story he comes to England just to keep an eye on things and crack down on backsliding. He is outraged to find corruption and sensual indulgence. The rules of the Order were specific and harshly maintained, and the Master himself must have been sexually frustrated.

This notion of him was in the script and not my invention. In the film he had to mortify the flesh. In the scene between him and the young Jewish girl, when he says, 'If you will but convert or confess your sins, I can help you,' the unspoken implication is 'if you become carnally involved with me'. This had to be conveyed in the way the line is said, together with my expression, from which she flinches away in disgust. This little exchange was awkward and could have been gross, but Susan Lynch is a very good actress.

The BBC had assembled a fine cast that ached more from the cold than from sexual frustration. The wind was brutal, howling through the huge gaps in the walls of the ruined castle of Craigmillar, near Edinburgh. It was one of the coldest springs I can remember, with the blossom in Edinburgh delayed until May. Somehow it was fiercer to me than Alaska, where the thermometer had registered forty below. Longjohns below our medieval clothing made no difference. There was a scene outside in the quadrangle of the castle where two knights joust and Ivanhoe wins, and there too, attached to the stake in her shift, was Susan Lynch. Poor girl, she must have considered lighting the pile of faggots. It was so cold I could barely speak. At the lunch break our director Stuart Orme, delightful man, asked, 'Are you all right?' I replied, 'No, I'm not, I'm not. I can't put on twenty mantles and longjohns while pretending to be a gaunt, ascetic Grand Master!' Considerate fellow, he had them bring on some heaters.

A more daring BBC venture, and in the event one of the best things in fiction it has done, was *Gormenghast*. For fifty years, ever since its first publication in 1950, Mervyn Peake's modern classic novel had been seen as 'unfilmable'. It was not that no one had tried, but the strangeness of the concept and the high intensity of the language had always defeated would-be scriptwriters, and their efforts had been rejected by the Peake family who looked after his estate, as not being in the spirit of his work. His whole oeuvre, in fiction, poetry and illustration, was unique and brilliant, a kind of oxbow off the mainstream of English writing.

He had been a war artist, an experience that some people have suggested accounts for the collapse of his mind, though it was Parkinson's disease that caused his tragically early death at the age of fifty-seven in 1968. I knew him only slightly, but when we encountered one another in Harrods' library we would talk briefly, because he knew my sister, and there were no signs then of the impending disaster. He was very quiet and good-looking, with wonderfully blue and slightly hooded eyes. I read two of the novels in the trilogy, *Titus Groan* and *Titus Alone*, but oddly not the best, *Gormenghast* itself, until the script was sent to me.

It was straight away extraordinary, on first reading, to appreciate how they had transferred his language, in itself a basic element of the story, into a practical vehicle for television, condensed as it had to be. Like other classic fantasies widely known to be unfilmable, such as *Gulliver's Travels* and *Alice in Wonderland*, it was to be filmed. At a lunch in Holland Park with the director, the wonderfully even-tempered intellectual Andy Wilson, we heard that the whole package of writer-producer-director-cast had been given the imprimatur of the Peake family. And such a cast, too! Peake's eccentric and rococo-named characters, Irma Prunesquallor, Fuchsia Groan, Dr Barquentine, would be safe in their hands. It was a splendid experience for me to be working with actors I'd never met before, among them Celia Imrie, Zoë Wanamaker and John Sessions. Ian Richardson produced a *tour de force* pretending to be an owl. Jonathan Rhys Meyers gave an extraordinary performance as Steerpike, the lynchpin of villainy, a murderous youth who hadn't even a nodding acquaintance with a conscience.

My role was Mr Flay, the butler, a nice contrast with the Grand Master in *Ivanhoe* – social mobility is demanded of and much enjoyed by actors. The important turn in Flay's development through the story is that while appearing at first to be a nasty piece of work because of his treatment in the kitchen of the vicious but unsuspected Steerpike, he is proven to be an ultra-loyal servant to the 77th Earl, the boy Titus. He has great pathos as the ancient retainer exiled in the Gormenghast forest, returning to expose the creature Steerpike, who wants to destroy the whole rickety, tottering family set-up. And finally, defending the young 'lordship', he pays with his life. (His reward in the book is to be buried in the cemetery dedicated only to the most devoted servants.) Having served several generations of Groan, he has the truest idea of the family history and its rituals. What appealed to me about the part was that it was a series of different layers of the same character.

The Devil of course is in the detail. It is not difficult for me to appear tall and cadaverous and taciturn, but it was a problem to have Flay's 'knee joints reporting his progress at every spider-like step'. I protested that 'the one thing we really can't have is that every time I walk there's a clicking noise. Click-click-click all the time will drive everyone mad in minutes.' Even when the clicking had been silenced, I still had to walk awkwardly. And talk awkwardly, too. The most difficult bit of *Gormenghast* for me was the dialogue. Flay does not speak normally, but in a staccato fashion, without connecting the phrases and never putting a recognizable sentence together. It was like somebody learning a language who has got hold of the vocabulary but not the grammar. The challenge in the film was to avoid this delivery becoming monotonous.

Scenes in which butlers fight duels are rare in the annals of dramatic art. But Mr Flay has one with the evil cook, played by Richard Griffiths. Cook and butler loathe one another. When he comes after me with his cleaver I snatch up a sword from somewhere in the castle furniture, and just as we join in mortal combat, Ian Richardson as Lord Groan comes sleepwalking out of his room into the corridor. I had to do all this tremendous sword work with Griffiths while retreating from the sleepwalker and taking care not to touch Ian with any of my tremendous swipes.

And then there was the risk of alienating the audience when I threw a cat at Steerpike. In practice it was a deception. I merely took hold of the beast by the scruff of the neck, as its own mother might, and the missile that hit Steerpike was a fluffy toy cat. I also dragged Steerpike along by his hair. Very cruel. But again, the apparent cruelty to Jonathan Rhys Meyers was mitigated by the skill of an unseen stagehand pushing him along by the legs, while Jonathan held on to my arm.

The great crumbling castle of the Groans was created at Shepperton out of cyclopean blocks by a brilliant and ingenious set-designer. You could feel as you traversed the long, curving corridors and courtyards that you were wandering through Agamemnon's palace. It was irresistible for a philistine gossip on a newspaper to dub this great production 'Gormenghastly', but on the whole it was received adequately in this country, and was an enormous success in America, South Africa and the Antipodes. Not that it was much use on a CV. When people in the business ask you what you've done, and you reply '*Gormenghast*', they just look at you as if you were clearing your throat.

It is a pity that dandy writing, which the English do so well, does not get more exercise on television. But then, there is little support for it in any medium. The great merit of television is the quality of naturalistic acting on view. It takes very little flicking around the channels to turn up examples of this any day of the week. To the extent that actors are distinguished by their careers in television or film, the latter are disadvantaged by their relative shortage of options. Of course television budgets are smaller, and except for long-stay players in soaps, actors make less money, but it does provide the discipline and experience that film actors crave and need. *Gormenghast* was a curiosity that belonged to both media, yet somehow floated free of the normal constraints of both. Besides, it was fun.

Surrounded by Pixels

'The most important thing is the story,' said George Lucas.

'Of course,' I replied. Because it usually is.

But actually, with *Star Wars* it's not. Well, there's a kind of onrush of events, which are an excuse for startling explosions, wholesale incineration of military equipment and personnel, odd and presumably extinct beasts, and a rainbow brilliance of amazing effects. The most important thing about *Star Wars* is the spectacle. The second most important thing about it is being in it. You do not turn down *Star Wars*, unless you're Harrison Ford and have already done three episodes. The third most important thing is that George wrote the story. George also wrote the sequels and the prequels, until there were half a dozen of them. The first of these blockbusters was made in 1977, and most of the complications of doing the rest, out of their supposed time sequence, derive from the increasing sophistication of the technology. Connecting the threads must have been like matching up the wires in a broken transatlantic cable.

The several episodes have made enough mega-bucks to fill a black hole in space, a phenomenal gross generated by stories reminiscent of Campbellian pulp science fiction in the thirties. George Lucas has a drive similar to that of those old writers, to make his customers pop-eyed with astonishment and wonder. The universe has never looked bigger, or planets more expendable. New constellations can be generated by the touch of a mouse. But computers can't yet contrive the most important thing, which is the story by George Lucas, who is also the director. And there are literally dozens of *Star Wars* books, some with the Lucas imprint, and all by storytellers authorized by George.

The action in my own story begins with a call from my agent, who said, 'The casting director for the next *Star Wars* is coming to London, and I think we should have lunch at the Ivy, the three of us.'

'Has she asked to see me?' I enquired.

'No, but I think it would be a good idea.'

Of course, I thought, and went.

The casting director was Robin Gurland and very charming. At lunch *Star Wars* was never mentioned. Indeed we hardly talked about films, and certainly not inter-galactic sagas. So it was apparently just a nice lunch at a fashionable restaurant. Yet it was obviously the right way to proceed, because in due course I heard that Lucas, away in Australia, perhaps pondering deserts, had accepted me for Count Dooku, alias Darth Tyrannus. This was for *Attack of the Clones*, already scripted, and for an as yet untitled and unscripted prequel or sequel.

In this case there was no book for me to read, because the usual process is reversed and the film precedes the book. Nevertheless at least I've been able to read the books of the films I did not appear in, and it was like being in my teens again. The only thing I couldn't remember was who is who in the galaxy and where all the planets are, partly because they are as the sands of the sea, and partly because they are all made up. Much of *Attack* takes place on the planet of Geonosis, where those skeletal bipeds with dragonfly wings are the Geonosians. Some Geonosian dialogue is difficult to put over because it is a mixture from an ancient time in a faraway galaxy – which George told me was considerably more than 7,000 years ago – and modern speech in our own galaxy of cinema duplexes.

The Count is the most malignant, dangerous and lethal force in the entire story, possibly in the entire galaxy. As a disenchanted Jedi who quits the Republic to serve the Emperor, I am a good guy gone wrong, though I have already engineered the death of Liam Neeson in an episode I wasn't in. My brief from the Emperor, who has appeared in several episodes with his face half-covered, is to initiate a war on a galactic scale between the two systems. I create clones for battle in huge numbers, 'a power so colossal that they will be the greatest army in the history of the galaxy'. I actually have to say that – surely the most over-the-top line in the history of drama, though 'My life for the world's future' in Shaw's *The Devil's Disciple* comes close.

Along the way to establishing my master as cock of the galactic walk, I have some local conflicts with people who cast a long shadow. I capture three people. One is Obi-wan Kenobi, who has in the next picture to change from Ewan McGregor into Alec Guinness (who rumour has it took two per cent of the gross profit, which could have been nothing but turned out to be much more than that). My second captive is the romantic lead, Anakin Skywalker, just a child in the first film, so his transformation is an even greater challenge. The third is Padmé Amidala, the glamour puss Senator. Explaining it all is more complicated than changing from a new computer to an old one, and it is surprising that a man so strong on story as George Lucas did not start at the beginning and go on to the end.

The character of Count Dooku is described as an accomplished swordsman – a *beau sabreur* in the light-sabre division. So I was given a good portion of fights. The climactic duel was with my erstwhile Jedi master, the tiny figure of Yoda. This time, instead of using a puppet, their Yoda was a computer animation, and cute as a lynx with his round face and long, pointed ears. Each character fought in a different style. I've never played a golfer in a film, but some of the movements I did with a light sabre were pretty close to a golf swing. However, the sabre is not what the viewer sees on the screen: the thing itself is only a rod, with the hilt on mine specially made curved – the only one of its kind. The sabre light and sound were added afterwards.

For my first two fights I could see my opponents. But with Yoda, the most furious contest of them all, there was no one to see. He wasn't there. I whirled and twirled and leaped and spun around, striking and parrying and darting about like a madman fighting his shadow. It was more difficult for me than sword fights had been in the past, because though my arms and hands do what I ask of them, my legs are slower and I had stunt men to do the running.

It is the invention of the 'blue screen' process that enables actors to perform with no direct perception of what is going on around them. When the film is shown they will find out, but in the meantime they have to rely on their own imaginations and the stirring words of the director. 'Blue movies' does not mean what it used to mean. *Attack* was my first experience of a set entirely surrounded by blue walls, which are compositions of zillions of minuscule points of light called pixels. If you are a photographer scanning your pictures on a screen you will know the importance of the density of pixels. I imagine that even for young actors brought up on computer manipulation the initial impact of a blue screen set, like the coldest part of a giant refrigerator, is bewildering, and for my own part it was indeed a case of pixellation.

But it is not for nothing that George's company is called Industrial Light and Magic, and once he has explained the routines you soon get used to it, and face yellow or red screen or any other pixels in the spectrum without a qualm, and without any fear of what is going on invisibly and silently, above you, below you, in front of you. And you do have points of reference, naturally, like a piece of tape for an eyeline stuck to the matte box, immediately beside the camera. The one thing you can't do in a film, in contrast with television, is look directly into the camera. Now, if anyone asks me what it is like to work with nothing behind the camera, I can say lightly, 'Oh, I've had that experience before, many times, from quite a few of my colleagues.' It must be said too that when George promised me it would be fun, he meant it. There is a common misconception that he is very reserved, not particularly approachable, and difficult to talk to. These are false assumptions. He knows in detail what he wants, and repeats the action until he gets it. But he couldn't have been easier to work with, and once started, could talk the stars down.

An incident I cherish from this film was the shooting of the scene in which Count Dooku makes his exit at speed to report the success of his mission to the Emperor. Once again with nothing but pixels all round, I had to mount a thing like a motorbike, covered in blue of course, with attachments to hold on to. I had to rocket across this landscape, revealed as extraordinary by the film, with people on either side of me who had not yet been brought into being. My task was to make slight movements suggesting that I was in control of this machine, and not to blink and thereby give away the fact that my cloak was billowing out behind because of a wind machine in front of me. True to my director's instructions I went through this scene with no expression on my face at all, absolutely none. It happened that George's director friend Francis Ford Coppola was visiting him that day and was sitting beside the monitor. When George finally said, 'I think we've got enough there – cut,' Coppola said to me, 'Amazing!' I asked him what he thought was amazing. Was it perhaps the process? 'No, no,' he said in sepulchral tones. 'It was all there. It was all there. Everything.' I objected that I'd had absolutely no expression on my face whatsoever, and did nothing.

'It was all there,' said Coppola. 'Every marvellous bit of it. Great stuff!'

Words and Music

The stylish small town of Parma, in the Emilia Romagna district of Italy, is famous for its cheese and for a special kind of ham called *culatello*, which is literally the gift at Christmas for princes who have everything. Another and perhaps greater distinction is its musical culture. Parma had the great good fortune to be allocated Napoleon's widow, the Archduchess Marie-Louise of Austria, to rule the region until her death, and she it was who built the splendid theatre for concerts and opera, and thereby gave the local composer Giuseppe Verdi the opportunity to show off his skills. In a parallel world my greatest happiness would be to indulge my operatic leanings in that theatre.

Unfortunately, great theatre breeds and depends on a great audience, and the regular habit of listening to fine performances has polished up the critical knowledge of the Parmigiani audience until it is downright intimidating. A story I heard there can illustrate this. There was a man notorious for being undependable as a tenor, and everybody waited for him to deliver his big aria in the expectation of seeing a rain of vegetables descending on the stage. He duly delivered, and it was pretty dreadful. But before the protest could start, a voice boomed out of the amphitheatre: '*Ancora*!' Surprised, orchestra and tenor nevertheless did the repeat. Even worse. Another deathly silence, broken again by the same voice shouting '*Ancora*!' and again they did it. The tenor's voice cracked, everything went wrong, and this time the voice shouted, '*Ancora*! Until he gets it right!'

Many much better singers than that poor tenor have cracked reaching for the note and brought immediate scorn on themselves. It must be unbearable. In that sense I'm glad that I never let it happen to me. And yet the one serious regret of my career is that I never gave singing a proper shot. I sang, as it were, in the wings, grateful for the help of such as Jussi Björling. If singing had events equivalent to golfing's Pro-Ams, I think I might have volunteered. I went so far as to take a couple of lessons in the fifties from Ezio Pinza, but by the time I was confident that I had a voice, and an ear, it was all I had. I sing, I make some records, but for all that I cannot to this day read music.

I tell myself that if I had gone for that other life instead of the B-movie heaven of my youth, my voice by now would have gone. As it is I keep it moving, give it a taste of Mozart or Wagner or Verdi, and sing every day provided I don't upset people in the hotel. As a boy I visited the Savoy with my mother, when we saw *The Mikado*, with the legendary Savoyard Sir Henry Lytton, then in his seventies, playing Ko-Ko. There were also on stage Darrell Fancourt as the Mikado, Sidney Granville as Pooh-Bah and Derek Oldham singing Nanki-Poo. These were the actors who virtually created the roles. I won't say that I felt able to recreate them, but there was a definite D'Oyley Carte style, and I copied that a bit, without picking out any particular English singers. My idol, because of his attack, has long been the Danish tenor Lauritz Melchior.

In most countries other than Italy, opera houses are few and far between, and when in range tend to ask a small ransom for a seat in a good place. In our years in Los Angeles there was no opera within easy reach except at two museums, the LA and the Norton Simon. People like me gradually fall into the fashion of thinking that recordings are the pillars of the art. Then we evolve into people on the outlook for a chance to make a recording. The material tends to divide into classics that have become popular, and popular numbers that have survived long enough to be reclassified as classics. Among the latter I have on my CV *The King and I*, whose male stars in the theatre and cinema have used a kind of *sprechgesang*, whereas I was challenged for the recording actually to sing the part, with a distinguished career opera singer, Valerie Masterson, as Anna.

The beginning for me of professional records was a 1976 Chrysalis production in Brussels of Knight and Johnson's *The King of Elfland's Daughter*. This was the only recording made of this work and was one of the most beautiful things I've ever been associated with. If I'd had the sense to realize that it would in due course become unobtainable I would have bought a few spare copies. I was the narrator and I sang the King, relatively simple by comparison with narrating all the voices, including the women, of Stravinsky's *The Soldier's Tale*. This was on a tour of Britain – Birmingham, Croydon, Cheltenham and Glasgow – with the Scottish Chamber Orchestra, a very small band with me out front, conducted by Lionel Friend. Then I went to Leominster and did

Prokofiev's *Peter and the Wolf*, conducted by Yehudi Menuhin. Having heard me sing, he was a little surprised to find I couldn't read music, but adjusted himself to the situation by giving me finger signals for my cue, and so on.

How does one get to do a solo album? In my case the title is self-explanatory: *Christopher Lee sings Devils, Rogues and other Villains – from Broadway to Bayreuth*. Equally well it could have been blurbed as 'From Sweeney Todd to Mack the Knife'. I sang it at the invitation of Nicholas Schreck, whose father-in-law was Sandor La Vey, a kind of American Alistair Crowley. It contains a linguistic miscellany of fifteen items that I sang in five days in 1997 in Los Angeles, some with piano and some with orchestra. And some, the most difficult, I sang with the Mighty Wurlitzer, played by a brilliant organist from Palm Springs. Despite his skill it sounds heavy; a Wurlitzer hasn't the flexibility of a piano. There is Iago's Credo from *Otello*, the two Mephistopheles arias from *Faust*, the Mikado's song, the Inquisitor's number from *The Gondoliers*, plus pieces from *The Rheingold*, *The Marriage of Figaro*, *Götterdämmerung* and so forth. I'm not sure where I found the nerve to do it. It did have a sales history but unfortunately the company, Wolf's Lair, just vanished, and the record with it.

An association that does go on is with Gary Curtis. Our first duet was Elvis's 'Now or Never', with Gary starting out in English, then my coming in on the top in the Neapolitan dialect, and overlapping all the way along. Our plan during 2003 is an album along Country and Western lines, using 'High Noon', songs from *Seven Brides for Seven Brothers*, a Pat Boone song, a smidgen of Nashville, a whiff of the Delta. An amazing number of people listen to this kind of thing. It is perfectly open. You pay so much to the copyright holder, and you do it, and there is no risk of being accused of plagiarism.

Apart from the bonus of a couple of songs in films, notably in *The Wicker Man*, that roughly encapsulates my excursions down the byroads of a medium that I regret not having more fully exploited. But a deep voice that carries is not just for singing, and every so often an opportunity pops up to read a book on radio or audio. Several jobs in the fantasy field have come my way. Mary Shelley's *Frankenstein* was a brave venture and an intriguing intellectual foray when first published in 1818, but as a story to be listened to two centuries later it comes across as incredibly turgid. *Dracula* holds up well, but the more recent *Phantom of the Opera* that made a fine vehicle for Lon Chaney in 1925 is not very interesting as a book. Stephenson's *The Strange Case of Dr Jekyll and Mr Hyde* was very interesting, one of the best. There were also works by Agatha Christie and Dennis Wheatley, straightforward stuff. These books have been huge bestsellers, but I believe that the publishers have never been able to activate a comparable market in audiobooks. It fluctuates, and so does the income an actor can expect from taking part.

Most of these books were condensed for reading aloud, and were done in various studios, usually in a couple of days. I just kept going until I made a mistake. If I fluffed a line I simply did it again and rolled on. Recently I took part in a hybrid: that is to say a video of M.R. James ghost stories in which I supposedly read them as he did at Christmas time to students gathered round a roaring fire. Unfortunately they were not his best stories, such as Count Magnus, because the best are too long for TV. Nevertheless, the shorter ones are well worth listening to.

The toughest that I had to deal with was William Peter Blatty's *The Exorcist*, not just because it's a very frightening story but because at one point there's a horripilating description of what takes place in a Black Mass, and the author had evidently done his level best to make it authentic. This was so vile that the reading of it gave me a sick feeling. I agreed when the producer said, 'This is really appalling, isn't it?', but whether it was excised from the finished product I don't know. Nor can I say who the audio publishers were: possibly the company that hired me was itself subcontracted by the distributors.

I reproach myself for not having more than two radio credits and for not having enquired further after playing in Somerset Maugham's *The Noble Spaniard* and Ray Bradbury's *Leviathan 99*, which was Moby Dick in outer space. I played Captain Ahab, who in Bradbury's retelling had been blinded by 'the white comet'. It's hard to play a blind man on radio.

Instead of Curtain Calls

There comes a time when a light shower of awards settles, like stardust, on the actor's shoulders. You feel slightly bemused because, as in the case of all awards, they are essentially for doing your job. People with awards in their gift worry lest they have left it too late, and are anxious to get them to you before you fall off the twig – but not so early as to encourage you to get above yourself. Generous and beautifully dressed people salute your 'lifetime achievement', and you wish that might mean 'most promising veteran'. You stand there clutching a piece of statuary, looking down at their smiling and expectant faces, and for a moment it feels like a prop that you will have to give back at the end of the scene. You wonder what to say. In your heart you know that the real achievement is to have reached eighty through such a turbulent century, and still be working.

But that won't do. The least you can offer in return is 'thank you'. Some people think it is more dignified to confine yourself to this. But it seems mean, an anticlimax. A cheerful song might suit the occasion, but no one seems to do that. On the other hand, on the showcase evenings of cinema awards the recipients now go to the other extreme and thank everyone involved in their film, perhaps thinking that it makes up for the credits having been rolled so fast in the cinema that the audience had no time to identify who did or played what. This can just about be managed when only one movie is in the frame, but for a 'lifetime' of more than 250 movies, there is no satisfactory formula. This book must do as a thank you for the opportunity, and if all the help I have been given were acknowledged it would be many times longer.

Not everyone is always helpful. It must be a temptation to an actor sometimes to take advantage of the situation and to condemn, as it were *ex cathedra*, the young producer with his hat on backwards who'd never heard of Garbo and Chaplin, and who demanded to know what else you had been in, the agents who never rang you back, the casting director who declined to sign you up as a wizard because there are already several wizards on your CV, the actor who finesses your part in a script you had bought and developed for yourself ... But no, this is a time for forgiveness.

A journalist friend (not necessarily a contradiction in terms) tells me that when you pass eighty everything is forgiven. If that may be too much to hope for, *sub specie aeternitatis*, he feels at any rate that readers cease to be angry with or jealous of profiles of you. There'll be no nasty e-mails contradicting what has been reported. People in the arts think that they no longer have anything to fear from you, that you are *hors concours*, and that following your example they'll all fetch up on the sunny uplands if the weather holds and pensions don't go out of fashion.

I was invited to Monte Carlo to receive an award for 'services to literature'. Perhaps that was forgiveness. It was certainly a surprise. But I had never willingly misrepresented the characters invented by Conan Doyle, Edgar Allan Poe, Alexandre Dumas, Molière, Mervyn Peake, J.R.R. Tolkien, Mary Shelley or, I suppose, George Lucas. In fact, this side of pedantry, I've always been on the side of the author against the scriptwriter. So what could I say to this well-intentioned gathering in the tiny principality? I felt it was incumbent on me to say something sonorous on behalf of The Book. 'In the beginning was the Word,' I told them. 'And the Word was made Flesh,' I intoned. 'And that's us,' I added.

It seemed to go down well. And while on classic literary figures I thought with regret that I had never had the chance to realize my great ambition of playing Don Quixote, and now it is too late. On the plane home from Monte I was congratulating myself on my impromptu performance when it suddenly occurred to me that so far as the cinema is concerned, its beginning was not the word but the image, and for a quarter of a century silent movies ruled, coming to grief pretty much at the time I was born. In an ideal celluloid world it would be an interesting requirement for every actor, producer and director, at least once in a lifetime, to take part in a silent movie.

For the winners, awards in the cinema are a substitute for curtain calls in the theatre, where the actors have nothing further to say, but just bow, though in some countries they clap the audience. In the same spirit I clap the London Film Critics' Circle, and the *London Evening Standard* and *Empire* magazine. Plus a bow in the direction of the Royal Box: thank you, Ma'am, for the extra initials. It's a shame about the

Empire though, redesignated by the present regime as Overseas Territories.

I'm also grateful to have been made a freeman of a couple of overseas cities, with large silver keys to prove it, which should unlock the gates of Palermo in Sicily, and Modena in the Emilia Romagna. Modena is my Italian family's seat, the Palazzo Carandini, half of which survives as a showpiece, with the other half a bank. The *bonne bouche* of the visit was a meeting with my archaeologist cousin Andrea Carandini who, during his dig-in-progress, had just turned up a pot with 'Carandinus' painted on it. Would I guess how old it was? I said the only records I have of the family go back to 1184 AD, when Cristoforo was created the first Count. 'It's first century,' he said. We felt that made some of the other families seem like *parvenus*. I dare say, however, that they won't lose any sleep over it.

The World Awards were founded in the year 2000. I was included in their third annual muster, and the bonus was a pleasant weekend in Vienna. Perhaps the most enjoyable part is the informal restaurant dinner on the eve of the ceremony. There you are at table with a most catholic range of participants – painters, writers, directors, scientists, wherever the wheel of fortune stops. The Man of the Year in our group was a middle-aged German teacher who had saved many lives at his school in Erfurt when he seized a crazy gunman who had already shot sixteen people.

We also had with us Mikhail Gorbachev, who next day at the gala in the vast Habsburg room of the royal palace always presents the statuary, looking you straight in the eye, and it was the unembroidered truth to say that there could not have been a greater honour than to receive it from the man who rescued the twentieth century from the Cold War. So that was an easy speech to make. Not quite so simple was carrying off the trophy, which weighs eight kilos. When the Pope received his he very wisely made no effort to pick it up. I was glad to relinquish mine at the airport to be transported in the hold.

Another hefty item, shaped like an Oscar, is the German award for the Best Actor in Video. This is eccentric because the actor is passive, unable to increase or reduce the number of his appearances on video, or enhance them, or for that matter prevent them from being butchered. So it is rather unfair on actors who might have given terrific importance to a film without commercial clout. Perhaps it could be named the Takeaway Trophy, to recognize the importance of videos to those who pick them up on the same trip as their dinner.

Collecting fantasy and science-fiction awards the actor does not have to travel or say anything. They are generally non-specific and arrive in the post. However, I did visit Washington for the Carl Laemmle award for the Best Actor in a Fantasy field, named after the man who founded Universal. The unexpected bonus at this convention was to meet Bela Lugosi's son, Boris Karloff's daughter, Lon Chaney's grandson, plus a very old lady who was a real niece of the man universally known as 'Uncle Carl'. I am still labouring in the fantasy field, with a nomination for Best Fight in a Film, for a wizards' duel. Even more specialized is the possibility of World Record for Swordplay in Front of a Camera, a bit of business in which I've been engaged since the days of leaping off balconies onto chandeliers and rushing up and down stone staircases, until present times wielding a light sabre against an invisible opponent.

This was all spread out for me recently, in what was otherwise a wretched cruise via bitterly cold Venice, rather dreary Messina, and Malta, where I heard in my head echoes of the gunfire of 1943. The saving grace was an encounter with an old acquaintance, Derek Ware, a stunt man on board as a lecturer. As the result of a formidable amount of research on swordplay in films, and duelling with axes, daggers, swords, knives, etc., he'd established a kind of chart, in the way that sports pages maintain lists of leading goal scorers. Derek's contained some redoubtable players, most of whom I know to bear physical scars from their experiences. Anthony Hopkins, Antonio Banderas and Tyrone Power all fought in the *Zorro* films, Ronald Colman in *Prisoner of Zenda*, and of course Douglas Fairbanks had several fights to his name. Basil Rathbone and Errol Flynn have both chalked up eight. And at the top Derek showed me Christopher Lee, with seventeen. It must be admitted that the others were generally victorious, whereas I was usually killed. Derek said that he meant to send the facts to the *Guinness Book of Records*.

Spellbinder

One story I had no need to read as homework was Tolkien's trilogy *The Lord of the Rings*, because I have been reading it every year since I was hooked by the first novel, *The Fellowship of the Ring*, when it came out in 1954. I'd been primed for it by discovering *The Hobbit* soon after my demob in 1945, and waited for the others to come out with the same kind of fiery suspense that J.K. Rowling seems to have kindled in children for her Harry Potter series, with the slight difference that I was in my thirties and recognizing it as a masterpiece on a level with *The Odyssey* and the Sagas of Iceland.

The Hobbit had been a book for children and was published by Stanley Unwin on the recommendation of a child, his son Rayner. It also appealed to adults – what today is called a 'crossover' book – and that must have reinforced its power as a bestseller. The trilogy was for adults, but appeals also to the dwindling band of bookish children. The Unwins had been looking forward to a follow-up to *The Hobbit* but were aghast when the author, J.R.R. Tolkien, the Merton Professor of Language and Literature at Oxford, turned up with an enormous manuscript that had taken him more than twenty years to compile. Stanley Unwin feared a £1,000 loss on publication of a doorstopper, but once again the astute and now grown-up Rayner dealt with it, by dividing the *The Lord of the Rings* into *The Fellowship of the Ring*, *The Two Towers* and *The Return of the King*. Nearly half a century later the whole sequence has been filmed with the same titles.

Until then, we enthusiasts wished that it could be filmed, and I furthermore wished that I could play the wizard Gandalf, an immortal dispatched in human form to Middle Earth to defend it from the evil ambitions of the apostate wizard Saruman and his dreadful master Sauron in the terrible land of Mordor. Well, this was obviously a pipe dream, since Tolkien's story of an epic journey called on Hobbits and

Orcs and Ents and Elves and Dwarves and other weird creatures from his own mythology, with the armies of good and evil battling in a vast landscape where even trees might move and take part, and the magic of the cinema was simply not up to it. Until one day it was. And the magician was Peter Jackson, a director from New Zealand. Not the least of his spells was the one he cast on New Line productions in America to back him to the tune of about $300 million.

Reading in a newspaper that there was a chance that my bedside book might actually be filmed had an impact on me like the first news that the Russians had put a sputnik on the moon. It was a glimpse of the infinite possibilities of technology. I immediately called my London agents and urged them to get me into the frame. This can be like putting a message in a bottle when you're on a desert island, but on this occasion it was picked up, and I was called to meet Jackson in a deconsecrated church off Tottenham Court Road in London. It was like a warren with the rabbits long gone, not what you'd imagine as an action centre for the biggest project in the history of the cinema. In the back somewhere I located three people, the casting director with a video camera, scriptwriter Fran Walsh and her partner Peter Jackson, a big stocky man with a huge black beard, glasses and a mass of black hair. Would I be prepared to read?

I'm not usually asked to read. But it's not a fraught moment for me when I am. Some actors don't read, won't read. But if they really want the part, it's a risky stance to take. It's very likely that somebody else will get the job. For a part in *The Lord of the Rings* I would have read anything, even one of Tolkien's early philological studies if required. As it was, Jackson prescribed some lines of Gandalf in a scene with Frodo, and added some directions to go with them. I read them knowing that I was too old for Gandalf and went away without being told what they had in mind for me, if anything, though they showed me some riveting photographs of New Zealand scenery. But within a short time – just a few months – I learned that I was to play the long, thin, bearded streak of immortal nastiness, Saruman the wizard. For their Gandalf they had chosen Ian McKellen, who in the event proved to be my Gandalf, Tolkien's Gandalf, everybody's Gandalf, as well.

The statistics of this film are eye-glazing. It was an operation on the scale of the book itself. Some 20,000 Kiwi soldiers were engaged and those who took part in the battles had not a few bruises for souvenirs. To get the terrifying roar and hubbub, Peter Jackson went out on the pitch at an international cricket match and whipped up the crowd. The variety of locations across lakes and mountains, calling on helicopters and adventurous catering trucks, are like a gazetteer to New Zealand. Whatever awards the films might garner, they are surely the world's champion tourist promotions. I truly believe, given the number of units and cameras turning on any given day, that five million feet of film were shot. Watching night and day, it would take you seven weeks to see it all.

They collected 50,000 sound effects, from storm to lull-in-the-storm. Walruses supplied grunts for the troll in the cave and a horse on heat did the same for Orcs. It's a standard formula for the movie/publishing industry to bring out an anatomy of every blockbuster, and not all read inspiringly, but for *The Lord of the Rings* Brian Sibley made a fizzing book, especially in his accounts of the ingenious mechanicians who built the forts and awful towers, gave shape to the ghastly Orcs and Uruk-hai and made the chaos of fire and flood convincing.

Much of this complex stuff happened in the Weta Workshop in Jackson's hometown, Wellington – a weta being a local, large and revolting insect. Under the brilliant Richard Taylor, I did almost all my work nearby in the headquarter studios that had at times been a paint factory, and a mental hospital. They were not soundproof, and stood at the end of an airport runway, which did not help us with the dialogue. We had people stationed by the runway to alert us to the imminence of planes landing and taking off.

I formed as strong an impression of Peter Jackson's power as a director when he had his back to me – usually in baggy shorts and often barefoot – as when he was addressing me. He seemed able to cope with several operations at once. He even, *à la* Hitchcock, made a brief appearance as a Hobbit in the first film. Over fifteen months they were making the three films simultaneously, and he'd be looking into the monitors showing the scene before him, and perhaps something else being shot fifty miles away, and yet again some night shooting from a few days before. He is a perfectionist. He knew what he wanted and that does not mean just recognizing it when it happened. His comment 'Good!' at the end of a take never meant 'Good enough'. We could not relax until he said, 'Excellent!' Everyone would witness to that. It sounds obsessional, and it meant some very long days, but the fund of his goodwill to his actors never dried up. The whole business was fun. Everyone would witness to that, too.

I made four visits to New Zealand, staying ten weeks for the longest period, with some post-synching in London. The only problem I had was not of the film's making. It's a long way for a tall man to sit in an aircraft seat, and Gitte and I would break our journey for a few days in Singapore. On one occasion I woke in the middle of the night, jetlagged, weaved about my hotel room searching for the bathroom, staggered, tripped, flung out my left hand and nearly severed two fingers. An immediate operation was necessary. That was soon done in super-efficient Singapore, but it remained agonizing because there were bandages and blood all over the place, and I still had to work. Luckily the wizards' duel with staves was already done, but it was awkward hiding my left hand whenever possible. It's hard to spot on the finished film.

Nobody could have been more helpful when I had this accident than Ian McKellen. Immortal enemies while the cameras rolled, we became great friends and shared a lot of laughs between times. In the film we were both several thousand years old, but in the real world he is some twenty years younger than me, which is young enough to have the habit of keeping a diary in a laptop, and to fly off to perform in scenes of dizzy heights and the virgin snow of New Zealand's tremendous mountains. Much younger people in the cast had a great time with the physical challenges of the country, and enjoyed games and contests among themselves. Back in Wellington, playing scenes in the adjacent national park, Ian and I had more verbal relaxations.

He set the tone straight away when we were walking in the garden under my tower, and he looked past me to where Orcs were leaping about in the trees. His line then was, 'Orcs? In Eisengard?' And, distinguished actor that he is, he tried to get me to reply, 'Well, we *are* near Auckland.' I hadn't the nerve, but I might have got away with it because at the insistence of the Australians in the crew I did intone, in robes and make-up as Saruman and looking up high, the whole of the Lord's Prayer – in Strine. It goes like this: 'Our 'arbour, which art an 'aven, Goodoh be thy name, Thy Bridge be done, in 1930 or '31. Give us this day our daily Bradman. Forgive us our trespasses as we forgive those cows in Melbourne. Lead us not into taxation, and deliver us from strikes, for thine is the 'arbour, the 'aven and the Bradman. For ever and ever, too right.' That exists on film, but I can't say whether or not it's an out-take.

An essential pleasure of the book to me is Tolkien's expertise with a raft of old languages, and his own creation of speech for his characters, which derives in part from Finnish, Old English, Welsh, and others. An instance of this in the film is the Sindarin language that he has most of the Elves speak – and an example of the attention to detail of the production was the presence of two experts in linguistics to check that the speakers got the pronunciation and the stresses right. My own love of correct detail must have become apparent, because once the crew had come to regard me as a Tolkien swot, I couldn't go into the workshop without somebody trying to catch me out with some abstruse question on the parentage of the characters or the royal succession in Gondor.

For all this, it was hard work. Starting out at 3.30 a.m. was an hour earlier than I could remember being on a set before. But that's nothing to what my monster Lurtz, an Uruk-hai played by a delightful Maori actor, Lawrence Makoare, went through, spending eleven hours in make-up. Everything had to be stuck down. Remembering the days when I had similar treatment it gave me a great fellow feeling. By the time the film opened one could only hope that the author's son Christopher, a considerable scholar himself, who had not believed it could properly convey the book, would come to accept it. Certainly it has expanded the Tolkien estate. In the first year the British publishers of the core books and their derivatives sold more than 12 million copies. And to take merely one more example from the overwhelming shower of statistics, *The Fellowship of the Ring* earned $850 million worldwide in its first year.

But that wasn't the end. People say to me, 'Is that the end, when those two young people, Frodo and Sam, go off in a boat?'

And I say, 'Of course it isn't. It's the beginning of the second book.'

But after the second film people ask me, 'Is that the end, when those trees are walking about in the water?'

And I say, 'Of course it isn't. It's the beginning of the third book.'

But after the third film if people ask, 'Is that the end, when the ring gets chucked into the Crack of Doom, or somewhere, and the handsome one gets crowned?'

I have to say, 'Of course it is. There are no more books. Unless you want prequels. So that is

The End (of That)

Envoi: Square View

I sit in the front room of our long, narrow flat, with the balcony that looks out on a Chelsea square, with its 'Pont Street Dutch' façades and 'private' central garden. To be key holders we pay the estate. Walking four times round the square adds up to a mile and that's my regular exercise when the weather's too foul for golf. To test my ability to play to my present handicap of eight, we escaped to Morocco for a holiday, bringing in the new year of 2003. The test was never completed because a chilling freak storm hit the course while I was on it, and I spent eight days in bed with bronchitis. So I'd have done better to restrict myself to practising my putting in the square.

Beside my chair on the right rises a cliff-face of books, a variegated miscellany that covers most of the wall to the high ceiling. It's a great resource, proven over years, but I could not just sit in my comfortable armchair with an occasional cigar, read books and listen to opera. I must be doing and, if not in work, looking for some. And here on my left is a small stand that holds the phone and a shuffle of documents, and on the carpet a landslide of scripts. My presence in *Star Wars* and *The Lord of the Rings* has kept the postman busy delivering offers. But sadly, by the same token, they are mostly a disappointment – spin-offs and imitations.

However, the year has had some bankables. Off to Australia again for another episode of *Star Wars*, knowing only that I must die along with all the other Jedis bar Anakin and Obi-Wan Kenobi. And then a bonus appearance in *The Return of the King*. I had not originally thought that I would be in it, being contracted only for the first two parts of *The Lord of the Rings*. But then my death was postponed, as it were, apparently because I am the only antagonist in human form in the entire story.

And just as Peter Jackson gears himself up to make a really *small* film by way of a relief from the pressures of the last eight years of his life, I'm able to follow his example and do something relatively small by playing a

342

German in three locations in France, in a fiction written by Luc Besson called *Angels of the Apocalypse*. Then another Holmes detective yarn in Germany, which appealed because I play the wicked opponent Moriarty, by way of a change from being Sherlock, or his brother, or indeed Dr Watson. Then there was a suggestion from the people who made *Jinnah* that I should take part in their project on *Saladin*, though not in the title role – I have to wonder whether they will get the finance together for it.

That might seem enough to be going on with, and I am not complaining about the hand that has been dealt to me. An actor's life has never been more precarious, for young and old alike. However good the performance, nobody will be interested unless the film makes money. In more sombre moments I even wonder if our occupation will be usurped by computer-generated images – such a common term now that people use the acronym CGIs. Then I rally, and think that it's not the camera that matters but the person behind it, and the persons in front as well.

It would not become a veteran to bite the hand that has fed him, and of the British film industry in particular it needs only be said that diagnosing its illness is easier than finding a cure – an extravagance expressed especially by its fondness for making pictures that have no chance of travelling. It's actually a self-inflicted wound. This makes it galling when a backer asks for scripts that are different, and you show them two or three that are excitingly different and exotic, usually breakthroughs by writers who have not been heard of before, and they recoil in alarm, saying 'Sorry, it isn't quite what we've been doing.' I quote verbatim.

Gitte and I have had our ruby wedding. We rarely dine out because, well, I prefer her Scandinavian cooking to the restaurants' menus. The exceptions are when we visit unfamiliar towns, when, being crazy about architecture, she disappears the entire day with her camera, photographing buildings. I've never made a film in Danish, and couldn't master her language. I tried, but my confidence drained away because she always said, 'You sound like a taxi driver.' Our daughter Christina married and lives nearby, and I can speak to her husband in his native tongue because he is Spanish, a language I enjoy. He created a marvellous website for me (in English), entirely his own doing, with a technology I do not understand or use, though he calls on me to chat with fans when I can. It holds the complete filmography, on *christopherleeweb.com*.

Actors get to be recognized as they go about their ordinary business. This has its drawbacks. I never travel on the Underground because it is hard to get off at the station of my choice. People ask me to sign things as small as a stamp, a postal order or even their passport. I say, 'This will get you into trouble,' but they're not bothered. Recently a bus conductor asked me to get off because a group of boys on the top deck were making such a fuss over discovering me. Being discovered, however, can have a rougher side. This became apparent not long ago when I visited St Mary's hospital in Paddington with Gitte, where she was being treated after an appalling accident that shattered most of the bones in her left elbow.

We were in the lift going down when a man got in, about forty, wearing a baseball cap. He shot me a keen look, and evidently recognized me.

'You're Peter Sellers, arn'cha?' It was said with an accusing expression.

'No, I'm not,' I said. I didn't so much mind his thinking I was Peter Sellers, who after all was a considerable actor and impersonator, as this man's aggressive manner.

'Yes you are, you lying git,' he retorted.

There were only the three of us in a confined space. I was anxious lest Gitte suffer further damage. Should I endure this, or take his head off? Then I would be prosecuted. As I hesitated, the lift door opened at street level, where the man appealed to the kiosk newspaper vendor to confirm his identification of Peter Sellers. The vendor knew me. I always bought a paper from him for Gitte.

'No, he's not Peter Sellers, he died years ago.'

The man came up to me with a piece of paper and thrust it out. 'Sign!' he commanded.

'Next time get it right,' I said, and gave it back to him signed,

Christopher Lee

Index

Index

Index

Index

Index